PRAISE FOR *LORD JESUS CHRI*

Lord Jesus Christ is a deeply informed confessional and exercise in constructive theology. From the introduction to the final chapter, Treier's volume abounds with biblical insights as well as careful syntheses of historical and contemporary issues. Perhaps most compelling is the way Treier allows Scripture's form and content to dictate the shape and categories of Christology, resulting in a Christology that is both from above and below. Thorough yet succinct, this is an exceptional scriptural, traditional, and contemporary account of the wonder of the Lord Jesus.

—*Uche Anizor, professor of theology, Biola University*

This book is an exceptional contribution to the doctrine of Christ and is certain to establish itself among the finest Christologies in the present generation and beyond. Highlights, of which there are many, include associate its creative and intriguing framework that traces the Christological arc from the Son's eternal communion with the Father and the Holy Spirit, through the creation of the world by and for the Son, to the consummation of all things that will be united in him; its affirmation of traditional yet recently challenged elements of Christology such as eternal generation, *extra carnem*, humiliation without kenoticism, and penal substitution; and its aspiration (accomplished well) to be both evangelical and catholic through retrieval of the first six ecumenical councils and its framework of Protestant confessionalism. *Lord Jesus Christ* offers an exquisite and paradigm-setting dogmatic account of Christology and has my highest recommendation!

—*Gregg R. Allison, professor of Christian theology,*
Southern Baptist Theological Seminary

Modern Christology has left a wasteland in its wake, from its bifurcation of Jesus of Nazareth and the Christ of faith to the rise of kenotic Christology's abandonment of Christ's divine attributes. Even evangelicals have been susceptible to revisionism by means of Spirit Christology. But Daniel Treier's *Lord Jesus Christ* is a shelter for refugees weary from the winds of modern Christology. The conspicuous strength of Daniel Treier is his ability to rigorously exegete Scripture by means of an orthodox commitment to Chalcedon. Treier is also refreshing because he demonstrates the entailments of Christology for the church's participation in Christ, though some will wish he substantiated such a move with a more pronounced commitment to the metaphysic of classical realism. Conversant with the vast landscape of contemporary literature, Treier is a long-anticipated sign that Reformed, classical Christology will have a future once more.

—*Matthew Barrett, professor of Christian theology,*
Midwestern Baptist Theological Seminary

Lord Jesus Christ does a masterful job exploring Christology through the lens of dogmatic theology. Treier couples his extensive knowledge of theology with his expertise in biblical exegesis, providing an excellent intermediate-level examination of key aspects of Christ's person and work. Written from a Reformed position, Treier engages a broad range of global, female, and minoritized voices, as well as numerous scholars in biblical studies. *Lord Jesus Christ* is a must-have resource pastors and scholars will return to again and again.

—**Lynn H. Cohick,** *distinguished professor of New Testament, Houston Theological Seminary*

Christian theology, if it is worth anything at all, must continually return to the scandalous claim that Jesus Christ is Lord. Daniel J. Treier's *Lord Jesus Christ* is an outstanding and illuminating examination of Christology in light of Holy Scripture's dramatic arc from God's life in himself to creation's eschatological communion with God. Rooted in a series of characteristically brilliant theological expositions of the names of Christ, this is a book you will find yourself reading and rereading to great benefit. It is a book that will drive you to the text of Holy Writ to hear anew its affirmation of the risen Lord. One would expect nothing less from a theologian of his caliber.

—**Daniel L. Hill,** *assistant professor of Christian theology, Truett Seminary, Baylor University*

This is an excellent book that leverages recent interest in the theological interpretation of Scripture to present a fresh and compelling account of Christology that is biblically based, faithful to the broad Christian tradition, and relevant and convincing in our present context.

—**Steve Holmes,** *senior lecturer in theology, University of St. Andrews*

Sophisticated and succinct, learned and lively, classically Reformed and deeply ecumenical, this elegant book presents an academically and historically rigorous evangelical Christology for today. *Lord Jesus Christ* should be a standard text in seminaries and for advanced undergraduates. Treier's rich theological exegesis and creative proposals make for a stimulating and vital read for anyone interested in the doctrine of Christ and praising the holy name(s) of Jesus.

—**Han-luen Kantzer Komline,** *Marvin and Jerene DeWitt Professor of Theology and Church History, Western Theological Seminary*

Daniel Treier has given the church a tour-de-force through the intricacies of Christological discussion across the ages, always keeping an eye on helping the reader inhabit the biblical story narrating the creation, redemption, and consummation of all things in the Lord Jesus Christ. What may appear on the surface to be a narrow doctrinal treatment of Christology has become in the hands of a remarkably skilled theologian a summing up of all things in Christ. Treier never loses sight of the deep conviction of Scripture, that it is Jesus who has written us into his story rather than us fitting Jesus into our own narratives. This book is a precious gift to the church and to any who want to dig deep into Christology writ large.

—*Richard Lints, senior advisor, Redeemer City-to-City*

Good theology should not only provide answers to questions but also provoke better ones. This book does both; through patient exegesis and careful reflection it offers insightful and helpful answers, and through exploration and inquiry it raises fresh questions that warrant further analysis. Many scholars talk about theological interpretation of Christian Scripture, but Dan Treier actually does it, and the result is a treasure trove of theological exegesis that strives to be both faithful to the biblical text and informed by the insights of the creedal and confessional tradition as well as attentive to the concerns of distinctly modern theologians. Careful readers—including not only those inclined to agree but also and perhaps especially those who might question various judgments or challenge certain conclusions—will benefit greatly. I know that I shall return to this book again and again.

—*Thomas H. McCall, Timothy C. and Julie M. Tennent*
Chair of Theology, Asbury Theological Seminary

There is not a more important question to ponder than "Who is Jesus?" In *Lord Jesus Christ*, Dan Treier offers an answer that is both evangelical and ecumenical. While acknowledging and engaging with contemporary Christological debates, Treier refreshingly lets Scripture set the agenda for the doctrine of Christ. He does so not only by providing theological exegesis of key texts but also by following the narrative arc of Scripture that begins with the eternal communion of the triune God and is consummated with the union of Christ and the church. This book equips the church to declare—with more depth and awe—that Jesus Christ is Lord.

—*Jeremy Treat, pastor for preaching and vision, Reality*
LA, adjunct professor of theology, Biola University

In *Lord Jesus Christ*, Dan Treier has given the church a precious gift, a fresh articulation—biblically based, historically informed, doctrinally aware, culturally alert, and elegantly structured—of the answer to the Christian's most important question: Who do we say Jesus is? In providing a clear, cogent, and comprehensive response, and in modelling healthy interaction between biblical exegesis and systematic theology, Treier's book is (to borrow one of its key terms) the epitome of evangelical dogmatic Christology.

—*Kevin J. Vanhoozer, research professor of systematic*
theology, Trinity Evangelical Divinity School

Neither merely iterating Christological commonplaces nor bedazzled by vogueish approaches, Treier's introduction to Christology treads an ancient path. It knows where theological sap is to be found, namely in the theological exposition of Scripture itself. Without ever losing sight of contemporary challenges and applications, Treier focuses the vision of the reader on the main thing, teaching her the peculiar Christological language of Scripture. The result is a measured, wise, and deeply nourishing Christology.

—*Adonis Vidu, Andrew Mutch Distinguished Professor of Theology, Gordon-Conwell Theological Seminary*

Grounded in exegesis of the biblical text, conversant with the history of theology, and engaged with contemporary debates of lasting significance—Daniel Treier offers a superb Christology. This text will not only prove useful in the classroom; it will also become a methodological standard. *Lord Jesus Christ* is modern theological interpretation of Scripture as it should be written. The chapter on Philippians 2 alone is worth the price of the book you hold in your hands, while the entire arc of this theodrama makes it priceless.

—*Malcolm B. Yarnell III, research professor of theology, Southwestern Baptist Theological Seminary*

NEW STUDIES IN DOGMATICS

LORD JESUS CHRIST

NEW STUDIES IN DOGMATICS

LORD JESUS CHRIST

DANIEL J. TREIER

MICHAEL ALLEN AND SCOTT R. SWAIN,
GENERAL EDITORS

To Mark Bowald and Jon Laansma, stalwart friends
on the pilgrimage of faith seeking understanding

ZONDERVAN ACADEMIC

Lord Jesus Christ
Copyright © 2023 by Daniel J. Treier

Requests for information should be addressed to: Zondervan, 3900 *Sparks Dr. SE, Grand Rapids, Michigan 49546*

Zondervan titles may be purchased in bulk for educational, business, fundraising, or sales promotional use. For information, please email SpecialMarkets@Zondervan.com.

ISBN 978-0-310-16045-8 (audio)

Library of Congress Cataloging-in-Publication Data
Names: Treier, Daniel J., 1972- author. | Allen, Michael, 1981- editor. | Swain, Scott R., editor.
Title: Lord Jesus Christ / Daniel J. Treier, Michael Allen, Scott R. Swain.
Other titles: New studies in dogmatics
Description: Grand Rapids : Zondervan, 2023. | Series: New studies in dogmatics | Includes bibliographical references and index.
Identifiers: LCCN 2023015843 (print) | LCCN 2023015844 (ebook) | ISBN 9780310491774 (paperback) | ISBN 9780310491781 (ebook)
Subjects: LCSH: Jesus Christ--History of doctrines. | Jesus Christ--Person and offices. | BISAC: RELIGION / Christian Theology / Christology | RELIGION / Christian Theology / Systematic
Classification: LCC BT198 .T74 2023 (print) | LCC BT198 (ebook) | DDC 232.09--dc23/eng/20230505
LC record available at https://lccn.loc.gov/2023015843
LC ebook record available at https://lccn.loc.gov/2023015844

"The Visitation" is reprinted with the kind permission of author Malcolm Guite from *Sounding the Seasons: Seventy Sonnets for the Christian Year* (London: Canterbury, 2012).

Small portions have been adapted from the following publications, used by permission.

Daniel J. Treier, "Incarnation," in *Christian Dogmatics: Reformed Theology for the Church Catholic*, ed. Michael Allen and Scott R. Swain (Grand Rapids: Baker Academic [a division of Baker Publishing Group], 2016), 216–42.

Daniel J. Treier, *Introducing Evangelical Theology* (Grand Rapids: Baker Academic [a division of Baker Publishing Group], 2019).

Daniel J. Treier, "'Mediator of a New Covenant': Atonement and Christology in Hebrews," in *So Great a Salvation: A Dialogue on the Atonement in Hebrews*, ed. Jon C. Laansma, George H. Guthrie, and Cynthia Long Westfall, LNTS (London: Bloomsbury T&T Clark, 2019), 105–19.

Cover design: Micah Kandros Design
Interior design: Kait Lamphere and Denise Froehlich
Interior typesetting: Sara Colley

Printed in the United States of America

23 24 25 26 27 28 TRM 9 8 7 6 5 4 3 2 1

CONTENTS

DETAILED CONTENTS

1. COMMUNION AS THE SON OF GOD (EPHESIANS 1:3–14)

As epitomized in **Ephesians 1:3–14**, Jesus Christ is the **Son of God**, who enjoys eternal **communion** with the Father and the Holy Spirit. *Confessing the eternal generation of the Son as the Logos asarkos is integral to properly naming the persons of the Blessed Trinity. The triune God elected to share the divine communion with human beings in a history of salvation, unifying the cosmos in the fellowship and praise of Jesus Christ.*

2. CREATION AS THE IMAGE
OF GOD (COLOSSIANS 1:15–29)

As epitomized in **Colossians 1:15–29**, Jesus Christ is the unique **Image of God**, who embodies the divine Wisdom active in the **creation** of the world. *In this Son the cosmos holds together, and the one true God has begun reconciling all things through the redemption of human beings, so that they may represent the glory and enjoy the shalom of their Creator's reign.*

3. COVENANT AS THE MESSIAH (LUKE 24:13–35)

As epitomized in **Luke 24:13–35**, Jesus Christ is the **Messiah**, who fulfills God's **covenant** promises. *Recognition of the resurrected Lord is given as Christ makes himself present through Word and* *sacrament. The inaugurated fulfillment of the Old Testament's prophetic witness authorizes christological interpretation of its promises, patterns, and proclamation for God's covenant people, then and now.*

4. ADVENT AS IMMANUEL (ISAIAH 7:14)

As epitomized in **Isaiah 7:14**, the Old Testament anticipated the first **advent** of Jesus Christ as **Immanuel**, God with us, incarnate in a fully human life. *This incarnate state began with the Holy Spirit overshadowing Jesus's virginal conception in Mary. Returning God's redemptive presence to the covenant people, the eternal Son thus assumed a fully human nature and identified impeccably with humanity's fallen history.*

5. REVELATION AS THE WORD (JOHN 1:1–18)

As epitomized in **John 1:1–18**, Jesus Christ is the **Word**, whose incarnation is God's ultimate self-**revelation**. *As the first six ecumenical councils recognized, the hypostatic union of full deity and full humanity in this Logos was essential for the triune God's redemptive love to illuminate us. Contra the seventh ecumenical council (787), though, the uniqueness of this incarnate Word requires continuing iconoclastic obedience to the second commandment. From revelatory alignment with Trinitarian missions there comes theological support for* filioque *regarding the Spirit's procession.*

6. HUMILIATION OF THE LORD AS SERVANT (PHILIPPIANS 2:5–11)

As epitomized in **Philippians 2:5–11**, Jesus Christ is the Lord, whose **humiliation** as **Servant** revealed the glory of God's love in rendering the ultimate human obedience. *His twofold earthly state intertwined humiliation with exaltation while also involving the redemptive sequence of suffering followed by glory. Contra kenotic Christologies, a classically Reformed account of the* communicatio idiomatum *addresses Christ's presence by affirming the* extra carnem, *Christ's knowledge by acknowledging his pilgrim faith, and Christ's power by articulating theandric agency.*

7. MISSION AS JESUS OF NAZARETH, THE SAVIOR (LUKE 4:14–30)

As epitomized in **Luke 4:14–30**, Jesus of Nazareth is the **Savior**, whose earthly **mission** inaugurated God's kingdom in person. *Uniquely anointed with the Holy Spirit, Jesus represented humanity as the perfectly faithful Israelite before God; fulfilled the threefold office of prophet, priest, and king; and proclaimed forgiveness, healing, and liberation in word and deed.*

8. PASSION AS THE SON OF MAN
(MARK 10:32–45; ISAIAH 52:13–53:12)

As epitomized in **Mark 10:32–45** (with **Isaiah 52:13–53:12** in
the background), Jesus Christ is the **Son of Man**, whose **passion** was the once-for-all act of atonement through which God
redeemed us. *Amid an array of biblical metaphors, penal substitution
is the central concept that clarifies how Jesus's crucifixion bore away sin's
deadly consequences. The extent of Christ's sinless identification with
fallen humanity is evident in his body's burial and his soul's descent to
the dead. Yet as Son of Man he also attained our eschatological triumph.*

9. EXALTATION AS THE MEDIATOR
(HEBREWS 7:22–8:6)

As epitomized in **Hebrews 7:22–8:6**, Jesus Christ is the theandric **Mediator** between God and humanity, whose bodily
resurrection and ascension inaugurated his **exaltation**. *As his
transfiguration anticipated, he now enjoys his heavenly session while
shepherding his church on its earthly pilgrimage—incorporating par-*

ticipants in the new covenant through baptism, indwelling them by his Spirit, instructing them as their Lord, and interceding for them based on his completed work of atonement.

10. CONSUMMATION AS THE BRIDEGROOM
(REVELATION 21:1–22:5)

As epitomized in **Revelation 21:1–22:5**, Jesus Christ is the **Bridegroom**, whose return will bring the **consummation** of creation and redemption, glorifying the covenant people to be fully at home with God. *After the final judgment, only righteousness will fill the new cosmos; with history's struggles ended and tragedies redeemed, we will enjoy intimate communion with God and each other in Christ. Until then, the Lord's Supper nourishes faith with a foretaste of such communion.*

SERIES PREFACE

New Studies in Dogmatics follows in the tradition of G. C. Berkouwer's classic series, Studies in Dogmatics, in seeking to offer concise, focused treatments of major topics in dogmatic theology that fill the gap between introductory theology textbooks and advanced theological monographs. Dogmatic theology, as understood by editors and contributors to the series, is a conceptual representation of scriptural teaching about God and all things in relation to God. The source of dogmatics is Holy Scripture; its scope is the summing up of all things in Jesus Christ; its setting is the communion of the saints; and its end is the conversion, consolation, and instruction of creaturely wayfarers in the knowledge and love of the triune God until that knowledge and love is consummated in the beatific vision.

The series wagers that the way forward in constructive theology lies in a program of renewal through retrieval. This wager follows upon the judgment that much modern theology exhibits "a stubborn tendency to grow not higher but to the side," to borrow Alexander Solzhenitsyn's words from another context. Though modern theology continues to grow in a number of areas of technical expertise and interdisciplinary facility (especially in both the exegetical and historical domains), this growth too often displays a sideways drift rather than an upward progression in relation to theology's subject matter, scope, and source, and in fulfilling theology's end. We believe the path toward theological renewal in such a situation lies in drawing more deeply upon the resources of Holy Scripture in conversation with the church's most trusted teachers (ancient, medieval, and modern) who have sought to fathom Christ's unsearchable riches. In keeping with this belief, authors from a broad evangelical constituency will seek in this series to retrieve the riches of Scripture and tradition for constructive dogmatics. The purpose of retrieval is neither simple repetition of past theologians nor repristination of an earlier phase in church history; Christianity, at any rate, has no golden age east of Eden and short of the kingdom of God. Properly understood, retrieval is an inclusive and enlarging venture, a matter of tapping into a vital root and, in some cases, of relearning a lost grammar of theological discourse, all for the sake of equipping the church in its contemporary vocation to think and speak faithfully and fruitfully about God and God's works.

While the specific emphases of individual volumes will vary, each volume will display (1) awareness of the "state of the question" pertaining to the doctrine under discussion; (2) attention to the patterns of biblical reasoning (exegetical, biblical-theological, etc.) from which the doctrine emerges; (3) engagement with relevant ecclesiastical statements of the doctrine (creedal, conciliar, confessional), as well as with leading theologians of the church; and (4) appreciation of the doctrine's location within the larger system of theology, as well as of its contribution to Christian piety and practice.

Our prayer is that by drawing upon the best resources of the past and with an awareness of both perennial and proximate challenges to Christian thought and practice in the present, New Studies in Dogmatics will contribute to a flourishing theological culture in the church today. Soli Deo Gloria.

MICHAEL ALLEN AND SCOTT R. SWAIN

ACKNOWLEDGMENTS

As always, I could not have written this book without the encouragement and forbearance of my wife, Amy, and daughter, Anna, along with our extended families and family of faith at Immanuel Presbyterian Church in Warrenville, Illinois. My office neighbor, Tim Larsen, and the rest of the Wednesday lunch group—even when we were Zooming, thanks to COVID-19—also provided a bulwark of (in)sanity. Time spent with Kevin and Sylvie Vanhoozer and Doug and Wilma Sweeney was a precious encouragement during the five challenging years of this project.

Colleagues Andy Abernethy and Marc Cortez graciously read the manuscript—usually with Andy making it clearer and Marc making it more complicated. Other colleagues such as Greg Lee, Richard Schultz, and Carlos Sosa Siliezar were helpful sounding boards, and Keith Johnson kindly gave me a sneak peek at an important new book. Several graduate students—Gerardo Corpeño, Craig Hefner, Dustyn Keepers, Sean Fei Long, Jeremy Mann, Joel Miles, Euntaek "David" Shin, Chris Smith, Nimrod Tica, and Michael Yoo—provided questions, research assistance, and support. During this project Ty Kieser went from graduate student to colleague, and this book is much better for his frequent help. In several iterations of a Christology seminar, numerous other students occasioned clearer thinking and contributed exegetical notes on the Scripture texts that anchor the chapters. I have tried to acknowledge specific debts along the way, but I ask for forgiveness if middle-aged forgetfulness triumphed.

I also express gratitude and a potential apology to the authors of many stimulating Christology books over the past decade or two. I am grateful for their intellectual contributions, even if the revived interest in this doctrine became overwhelming. If interlocutors like Bruce McCormack, who has always been generous to me, see this book, they could legitimately ask for more explanation about roads not taken. Yet the assigned task and word limit precluded engaging them in my preferred way—by summarizing their best arguments before stating summary judgments.

Alas, paragraphs became footnotes, and then tens of thousands more words hit the cutting-room floor.

Greg Morrison and staff members at Buswell Library did yeoman work to sustain our teaching and scholarship during these pandemic years. For several months these poor souls were scanning specific pages or entire sections upon request, and I kept requests coming every few days.

Michael Card's music, especially his trilogy on *The Life*, has been a christological provocateur and companion throughout my adult life. I am thankful for such help with turning theological contemplation into awestruck praise.

Michael Allen and Scott Swain have been among my closest friends for over twenty years. Here I owe them much for entrusting me with Christology, where their conceptual footprints will also be apparent. Katya Covrett, Matthew Estel, and the rest of the Zondervan team have been generous throughout the editorial process.

This book's dedicatees have shaped my life—and endured my snoring at the annual conferences—for nearly thirty years. Although cousins by blood, they offer distinct intellectual gifts, together keeping me exegetically honest and theologically alert. Despite their ignorant support for the Wolverines, we find common ground on the Detroit Tigers, and, more importantly, they have treated this Buckeye as more than a worthless nut.

ABBREVIATIONS

AARAS	American Academy of Religion Academy Series
AB	Anchor Bible
ACCS	Ancient Christian Commentary on Scripture
AnBib	Analecta Biblica
ASBT	Acadia Studies in Bible and Theology
ASET	Africa Society of Evangelical Theology
BBR	*Bulletin for Biblical Research*
BECNT	Baker Exegetical Commentary on the New Testament
BibInt	Biblical Interpretation Series
BS	Barth Studies
BST	The Bible Speaks Today
BTCB	Brazos Theological Commentary on the Bible
BTNT	Biblical Theology of the New Testament
CB	The Church's Bible
CBQ	*Catholic Biblical Quarterly*
CCT	Challenges in Contemporary Theology
CD	*Church Dogmatics*. Karl Barth. Edited by G. W. Bromiley and T. F. Torrance. 4 vols. in 14 parts. Edinburgh: T&T Clark, 1956–75
CIT	Current Issues in Theology
CNTOT	*Commentary on the New Testament Use of the Old Testament.* Edited by G. K. Beale and D. A. Carson. Grand Rapids: Baker Academic, 2007
CSCD	Cambridge Studies in Christian Doctrine
CSR	*Christian Scholar's Review*
DBWE	Dietrich Bonhoeffer Works in English
DJG	*Dictionary of Jesus and the Gospels*. Edited by Joel B. Green, Jeannine K. Brown, and Nicholas Perrin. 2nd ed. Downers Grove, IL: InterVarsity Press, 2013

DTIB	*Dictionary for Theological Interpretation of the Bible.* Edited by Kevin J. Vanhoozer, Craig G. Bartholomew, N. T. Wright, and Daniel J. Treier. Grand Rapids: Baker Academic, 2005
EDT	*Evangelical Dictionary of Theology.* Edited by Daniel J. Treier and Walter A. Elwell. 3rd ed. Grand Rapids: Baker Academic, 2017
EGGNT	Exegetical Guide to the Greek New Testament
EGNT	Exegetical Guide to the New Testament
ES	Emerging Scholars
FET	Foundations of Evangelical Theology
FZAW	Forschungen zum Alten Testament
GDT	*Global Dictionary of Theology: A Resource for the Worldwide Church.* Edited by William A. Dyrness and Veli-Matti Kärkkäinen. Downers Grove, IL: InterVarsity Press, 2008
ICC	International Critical Commentary
IJST	*International Journal of Systematic Theology*
Int	*Interpretation*
ITC	International Theological Commentary
JETS	*Journal of the Evangelical Theological Society*
JRT	*Journal of Reformed Theology*
JSNT	*Journal for the Study of the New Testament*
JSNTSup	*Journal for the Study of the New Testament* Supplement Series
JTI	*Journal of Theological Interpretation*
JTS	*Journal of Theological Studies*
LBS	Library of Biblical Studies
LCC	Library of Christian Classics
LNTS	The Library of New Testament Studies
ModTheo	*Modern Theology*
MWT	Majority World Theology
NAC	New American Commentary
NIB	*The New Interpreter's Bible.* Edited by Leander Keck. 12 vols. Nashville: Abingdon, 1994–2004
NICNT	New International Commentary on the New Testament
NICOT	New International Commentary on the Old Testament
NIGTC	New International Greek Testament Commentary
NovT	*Novum Testamentum*
NovTSup	Supplements to *Novum Testamentum*

NPNF2	*Nicene and Post-Nicene Fathers*, Series 2. 14 vols. Edited by Philip Schaff and Henry Wace. Reprint, Peabody, MA: Hendrickson, 2004
NSBT	New Studies in Biblical Theology
NSD	New Studies in Dogmatics
NTL	New Testament Library
NTT	New Testament Theology
OECS	Oxford Early Christian Studies
OSAT	Oxford Studies in Analytic Theology
OTL	Old Testament Library
OTM	Oxford Theological Monographs
OWC	Oxford World's Classics
PP	Popular Patristics
ProEccl	*Pro Ecclesia*
PRRD	*Post-Reformation Reformed Dogmatics*. Richard A. Muller. 4 vols. Grand Rapids: Baker Academic, 2003
RBL	*Review of Biblical Literature*
RCS	Reformation Commentary on Scripture
SBET	*Scottish Bulletin of Evangelical Theology*
SCDS	Studies in Christian Doctrine and Scripture
SHS	Scripture and Hermeneutics Series
SJT	*Scottish Journal of Theology*
SNTSMS	Society for New Testament Studies Monograph Series
SST	Studies in Systematic Theology
TC	Theology in Community
THNTC	Two Horizons New Testament Commentary
TS	*Theological Studies*
TynBul	*Tyndale Bulletin*
WUNT	Wissenschaftliche Untersuchungen zum Neuen Testament

INTRODUCTION

Theology is "an integrating discipline that studies how the church may bear enduring, timely, and truthful—that is, wise—witness to the Triune God revealed in Jesus Christ";[1] dogmatic theology focuses on exposition of the church's authoritative teaching. The present book's dogmatic Christology is accountable to both ecumenical dogma and additional Protestant confessions. Authoritative doctrine is not the exclusive reference point for the exposition, but it establishes the realm within which faith seeks understanding. Because so much modern Christology is preoccupied with methods of understanding, it is tempting instead to plunge immediately into the subject matter. However, knowledge of Christ is a gift; its reception is a christological subject that needs a proper introduction. So, first, a brief survey of Christology's historical development identifies four crucial factors shaping contemporary debates. Second, a sketch of the present book's approach identifies four paired aspirations. Third, a short synopsis explains the book's title, identifies its distinct perspective, and charts the theses of its chapters.

I. CRUCIAL FACTORS SHAPING CHRISTOLOGY

Dogmatic Christology started with a biblical foundation and built traditional structures during the patristic, medieval, and Reformation periods—only to suffer the modern collapse of its "incarnational narrative," which made space for competing reconstruction sites today.[2] Christology has gathered its biblical materials from theological exegesis

---

1. Daniel J. Treier, "Systematic Theology," in *EDT*, 853.
2. This broad outline appears in the hermeneutical survey of Daniel J. Treier, "Jesus Christ, Doctrine of," in *DTIB*, 363–71. Reflecting later scholastic divisions, the word *Christology* is first attested in English in 1673 and was not widely used until the nineteenth century, according to Brian E. Daley, SJ, *God Visible: Patristic Christology Reconsidered*, Changing Paradigms in Historical and Systematic Theology (Oxford: Oxford University Press, 2018), 8n24.

of specific texts along with various forms of biblical-theological synthesis, including the "titles" of Christ. Biblical materials grounded the creedal cornerstones of Nicaea (325), Constantinople (381), and Chalcedon (451): the fully divine and fully human natures of Jesus Christ as one incarnate person of the Blessed Trinity.[3] Beyond the creedal cornerstones, Christology's traditional structures included medieval scholastic contemplation and mystical devotion. Protestant Christology added emphasis upon Christ as the one Mediator who fully accomplished our gracious redemption when he died on a Roman cross. The incarnational narrative's modern collapse stemmed from the rise of historical criticism and human subjectivity: a historical split emerged between Jesus of Nazareth and the Christ of faith, a Hellenization thesis emerged with a split between early Jewish Christianity and Christology's gradual corruption by Greek philosophy, and a hermeneutical split emerged between faith and reason. In the twentieth century Karl Barth (1886–1968) epitomized rebuilding efforts "from above," that is, by relating Christ to human subjectivity through a Trinitarian account of God's self-revelation, and Wolfhart Pannenberg (1928–2014) epitomized rebuilding efforts "from below," that is, by relating Jesus to historical criticism through a Trinitarian and eschatological account of his resurrection. In a variation on the latter theme, Jürgen Moltmann (1926–) has encouraged global hopes for liberation by relating Jesus as the crucified God to the appalling depths of creaturely suffering.

As christological reconstruction sites proliferated in recent decades, the categories and even the claims of the Chalcedonian Definition remained under pressure. Among the proposals engaged in ensuing chapters, (1) kenotic Christologies that began to arise in the nineteenth century retain broadly Chalcedonian claims, but they depart from traditional categories by having the incarnate Christ "empty himself" (Phil 2:7) of divine attributes or at least their use. (2) Similarly, Barthian Christologies remain broadly Chalcedonian, but they embrace an actualistic ontology and debate the extent of its (in)compatibility with the substance metaphysics reflected in conciliar categories. (3) Liberationist Christologies range from suspicion to rejection of Chalcedon's claims,

---

3. The impetus for the foundation metaphor(s) comes from 1 Corinthians 3:10–11. But for a "building block" narrative that also surveys recent scholarship on creedal development, see Wolfram Kinzig and Markus Vinzent, "Recent Research on the Origin of the Creed," *JTS* 50, no. 2 (October 1999): 535–59.

not least because its context aligned the divine Christ with the human emperor. (4) Postcolonial and enculturationist Christologies worry that liberationist critiques of Scripture and tradition do not prioritize social context enough, although liberationists may worry in return that any cultural status quo can be oppressive. (5) Feminist Christologies wonder whether the Chalcedonian Christ, identified as male because of the Bible's Jesus, can be redemptive for women.

The upshot of this historical survey is that four crucial factors confront Protestant Christology with challenging questions. Indeed, the traditional distinction between the person and work of Christ, with the former being the focus of Christology and the latter occupying the intersection between soteriology and atonement, is challenged by modern critiques of metaphysics and late- or postmodern concerns for ethics. It seems as if we cannot understand who Jesus is apart from what he has done and how he calls people to live. Before sketching a response, we examine these crucial factors more closely.

A. The Gospel(s): The One, the Four, the Fifth, and the Many

Contemporary Christology reflects diverse biblical ways of integrating Jesus's person and work. *Gospel* is both a biblical genre and a theological concept. This good news is ultimately identified with God's gracious presence in the person of Jesus. Scripture's short summaries of the gospel focus on him, particularly his death and resurrection (e.g., 1 Cor 15:3–4). Yet the New Testament also contains four books that narrate his earthly life and ministry, culminating in his passion. The need for four Gospels to render Jesus's identity indicates its sheer fullness, adding both credibility and complexity: the Bible meets the historical criterion of multiple attestation without harmonizing details too neatly. And Isaiah is a so-called fifth Gospel, evoked by all four of the others within their first chapters. The terminology *gospel* itself, along with its core announcement regarding YHWH's return as Redeemer, stems from this prophet (Isa 40:9; 52:7).

While the gospel's theological content is relatively singular, its communicative contexts are plural. The four Gospels are "passion narratives with extended introductions," as Martin Kähler's famous saying goes—culminating in the protagonist's death, as ancient biographies would expect to do, and then, shockingly, his resurrection.[4] Yet these extended introductions vary considerably, not just between John and the Synoptics but even among Matthew, Mark, and Luke. Meanwhile, some New Testament epistles contain confessional formulae (e.g., 1 Cor 12:3; 15:3–4), whereas others scarcely refer to Jesus (e.g., James). Given this credible variety and complex unity, questions ensue concerning how to relate the Gospels and epistles. The former are saturated with "the kingdom of God," whereas the latter scarcely mention "discipleship." In many eyes, renewed attention to the incarnate Christ of the Gospels challenges the soteriology that classic Protestants draw from the epistles. And yet the resurrection fundamentally changed the redemptive-historical context between Jesus's earthly ministry and the church's missionary situations, understandably drawing classic Protestant attention toward Pauline soteriology.

B. Greek Philosophy: Substance Metaphysics and the Hellenization Thesis

Contemporary Christology reflects lively debate about Greek philosophy's influence upon Christian dogma. The Nicene Creed's decisive term *homoousios* asserts that the "one Lord, Jesus Christ, the only Son of God," is "of one being with the Father." *Ousia* designates an unchanging essence. Every visible creature has a physical substrate that incorporates change. Metaphysics is an inquiry into the essences of creaturely beings, going beyond changeable aspects in defining their natures. Because physical substrates are involved, the metaphysical tradition spawned by Greek philosophy also speaks in terms of substances—secondary substances that are universals containing properties shared by all members ("dog"), and primary substances that are individual members of such classes (my dog, "Gizmo"), having unique accidental properties ("jumpy"). It was not obvious how metaphysical categories might apply christologically, or else the history of early church councils might not have been so complicated. Identifying Christ the Word as *homoousios* with the Father seemed to diminish God's transcendence or the Father's precedence in generating the Son. Later, identifying Christ as *homoousios* with other human beings seemed to diminish his deity or personal unity. But conciliar dogma gradually

---

4. On the Gospels vis-à-vis biography and memory, see most recently Craig Keener, *Christobiography: Memory, History, and the Reliability of the Gospels* (Grand Rapids: Eerdmans, 2019).

appropriated metaphysical terminology for summarizing fundamental claims of biblical Christology, excluding deviations that would undermine Christian worship or salvation.

Many modern Christologies, however, are unconvinced about the viability of such metaphysics. Even theologians who embrace the "values" of Chalcedon worry about identifying the incarnate Christ with the classic understanding of deity. It seems impossible for an immutable Logos to become flesh or an impassible God to suffer for our salvation. Even if incarnation and crucifixion can somehow be attributed to the divine Logos, it at least seems impossible for him to be genuinely united with a Jesus who is fully human in the sense that modernity values—rendering self-activated obedience to God.[5] Hence numerous Protestants have insisted on finding new forms for conveying the catholic substance of conciliar dogma.[6] Even some who affirm the dogma worry that modern dualism between God and humanity emerged from conciliar use of Greek metaphysics in the first place.[7] And yet current patristics scholarship challenges modern assumptions about both the extent and the evaluation of Hellenization, while Protestant retrieval efforts challenge several aspects of the newer Christologies.

C. German Enlightenment: Historical Quests and the Human Ego

Contemporary Christologies reflect two lingering influences from early modern Germany: quests for the historical Jesus and newfound emphasis on the *psyche* as essential to full humanity. Modernity involved a new attentiveness to location in history.[8] In the nineteenth century, "lives" of Jesus began treating history as a critical discipline: the truth of the church's Scriptures and tradition could not be presupposed, but impartial judgments must be made using criteria like analogy and

---

5. Rejecting divine impassibility and affirming such human obedience are core moves in the Reformed kenoticism of Bruce L. McCormack, *The Humility of the Eternal Son: Reformed Kenoticism and the Repair of Chalcedon*, CIT (Cambridge: Cambridge University Press, 2021).

6. So, e.g., given the "very inadequate" conceptual tools of the catholic tradition, according to part III, C, in Paul Tillich, *Systematic Theology*, vol. 3 (Chicago: University of Chicago Press, 1963).

7. E.g., Colin E. Gunton, *Yesterday and Today: A Study of Continuities in Christology* (Grand Rapids: Eerdmans, 1983).

8. For profound wrestling with this new sensibility, see both the poem itself and the introduction by Alan Jacobs in W. H. Auden, *For the Time Being: A Christmas Oratorio*, ed. Alan Jacobs (Princeton: Princeton University Press, 2013).

correlation.[9] These criteria actually treat biblical narratives and conciliar dogma as guilty until proven innocent, because the incarnation, miracles, and resurrection involve unique or at least unusual events—for which arguments from analogy would never lead to historical probability.[10] Epitomizing assumptions in play, Rudolf Bultmann (1884–1976) famously suggested, "It is impossible to use electric light and the wireless and to avail ourselves of modern medical and surgical discoveries, and at the same time to believe in the New Testament world of spirits and miracles."[11] Whereas earlier British skeptics simply rejected biblical miracles out of hand, Bultmann paradigmatically reinterpreted them in terms of "myth"—legendary or literary representations of powers beyond ancient comprehension in terms of supernatural forces or events.[12] Such rejection or reinterpretation of miracles and the resurrection had rebound effects on the reality of incarnation.[13] One critic suggested that many new lives of Jesus were written out of "hate" in the first place,[14] and the authority of the Old Testament fared poorly in early modern Christologies as well.[15]

Although historical Jesus quests faced substantial criticism, they accompanied newfound interest in human subjectivity, and they accentuated a shift from examining the person of Christ to experiencing his saving work.[16] Skeptical about metaphysical knowledge, modernity

9. An influential treatment of these competing orientations is Van Austin Harvey, *The Historian and the Believer; The Morality of Historical Knowledge and Christian Belief* (New York: Macmillan, 1966).

10. Whatever his intentions, David Hume's definition of miracles in opposition to probabilistic natural laws stacked the deck against their historical plausibility and then made some defenders too nervous about claiming divine intervention within the natural order—this despite the salvage attempt in Robert J. Fogelin, *A Defense of Hume on Miracles* (Princeton: Princeton University Press, 2003). But see, e.g., Timothy McGrew, "Review of Fogelin," *Mind* 114, no. 453 (January 2005): 145–49.

11. "New Testament and Mythology: The Problem of Demythologizing the New Testament Proclamation (1941)," in Rudolf Bultmann, *The New Testament and Mythology and Other Basic Writings*, ed. Schubert Ogden (Philadelphia: Fortress, 1984), 4.

12. See Rudolf Bultmann, *Jesus Christ and Mythology* (New York: Scribner's, 1958). On the early modern contrast between British and German critics, see Hans W. Frei, *The Eclipse of Biblical Narrative: A Study in Eighteenth and Nineteenth Century Hermeneutics* (New Haven, CT: Yale University Press, 1974).

13. Infamously, John Hick, ed., *The Myth of God Incarnate* (Philadelphia: Westminster, 1977).

14. So Albert Schweitzer, according to Alister E. McGrath, *The Making of Modern German Christology: From the Enlightenment to Pannenberg* (Oxford: Blackwell, 1986), 2.

15. See the stunning quotation from Adolf von Harnack—that only Protestantism's "crippling" maintained the Old Testament's canonical status—in John Behr, *The Way to Nicaea*, vol. 1 of *Formation of Christian Theology* (Crestwood, NY: St. Vladimir's Seminary Press, 2001), 18.

16. This shift is summarized by, e.g., Walter Lowe, "Christ and Salvation," in *Christian Theology: An Introduction to Its Traditions and Tasks*, ed. Peter C. Hodgson and Robert H. King (Minneapolis: Fortress, 1994), 222. To trace its effects on theologians like Barth, see Kathryn Tanner, "Jesus Christ," in *The Cambridge Companion to Christian Doctrine*, ed. Colin E. Gunton

prioritized Christology over Trinitarian theology proper—in a particular way. Lacking confidence in identifying who Jesus really was or is, modernity therefore prioritized soteriology and ethics—what Christ reveals about divine benevolence and human responsibility: "A God without wrath brought men without sin into a Kingdom without judgment through the ministrations of a Christ without a Cross."[17] Perhaps the Christology of Friedrich Schleiermacher (1768–1834) epitomizes the challenge faced by even sophisticated accounts: "Is Christ a teacher who could be surpassed and left behind, once the lesson is mastered? Or is he a teacher who can never be excluded from the lesson he conveys, for he is source but also sustenance, without whom no lesson can be mastered?" Wanting to affirm the latter, Schleiermacher and many since struggled to prevent the historical church from swallowing up the original Christ.[18] Modernity's historical methods did not produce consensus about Jesus's identity, but they reduced confidence in the Bible's traditional message while refocusing critical study on the church's praxis.[19] Yet, for all its historical overconfidence and lack of christological confidence, modernity can both reflect the influence and renew the church's understanding of Jesus, especially with its attention to Christology's human factors.

D. Global Contexts: Conciliar Ecumenism and Cultural Engagement

Contemporary Christology reflects increasing attention to both global contexts and marginalized voices within the previously dominant Anglo-European world. The twentieth century saw rapid indigenous and missionary Christian expansion throughout the global South, which theologians eventually noticed; other factors like decolonization and globalization also fostered "Majority World" Christology. Closer to North American homes, Black and feminist theologians gradually drew others' attention to race and gender. A long history of marginalizing

(Cambridge: Cambridge University Press, 1997), 245–72. Perhaps the paradigmatic theological example comes from the intertwining of Christ with redemption through God-consciousness in Friedrich Schleiermacher, *Christian Faith: A New Translation and Critical Edition*, trans. Terrence N. Tice, Catherine L. Kelsey, and Edwina Lawler, 2 vols. (Louisville: Westminster John Knox, 2016).

17. H. Richard Niebuhr, *The Kingdom of God in America* (New York: Harper & Row, 1937), 193.

18. Katherine Sonderegger, "Jesus Christ and the Incarnation," in *The Oxford Handbook of Christmas*, ed. Timothy Larsen (Oxford: Oxford University Press, 2020), 94–97.

19. Finding the historical stalwart Ernst Troeltsch (1865–1923) most instructive where he is most negative, namely regarding a social phenomenology of faith's referent for *Christ*, is Sarah Coakley, *Christ without Absolutes: A Study of the Christology of Ernst Troeltsch* (Oxford: Clarendon, 1988).

Jesus's Jewish body catalyzed colonialism and sustained complicity with racism and slavery.[20] Neglecting Jesus's empowerment of women favored existing cultural stereotypes, alienating marginalized people from the power of self-giving love.[21] Similarly, Christologies outside the West highlight otherwise neglected questions—especially poverty and oppression in Latin America, identity vis-à-vis tribal cultures in Africa, and religious pluralism in Asia.[22]

Such newfound cultural engagement confronts evangelical Christology with both opportunities and challenges.[23] Challenges emerge from the need for liberation alongside and after enculturation, and for reconciliation alongside and after liberation.[24] Moreover, previous generations of evangelical Christology neglected conciliar ecumenism along with cultural engagement. Biblical Christology calls for both rather than simply replacing assumed orthodoxy with passion for justice. In embodying God's embrace of human particularity, Jesus personalizes a universal challenge: all theologies must do justice to *this* Word, sharing

---

20. Willie James Jennings, *The Christian Imagination: Theology and the Origins of Race* (New Haven, CT: Yale University Press, 2011). See also provocative essays in George Yancy, ed., *Christology and Whiteness: What Would Jesus Do?* (London; New York: Routledge, 2012). Yancy's introduction relates whiteness to power and privilege rather than skin color per se, and the book makes intriguing conceptual appeals to Samaritans. But the framing WWJD? question is problematic, especially when some authors propose that Jesus himself might be wrong.

21. For christological intersections with feminist concerns, see Sarah Coakley, "*Kenōsis* and Subversion: On the Repression of 'Vulnerability' in Christian Feminist Writing," in *Powers and Submissions: Spirituality, Philosophy and Gender*, CCT (Oxford: Blackwell, 2002), 3–39; Ruth Groenhout, "Kenosis and Feminist Theory," in *Exploring Kenotic Christology: The Self-Emptying of God*, ed. C. Stephen Evans (Oxford: Oxford University Press, 2006), 291–312.

22. See, e.g., Volker Küster, *The Many Faces of Jesus Christ: Intercultural Christology*, trans. John Bowden (Maryknoll, NY: Orbis, 2001). Of course these are textbook generalizations, yet such foci had their initial moments. For additional surveys, see Veli-Matti Kärkkäinen, *Christology: A Global Introduction* (Grand Rapids: Baker Academic, 2003); Gene L. Green, Stephen T. Pardue, and K. K. Yeo, eds., *Jesus without Borders: Christology in the Majority World*, MWT (Grand Rapids: Eerdmans, 2014). For more contextual tensions, see the epilogue of R. S. Sugirtharajah, ed., *Asian Faces of Jesus*, Faith and Cultures (Maryknoll, NY: Orbis, 1993).

23. For culturally framed christological analysis, see Colin J. D. Greene, *Christology in Cultural Perspective: Marking Out the Horizons* (Grand Rapids: Eerdmans, 2004). Earlier evangelicals did not entirely ignore global contexts and injustice. See, e.g., Vinay Samuel and Chris Sugden, eds., *Sharing Jesus in the Two Thirds World: Evangelical Christologies from the Contexts of Poverty, Powerlessness and Religious Pluralism* (Bangalore: Partnership in Mission-Asia, 1983). Chapters addressed every major region, Islam as well as Buddhism, and marginalized groups in the "West," while the original conference modeled genuine dialogue. However, a decade later evangelical students like me never heard of them.

24. See, e.g., discussion of "social reconstruction" in Diane B. Stinton, *Jesus of Africa: Voices of Contemporary African Christology* (Maryknoll, NY: Orbis, 2004), 222–26. Stinton's book reflects an important, albeit contested, effort to study popular and not just professional theology. On liberation and enculturation consider, e.g., the Dalits vis-à-vis the Hindu caste system as mentioned by Ivor Poobalan, "Christology in Asia: Rooted and Responsive," in *Asian Christian Theology: Evangelical Perspectives*, ed. Timoteo D. Gener and Stephen T. Pardue (Carlisle, Cumbria, UK: Langham Global Library, 2019), 96.

what the Spirit illuminates in their contexts while likewise seeking to understand the truth that others have seen. And yet in these challenges lie opportunities for needed repentance and fresh insight, especially concerning holistic mission. Perhaps, when we enjoy the heavenly worship promised in Revelation 7:9–10, "there will be a Bach–inspired version of this song of praise, and a hip–hop version, and a bluegrass version."[25]

II. CHRISTIAN FAITH SEEKING CHRISTOLOGICAL UNDERSTANDING

The current book approaches dogmatic Christology as an exercise of faith seeking understanding, written primarily as an expository argument. When theologians contemplate God and all things in relation to God, they make judgments and communicate arguments to support them. Bound by authoritative doctrine, though, dogmatic theology is not primarily a constructive task. Instead, dogmatic theology articulates fundamental truths, examining their coherence and ramifications. Renewed by biblical exegesis, informed by the church's history, stimulated by philosophy and other intellectual disciplines, and challenged by praxis, dogmatics must not be reduced to any of these tasks. It engages their contributions while prayerfully expounding the Christian faith. The current book enacts this commitment to faith seeking christological understanding with four primary, paired aspirations.

A. Evangelical and Ecumenical Faith

First, this dogmatic Christology aspires to be both evangelical and ecumenical by upholding the creedal "rule of faith" and more specifically the Reformed confessions. For Protestant Christology, being ecumenical focuses initially on the seven ecumenical councils. That conciliar dogma comes as close as anything to the Vincentian canon of "what has been believed everywhere, always, and by all." Yet caveats are necessary, given the addition of the *filioque* clause to the Nicene Creed (rejected by the Orthodox East) and the anathematizing of iconoclasm in 787 at Nicaea II (later accepted by much of the Reformed tradition). Thus, to be ecumenical focuses secondarily on the church's peace, unity, and purity from a confessional, albeit teachable, standpoint. In commending a classically

---

25. J. Todd Billings, *Remembrance, Communion, and Hope: Rediscovering the Gospel at the Lord's Table* (Grand Rapids: Eerdmans, 2018), 192.

Reformed Christology, this volume does not labor over the definition of *Reformed* or the preservation of a tradition for its legacy's sake. There is no denying variety among Reformed Christologies or usurping churches' prerogative of dogmatic discipline. Like other Reformed thinkers, if I became convinced that biblical Christology contradicted the confessions, I would align with Scripture as the final authority under Christ. Still, beyond corresponding to my convictions and churchly location, "classically" Reformed adherence to earlier confessions provides a "reference point"—neither Catholic in certain respects, nor Lutheran with respect to Eucharistic presence, nor kenotic with respect to divine perfections.[26]

For Protestant Christology, being evangelical is prior to being ecumenical because Jesus Christ graciously assembles the church. Thus, being evangelical focuses primarily on bearing witness to the gospel: "the joyful *announcement* that the Triune Creator has returned to redeem Israel in Christ, who bore human sin on the cross and was raised from the dead as the firstfruits of our new life; the Holy Spirit is regathering the covenant people around Jesus as Lord and is welcoming gentiles into this redeemed community; ultimately Christ will return to establish the *shalom* of God's comprehensive reign."[27] Consequently, juxtaposing Christology "from above" and "from below" generates false dichotomies. The methodological question of whether the historical Jesus is privileged becomes confused with the material question of whether Christ's full deity is affirmed. Once we confess the incarnation, surely faith acknowledges God's gracious initiative "from above"—not least in sending the Holy Spirit to raise Jesus from the dead and unite us with him. We do not ascend to bring Christ down on our own (Rom 10:6).[28] Of course, the incarnation should incline us to take our humanity and earthly history seriously as matters in which faith should seek lived understanding. Unfortunately, to be evangelical in

---

26. Although it defies a brief summary, see the excellent survey of Reformed diversity and enduring discussions in Ivor J. Davidson, "Christ," in *The Oxford Handbook of Reformed Theology*, ed. Michael Allen and Scott R. Swain (Oxford: Oxford University Press, 2020), 446–72. "Reference point" comes from p. 449. Recent treatments of Reformed identity frequently emphasize the scope of possible exceptions, but perhaps it is equally important to characterize normal tendencies.

27. Italics original in Daniel J. Treier, *Introducing Evangelical Theology* (Grand Rapids: Baker Academic, 2019), 272.

28. Given Christ's presence, distance need not be bridged from our end; so John Webster, *The Culture of Theology*, ed. Ivor J. Davidson and Alden C. McCray (Grand Rapids: Baker Academic, 2019), 87. On the living Christ gathering a congregation, see "Resurrection and Scripture," chap. 2 in John Webster, *The Domain of the Word: Scripture and Theological Reason* (London: T&T Clark, 2012), 41–45. See also the caution about juxtaposing Jesus "then" with faith "now" from "Jesus in Modernity: Reflections on Jüngel's Christology," chap. 5 in John Webster, *Word and Church: Essays in Christian Dogmatics* (New York: T&T Clark, 2001), 165.

a secondary sense—participating in evangelical theology as a subculture—has rarely fostered such christological excellence. We can be grateful for evangelical strength at practically teaching fundamental truths.[29] Corresponding weaknesses, however, reflect overreactions to modern culture "from below": apologetic defensiveness, historical obsessiveness in biblical interpretation, and perhaps intellectual naivete.[30] Most evangelical Christology has been broadly Reformed, intentionally or not, although increasingly tempted by moderate kenoticism.[31] The present book seeks to be theologically evangelical and ecumenical, first and foremost, but on the ground that means expounding classically Reformed confessional commitments while interacting with other evangelical subcultures and contemporary global contexts.

B. Biblical and Historical Seeking

Second, this dogmatic Christology aspires to be both biblical and historical by undertaking theological interpretation of Scripture, engaging accounts of early high Christology, and appropriating historical-Jesus research with theological realism. A theological interpretation of a Scripture text introduces each chapter. Such an approach is not essential for every dogmatic project, but it is strategic in the current environment. Much modern Christology does not engage the Bible deeply, focusing instead on retrieving certain figures or constructing new arguments or championing noble causes. Accordingly, much modern Christology does not connect with ordinary Christians or convince pastors that church doctrine should be preached. If the present book exemplifies how biblical exegesis contributes to exposition of christological teaching, then some of the promise of theological interpretation of Scripture would be fulfilled.[32] Undoubtedly, other passages could have been chosen, but the

---

29. E.g., organized by Story/Images/Practices, Jonathan R. Wilson, *God So Loved the World: A Christology for Disciples* (Grand Rapids: Baker Academic, 2001).

30. For this sobering assessment, see John Webster, "Jesus Christ," in *The Cambridge Companion to Evangelical Theology*, ed. Timothy Larsen and Daniel J. Treier (Cambridge: Cambridge University Press, 2007), 51–63. However, its standard regarding Christology's intellectual deployment should perhaps be tempered.

31. On evangelical Christology from a pietistic perspective, see chap. 3 in Tyron Inbody, *The Many Faces of Christology* (Nashville: Abingdon, 2002).

32. See the promising book (although it arrived too late for careful interaction) by R. B. Jamieson and Tyler R. Wittman, *Biblical Reasoning: Christological and Trinitarian Rules for Exegesis* (Grand Rapids: Baker Academic, 2022). For my accounts, see Daniel J. Treier, *Introducing Theological Interpretation of Scripture: Recovering a Christian Practice* (Grand Rapids: Baker Academic, 2008); Kevin J. Vanhoozer and Daniel J. Treier, *Theology and the Mirror of Scripture: A Mere Evangelical Account*, SCDS (Downers Grove, IL: IVP Academic, 2015). As indicated elsewhere, I am not overly attached to "TIS" terminology, which has limitations. But Jamieson and Wittman

present selection embodies a material claim: biblical Christology presents a coherent, dramatic arc from the eternal communion of the triune God through creation to the consummation of redemptive history. This arc emerges through a canonical reading that incorporates not only Pauline and catholic epistles but also the Synoptic Gospels, the Gospel of John, Isaiah's fifth Gospel, and John's Apocalypse.[33]

Early high Christology bears on both biblical texts and theologically vital aspects of the historical Jesus. The question of how early Christ was understood as included in the identity of YHWH goes beyond the apostolic writers and their audiences to Jesus's self-understanding. If there is good reason to believe that Christ rose from the dead and authorized witnesses who rooted their testimony in Spirit-guided memory, then its content is historically noteworthy.[34] When this testimony includes Jesus's expectation of his death and resurrection as shaped by Isaiah's eschatological monotheism and the Psalter's intradivine dialogue, then there is good reason to believe that Jesus understood himself to be the Son of God.[35] Early high Christology arguments both provide resources and pose challenges for the dogmatic tradition. They provide resources for biblically supporting Jesus's full deity beyond the confines of John's (supposedly late, Hellenistic) Gospel. Their preoccupation with Jesus's human self-understanding and their suspicions of Hellenistic metaphysics pose challenges, though, especially when they prefer Spirit Christology as the sole explanation for Jesus's miracles or tacitly presume a kenotic account of his earthly attributes. Accordingly, the present book will both appropriate and assess historical arguments for early high Christology.

More broadly, historical Jesus research should be appropriated with

---

may not be quite right about reducing it to a "crisis measure" with "little descriptive value" (p. xxiv).

33. Interpretation needs to integrate "ground (Jesus the Lord), foreground (the salvation of humanity and cosmos), and background (Trinity)." Since "one cannot simply read the Bible as a whole at one moment," it is necessary to "move from particular texts in an ever expanding circle. But the inner dynamism of the texts is to so expand." See William M. Thompson, *The Struggle for Theology's Soul: Contesting Scripture in Christology* (New York: Crossroad, 1996), 242, 244.

34. For a historical argument treating the Gospels as testimony, see Richard Bauckham, *Jesus and the Eyewitnesses: The Gospels as Eyewitness Testimony* (Grand Rapids: Eerdmans, 2006). For a philosophical argument appealing to testimony in a critique of historical-critical hubris, see C. Stephen Evans, *The Historical Christ and the Jesus of Faith: The Incarnational Narrative as History* (Oxford: Clarendon, 1996).

35. It is difficult to explain Jesus's impact apart from his self-understanding, as noted, e.g., by Douglas D. Webster, *A Passion for Christ: An Evangelical Christology* (Grand Rapids: Zondervan, 1987), 106. Filial communion was central to this self-understanding (otherwise Jesus's teaching would be presumptuous); so Pope Benedict XVI, *Jesus of Nazareth: From the Baptism in the Jordan to the Transfiguration*, trans. Adrian J. Walker (New York: Image, 2015). See especially pp. xiv, xxii, 332.

theological realism. The christological order of knowing moves backward and upward. Having encountered the risen Christ and experienced his ascension to heaven, his earliest followers remembered his earthly words and deeds. They gradually recognized that he was more than a man sent from God; the Creator of Israel came in person as the saving Mediator between God and humanity. This process makes historical sense: rather than applying criteria of criticism, analogy, and correlation to the point of authenticating only dissimilarity between Jesus and the church's Christology, a double similarity and double dissimilarity are needed. A historically plausible Jesus should make sense within Second Temple Judaism yet be dissimilar enough that he would be crucified; likewise he should make sense as the church's Lord yet be dissimilar enough that he would fit within prior decades and debates.[36] Given testimony's epistemological prominence, the primary christological contributions of historical research involve nuancing the interpretation of biblical texts, falsifying implausible reconstructions, and underscoring Jesus's inextricable link with Israel.[37] Its apologetic value is primarily defensive and internal, supporting believers who doubt more than winning over skeptics.[38] Thus, the present book seeks to be biblical and historical as the way in which the risen Christ evokes faith seeking dogmatic understanding.[39]

---

36. For this reframing, see N. T. Wright, *Jesus and the Victory of God*, Christian Origins and the Question of God 2 (Minneapolis: Fortress, 1996). For constructively critical engagement with Wright's work, see Carey C. Newman, ed., *Jesus and the Restoration of Israel: A Critical Assessment of N. T. Wright's* Jesus and the Victory of God (Downers Grove, IL: InterVarsity Press, 1999); Nicholas Perrin and Richard B. Hays, eds., *Jesus, Paul, and the People of God: A Theological Dialogue with N. T. Wright* (Downers Grove, IL: IVP Academic, 2011); James M. Scott, ed., *Exile: A Conversation with N. T. Wright* (Downers Grove, IL: IVP Academic, 2017).

37. An increasing tendency to criticize church creeds for marginalizing Israel is on display, e.g., in chap. 11 of N. T. Wright, *How God Became King: The Forgotten Story of the Gospels* (New York: HarperOne, 2012). It was already recognized decades ago that newer Christologies were rectifying dogmatic inattention to Israel; so Klaas Runia, *The Present-Day Christological Debate* (Downers Grove, IL: InterVarsity Press, 1984), 97–98. This legitimate concern (and some allowance for popular imprecision) notwithstanding, Wright and others write unrealistically as if creeds were to be christologically comprehensive rather than boundary setting and thus minimalist.

38. As Evans indicates and Wright's work illustrates. For an attempt to blend radical historical consciousness with formally conciliar Christology, see Paul J. DeHart, *Unspeakable Cults: An Essay in Christology* (Waco, TX: Baylor University Press, 2021). Although argued with DeHart's usual genius, the proposal is unconvincing. Materially, similar risks arise as those that are mentioned later regarding Rowan Williams's and Ian McFarland's recent books: Christ's deity becomes a formal affirmation without robust divine agency. Methodologically, DeHart allows for—yet supposedly demurs from—radical reconstructions that severely falsify biblical accounts, alongside insistence on the gift of historical consciousness. Notwithstanding Christian apologetic bias, it seems odd to champion high confidence in historical consciousness yet leave the field open to a wide array of reconstructions with few criteria for winnowing them.

39. For a bracing insistence (contra Bultmann) that the *skandalon* of faith is perennial rather than new in modernity, see Oscar Cullmann, *The Christology of the New Testament*, trans. Shirley C. Guthrie and Charles A. M. Hall, rev. ed., NTL (Philadelphia: Westminster, 1963), 327.

C. Ontological and Analogical Understanding

Third, this dogmatic Christology aspires to be both ontological and analogical in a particular way, by focusing on the identity of Jesus Christ and incorporating dialectic in articulating that identity. Dogmatic Christology inevitably addresses the being of the person of Christ; even theologies that reject christological dogma are implicitly ontological. Whereas the christological order of knowing moves backward and upward, the confessional order of being moves downward and forward—from divine eternity into human time. Consequently, faith's understanding is always analogical, with similarity yet greater dissimilarity between human words and divine referents. Christology's supposed intellectual problems—precritically "portraying a world of timeless supersensible objects"—are primarily addressed by God's dynamic "turning" to us in reconciliation, "a history of repentance, rebirth, justification and sanctification."[40] We only see as far as the light of redemptive revelation shines, though it will often seem as if we are staring into the sun; this revelation illuminates who Christ is via what he has done in redeeming us.

Despite its problems, the category of identity enables making ontological claims without turning the dogmatic distinction between Christ's person and work into a problematic separation. Modern challenges to substance metaphysics and recent emphases upon biblical narrative lend additional weight to *identity* as a fashionable alternative to *persons* and *natures*.[41] Identity references the uniqueness of agents that narratives render in plots, thus cohering with the fourfold Gospel specifically and the biblical drama generally. Identity focuses on *who* the incarnate Christ is in relation to what he has done, rather than *how* the divine and human natures could be united in one person.[42]

---

40. John Webster, "Prolegomena to Christology: Four Theses," in *Confessing God: Essays in Christian Dogmatics II* (London: T&T Clark, 2005), 149.

41. See, building on earlier attention to biblical narrative, Hans W. Frei, *The Identity of Jesus Christ: The Hermeneutical Bases of Dogmatic Theology* (Eugene, OR: Wipf & Stock, 1997). Notwithstanding its overly formal and theologically limited treatments of identity (as "a person's uniqueness," described via connections between intention and action) vis-à-vis divine presence, this project highlighted the resurrection's importance for the Gospels' depiction of Jesus. Using the category to defend early high Christology while being suspicious of creedal metaphysics is Richard Bauckham, *Jesus and the God of Israel: God Crucified and Other Studies on the New Testament's Christology of Divine Identity* (Grand Rapids: Eerdmans, 2008).

42. For a well-known expression of this contrast, see Dietrich Bonhoeffer, "Lectures on Christology (Student Notes)," in *Berlin: 1932–1933*, ed. Larry L. Rasmussen, trans. Isabel Best and David Higgins, DBWE 12 (Minneapolis: Fortress, 2009), 299–360.

However, the category is rarely described, let alone defined.[43] It is often ambiguous regarding whether identity is based in psychological self-awareness, vocational self-understanding, or third-person characterization. If biblical and creedal narratives are cut loose from the "what" of the Son's eternal preexistence or Jesus's earthly history, then his identity becomes a mere plot cipher rather than revealing a real person who enacts both divine and creaturely freedom. Like *person*, perhaps *identity* is a primitive concept—so basic that its definition remains somewhat ineffable, yet vital for just that reason.[44] Christologically, identity applies to the Trinitarian proper naming of the eternal Son, the vocational self-understanding of the incarnate Logos, the psychological self-awareness of Jesus as human, and his biblical characterization. Identity is the conceptual rendering of who this person is; we lack access to his experiential self-rendering beyond what Scripture modestly attests.

Yet speaking of identity need not be an evasion of ontological claims, because dialectic can apply to thought forms and not just specific statements. While identifying the being of entities is an inescapable human practice, ontological claims may take multiple forms. Thus, Christology needs to discern whether to prioritize enduring metaphysical essences or dynamic historical agents and events. The virtue of metaphysics lies in retaining objective otherness regarding God's revelation in Christ, thereby resisting conceptual idolatry.[45] But much of what passes for metaphysical reflection has the potential to conflict with biblical dynamism, categorize God vis-à-vis creaturely limitations, and constrain

---

43. Entries on "Identity" and "Personal Identity" in the online Stanford Encyclopedia of Philosophy describe numerous debates but provide no definitions. Similarly, Charles Taylor's famous *Sources of the Self: The Making of the Modern Identity* (Cambridge, MA: Harvard University Press, 1989) provides historical description more than definition. One of the few theological treatments, which focuses on human faithfulness to God amid temporal and social change (but, again, without a definition), is Vernon White, *Identity* (London: SCM, 2002). To "identify" can mean that two or more items are the very same thing, or they are closely associated, or one is the proper name of the other(s), and this verb's christological deployment is "spongy" according to Paula Fredriksen, "How High Can Early High Christology Be?," in *Monotheism and Christology in Greco-Roman Antiquity*, ed. Matthew N. Novenson, NovTSup (Leiden: Brill, 2020), 293n1. Hence, for relating Jesus to YHWH the present book usually avoids the verb, using Bauckham's more precise phrase "included in the identity of" when possible.

44. This approach is similar to what is apparently the most substantive theological discussion of the concept: Robert W. Jenson, "Identity, Jesus, and Exegesis," in *Seeking the Identity of Jesus: A Pilgrimage*, ed. Beverly Roberts Gaventa and Richard B. Hays (Grand Rapids: Eerdmans, 2008), 232–48. The larger volume has many fine essays.

45. John Webster, "'Where Christ Is': Christology and Ethics," in *God without Measure: Working Papers in Christian Theology*, vol. 2, *Virtue and Intellect* (London: Bloomsbury T&T Clark, 2016), 23.

missional contextualization.[46] Recent christological attention to identity emerged in tandem with appreciation for Barth's actualistic—dynamic and dialectical—approach to ontology. Barthian dialectic goes beyond Plato's "process of dialogical argumentation aimed at discovering truth amid contradiction" yet resists Hegel's use of the concept "to explain the whole process of history" as identified with God's being.[47] Barth dialectically juxtaposed strong, seemingly contradictory statements—regarding Christ's full deity and full humanity—bearing witness to a reality that transcended the grasp of human cognition.[48] Some use of dialectic seems to be necessary given the analogical nature of theological language. Dialectic formally mirrors analogy's *is* and *is not* in a way that may be especially pertinent to the singular case of the incarnation. The present volume presses dialectical juxtaposition beyond statements to thought forms. On one hand, substance metaphysics played a providential role in Christology's creedal definition and plays a useful role in identifying the agent(s) of biblical narratives. On the other hand, substance metaphysics cannot, strictly speaking, apply to the Creator God, and actualistic ontology plays a useful role in critiquing the conceptual aporias that ensue. Dialectic does not dominate this book's idiom, but it undergirds the analysis of others' party lines and acknowledgment of speculative limits.

D. Conceptual and Contextual Christology

Fourth, this dogmatic Christology aspires to be both conceptual and contextual by engaging numerous voices yet coherently expounding Scripture's theodramatic ontology of Jesus Christ. Our heavenly Father is Christology's initial context and ultimate audience.[49] Both academic trendiness and its populist avoidance should fade to the background in that light. Evangelical Christology's attention to human contexts has recently been expanding through engagement with the church fathers and their scholastic heirs as well as the global South and other marginalized communities. More light remains to be shed from Holy Scripture, and our myopia can only be healed as we receive Christ's instruction

46. Strictly speaking, metaphysical concepts cannot encompass God as an immaterial being, a point to glean from Steven Duby, *God in Himself: Scripture, Metaphysics, and the Object of Christian Theology*, SCDS (Downers Grove, IL: IVP Academic, 2019).

47. James R. Gordon, "Dialectic," in *EDT*, 244–45.

48. George Hunsinger, "Karl Barth's Christology: Its Basic Chalcedonian Character," in *Disruptive Grace: Studies in the Theology of Karl Barth* (Grand Rapids: Eerdmans, 2000), 131–47.

49. Paul R. Hinlicky, *Beloved Community: Critical Dogmatics after Christendom* (Grand Rapids: Eerdmans, 2015), 509.

with and from other members of his body. In addition to contextual attentiveness, evangelical Christology should also have the contextual aim of furthering catechesis. Although this series assumes a measure of theological literacy, this book's desired audience is not primarily professional scholars but those who are enhancing their preparation for various kinds of gospel ministry. Because conciliar Christology seems to be assumed or avoided more than biblically taught, these contextual factors have concrete effects on how this book pursues its aim. First, as noted earlier, a pastoral aim of incorporating theological exegesis in each chapter is to connect dogmatic concepts and current debates more organically with biblical passages. Second, contemporary scholars are engaged in footnotes but almost never named in the main text. This practice is not always necessary, but it seems contextually appropriate, focusing dogmatic arguments on exposition of Scripture and christological concepts rather than scholarly literature or prestige. Third, to promote clarity, chapters expound large-scale theses, and paragraphs' topic sentences encapsulate major arguments step by step. Of course, the preceding aspirations—even regarding Christology's contextual aspects—situate this book in ways that its author can only begin to recognize.

Still, although always contextual, dogmatic Christology should do conceptual justice to Scripture's theodramatic ontology—hence the structure of the chapter theses. Admittedly, *theodramatic ontology* is barely adequate terminology.[50] *Ontology* properly applies to the study of being rather than being itself, and *Christology* is inevitably ontological, but the term indicates claims about who Christ is.[51] *Theodramatic* indicates the progressive revelation of the eternal Son of God and the historical enrichment of his identity, especially by the incarnation.[52] Accompanying this revelatory and redemptive history are biblical names that have long

---

50. Similar but less satisfying alternatives include "theological metaphysics" from "'It was the will of the Lord to bruise him': Soteriology and the Doctrine of God," chap. 10 in John Webster, *God without Measure: Working Papers in Christian Theology*, vol. 1, *God and the Works of God* (London: Bloomsbury T&T Clark, 2016), 154. Webster's "evangelical metaphysics" is referenced in Paul T. Nimmo, "Ethics," in *A Companion to the Theology of John Webster*, ed. Michael Allen and R. David Nelson (Grand Rapids: Eerdmans, 2021), 288. "Historical ontology" appears in "Incarnation," chap. 4 in Webster, *Word and Church*, 144.

51. Thus refusing to let the Son's temporal career expand enough to fill up Christology entirely, as cautioned against by Webster, "'In the society of God': Some Principles of Ecclesiology," in *God without Measure*, 1:184.

52. This term is obviously indebted to recent works by Kevin Vanhoozer. One reason for privileging *drama* is that the action in its narrative is carried forward by speech, as is often the case in Scripture.

informed dogmatic Christology. Speaking of *names*, on analogy with the tradition of divine names in theology proper, is less connotatively specific than *titles*, the term often used in Christology: some may be proper names; others may be honorific titles; still others may be leading metaphors or loose identifiers. Of course, it would be improper to load comprehensive, identical, or important theological content into every biblical use of a name. Yet the titles' recent fall from favor may reflect excessive zeal about such worries, or excessive suspicion about unity in Scripture and tradition: the names signal patterns of biblical teaching about who Christ is in relation to what he has done and will do.

Prioritizing Scripture's theodramatic ontology promotes Christology's appropriate dogmatic prominence. Most broadly, dogmatics can be said to expound one doctrine, the Trinity, in inward and outward movements respectively.[53] Simultaneously, dogmatics can begin with any doctrine—whether teaching about creatures like angels or aspects of the divine economy like providence—and properly connect it with the fullness of biblical teaching about the triune God. Yet dogmatics must also enact more specific structural decisions, some principled, others prudential. In principle, dogmatic Christology will be distinctly prominent: it teaches about one of the divine persons, and it treats a unique hinge point between God and God's economy.[54] Indeed, it is creedally and historically fundamental to the recognition of God's triunity. In practice, then, Christology could be a dogmatic starting point; the ensuing contemporary risk would be diminishing the attention given to divine perfection apart from, and divine prevenience within, the economy of creation and redemption. Or, given Christ's identity as the one Mediator, dogmatic theology could be "Christ-centered" to celebrate the climax of covenant history; the ensuing contemporary risk would be domesticating the authority of the biblical Creator of Israel with appeals to later revelation in the economy of redemption. As with any good mystery story, a second reading of Israel's Scriptures provides new insight into steps leading toward the surprise ending, yet such a

---

53. Webster, "Principles of Systematic Theology," in *Domain of the Word*, 145.

54. On Christology as a "distributed" doctrine, see Webster, "Christology, Theology, Economy: The Place of Christology in Systematic Theology," in *God without Measure*, 1:47. Webster prioritized Christ's identity as the ascended Lord and the Trinity's prior perfection, according to Katherine Sonderegger, "Jesus Christ," in *A Companion to the Theology of John Webster*, ed. Michael Allen and R. David Nelson (Grand Rapids: Eerdmans, 2021), 208–22. The hope of this book is to laud the perfection of the Blessed Trinity while robustly expounding the biblical economy, avoiding overreaction to modern christological excesses.

reading cannot come first and must not rewrite the story's structure or characters.[55] Dogmatic Christology can be undertaken in multiple ways, and no structure guarantees success. The present volume, however, embodies not only a material but also a structural claim: by organizing dogmatic Christology around Scripture's dramatic arc from the eternal communion of the triune God through creation to the consummation of redemptive history, and by tracing this arc through exegeting key texts connected with Christ's biblical names, the doctrine's prominence can be honored while minimizing the contemporary risk of its overinflation.

III. THE FUNDAMENTAL CONFESSION: JESUS CHRIST AS LORD

As the title indicates, this dogmatic Christology is rooted in what was apparently the earliest, tersest Christian confession: "Jesus Christ is Lord" (Rom 10:9; 1 Cor 12:3; Phil 2:11). The Nicene Creed begins its second article by affirming faith "in one Lord, Jesus Christ." It is tempting to parse the name Jesus Christ in terms of humanity and deity respectively, but those associations are misleading. *Christ*, from the Greek term for Messiah, identifies the divinely anointed human being who fulfills the offices of prophet, priest, and king. Jesus is not a generically godlike Christ-figure who represents something divine in all of us. And although it is a human proper name, *Jesus* identifies him as Savior, an identity that characterizes God alone. In rescuing us, Christ reveals the true God. Then, as we shall see, some uses of *Lord* include him in the identity of the God of Israel through the word's equivalence in the Septuagint (a Greek translation of the Old Testament; hereafter LXX) with YHWH. God fulfilled the Old Testament promises of a saving Messiah in a mysterious, superabundant way—by coming in person.

Although dogmatic Christology does not aspire to novelty—far from it—this book's exposition of a classically Reformed perspective is somewhat distinctive. On one hand, there are obvious affinities with recent Reformed-catholic defenses of classical theism and metaphysical Christology—consistent with a nonkenotic account that is cautious in

---

55. See David C. Steinmetz, "Uncovering a Second Narrative: Detective Fiction and the Construction of Historical Method," in *The Art of Reading Scripture*, ed. Ellen F. Davis and Richard B. Hays (Grand Rapids: Eerdmans, 2003), 54–65.

appropriating Spirit Christology.[56] On the other hand, there is dialectical openness to limiting the reach of substance metaphysics and tempering the relentlessness of analytical inquiry—content with a more biblical-historical account of the earthly Jesus's growth in faith toward a beatific vision reserved for postresurrection glory. A tentative proposal that can hold these elements together involves Jesus's virginal conception and Isaianic self-understanding: if he understood himself to be the "God with us" Son of Isaiah 7:14 and the ensuing Servant, then he could plausibly know himself to be Yʜᴡʜ incarnate as a human being. Neither beatific vision nor a constant extension of full omniscience would be required for acquiring human knowledge, as a student of Israel's Scriptures, regarding his divine identity. To my knowledge, this proposal has not appeared elsewhere. Probably that is because classic Christologies have been less preoccupied with historical questions about Jesus's humanity, whereas historical quests—even by evangelicals—have almost universally denied or marginalized the virginal conception. Of course, this proposal must be tentative because it is inferential. Although the virginal conception is biblical and Isaiah's contribution to early high Christology is vital, Jesus's acquaintance with his parentage is not biblically explicit. Even if the proposed inference is incorrect, however, a classically Reformed Christology would remain viable, with its nonkenotic account of Christ's self-knowledge open to alternative nuances.

Thus, as the book's title follows a central arc from humiliating incarnation to exalted ascension, its broader arc flows from eternal communion to consummation, starting with Jesus's first and fundamental name: Son. The eternal Son of God, enjoying the communion of the blessed Trinity, gives human beings a creaturely share in such blessedness, becoming the Bridegroom through whom we will enjoy the eternal consummation of our union with God. These summary theses from the coming chapters recapitulate Christ's theodramatic ontology:

1. As epitomized in **Ephesians 1:3–14**, Jesus Christ is the **Son of God**, who enjoys eternal **communion** with the Father and the Holy Spirit.

---

56. Most notably (arriving after most of this book was drafted), Steven Duby, *Jesus and the God of Classical Theism: Biblical Christology in Light of the Doctrine of God* (Grand Rapids: Baker Academic, 2022). Duby explains the meaning and shows the viability of many classical concepts, even if he explores their depths and defends them to a degree that the present approach occasionally finds unnecessary.

2. As epitomized in **Colossians 1:15–29**, Jesus Christ is the unique **Image of God**, who embodies the divine Wisdom active in the **creation** of the world.
3. As epitomized in **Luke 24:13–35**, Jesus Christ is the **Messiah**, who fulfills God's **covenant** promises.
4. As epitomized in **Isaiah 7:14**, the Old Testament anticipated the first **advent** of Jesus Christ as **Immanuel**, God with us, incarnate in a fully human life.
5. As epitomized in **John 1:1–18**, Jesus Christ is the **Word**, whose incarnation is God's ultimate self-**revelation**.
6. As epitomized in **Philippians 2:5–11**, Jesus Christ is the LORD, whose **humiliation** as **Servant** revealed the glory of God's love in rendering the ultimate human obedience.
7. As epitomized in **Luke 4:14–30**, Jesus of Nazareth is the **Savior**, whose earthly **mission** inaugurated God's kingdom in person.
8. As epitomized in **Mark 10:32–45** (with **Isaiah 52:13–53:12** in the background), Jesus Christ is the **Son of Man**, whose **passion** was the once-for-all act of atonement through which God redeemed us.
9. As epitomized in **Hebrews 7:22–8:6**, Jesus Christ is the theandric **Mediator** between God and humanity, whose bodily resurrection and ascension inaugurated his **exaltation**.
10. As epitomized in **Revelation 21:1–22:5**, Jesus Christ is the **Bridegroom**, whose return will bring the **consummation** of creation and redemption, glorifying the covenant people to be fully at home with God.

CHAPTER 1

COMMUNION AS THE SON OF GOD

Ephesians 1:3–14

As epitomized in **Ephesians 1:3–14**, Jesus Christ is the **Son of God**, who enjoys eternal **communion** with the Father and the Holy Spirit. *Confessing the eternal generation of the Son as the Logos asarkos is integral to properly naming the persons of the Blessed Trinity. The triune God elected to share the divine communion with human beings in a history of salvation, unifying the cosmos in the fellowship and praise of Jesus Christ.*

Scripture's theodramatic ontology begins with the eternal communion between God the Son and God the Father in the love of God the Holy Spirit. Before and outside of earthly time, the life of the Blessed Trinity remains mysterious even with the provision of divine revelation. Within that revelation, Ephesians 1:3–14 highlights both the eternal communion of the triune God and the glory of the divine Son. The passage celebrates God's decision, before time began, to redeem sinful human beings and the surrounding cosmos. For relating the communion between the Father and the Son to creaturely communion with God in Jesus Christ, Scripture offers no better starting point than Ephesians 1. After initially expounding aspects of that crucial text, this chapter focuses upon two related doctrines. The eternal generation of the Son and election in Jesus Christ frame our understanding of communion—both within the divine life and in the historical outpouring of divine love, through which we enjoy filial fellowship with God. In that light, the chapter concludes by summarizing the significance of naming Jesus Christ the Son of God.

I. FILIAL COMMUNION IN EPHESIANS 1:3–14

Communion fundamentally communicates the eternal blessedness of the triune God because "God is love" (1 John 4:8)—one of Scripture's most direct theological claims. Of course, "God is light" (1 John 1:5) too, and Jesus's cross demonstrates that divine love is infinitely far from selfish desire or tolerant sentiment. Whereas we may come to have or enact love, God *is* love. Beginning dogmatic Christology with Ephesians 1:3–14 shines a spotlight on the familial love enjoyed by the *Son* of God. Even without using that name, the passage pervasively celebrates filial communion: how Christ's divine sonship shapes our understanding of and communion with God. This christological focus emerges from the passage in four primary ways.

First, *the greeting in Ephesians 1:1–2* introduces the multifaceted communion that this epistle celebrates. In verse 1 Paul identifies himself as an apostle of Christ Jesus by God's will, addressing those who are holy and faithful in this Messiah. They have been set apart, and they have been faithful to God's claim upon their lives. Both this sanctity and their faithfulness have transpired *in* Christ Jesus. The meaning of this prepositional relationship needs further contemplation, but for now it is vital to highlight its frequency: at least eleven occurrences (1:3; 1:4 [arguably twice]; 1:5 [with *dia*]; 1:6; 1:7; 1:9; 1:10 [twice]; 1:11; 1:12; 1:13 [twice]). Verse 2 conveys the content of Paul's greeting: peace—shalom, holistic flourishing—rooted in unmerited favor from God, identified as our Father, and Jesus the Messiah, identified as Lord. The frequent New Testament pattern of both personal distinction and divine identity is present. Personal distinction: God our Father and (our) Lord Jesus Christ. Divine identity: Lord (*Kyrios*) renders the covenantal divine name, YHWH, in the LXX. Such an association may be in the background here, and strong association with God may be suggested by the lack of a definite article preceding "Lord Jesus Christ."[1] Yet Psalm

---

1. Of course this claim does not involve grammatical proof, since anarthrous nouns are often definite objects of prepositions; so Daniel B. Wallace, *Greek Grammar Beyond the Basics: An Exegetical Syntax of the New Testament* (Grand Rapids: Zondervan, 1996), 247. Plus, *Theos* is usually identified with the Father in the New Testament—as is sensibly treated in Murray J.

110:1 may provide the more immediate context for this *Kyrios*, given Ephesians's celebration of Christ's supremacy over all creaturely powers: "The LORD says to my lord: 'Sit at my right hand until I make your enemies a footstool for your feet.'"[2] In any case, Paul's greeting celebrates the communion of the Father with the messianic Lord, and of God with those who are in Jesus.

Second, *the blessing in Ephesians 1:3* immediately repeats yet varies this identification of the Lord Jesus Christ vis-à-vis God the Father. Paul begins one breathlessly long Greek sentence, which runs all the way through verse 6, with "Blessed be God." The subsequent phrase identifies this God with reference to our Lord Jesus Christ. Now God is Father not with immediate reference to us, as in verse 2, but with reference to Jesus Christ, who is identified with God as our Lord. The *and* introduces a complementary identifier of God—Father—as in most translations: "Praise be to the God and Father of our Lord Jesus Christ," with the absence of a definite article before *Father* supporting this interpretation.[3] In thus identifying God as the Father, yet the Father of Jesus Christ as our Lord, Paul celebrates a filial relationship that entails both personal distinction and the Son's divine identity.

Incipient Trinitarian theology continues in the second half of verse 3: God has blessed us with every spiritual blessing. The same reality ascribed to God—blessing—characterizes what God has accomplished for us in Christ. These blessings in the heavenly realms are spiritual; in the larger context, not to mention the rest of the epistle and Paul's theology, this term draws our minds to the Holy Spirit. The Spirit is the seal (v. 13) and guarantee of our heavenly inheritance (v. 14), through whom we begin to comprehend our glorious hope (vv. 17–18), because the filial communion of the Father and the Son is spiritual and heavenly in the first place. Through the Spirit God raised Jesus from the dead, and through the Spirit God relocates us *in* Christ so that we may have a share in filial communion.

Paul begins to explicate the divine blessing of verse 3 in terms of

---

Harris, *Jesus as God: The New Testament Use of* Theos *in Reference to Jesus* (Grand Rapids: Baker, 1992). The suggestion here concerns a possible implication of this grammatical feature in this theological context.

2. See Gordon D. Fee, *Pauline Christology: An Exegetical-Theological Study* (Peabody, MA: Hendrickson, 2007), 351–59.

3. For further support, involving other texts along with the Granville Sharp rule, see Harold W. Hoehner, *Ephesians: An Exegetical Commentary* (Grand Rapids: Baker Academic, 2002), 164.

subordinate actions, with verse 4 focusing on election.[4] Again, this action occurred in Christ (the aorist *chose* views the action in terms of completion, especially in tandem with "before the creation of the world"). The purpose of this action is already being realized: that we might be holy (a term that appeared in v. 1) and blameless before God. "Before him" creates an intriguing ambiguity. Blamelessness deals ultimately with God; previously, though, the pronoun refers to Christ, in whom we were chosen. Presumably this *autou* still refers to God as the implied subject of the clause that comprises verse 4, yet the rhetorical effect tightly associates Jesus Christ with the realization of God's chosen purpose. At the verse's end, "in love" could complete the thought—identifying the manner or realm in which we will be blameless. More commonly today, interpreters take this phrase to introduce the next clause, identifying the motive or manner of the predestination in verse 5. In either case, this reference to love prepares for another line of emphasis upon filial communion.

Third, rather than retaining an altogether exclusive relationship with God the Father, the divine Son incorporates human beings into *a creaturely form of filial communion that is introduced in Ephesians 1:5*. Spelling out what the eternal election of verse 4 involves, verse 5 speaks of God predestining us for *huiothesian*.[5] This adoption is "through Jesus Christ," adding to the litany of "in Christ" references. The ground of this predestination is "the good pleasure of God's will." Amazingly enough, the heavenly Patriarch—subverting expectations that might accompany this loaded term—has predestined us to join the divine household. Verse 6 spells out the result: the praise of God's glorious grace. The syntax is lavish: just as Paul blessed the God who has blessed us with every blessing (v. 3), so now he lauds the grace with which God has graced us. For present purposes, the key phrase appears at the end of verse 6: "in the One he loves."

The grace of adoption has come to us in Jesus Christ, God's beloved Son. His unique filial identity is unmistakable. We are adopted into a filial relationship with God as Father; Jesus Christ already enjoyed such a relationship, and our adoption only happens in connection with him.

---

4. The comparison established by the opening *kathōs* suggests that election begins to tell us how God effected the blessing.

5. For a helpful caution against overinterpreting distinctions between electing and predestining, allowing instead for redundancy in praise, see Frank Thielman, *Ephesians*, BECNT (Grand Rapids: Baker Academic, 2010), 51.

God has lavished this eternally predestined grace upon us in history—after creation (v. 4), through predestined lives (v. 5), and by Christ's redemptive work (introduced in v. 7). This identification of Christ calls to mind his baptism, when a voice thundered from heaven to praise this beloved Son (Matt 3:17). The voice was accompanied by a dove, signifying that the empowering presence of God's Spirit would rest upon him. Already, at his baptism, Jesus fulfilled all righteousness in his identification with Israel's vocation and plight. Whereas that generation laid claim to being God's children, they were in danger of losing their Abrahamic inheritance due to unfruitful living (Matt 3:1–12). With Jesus, by contrast, God was well-pleased (3:13–17). In saying so, God alluded to Psalm 2, taken from a generic context of installing Israel's king into its specific, ultimate context of lauding Christ as God's Son.

Naming Jesus as God's beloved Son highlights both the Trinitarian identity of God and the adoptive character of Christian salvation. The Trinitarian identity of God is apparent in the structure of Ephesians 1:3–14: subsections focused on the Father (vv. 3–6), the Son (vv. 7–12), and the Holy Spirit (vv. 13–14), each reverberating with praise. Matching verse 6, "to the praise of his glorious grace," verses 12 and 14 refer to "the praise of his glory." The adoptive character of Christian salvation has already appeared in verse 5 as the outcome of our predestination. In verse 6 adoption connects us with Christ as the beloved Son. Adoption also resonates with household administration language in verse 10 and inheritance language in verse 14.

A fourth, indirect emphasis upon filial communion emerges from *the passage's overwhelming Christ-centeredness*. The structure is Christ-centered, as we have just seen: in verses 7–12 Jesus's work forms the crux of how his human brothers and sisters come to enjoy filial communion. Thus, the theme is Christ-centered as well: in verse 10 the apex of God's plan involves summing up all things in Christ. References to the Father's loving predestination of our adoption are legion, and the passage concludes with the Spirit's loving reassurance regarding this extraordinary inheritance. In between stands Jesus Christ, the divine Son through whom God adopts us: He stands between not just the Father and the Spirit but also God and humanity.

The introduction of redemption in verse 7 contains shifting pronouns through which God and Christ overlap. The opening "in him" clearly refers to Christ; we have redemption through his blood, which crucially involves forgiveness of sins. At the verse's end, this forgiveness comes according to the riches of "his" grace, which presumably refers to God—who predestined us according to the good pleasure of "his" will (v. 5), unto the praise of "his" glorious grace (v. 6). God the Father is also the agent of the lavishing, the making known, and the purposing of verses 8–9. Yet the nearer pronouns, from "in him" and "his blood," keep Christ in our minds throughout verse 7. He is the agent through whom—indeed, the One in whom—the Father's initiative is realized, as verse 10 climactically asserts. Jesus Christ brings heaven and earth together.

The preceding exposition has offered a fourfold rationale for highlighting filial communion: (1) multifaceted communion is emphasized in the greeting of verses 1–2; (2) the Lord Jesus Christ is identified vis-à-vis God the Father, beginning in verse 3; (3) the divine Son eventually incorporates others into filial communion, beginning in verse 5; and (4) the passage is structurally and thematically Christ-centered in a way that integrates the Son's filial communion with ours. The concept of filial communion intersects with two primary aspects of dogmatic Christology to which we now turn: the eternal generation of the Son and election in Christ. These dogmatic subjects briefly evoke corresponding aspects of biblical theology: Christians' adoption and union with Christ.

II. THE ETERNAL GENERATION OF THE SON

The eternal generation of the Son anchors the ecumenical orthodoxy of the Nicene Creed: "We believe in one Lord, Jesus Christ, eternally begotten of the Father; God from God, light from light . . . begotten, not made, of one being [homoousios] with the Father." To be sure, this christological anchor gained its foundational place over more than a century of controversy. In various forms, winds of heretical Arianism perennially buffet the church. What is more, some well-intended Protestants have periodically attempted to toss aside eternal generation without turning away from ecumenical orthodoxy. In both cases, detractors have misunderstood the doctrine's basic claims and biblical character.

A. Eternal Begetting and the Analogy of Faith

To begin with, "the relation between the divine Father and the divine Son whereby the Father naturally radiates the Son and consequently the

Son is the exact imprint of the Father's substance is in essence all that the doctrine of eternal generation seeks to identify."[6] Eternal generation fits among four possible ways of being *from* the Father: (1) The world comes from God by *creation*, whereas the Son is "begotten, not made"; (2) the incarnate Son comes from God by the assumption of a human nature for his earthly *mission*; (3) other human beings who are united with Christ become children of God by *regeneration*; and (4) by an eternal *procession* the second person of the triune God *is begotten* from the first person as "God of God, light of light."[7] Eternal generation identifies Father and Son as *proper* names for these divine *persons*, specifying their relations of origin and modes of subsistence in what human beings cannot help but perceive as *metaphorical* terms.[8]

Because of its metaphorical aspect, eternal generation generates periodic clashes between apophatically, aesthetically, and analytically oriented theologians—that is, between those who emphasize mystery, beauty, and logic, respectively. The former two embrace this doctrine's speculative limits more than the latter, who often worry about its supposedly nonsensical character. From a human standpoint, eternal generation epitomizes a concept that not only began as a metaphor—like all concepts do, by a lively new use of language—but also remains metaphorical. God is Spirit, to whom no earthly concept of begetting readily applies, insofar as all human parenting relationships assume physical birth at some point in time. From the standpoint of revelation, however, divine filiation is the primary reality, to which human parenting has merely analogical correspondence. Among its other purposes, human parenting is a vehicle of creaturely witness to God's self-communication.

Father and Son are distinctly personal proper names.[9] Without eternal generation, there would be no corresponding relations of origin between

---

6. Scott R. Swain, "The Radiance of the Father's Glory: Eternal Generation, the Divine Names, and Biblical Interpretation," in *Retrieving Eternal Generation*, ed. Fred Sanders and Scott R. Swain (Grand Rapids: Zondervan, 2017), 41 (original italics removed).

7. Fred Sanders, "Eternal Generation and Soteriology," in *Retrieving Eternal Generation*, 268.

8. The "modes of subsistence are modes of relation"; so Webster, "Eternal Generation," in *God without Measure*, 1:31.

9. See Marianne Meye Thompson, *The Promise of the Father: Jesus and God in the New Testament* (Louisville: Westminster John Knox, 2000), 155–85. Thompson shows that the Old Testament treats God as Israel's Father, even if not by name; the Jewish context of early Christianity may have been reticent to speak God's name, but the name Father is distinctive to the New Testament mode of addressing God, and addressing God as Father depends ultimately upon eschatological hope in God's faithfulness, not human gender analogies. See also the important treatment of the larger issues (which arrived too late for detailed interaction) in Amy Peeler, *Women and the Gender of God* (Grand Rapids: Eerdmans, 2022).

these eternally self-existing persons; their naming would be inconsistent with biblical patterns of intradivine dialogue and prayer.[10] Thus, the metaphor (in one sense) of eternal generation is truly a concept (in another sense) because of the divine names: *Father* and *Son* are habitual, proper ways of speaking to and about these persons; the underlying relation of origin is articulated by the metaphor of generation when it is analogically qualified by *eternal*. In a poetic text like the Psalter, God is named *a rock* in a different (fundamentally metaphorical) sense than God is named *love* in a more prosaic text. Such a term still applies analogically, not univocally, to human beings, insofar as we receive the gift of participating in God's love.[11] Father and Son are proper for naming personal relations within God's life, whereas concepts like love name the common character of this living God and metaphors like rock convey concepts more poetically. Eternal generation, then, is a fundamentally metaphorical background claim (as human thought encounters it) that makes sense of properly naming divine persons in this relational way.

The biblical character of this background doctrine emerges from such patterns of divine naming and a corresponding emphasis upon kinship. As Isaiah 63:16 (NRSVue) illustrates, three kinds of nouns preeminently name God: personal proper names ("O LORD"), kinship terms ("our father"), and common nouns ("our Redeemer from of old"). Eternal generation, while focused on the Father and the Son, is fundamental for naming God because it reflects a kinship emphasis along with patterns like the divine Word's procession from God, which is accompanied by the Spirit's procession from God in the speaking of the divine Name. The Father bears the divine Name, gives to the Son to bear the divine Name, and in so doing breathes out the Spirit to speak the divine Name.[12]

This doctrine's early development did not ignore Israel's Scriptures. Proverbs 8:22–36 played a crucial role. Although its patristic contribution is debated by modern interpreters, at minimum this text reflects

---

10. For impersonal parallels, see Swain, "Radiance of the Father's Glory," 42. Divine "glory that radiates divine effulgence, a divine speaker that utters a divine word (John 1:1–18) and a divine exemplar who produces a divine image (Col 1:15–18)" epitomize this pattern, but these could not be addressed in personal prayer as a "Father who has life in himself and who has granted his Son to have life in himself (John 5:26)" can be.

11. Swain, "Radiance of the Father's Glory," 35.

12. R. Kendall Soulen, "*Generatio, Processio Verbi, Donum Nominis*: Mapping the Vocabulary of Eternal Generation," in *Retrieving Eternal Generation*, 132–46.

the self-expression of divine Wisdom in the created order.[13] For those who were seeking to renew biblical wisdom in a Hellenistic Jewish environment, divine Wisdom's self-revelation tied together Jesus Christ's identities as Son and Word. We can certainly appreciate the ancients' frequent efforts to read the Old Testament Christianly rather than ignoring it. Relatedly, as recognized by recent scholarship, prosopological exegesis read certain texts in terms of the Father and the Son talking face to face. Prosopological exegesis bears on the present doctrine in texts like Hebrews 1:5, where the appropriation of Psalm 2:7 ("today I have become your Father") may support an eternal grant of the Son's divine life.[14]

At the heart of this doctrine, of course, stands the New Testament, especially John's Gospel. *Monogenēs* ("the one and only Son," John 1:18) has come under intense modern scrutiny—as if it only connotes unique privilege, as if that clears away "begotten" as an otherwise logically problematic, subordinationist concept. Contemporary retrievals of eternal generation offer two lines of response. First, even if "one and only" (or the like) rather than "only begotten" were the correct translation, the doctrine of eternal generation would not suffer.[15] The begetting language has additional source texts (like Proverbs 8) and is metaphorical (as noted above). The relevant claims about the Father-Son identities and relations remain intact whether or not *begetting* is conceptually integral to the Greek term's biblical use. Second, a revisionist account of the lexical evidence has recently been offered in favor of the traditional language. If this account holds up under ongoing scrutiny, then treating *Monogenēs* as "only Begotten" surfaced long before fourth-century christological debates; "only Begotten" is consistent with the etymological evidence; and "only Begotten" is consistent with biological dimensions that were internal to the word's original meaning (whereas nonbiological, "one and only" dimensions were subsequent metaphorical extensions).[16]

After John 1:18, John 5:26 asserts, "For as the Father has life in himself, so he has granted the Son also to have life in himself." Despite its complexity, for several reasons "the best response remains that adopted

---

13. See Daniel J. Treier, *Proverbs and Ecclesiastes*, BTCB (Grand Rapids: Brazos, 2011), 44–57.

14. Madison N. Pierce, "Hebrews 1 and the Son Begotten 'Today,'" in *Retrieving Eternal Generation*, 123. Prosopological exegesis gets further treatment in chapter 4.

15. See further discussion of this terminology vis-à-vis John 1:18 in chapter 5.

16. Charles Lee Irons, "A Lexical Defense of the Johannine 'Only Begotten,'" in *Retrieving Eternal Generation*, 98–116.

by Augustine and other fathers of the church: this is an eternal grant."[17] (1) The immediate context involves the Jewish leaders' rage over Jesus's apparent challenge to monotheism. (2) Jesus clarifies that he claims no independent deity; his activity is coextensive with the Father's but also dependent, while his reasoning (signaled by *gar*: "For as the Father . . . so he has granted the Son . . .") claims equality with God in terms of filial apprenticeship. (3) The structure of 5:26 tightly links the meaning of "life in himself" for the Father and the Son. (4) The rest of the passage voices the same tension: coextensive existence and action of Father and Son, utter dependence of the Son upon the Father. (5) Other texts in John voice both sides of this apparent tension. Accordingly, affirming eternal generation does not dispense with mystery concerning the incarnation and intra-Trinitarian personal relations. Instead, affirming eternal generation means confessing the metaphorical background that is necessary to speak the Bible's proper names Father and Son for the first and second persons of the triune God.

B. Autotheos *and the Gift of Aseity*

Despite the integral role of the Son's eternal generation within Nicene orthodoxy, some Protestants have had conceptual reservations about the doctrine, not least regarding potential subordination among the divine persons. Classical Trinitarian theology recognized that insofar as aseity—eternal self-existence—pertained to the shared divine essence, it must be predicated of the Son. Simultaneously, however, classical Trinitarian theology insisted that the Father's communication of the shared essence in eternal generation undergirded the persons' essential unity and relational distinction. Once John Calvin (1509–64) and Reformed orthodoxy emphasized divine aseity, full equality with the Father entailed robustly affirming the Son's aseity in order to avoid ontological subordination. Accordingly, Calvin insisted that the Son was *autotheos*—self-existing as God. While Calvin affirmed eternal generation, he did not affirm the traditional inference of the Son's "essential communication" from the Father.[18] He focused on

---

17. D. A. Carson, "John 5:26: *Crux Interpretum* for Eternal Generation," in *Retrieving Eternal Generation*, 82. The rest of this paragraph summarizes Carson's exegetical reasoning, which includes a judicious appraisal of Irons's work.

18. Calvin's initial discussion of whether the Father is the "essence giver" appears in a polemical context—dealing with heretics who would subordinate the Son and the Spirit—and he goes on to acknowledge that the Father "is rightly deemed the beginning and fountainhead of the whole of divinity." See John Calvin, *Institutes of the Christian Religion*, vol. 1, ed. John

the eternal relationship expressed in the names Father and Son, rather than any mysterious giving of the divine essence by the Father to the Son. A minority of later Reformed leaders went further, denying not just essential communication but also eternal generation, lest the affirmation of any immanent order within the Godhead should entail the Son's ontological subordination.

So three divergent Reformed approaches to affirming eternal generation had arisen by the end of the seventeenth century.[19] The first approach retained the ancient assertion of essential communication through eternal generation. The second approach rejected essential communication. A third, mediating approach proposed that only the *person* (not the *existence*) of the Son is begotten of the Father, yet the divine essence is thereby communicated because the person of the Son is begotten. Meanwhile, against perceived Reformed excesses associated with the *autotheos* concept, other traditions became nervous about explicitly predicating aseity of the Son. Their position "may be encapsulated as 'the Son is the selfsame God with the Father, but *by communication from the Father*, and therefore it is inappropriate to call him self-existent,'" whereas "the majority Reformed position may be summarized as 'the Son is *the selfsame God* with the Father, even by communication from the Father, and therefore it is appropriate to call him self-existent.'"[20]

As noted above, biblical texts like John 5:26 suggest both the Son's aseity and his particular mode of possessing that divine perfection: the Son has life in himself as an eternal grant from the Father. Whereas Trinitarian appropriation "tethers particular actions to specific divine persons (normally for reason of emphasis)" even as God's external works are indivisible, here dogmatic speech requires "redoubling or reduplication" to reflect "the eternal Son's receptivity in relation to his Father." Reduplication ascribes the same perfections to the three divine persons along with different modes of possession. Hence the Son's receptivity characterizes not only "his free enactment of his proper activity in the divine economy, which is time and again characterized as obedience," but also his immanent mode of possessing divine

---

T. McNeill, trans. Ford Lewis Battles, LCC 20 (Philadelphia: Westminster, 1960), 1.13.23–25 (pp. 149–54).

19. This historical account is indebted to Brannon Ellis, *Calvin, Classical Trinitarianism, and the Aseity of the Son* (Oxford: Oxford University Press, 2012).

20. Ellis, *Calvin, Classical Trinitarianism*, 14.

perfections.[21] Receptivity even characterizes the Son's possession of the divine perfection of necessarily existing life. Trinitarian reduplication carefully speaks of the divine persons' common life—their unity and equality—along with specific characteristics reflecting their processions, each qualifying the other.

Both the divine essence and the divine will are one, with no hint of ontological subordination. The Father's eternal grant of aseity does not indicate any temporal or logical moment when the Son or the Spirit "was not": "To speak of these as relations of origin is not, of course, to refer to events in the past, for they are eternal relations and not completed acts of self-constitution. The Son is the Son, not because he *has been* originated by the Father's paternal act, but because God *is* eternally the relation of paternity and filiation."[22] The Father possesses the divine essence in a giving mode while the Son and the Spirit possess the divine essence in receiving and proceeding modes.[23] As for the divine will, its ontological oneness precludes at least many accounts of the Son's functional subordination to the Father. The Son's economic obedience can properly reflect immanent receptivity within the relational order of the triune Godhead only when reduplication carefully references three personal modes of participation within the one divine will. Indeed, terms like *dependence* and *subordination* require caution due to misleading connotations.[24] Speaking of the Son's obedience stems from the hypostatic union of the divine and human in the incarnation, and such language remains analogical. Even speaking of mutual love between the Father, Son, and Spirit remains analogical, since the divine persons share one will rather than loving each other via discrete, deliberate actions. Therefore, speaking of a relational order and modes of possession or participation can account for biblical teaching about the immanent Trinity and the incarnate

---

21. Scott R. Swain and Michael Allen, "The Obedience of the Eternal Son: Catholic Trinitarianism and Reformed Christology," in *Christology, Ancient and Modern: Explorations in Constructive Dogmatics*, ed. Oliver D. Crisp and Fred Sanders (Grand Rapids: Zondervan, 2013), 94–95.

22. Italics original from Webster, "'It Was the Will,'" in *God without Measure*, 1:152.

23. The language of act and will for eternal generation and the grant of aseity does not indicate a discrete performance but only precludes impersonal emanation and celebrates the delight of Father and Son; so Herman Bavinck, *Reformed Dogmatics*, vol. 2, *God and Creation*, ed. John Bolt, trans. John Vriend (Grand Rapids: Baker Academic, 2004), 309–10.

24. See the sensible comments of Swain and Allen, "Obedience of the Eternal Son," 88; Carson, "John 5:26," 94–97.

Son without running the unnecessary risk of subordination language. While contemplating the fullness of God's revelation in Scripture, Christian theology must acknowledge the modest human capacity for comprehending the doctrine of eternal generation with its mystery of an eternal, ontological grant.

C. The Blessed Trinity

An intricate grammar for speaking about the triune God emerged from the church's gradual understanding of the Son's eternal generation, and it is everywhere presupposed by dogmatic Christology. To spell out this grammar with the necessary brevity: God has a singular Name that belongs to the Father, the Son, and the Holy Spirit, as the baptismal formula of Matthew 28:18–20 epitomizes. Common predication identifies the three persons with the one God; proper predications distinguish the three within the one God. These personal distinctions stem from unique relations of origin—paternity, filiation, and spiration, reflecting the eternal processions of the Son and the Spirit. Biblical texts underlie this doctrine in terms of inner-Trinitarian conversation, a cosmic framework, and redemptive missions.[25] Neither divine perfections nor the three divine persons comprise parts of God, who is fully actualized, infinite Spirit. Accordingly, the Trinity's external operations—in the economy of creation, redemption, and consummation—are inseparable. Aspects of these works can be appropriated to specific divine persons, as reflected in the triadic creedal structure that associates creation with the Father, redemption with the Son, and consummation with the Spirit. Such appropriation reflects the internal order (*taxis*) of the immanent Trinity in which the Father initiates, the Son effects, and the Spirit perfects; correspondingly, only the Son assumed human flesh. Yet appropriation must never obscure the perichoretic—mutually interwoven—being of the three persons; we must also say that "God became incarnate," for the incarnation is an inseparable operation of the Blessed Trinity. Thus the historical *missions*—the Son becoming incarnate, the Spirit overshadowing him and indwelling us—reveal the eternal *processions* of generation and spiration.

---

25. This paragraph depends on the elegant, readable summary of Scott R. Swain, *The Trinity: An Introduction*, Short Studies in Systematic Theology (Wheaton, IL: Crossway, 2020). On the biblical interpretation involved, see Scott R. Swain, *The Trinity and the Bible: On Theological Interpretation* (Bellingham, WA: Lexham, 2021).

III. ELECTION IN CHRIST

Ephesians 1:3–14 has introduced the Son's eternal communion with the Father as the ontological starting point in biblical teaching about the Lord Jesus Christ. The Son's eternal generation is the first dogmatic implication of this starting point, focused on the One who is beloved *by nature*. Now a second dogmatic implication focuses on the divine election of others to become beloved children of God *by grace*. This inquiry into election will not be soteriologically comprehensive but christologically focused: election *in Christ* flows from the Son's identity as the Logos *asarkos*—considered in his eternal deity apart from the assumption of flesh—and frames the adoptive nature of Christians' union with him.

A. The Logos Asarkos and the Dialectic of Revelation

Appealing to Ephesians 1, Barth presents this revisionary thesis in §32 of *Church Dogmatics* II/2:

> The doctrine of election is the sum of the Gospel because of all words that can be said or heard it is the best: that God elects man; that God is for man too the One who loves in freedom. It is grounded in the knowledge of Jesus Christ because He is both the electing God and elected man in One. It is part of the doctrine of God because originally God's election of man is a predestination not merely of man but of Himself. Its function is to bear basic testimony to eternal, free and unchanging grace as the beginning of all the ways and works of God.[26]

Barth claims that God's self-determination to be *for* humanity is irrevocable; having entered the relation, God could not be God without it.[27] In Barth's account, election does not determine each human being's final destiny as either elected or rejected: "its direct and proper object is . . . but one individual—and only in Him the people called and united by Him, and only in that people individuals in general in their private relationships with God." This individual, Jesus Christ, is both elected and rejected.[28] By contrast, Barth accuses traditional Protestant accounts

---

26. Originally printed in bold, in Barth, *CD* II/2:3.
27. Barth, *CD* II/2:7.
28. Barth, *CD* II/2:43.

of being dominated by general concepts of providence, referring to election "in Christ" as a decision "which is independent of Jesus Christ and only executed by Him."[29]

The "simplest form" of Barth's doctrine involves "the two assertions that Jesus Christ is the electing God, and that He is also elected man."[30] Barth accuses the Protestant Reformers of appealing to Christ merely as the first of the elect according to his human nature, a view that he deems incapable of explaining Ephesians 1:4: their view does not keep our eyes fixed on Jesus, to know that we will enjoy his benefits, since "the electing God is not identical . . . but behind and above Him."[31] The Barthian fear is that individual predestination and reprobation generate a "hidden God" that might not be consistent with the God who is revealed to be for us in Jesus Christ. With God so decisively "for us," Barth's view seems to entail universal salvation. Due to divine freedom, however, he refused to make that affirmation—ironically, perhaps, leaving unspecified the divine determination regarding personal destinies. Thus championing divine freedom may leave the loophole of a hidden God in a different form. Having banished predestination as a prehistorical decree constraining God in time, Barth's dialectical account fostered lingering debates about its meaning and implications.

References to Ephesians 1 are widespread throughout *Church Dogmatics*, but detailed exegesis—not least of the crux, 1:4—is absent.[32] Barth simply stakes his major claim, to which he subsequently appeals on numerous occasions. Christological attention should be paid to four facets of Barth's account: (1) Jesus Christ *as* the electing God, (2) the

---

29. Barth, *CD* II/2:64.

30. Barth, *CD* II/2:103.

31. Barth, *CD* II/2:110. Among the Reformed orthodox he credits only Polanus with even recognizing that Ephesians 1:4 credits election to God, not just the Father.

32. An early sermon on this text focused largely on existential themes and eschewed textual details; see Karl Barth, "Epheser 1,1–14 (Safenwil, Sonntag, Den 4. Mai 1919)," in *Predigten 1919*, ed. Hermann Schmidt, Karl Barth Gesamtausgabe 39 (Zurich: Theologischer Verlag Zürich, 2003), 173–80. Thanks to Jeremy Lundgren for noticing the sermon and translating portions. Barth also taught a lecture course on Ephesians in 1921–22. More than a decade prior to his "breakthrough" regarding election, he was already criticizing Calvin for misinterpreting this text due to "anthropological concerns"; see Karl Barth, *The Epistle to the Ephesians*, ed. R. David Nelson, trans. Ross M. Wright (Grand Rapids: Baker Academic, 2017), 94–95. All of these treatments lack detailed exegetical comments regarding the object of election in Ephesians 1:4. This case study certainly illustrates that Barth never felt bound by historical-critical criteria, as indicated in Mary Kathleen Cunningham, *What Is Theological Exegesis? Interpretation and Use of Scripture in Barth's Doctrine of Election* (Valley Forge, PA: Trinity Press International, 1995). But even those who are sympathetic to theological exegesis may worry that here "the way the words run" has been eclipsed.

election of *all* in Christ, (3) the objective completion of *anakephalaiōsis*, and (4) divine *self*-determination.

First, does Ephesians 1:4 identify Jesus Christ *as* the electing God? Not explicitly. As we saw above, while the passage's repeated "in him" refers to Christ, sometimes even with the name Jesus, the grammatical subject of the relevant verbs is God as Father. Admittedly, identifying Christ as the electing God could also find support from the emphasis upon filial communion. While the Father initiates the predestination, the Son is integral to its execution and the Spirit to its reception. The Father chose us in, not apart from, the Son. The ensuing question concerns whether this choice involves a Logos *asarkos*, "without flesh" from the incarnation, and what such a concept would mean. Biblical texts create rhetorical surprise from having election occur in *Jesus* Christ, seemingly long before the incarnation. There is surely a conceptual mystery in having election occur before the world's creation, seemingly "before" time. Hence Barth critiques any Logos *asarkos* beyond the minimally necessary affirmation of divine freedom, namely that God did not have to create us or assume flesh to redeem us. Even so, the grammar of Ephesians 1 appropriates election's initiative to God the Father as much as it locates election in Christ.

Second, does Ephesians 1:4 teach the election of *all* in Christ? Again, not explicitly. The incarnation is present insofar as all of redemption's blessings depend upon it. Although the incarnation identifies Jesus with all human beings, its background role in this passage does not relate election to absolutely everyone.[33] To the contrary, verse 12 particularizes the *us* or *we*: those who were first to hope in Christ. Whether between Jews and gentiles, anticipating Ephesians 2:11–22, or between initial groups of Christians, some distinction is present.

Third, does Ephesians 1:10 support objective *anakephalaiōsis* that mitigates this distinction? Not really. There certainly is objective *anakephalaiōsis*: all things in heaven and on earth will be under Christ, as this concept names the climax of God's redemptive purpose. Numerous references to God's choosing, predestining, pleasure, willing, and

---

33. See Kevin J. Vanhoozer, "The Origin of Paul's Soteriology: Election, Incarnation, and Union with Christ in Ephesians 1:4 (with Special Reference to Evangelical Calvinism)," in *Reconsidering the Relationship between Biblical and Systematic Theology in the New Testament: Essays by Theologians and New Testament Scholars*, ed. Benjamin E. Reynolds, Brian Lugioyo, and Kevin J. Vanhoozer, WUNT II (Tübingen: Mohr Siebeck, 2014), 177–211. When assessing "evangelical Calvinism," however, pastoral concerns about popular "contractual" soteriologies, as well as patristic concepts of corporate solidarity in Christ, need additional reflection.

purposing leave no doubt about this climactic result. Paul is blessing God in rapture from contemplating redemptive grace, not nuancing details about exactly who is in Christ or what happens to any who are not. Just so, 1:10 cannot simply undo the prior distinction, which reappears nearby in 1:12. The *anakephalaiōsis* is not limited to human beings with whom Christ identified in the incarnation; all things in heaven and on earth are involved. The *anakephalaiōsis* unifies all things in the fulfillment of God's historical purpose; it is not directly equivalent to the forgiveness of sin in 1:7.[34] Those who are God's possession are redeemed (1:14); what happens otherwise to effect cosmic unity in Christ goes unsaid.

Fourth, does Ephesians 1:4 authorize speaking of divine *self-determination* to be "for us"? Cautiously at most. The grammatical focus of 1:3–14 is consistent. *We* or *us* are objects receiving divine actions in every verse except verse 10. The Father's initiative comes to completion in and through Jesus Christ and the Holy Spirit, but the divine "self" is not expressly an object of action—with the possible exception of Christ as the beloved Son (v. 6). This fourth question introduces a more extensive issue.

Barth's doctrine of God's Trinitarian "self-determination" eventually spawned what has been labeled "the most important debate in contemporary systematic theology."[35] In the 1990s, Bruce McCormack (1952–) introduced a revisionist account of Barth's development. He argued that Barth retained dialectical alongside analogical modes of thinking throughout *Church Dogmatics*, rather than shifting from dialectic to analogy in the early 1930s.[36] In 2000, McCormack followed with a revisionist account of the Trinity and election.[37] He argued that Barth's

---

34. On three major views of *anakephalaiōsis*, as (1) sum up or unite (with lexical support), (2) renew (with patristic support, not least from Irenaeus's theme of recapitulation opposing Gnostic rejection of Israel's Scriptures), and/or (3) make [Christ] the head (with an etymological approach), see Markus Barth, *Ephesians 1–3: A New Translation with Introduction and Commentary*, AB (New York: Doubleday, 1974), 89–91. Whether or not there is an element of restoration, emphasis on predestination points Ephesians 1:10 toward the unity of all history from creation onward, and of the entire cosmos in this One who heads up a new humanity: "Headship is the means, reconciliation the purpose, of his appointment."

35. Francesca Aran Murphy, "Afterword: The Breadth of Christology: The Beautiful Work of Christ," in *The Oxford Handbook of Christology*, ed. Francesca Aran Murphy (Oxford: Oxford University Press, 2015), 628. This comment slightly expands the scope, however, by including related controversy over the work of Catholic theologian Hans Urs von Balthasar.

36. Bruce L. McCormack, *Karl Barth's Critically Realistic Dialectical Theology: Its Genesis and Development 1909–1936* (Oxford: Clarendon, 1995).

37. Bruce L. McCormack, "Grace and Being: The Role of God's Gracious Election in Karl Barth's Theological Ontology," in *The Cambridge Companion to Karl Barth*, ed. John Webster (Cambridge: Cambridge University Press, 2000), 92–110.

revisionist doctrine of election in the later 1930s gradually reshaped his understanding of God's triune being. As Barth shifted from beginning with the logic of revelation to focusing on the history of Jesus Christ, he more effectively closed a "metaphysical gap" that lurked in the dogmatic tradition: a potentially hidden God lurking in between the eternal divine processions and the temporal divine missions. Logically speaking, on McCormack's account, God's election to be "for us" in Christ preceded God's triunity; indeed, the eternal act of election constitutes God's being as triune. The decision to become incarnate for our salvation just is the eternal generation of the Son, or else a metaphysical gap ensues.

Traditionalists quickly objected to both McCormack's interpretation of Barth and his ensuing proposal.[38] They cited passages in which Barth continued to affirm what McCormack's account should have him gradually denying. On their account, Barth critiqued mistaken appeals to the Logos *asarkos* but never rejected the concept. Electing the incarnation does not constitute but determines and reveals God's triune being. Traditionalists accused the revisionist proposal of losing the divine freedom that Barth consistently affirmed—making creation constitutive of God's being by making the incarnation a necessary revelatory act. Regarding Barth's intended view, then, traditionalists have persuaded many to understand ambiguous statements charitably in context rather than seizing upon apparent inconsistencies or developments to appropriate Barth in favor of positions he did not express.[39]

It remains possible, however, to wonder if McCormack sees "the direction in which Barth's doctrine of election points" whereas traditionalists "turn back" when doing so.[40] McCormack does not deny divine freedom—"God would be God without us"—but rather any possibility to know what God would be, triune or otherwise, in that case. God need not have created, but we cannot know "how the divine being would have been structured had God not determined to be God for us in Jesus Christ."[41] Of interest, ultimately, is not what Barth thought

---

38. Key texts from the ensuing debate are collected in Michael T. Dempsey, ed., *Trinity and Election in Contemporary Theology* (Grand Rapids: Eerdmans, 2011).

39. So George Hunsinger, *Reading Barth with Charity: A Hermeneutical Proposal* (Grand Rapids: Baker Academic, 2015).

40. Kevin W. Hector, "God's Triunity and Self-Determination: A Conversation with Karl Barth, Bruce McCormack, and Paul Molnar," in *Trinity and Election in Contemporary Theology*, 46.

41. Bruce L. McCormack, "Foreword to the German Edition of *Karl Barth's Critically Realistic Dialectical Theology*," in *Orthodox and Modern: Studies in the Theology of Karl Barth* (Grand Rapids: Baker Academic, 2008), 297.

but what Scripture teaches. If McCormack presents a logical possibility toward which Barth's thinking points in its early modern, German, anti-metaphysical context, then regardless of whether Barth tried to stop along the way, we must evaluate the possible journey.

Without resolving all the conundrums, both material and formal considerations are christologically pertinent. Materially speaking, first, classic accounts opposed the metaphysical gap that Barth feared and McCormack alleges.[42] By definition the immanent Trinity and the economic Trinity are identical in every sense that does not deny the loving freedom of divine action in creation and redemption. Relational distinctions are not essential separations, so there is no hidden God behind the God revealed in Christ. Second, *decision* is a technical term for Barth, meaning a "willed act" of "self-determination" in an "intellectualist" rather than "voluntarist" sense—that is, in concert with God's self-knowledge.[43] Those who overlook Barth's theological intellectualism may worry needlessly about divine arbitrariness or self-constitution. Yet, granted that this distinction allays some potential worries, it is still possible that the early modern language of self-determination is neither theologically preferable nor even prudent. Admittedly, third, Barth pinpointed some traditional neglect of the "in Christ" emphasis, while highlighting a larger New Testament speech pattern relating "Jesus" to eternity. Among other texts, John 17:24 and 1 Peter 1:20 speak of Christ being beloved before creation; Revelation 13:8 speaks of his being slain before creation; and John 1:2–3, Romans 11:36, 1 Corinthians 8:6, and Colossians 1:16 involve him by that name in the work of creation.[44] The question is whether that speech pattern demands a historicized, "actualistic" account of divine self-determination or, instead, refers more loosely to that person of the Blessed Trinity whom we now know as our theandric Mediator. Chapter 6, when treating Philippians 2:5–11, provides one example of arguing for the latter, more modest conclusion.

Speaking more formally, first, allegations of unbiblical speculation cut both ways. If classical metaphysics, when poorly appropriated, contributes to a speculative God behind God, conversely modern, antimetaphysical

---

42. As detailed in the case of St. Thomas Aquinas (1225–74) by Matthew Levering, "Christ, the Trinity, and Predestination: McCormack and Aquinas," in *Trinity and Election in Contemporary Theology*, 264–65.

43. Matthew J. Aragon Bruce, "Election," in *The Oxford Handbook of Karl Barth*, ed. Paul Dafydd Jones and Paul T. Nimmo (Oxford: Oxford University Press, 2020), 309–24.

44. These texts are itemized in Hunsinger, *Reading Barth with Charity*, 41–42.

theology generates its own forms of speculation: "McCormack's transcendental argument for his doctrine of God appears to claim to have the force of a necessary deduction rather than an explanatory hypothesis" and ironically would appear "speculative and uncritical" from a premodern perspective.[45] Put differently, second, Barthian debates about divine self-determination stem from dogmatic implications more than direct biblical statements. Correspondingly, while these dogmatic implications emerge from wrestling with the biblical mystery of election, they also reflect philosophical questions and assumptions. In other words, they are located: the language of self-determination stems as much from early modern German thought as from biblical Trinitarianism. The point is not that theological exegesis can be free of philosophy but that Barthian actualism does not occupy uniquely high biblical ground. Third, accordingly, Barth's way of reading Scripture is more conceptual-thematic than technical-verbal, an approach that contributes distinctive strengths but may also have relevant weaknesses in his appropriation of Ephesians 1:4.

Given these material and formal considerations, there is a need to contemplate the dialectical aspect of revelation. Since the Son's eternal generation underscores the analogical nature of theological language, the Logos *asarkos* indicates an ensuing need to juxtapose forceful articulations of the two sides within apparent biblical tensions. Analogous language can bear faithful witness to revealed truth despite the fundamental dissimilarity between creaturely concepts and the divine being. Creaturely forms, not least the incarnate Son's human nature, are essential for God's unveiling to finite beings. Yet those essential forms simultaneously veil God's infinite being before human eyes. The relation between time and eternity suggests a need for dialectical modes of speech regarding historical events and divine actions. Human beings encounter choices in sequential terms with (more or less) discursive reasoning. God, to our knowledge, does not choose or act as we do; we are so bound in time that even our efforts to speak of "logical" rather than "temporal" relationships in eternity may be impertinent.

Thus, the apparent contradictions in dialectical forms may bear witness to aspects of divine revelation that transcend our human grasp. Dogmatics may use such human expressions with twofold openness—to further inquiry and to the possibility that we may never comprehend

---

45. Nicholas M. Healy, "Karl Barth, German-Language Theology, and the Catholic Tradition," in *Trinity and Election in Contemporary Theology*, 242.

the divine reality behind the rhetorical tensions. In the present case, on one hand, the election of human beings is an *eternal* act that the Bible characterizes "in Christ," seemingly breaking temporal propri- eties in its mode of speech. In some sense Jesus existed in the divine will before time, and the Son was "always" *incarnandus*, the Logos who would become *incarnatus*, enfleshed. On the other hand, the election of human beings is an eternal *act* that determines a temporal history. As a divine person (and hence Spirit) participating in this freely willed act, the Logos "was" *asarkos*, without human flesh or name except by anticipation. This affirmation does not domesticate the biblical way of speaking but instead articulates the second-order coherence of another set of biblical statements. The Logos assumed the human nature and name of Jesus in creaturely time. During his earthly ministry, the incar- nate Logos still transcended the humanity assumed in Christ. Even now the ascended Lord remains incarnate, yet his deity continues to transcend his humanity. This transcendence never hides a God of a different character; rather, it grounds the love revealed in Christ within an infinite reservoir of divine freedom: God's love for us is joyfully willed and will never be otherwise. The biblical revelation of the triune God inherently limits how much we can say about this mystery—both affirming a Logos *asarkos* and accepting irregular speech regarding Jesus Christ in the eternal divine act that encompasses creaturely history. This irregular speech celebrates the triune God's gracious election to be "for us" in incarnate self-revelation.

B. The Trinitarian Decree

Recent debate over the Trinity and election intersects with both classic Protestant debate about the divine decree's logical order and a recent tendency toward affirming incarnation "anyway," regardless of humanity's fall into sin and death. By placing creation and fall logically prior to redemption, an "infralapsarian" view of God's decree honors the narrative structure of nature and grace along with the biblical priority of salvation in Christ's earthly ministry (e.g., Matt 1:21). By placing reconciliation logically prior to creation and fall, a "supralapsarian" view honors biblical statements about the ultimate purpose of unifying all things in Christ (e.g., Eph 1:10) and the incarnation's apparent necessity for knowing the *triune* God. Although stipulating only a logical order within the decree, however, these positions easily—perhaps, for temporal creatures, inevitably—start projecting falsely sequential dichotomies onto divine predestination. Alternatives to supralapsarianism seem to entail a *felix culpa*, a fortunate fall, that makes the triune God's self-revelation possible. Otherwise, if the incarnation's occasion were solely redemptive, how would Trinitarian self-revelation have occurred without a fall?

Whereas much of the premodern tradition saw the incarnation as biblically focused on fallen humanity's salvation, seemingly qualifying as infralapsarian, "incarnation anyway" supralapsarianism has become increasingly popular.[46] A *felix culpa* now seems odious to many, as if it were making God responsible for necessary evil. However, we should be cautious about making that charge, lest God's mysterious permission of sin be equated with moral responsibility for authoring evil or setting creatures up for a fall. Rejecting a *felix culpa* altogether virtually denies the moral integrity or actuality of divine predestination, whereas it could also be affirmed alongside "incarnation anyway" in some form.[47] Still, the actuality of God's love in Christ may resist speculation about "what if" the fall had not occurred. The question of Trinitarian self-revelation apart from the fall may also resist such speculation.[48] We know little about the initial fellowship that Adam and Eve enjoyed with God or the blessedness they would have enjoyed in confirmed righteousness apart from the fall. Thus, we should not confidently speculate about hypothetical scenarios, and we should be cautious about logical ordering that easily projects human temporality or discursive reasoning onto

---

46. For historical tracing of infralapsarianism and supralapsarianism as names eventually applied to Christology, see Edwin Chr. Van Driel, *Incarnation Anyway: Arguments for Supralapsarian Christology*, AARAS (Oxford: Oxford University Press, 2008), 5. Van Driel follows David Kelsey in fundamentally distinguishing the narrative logic of creation, redemption, and consummation. Then he argues that God's distinct purpose for eschatological consummation requires supralapsarianism. But such strong narrative distinctions are biblically problematic. For a more Pauline argument, see Edwin Chr. Van Driel, *Rethinking Paul: Protestant Theology and Pauline Exegesis*, CIT (Cambridge: Cambridge University Press, 2021). Its appeal (e.g., p. 283) to passages like Ephesians 1:10 is important. But the larger argument adopts "newer" perspectives on Paul in a way that redefines faith and marginalizes soteriology (baptismal regeneration supplants faith for participation in Christ, and faith expresses eschatological trust rather than embracing Jesus's saving work in the gospel).

47. God neither caused nor necessitated that human beings would cause the fall, yet neither did God "play the idle spectator": "Would the one who cares for everything, down to little sparrows and even the least hair, consider the fate of the whole human race a matter of indifference? Notwithstanding that on this violation depended both the sending of the Mediator and the whole economy of redemption?" So Petrus van Mastricht, *The Works of God and the Fall of Man*, ed. Joel R. Beeke, trans. Todd M. Rester, vol. 3 of *Theoretical-Practical Theology* (Grand Rapids: Reformation Heritage, 2021), 418.

48. But for one of the strongest cases that speculation is appropriate in this instance, see the "incarnational union" account of supralapsarianism in Oliver D. Crisp, "Incarnation without the Fall," *JRT* 10 (2016): 215–33.

God. As we shall see in chapter 10, the unitive name *Bridegroom* relates Christ to nature, grace, and glory: we must incorporate the anticipated consummation of passages like Colossians 1:20 into our appreciation of the incarnation, even if we do not fully know how.

C. Union with Christ as Adoption by Grace

Along with the loving participation of the Logos *asarkos* in God's eternal decree, election "in Christ" entails an outcome: in union with God's Son by nature, we become children of God by grace. In other words, union with Christ fundamentally involves adoption. Of course, adoption does not exhaust this blessing; Scripture uses marital imagery to depict the consummation of the church's union with Christ. We will enjoy a wedding feast as his bride, and we will dwell in God's household forever. Relationally, union with Christ connotes a settled state, whereas participation language connotes more dynamic interaction—alongside identification with Christ's lordship and incorporation into Christ's body. The relevant plethora of prepositional relationships, nouns, and motifs in numerous Scripture passages cannot be reduced into one core concept at the center of a complete system of thought. That said, union with Christ encapsulates "the essential ingredient" that binds together Pauline theology.[49] Notwithstanding the splendid chaos in Pauline celebrations of this crucial reality, there is profound coherence with our initial theme of filial communion.

So, first, *God's triunity* is essential to our union with Christ. Coming to have God as our loving Father is one way of summarizing the gospel;[50] the Spirit liberates people from slavery to sin and makes them children of God by uniting them with Jesus.[51] Pauline texts are replete with familial metaphors for life in Christ.[52] The Roman empire knew of succession stories involving powerful fathers with natural versus adoptive sons; tellingly, Paul ignores those imperial stories in telling Christ's.[53]

---

49. Constantine R. Campbell, *Paul and Union with Christ: An Exegetical and Theological Study* (Grand Rapids: Zondervan, 2012), 30, 413.

50. Julie Canlis, "The Fatherhood of God and Union with Christ in Calvin," in *"In Christ" in Paul: Explorations in Paul's Theology of Union and Participation*, ed. Michael J. Thate, Kevin J. Vanhoozer, and Constantine R. Campbell, WUNT II (Tübingen: Mohr Siebeck, 2014), 414.

51. Darren Sarisky, "Augustine and Participation: Some Reflections on His Exegesis of Romans," in *"In Christ" in Paul*, 369.

52. Susan G. Eastman, "Oneself in Another: Participation and the Spirit in Romans 8," in *"In Christ" in Paul*, 116–17.

53. Michael J. Thate, "Paul and the Anxieties of (Imperial?) Succession: Galatians and the Politics of Neglect," in *"In Christ" in Paul*, 241.

The Jewish Jesus's identity as the divine Son honors God's redemptive presence in the prior history of Israel's adoption. It also indicates the fullness of his identification with sinful humanity, even as the New Testament avoids using adoption language for him.[54]

Second, *adoption* is the neglected "epitome" of our union with Christ, celebrating its nature as "not only *legal* but also *familial*."[55] This neglect has been tempting because explicit adoption texts are modest (Rom 8:15, 23; 9:4; Gal 4:5; Eph 1:5). Ephesians 1:5 is the only instance where adoption is "*explicitly* connected to the language of union," and in that case adoption comes "through" union.[56] However, since Scripture regularly grounds our identity as God's children by grace within the divine sonship that is Christ's by nature, adoption may be secondary as an explicit metaphor yet primary as an implicit soteriological reality: "Our understanding of Christianity cannot be better than our grasp of adoption."[57] This primacy stems from the *filial* character of the Son's eternal communion with the Father and the gracious communication of a creaturely share in that communion.

Thus, Calvin celebrated union with Christ not merely as a prominent Pauline doctrine or a soteriological end in itself but ultimately as a Trinitarian mystery befitting the biblical depiction of God as Father.[58] Although the Bible does not explicitly speak of Abraham's adoption, Calvin felt free to do so, given the narrative dynamics involved.[59] He preferred the Trinitarian language of adoption over Martin Luther's (1483–1546) tendency to use nuptial—biblical but also medieval—imagery.[60] Perhaps increased attention to adoption as an epitome of union with Christ would not only reframe soteriological debates but also increase attention to the Holy Spirit. For adoption points toward

54. Grant Macaskill, "Incarnational Ontology and the Theology of Participation in Paul," in *"In Christ" in Paul*, 95, 98–99.
55. Italics original in Kevin J. Vanhoozer, "From 'Blessed in Christ' to 'Being in Christ': The State of Union and the Place of Participation in Paul's Discourse, New Testament Exegesis, and Systematic Theology Today," in *"In Christ" in Paul*, 21. Vanhoozer highlighted adoption's neglected soteriological importance in "Wrighting the Wrongs of the Reformation? The State of the Union with Christ in St. Paul and Protestant Soteriology," in *Jesus, Paul and the People of God: A Theological Dialogue with N. T. Wright*, ed. Nicholas Perrin and Richard B. Hays (Downers Grove, IL: IVP Academic, 2011), 235–59.
56. So, e.g., Campbell, *Paul and Union with Christ*, 407n1.
57. J. I. Packer, *Knowing God* (Downers Grove, IL: InterVarsity Press, 2018), 201. Packer's chap. 19 offers a classic exposition.
58. Canlis, "Fatherhood of God," 401–2.
59. Canlis, "Fatherhood of God," 406.
60. Canlis, "Fatherhood of God," 417n114.

another aspect of the Christ-centered salvation celebrated in Ephesians 1: our future inheritance, of which the Spirit is a transformative guarantee. The Spirit is integral to both the eternal, filial communion between Father and Son and the temporal communication of that love, bringing us into covenantal communion.[61]

Third, in addition to its Trinitarian and adoptive grounds, union with Christ has vitally *royal* dimensions, extending Jesus's proclamation of God's kingdom into the life of the church and ultimately the fullness of the cosmos. The next chapter, relating the *anakephalaiōsis* of Ephesians 1 to the reconciliation of creation highlighted in Colossians 1, reinforces this royal aspect. The Creator installed bearers of the divine image in the cosmic temple, but they rebelled and were removed from God's life-giving presence. As our Redeemer, Christ not only rescues us from hostile powers and reconciles us to God; he also reflects the fullness of the divine image and renews us so that we may again represent the royal family as we were created to do.

IV. SON OF GOD

Thus the name Son of God encompasses the scope of this inaugural chapter. In Scripture's theodramatic ontology, the identity of the Lord Jesus Christ "begins" in the Son's eternal communion with God the Father. Ephesians 1:3–14 may not use this name with explicit frequency, but this identity is implicitly vital for the text's paean to filial communion. The ensuing dogmatic questions focus on the eternal generation of the Son and election in Christ. Understood with reference to Ephesians 1, together these doctrines celebrate union with Christ—characterized by adoption. We participate by grace in the filial communion that belongs to Jesus Christ as the Son of God by nature.

Son of God does not straightforwardly assert Christ's deity in every New Testament appearance, but the name gradually points in that direction.[62] Despite not being recorded on Jesus's own lips, in the Gospels this name periodically proclaims his supernatural power over

---

61. On these "material" concepts of union with Christ, see Vanhoozer, "From 'Blessed in Christ,'" 26–28.

62. For a survey of ways in which the name Son of God attaches to Jesus, see D. A. Carson, *Jesus the Son of God: A Christological Title Often Overlooked, Sometimes Misunderstood, and Currently Disputed* (Wheaton, IL: Crossway, 2012), 34–42.

the spirit world (e.g., Mark 3:11; 5:7). In various epistles the name is a favorite. In Hebrews, Christ's divine sonship establishes his uniqueness as Mediator in contrast with earlier prophets, angels, and Moses or any other human servant in God's household. In Paul's letters, at least some passages entail the Son's divine "preexistence," as later chapters discuss in terms of early high Christology (see, e.g., Rom 8:3; Gal 4:4; Col 1:15–17; plus, using other names, 1 Cor 10:4, Phil 2:5–11, and 1 Tim 3:16). Whereas some have worried that Romans 1:4 supports adoptionism rather than eternal divine sonship, there are good reasons to the contrary. Son of God is not an adoption category elsewhere in Romans, let alone elsewhere in Paul's writings. Whether *en dynamei*, "with power," grammatically attaches to the name or the verbal action, "the contrast is not between a time when he was Son and a time when he was not Son, but between a time when he was Son in weakness and a time when he became Son with power."[63]

The Son is eternally begotten, not made, *homoousios* ("of one being") with the Father. Any subordination that appears in John's Gospel, for instance, involves no ontological inequality but only an appropriate response from the enfleshed Word to the eternal Speaker—the theandric Son being apprenticed to the divine Father whose historical work and eternal honor he shares (John 5:19–27). Such internal ordering of the persons of the triune God makes it fitting for the Son to be the Incarnate One, embodying divine grace and truth (John 1:14–18). Shared exaltation ensues: the Father will not be glorified apart from the Son but rather *through* the Son's exaltation in the Spirit. A larger New Testament pattern follows: the Son's glorified existence after the resurrection and by virtue of the ascension enabled the church to recognize his preexistence as Creator.

---

63. Donald Macleod, *The Person of Christ*, Contours of Christian Theology (Downers Grove, IL: InterVarsity Press, 1998), 90–92. Alternatively, addressing reception history while attaching the power to the office of messianic sonship—but arriving at similar dogmatic implications—is Matthew W. Bates, "A Christology of Incarnation and Enthronement: Romans 1:3–4 as Unified, Nonadoptionist, and Nonconciliatory," *CBQ* 77 (2015): 107–27. Also addressing reception history and arguing for a non-adoptionist emphasis on Christ's Davidic humanity is Joshua W. Jipp, "Ancient, Modern, and Future Interpretations of Romans 1:3–4: Reception History and Biblical Interpretation," *JTI* 3, no. 2 (2009): 241–59. Treating the passage in terms of two perspectives, not two stages, is Jens Schröter, "Präexistenter Sohn und Messias Israels. Zu einer Christologischen Denkstruktur bei Paulus," in *Perspektiven zur Präexistenz im Frühjudentum und Frühen Christentum*, ed. Jörg Frey, Friederike Kunath, and Jens Schröter, WUNT (Tübingen: Mohr Siebeck, 2021), 116. For a contemporary response to adoptionist exegesis and historiography, addressing not only this text but also Mark's Gospel, see Michael F. Bird, *Jesus the Eternal Son: Answering Adoptionist Christology* (Grand Rapids: Eerdmans, 2017).

In short, biblical Christology celebrates the lengths to which God sent the Lord Jesus Christ so that we might come to enjoy filial communion through his Holy Spirit. These historical lengths of God's love reflect the eternal communion between the Father and the Son in the Blessed Trinity.

CHAPTER 2

CREATION AS THE IMAGE OF GOD

Colossians 1:15–29

As epitomized in **Colossians 1:15–29**, Jesus Christ is the unique **Image of God**, who embodies the divine Wisdom active in the **creation** of the world. *In this Son the cosmos holds together, and the one true God has begun reconciling all things through the redemption of human beings, so that they may represent the glory and enjoy the shalom of their Creator's reign.*

Colossians 1:15–29 complements the celebration of communion in Ephesians 1:3–14. In Jesus Christ, who is the eternal Son of God by nature, we have been elected for adoption as God's children by grace. Correspondingly, by grace we become part of the body of Christ, who is the ultimate image of God by nature. In this way God's royal glory goes on display throughout the universe. Thus, the present chapter begins by expounding Colossians 1, a passage renowned for celebrating the "cosmic" Christ. Next, this chapter addresses two dogmatic intersections between Christology and creation. First, biblical monotheism: a preliminary examination of early high Christology raises questions about the Creator-creature distinction. How did the earliest Christians maintain biblical monotheism yet include Jesus in the identity of Israel's God? Second, christological mediation: a preliminary examination of participation in Christ raises questions about the resurgence of Christian Platonism and sacramental ontology. How should contemporary

Christians maintain that all things hold together in Christ yet identify union with Christ as a specific redemptive reality? Eventually, the significance of naming Jesus the image of God draws together the threads of this chapter regarding Christ and creation.

I. ROYAL GLORY IN COLOSSIANS 1:15–29

Amid the wonders of Colossians 1:15–29, three concepts are crucial for the overarching theme, the royal glory of Jesus Christ. First, Colossians 1:15–29 makes explicit the name that was only implicit in Ephesians 1:3–14: *Son* of God. Second, the passage identifies this Son as the *image* of God, who makes God's glory visible and God's reign comprehensive. Third, the passage celebrates the Son's life-giving fullness as *head* of a new social body, the church, through which God reconciles the entire creation.

A. The Son: Agent of Creation

Colossians 1:13–14 introduces the figure whose title is so debated in 1:15. Verse 13 refers to the kingdom of the Father's beloved Son, and verse 14 locates our redemption—glossed as forgiveness of sins—*in* him. In the realm of the Son we enjoy by grace a taste of the communion that the Son enjoys with the Father by nature. The pronoun *hos*, the grammatical subject of verse 15 and the thematic subject of the ensuing hymn, refers back to this Son. Soon the verse reinforces this sonship with *prōtotokos*—"firstborn of all creation," a phrase that became legendary in fourth-century christological debates.

Arianism wrongly interprets the phrase as indicating that the Son was not fully divine. On that view, the Son was not coequal with the Father but merely the preeminent creature through whom God created everything else. As in Proverbs 8:22, however, the "firstborn" language does not refer literally to a birth or the first in a series. The begetting involved is metaphorically appropriate to both the parenting motif that surrounds Wisdom in Proverbs 8 and the Father-Son naming here. Having characterized God as invisible in its first phrase, Colossians 1:15 does not descend completely into the visible realm with this second, appositional description. It is true that for *prōtotokos* "the Hebrew equivalent can mean the distinctive eldest," that is, "the firstborn son who inherits," which by itself could leave the door ajar for Arianism, because in that case he might be the start of a creaturely series. But "already in the Old Testament the term has been drawn into a wider circle of significance," namely Israel as God's firstborn son and David as the king uniquely appointed by YHWH. Such sonship connotes a *sui generis* relationship with God, being "heir of all things of the Father."[1] Whatever the exact genre of Colossians 1:15–20, its hymnic repetition parallels the Psalter and points to Israel's Scriptures as the primary background for proper interpretation. The text celebrates Christ not as a rival or replacement for Torah or Wisdom but as the ruler over all other authorities.[2] So "firstborn of all creation" does not index the Son within a temporal or logical sequence, nor does it merely laud him via degrees of association with venerated intermediaries or revelatory figures.

Linguistic support for this reading of *prōtotokos* comes from "all creation," which should not be read as a partitive genitive (as if Christ were the firstborn part of it): "(1) v. 16a distinguishes Jesus from 'all creation' when it affirms that 'the whole universe' (τὰ πάντα) was created 'in' him; (2) if Paul had believed that Jesus was the first of God's creatures to be formed, the adj. πρωτόκτιστος ('created first') or πρωτόπλαστος ('formed first') might have been expected instead of πρωτότοκος, and v. 16a would have continued 'for all other things were created in him.'" Hence, the genitive is either objective, meaning "supreme over all creation," or comparative, meaning "prior to all creation" and thus "begotten before all creation."[3] Paul links this One uniquely to the sustaining sovereignty of the eternal Creator.

Colossians 1:16 makes explicit the implication of Ephesians 1 that all things were created *in* this unique Son. The pronoun *autos* repeatedly—eleven times in six verses—underscores his cosmic uniqueness.[4] He is unquestionably the subject of this paean. Every apparent rival is simply a creature, powerless by comparison.[5] The related prepositional phrases, indicating that all things were created "through" and "unto" the Son,

---

1. Christopher R. Seitz, *Colossians*, BTCB (Grand Rapids: Brazos, 2014), 95–96.
2. Seitz, *Colossians*, 86–94. Genesis, standing in the background, is both part of and prior to the Torah, as noted by Seitz, 105.
3. Murray J. Harris, *Colossians and Philemon*, EGNT (Grand Rapids: Eerdmans, 1991), 43–44.
4. Harris, *Colossians and Philemon*, 52.
5. In defense of reading "in him" as the sphere and not just the instrument of creation, as well as reading the passive "were created" to make space for the Son's participatory agency in creation along with the Father, see Scot McKnight, *The Letter to the Colossians*, NICNT (Grand Rapids: Eerdmans, 2018), 150–51.

underscore the *unity* of Father and Son. . . . The point of such formulations was surely to *include* Christ in God's act of creating the world, rather than to *limit* the character of his power or to indicate his inferior status or role. . . . Without some such ordering monotheism [these phrases] would clearly have been discarded. Put differently, Paul's arguments in Colossians are not that Christ is a "being like God" who does things that are like the things that God does, but rather that the work of God the Father in creation and redemption is mediated through Christ the Son of God. . . . an argument . . . [that] put the church on the road to trinitarianism rather than tritheism.[6]

The language of verse 17, then, conveys both temporal and hierarchical supremacy: the Son is *pro*, which can mean "before" or "above," all things; the present tense *is* resists an exclusively temporal reading in favor of a more customary or gnomic sense. In him, again, all things "hold together." Accordingly, in various New Testament references to Jesus as the *prōtotokos*, "his status, not his birth order, is in view. . . . His status is superior because temporally he is before all things, hierarchically he is above all things, and ontologically he sustains all things."[7]

B. The Image: Divine Glory Incarnate

The beginning of Colossians 1:15 further identifies this unique Son in whom we have redemption: he is "the image of the invisible God." According to 1:19 "God was pleased to have all his fullness dwell in him," and according to 2:9 "in Christ all the fullness of the deity lives in bodily form." These statements are striking: God is invisible, yet God (the Father) has an image, an icon. Subsequent references in 1:19 and 2:9 suggest that this title relates to the Son's incarnation. The immediate context of 1:15, regarding sovereign agency in creation, suggests that image refers not just to the incarnate God-man but also to the preexistent divine Son.

While these statements are commonly connected with Wisdom texts from Second Temple Judaism,[8] those proposed connections should

---

6. Italics original in Marianne Meye Thompson, *Colossians and Philemon*, THNTC (Grand Rapids: Eerdmans, 2005), 164–65. See further Sean M. McDonough, *Christ as Creator: Origins of a New Testament Doctrine* (Oxford: Oxford University Press, 2010).

7. McKnight, *Colossians*, 149.

8. See McKnight, *Colossians*, 138–43. Regarding Proverbs 8, a key influence was C. F. Burney, "Christ as the APXH of Creation," *JTS* 27 (1925): 160–77.

complement rather than eclipse image vocabulary. In Proverbs 8:31, personified Wisdom delights in the Creator's world and especially in humankind, establishing a link to other creation and wisdom texts like Proverbs 3:19. From there, intertestamental Jewish texts like Wisdom of Solomon began to celebrate the pervasiveness, purity, power, and presence of divine Wisdom. In Philo of Alexandria (c. 20 BC–c. AD 50), such wisdom involved the divine image serving as the archetype or pattern for the rest of creation. This image was frequently identified with the divine Logos by which God created. Sirach 43:26 even refers to all things holding together by God's Word, an obvious parallel to Colossians 1:17. The image "could thus bridge the otherwise unbridgeable gulf between the invisible world and God on the one side and visible creation and humanity on the other . . . safeguarding the unknowability of God by providing a mode of speaking of the invisible God's self-revelatory action (his 'image/likeness' being stamped, his 'word' spoken) by means of which he may nevertheless be known."[9]

Possible Wisdom connections focus on one of the image's two prominent aspects in Colossians 1: divine revelation. The immediate phrase in 1:15 highlights God's invisibility. A contrast between the visible and the invisible appears again in 1:16. Additionally, the Son's visibility is implied when 1:18 identifies him as head of the body and indicates the aim of his preeminence in all things. Yet this revelatory aspect should not mislead us into depersonalizing or dethroning the image. Depersonalizing could arise from interpreting the image via divine Wisdom understood in terms of mere personification, leaving the divine Son's ontological preexistence unclear.[10]

Dethroning could arise from neglecting the second prominent aspect in Colossians 1: divine rule. This Son has brought the divine reign toward its consummation through a peacemaking victory over all hostile powers.[11] God's kingdom has already become prominent, notably in 1:13. Terms pile up in 1:16 regarding various powers—all of which, whether heavenly or earthly, were created in and through and unto this

---

9. James D. G. Dunn, *The Epistles to the Colossians and Philemon*, NIGTC (Grand Rapids: Eerdmans, 1996), 88.

10. E.g., Dunn, *Colossians and Philemon*, 88–90.

11. On ruling and revealing, see McKnight, *Colossians*, 147. For the intriguing suggestion regarding creation's principalities and powers that "their role in structuring gentile societies corresponds to the role of the covenant of Moses in bringing up Israel," which learned not to fear them as pagans do, see Telford Work, *Jesus—the End and the Beginning: Tracing the Christ-Shaped Nature of Everything* (Grand Rapids: Baker Academic, 2019), 150.

Son. To creation 1:17 adds providence, in which he is "above" as well as "before" all things. Then 1:18 celebrates his redemptive preeminence in the church. This resurrected Son is the Lord of creation, providence, and now a new humanity by virtue of his victorious crucifixion (1:20). He not only reveals what God is like; he restores God's comprehensive rule over creation. As the divine image, the Son represents God within the created order, making God present in the twofold sense of revealing and ruling.

Colossians depicts believers "not only as benefiting from Christ's rule but also *as sharing in numerous aspects of Christ's rule*."[12] The transfer of 1:13b plays out in 1:15–20, aspects of which reappear elsewhere in the epistle. So the new humanity is being renewed in Christ's image (1:15a; 3:10b). This new humanity shares in Christ's victory over hostile powers (1:15–16; 2:10, 14–15). The unity of the new humanity is fitting given the integration of all things in Christ (1:17; 3:10–11). The head of this new body directs its nourishment (1:18; 2:19). This new body has been raised with him (1:18; 2:12–13, 3:1). Christ's fullness leads to our being filled up in him (1:19, 2:9; 2:10). Churchly reconciliation is an inaugural and integral aspect of cosmic redemption (1:20; 1:21–22; 3:15). The Old Testament anticipates these themes concerning God's dominion, not least the language of fullness and glory.[13] There is another relevant context though: contemporaneous expectations of rulers. Christ's pacifying victory fulfilled first-century expectations for a king, albeit with an unexpected form of bloody warfare.[14] As God's Son, he reconciles us, brings us into the family, keeps us safe, and dwells with us in a way that conforms our lives to our new identity: "In Paul's Christ-discourse, then, the kingdom of God is seen . . . in Christ's sharing of his own rule with his subjects. Given that in kingship discourse, the king or emperor is often conflated *with the empire* or *body politic*, Paul creates a discourse that makes the closest possible connection between king and

---

12. Italics original in Joshua W. Jipp, *Christ Is King: Paul's Royal Ideology* (Minneapolis: Fortress, 2015), 143–45. The rest of the paragraph summarizes some of his claims. Jipp promotes kingship rather than Wisdom as the background of Colossians 1:15–20, but connections between the two (in passages like Proverbs 8) suggest that they are not mutually exclusive.

13. Jipp, *Christ Is King*, 120–21. For an account of glory in Pauline Christology, see Carey C. Newman, *Paul's Glory-Christology: Tradition and Rhetoric*, NovTSup (Leiden: Brill, 1992). Newman suggests Paul's own Christophany as the interpretive origin of this account, emphasizes the resurrection as its crux, and also relates *eikon* language to Jewish mysticism.

14. Jipp, *Christ Is King*, 123.

subjects."[15] The body shall now participate in the unexpected form of the head's reconciling rule.

This revealing and ruling image makes divine glory visible. God's kingdom is characterized by light (1:12). The effusive language of totality and preeminence puts the Son under, behind, before, above, and at the center of everything. Christ's ministry is a long-hidden mystery that has now, finally, been disclosed (1:26). Accordingly, the language of glory appears when 1:27 begins summing up the Pauline ministry and message. The mystery itself is "glorious" (this genitive likely characterizing its richness), and Christ in us is "the hope of glory." The divine glory and the divine image are closely related. Like the image, divine glory is not only a reflection but a reality of God's being. People do not merely see a reflection of the sun; they experience its heat. The sun's visibility is a function of its life-giving reality. Similarly, to encounter God's glory is not to see some purely external reflection but to enjoy the splendor of who and what God is. God's rule is a major aspect of God's revelation.

Yet the divine image's visibility is qualified by transcendence—in the first instance, temporally. The goal of Paul's ministry is to make known the newly revealed mystery of Christ in us (1:27), by Christ's power at work in Paul (1:29), so that someday everyone may be presented to God as completely mature in Christ (1:28). The relational realm at the beginning of this passage, "in the Son," is bidirectionally "Christ in us" and us "in Christ" by the end.[16] In Christ are hidden all treasures of wisdom and knowledge (2:3); we trust in him (2:5); we live in Christ and grow in this faith (2:6–7); baptism has so identified us with his resurrection life that our former, sinful existence is dead (2:10–15). Hence, while the Son has personally revealed God's character and definitively reestablished God's earthly rule, our enjoyment of this reconciliation is inaugurated but not complete. Christ is in us and our lives are now reborn in him, but we need to grow up into adulthood as we live by faith and seek wisdom's treasures. Christ in us is the hope, not yet the full display, of glory.

In the second place, the transcendence of the divine image is qualitative. Christ's life is definitive for ours because of the incarnation (2:9), because in him we encounter the fullness of God outshining any human

---

15. Italics original in Jipp, *Christ Is King*, 140.

16. For a helpful warning against falsely dichotomizing "in you [all, individually]" and "among you [corporately]" in Pauline texts, and relatedly against following trendy anti-individualist readings, see McKnight, *Colossians*, 199.

or cosmic forces (2:8). Parallel to 2:9, where the transcendent content is specified as "the fullness of the Deity," in 1:19 the grammatical subject "all the fullness" conveys "God in all his fullness"; the subject is personal given the surrounding language of reconciliation.[17] Given this qualitative transcendence, Jesus's human body is integral to the Son's representation of divine glory, making visible the enacted love that would otherwise remain invisible. Secondarily, the social body of which Christ is head, the church, is also integral to his visible bearing of the image. After all, human sin was the wedge through which hostile powers wreaked havoc upon earthly community and the entire cosmos. The Son displays divine glory by demonstrating God's redeeming love and defeating the enemies of God's peaceful reign, representing God in both a single human life and the restoration of other human lives.[18] When this reconciliation is completely realized, the head of the body will be properly preeminent in all things. Even when other human beings bear the divine image as they were created to do by grace, by nature all of God's fullness will continue dwelling uniquely in the Son. God's unveiling happens in a human being, Jesus Christ, and just so God's fullness remains inevitably veiled to us. This image is temporally and qualitatively transcendent, yet graciously condescends to become an immanent dwelling of divine glory.

C. The Reconciler: Head of a New Community

So far the exposition has not focused on conciliar, two-natures Christology but followed the passage's development of key concepts. Its first christological identity is the divine Son, the grammatical subject whose association with the activity of creation and the authority of providence is so strong as to suggest participatory agency as Creator. Its second christological identity, the image of the invisible God, is temporally and qualitatively transcendent. In this image, however, God's fullness dwelt in bodily form—eventually being crucified and becoming the firstborn from the dead, not just remaining the firstborn over all creation. Here preeminence involves historical becoming, not just eternal being. The end of Colossians 1 and the beginning of Colossians 2 reiterate another

---

17. So Harris, *Colossians and Philemon*, 49–50.

18. While the account may identify Christ as the image too strongly with the many members of his churchly body, there are helpful reflections on discerning it in Ian A. McFarland, *The Divine Image: Envisioning the Invisible God* (Minneapolis: Fortress, 2005). God is refracted in finite plurality, since neither a single creature nor the sum of all creatures could adequately reflect the fullness of the divine being; so Ian A. McFarland, *The Word Made Flesh: A Theology of the Incarnation* (Louisville: Westminster John Knox, 2019), 54.

identity of this one, Messiah, which was attached to the human name Jesus at the epistle's beginning. Thus, Colossians presents him as both the "essential" image of God, by eternal generation, and the "representative" image of God, by incarnation.[19]

The passage's third christological identity, the head of the body that is the church, appears in 1:18. While the focus of 1:15–17 on creation implies the Son's deity, the focus of 1:18–20 on redemption insists on the image's humanity.[20] The *archē* evokes creation but signals a new beginning. Now this Son is the firstborn from the dead by virtue of resurrection (1:18a). The Son is the prototype of a new humanity. He will have preeminence in all things (1:18b) not only because God's fullness dwells in him (1:19) but also because all things are being reconciled to him through his crucifixion (1:20). By implication the new humanity will be characterized by Christ's preeminence in this twofold way: celebrating God's fullness dwelling in him and spreading the peace established by his reconciling work.

In this context the language of head, body, and assembly (church) had counterimperial implications.[21] An assembly (*ekklēsia*), after all, could designate the gathering of a political body (as Acts 19:23–41 dramatically illustrates). Strengthening this case is nearby reconciliation language, which "comes not from the sacrificial cult but from the discourse of political negotiation."[22] In this passage, the head "is the one who grants and sustains life, while also creating a new kind of unity among the members." In extracanonical literature the body may be the cosmos, but here the body is the church.[23] Rather than removing the metaphor's political implications, that contrast indicates the nature of Christ's peacemaking work. As God's Son he both reconciles all things through an extraordinary sacrifice and pacifies all opponents through a newly creative exercise of power: this warrior's victory involves his own,

---

19. John Owen, "Christologia: Or, a Declaration of the Glorious Mystery of the Person of Christ," in *The Works of John Owen*, vol. 1, ed. William H. Goold (repr., London: Banner of Truth Trust, 1965), 71–72.

20. Tracing three possible divisions of the hymn and opting for the basic twofold distinction adopted here (with *prōtotokos* appearing in each, and some paired elements without a fully chiastic structure) is Harris, *Colossians and Philemon*, 42. In both sections there are claims followed by causal clauses, but refrains are stacked in the middle, as noted by McKnight, *Colossians*, 144–45.

21. For a version (perhaps overly strong) of this claim, see Brian J. Walsh and Sylvia C. Keesmaat, *Colossians Remixed: Subverting the Empire* (Downers Grove, IL: InterVarsity Press, 2004), 153. Contraimperial overtones may not be overt, but such readings suggest that Paul need not have named names (and it may have been wiser not to; so pp. 89–91).

22. Thompson, *Colossians and Philemon*, 33.

23. McKnight, *Colossians*, 156.

not others', blood. The apparent triumph of hostile powers in Christ's death is overturned in his resurrection, inaugurating a new humanity.

Paul's teaching echoes the Old Testament's critique of idolatry while celebrating our liberation from false gods.[24] Idols have no reality other than the human rearrangement of created materials for religious projection. Despite their illusory reality, false gods exercise a form of power with deadly effects. Realignment of all things with the One in whom they hold together (1:17) is the only way to genuine harmony. Correspondingly, the hymn asserts the created character of all earthly powers in 1:16 and their redemptive pacification in 1:20.[25] The reference to Christ's blood may highlight the costly nature and not just the means of his victory.[26] This costly victory, though, is not just a reversal of human fortunes but a realization of God's ultimate design. Rather than truly reflecting the divine image they bear, humans were deceived and became idolatrous. Only through reconciliation to the Son, in whose image we were made, can we live before God as we ought (1:21–22)— but so we shall (1:28).

In the meantime, Paul suffers on behalf of this maturing body. Paul's claim to "fill up in my flesh what is still lacking in regard to Christ's afflictions, for the sake of his body, which is the church" (1:24) is christologically bracing. The same vocabulary for supplying what is not yet complete appears elsewhere when Paul speaks of churches' gifts to meet others' needs (e.g., 1 Cor 16:17; 2 Cor 9:12; 11:9). Here the claim cannot imply that Christ's atoning work is incomplete until Paul and the church provide a supplement. That would be inconsistent with the church's present possession of redemption (1:14), Christ's preeminence in all things (1:18), and the reconciliation accomplished through his blood (1:20, 22). "Afflictions" (*thlipseōn*), of which Paul speaks rather than using "cross" or "death" language, never designate the crucifixion as such but broadly reference the Messiah's suffering as the representative of God's people.[27] Paul's oppression, particularly at imperial hands, involves what the church generally undergoes in identifying with Jesus. It should be unsurprising to find glory and suffering in close proximity.[28] As passages

---

24. As itemized in Walsh and Keesmaat, *Colossians Remixed*, 142–43.

25. For an excursus discussing these principalities and powers, which likely include but may transcend the demonic realm, see Thompson, *Colossians and Philemon*, 36–39.

26. Dunn, *Colossians and Philemon*, 103–4.

27. The discussion of these points in J. B. Lightfoot, *St. Paul's Epistles to the Colossians and Philemon* (repr., Peabody, MA: Hendrickson, 1993), 164–67, remains helpful.

28. See Walsh and Keesmaat, *Colossians Remixed*, 228–30.

like Romans 15:20–21 suggest, Paul understood his ministry in Isaianic terms. The anticipated messianic woes may stand in the background, but the point is not exactly that Paul endures them. The point is that Christ has endured them; now Paul missionally participates in those sufferings and anticipates the ensuing glory.[29]

Thus, the christological implications of Colossians 1:15–29 are manifold, and occasional glances at verses 21–29 have not been extraneous to the exposition of verses 15–20. An understanding of Christ's life-giving relationship to the church, his body, is integral to Paul's ministry. This ministry flows from an understanding of the gospel in which creation and reconciliation are inextricably linked. In continuity with Ephesians 1:3–14, the passage points upward and backward, so to speak, to the Son's communion with the Father as eternal Creator. The passage also points downward, to the Messiah's redemptive passion, and forward, to his glorious reign of cosmic shalom. Every opponent of this reign is already defeated in principle. Now, in practice, the head of a new humanity is helping his body to grow into maturity, conforming our lives to the wisdom of the divine image. Granted this comprehensive scope of its salvation history, though, this passage's christological spotlight shines on creation. Accordingly, the next two sections address how the "cosmic Christ" of Colossians 1 aligns with the Creator-creature distinction.

II. BIBLICAL MONOTHEISM

The Creator-creature distinction has christological import for both biblical interpretation and dogmatic theology. In biblical scholarship— the focus of this section—historical hypotheses challenge the clarity of the distinction: at issue in the development of Jewish monotheism is the possibility that worship of intermediary beings anticipated the divinity of Jesus. In dogmatic theology—the focus of the next section— contemporary voices champion the recovery of sacramental ontology or even Christian Platonism: at issue is the nature of all creatures' participation in the divine Logos. Both discussions intersect with the cosmic Christ celebrated in Colossians 1.

When it comes to biblical monotheism, our focus is not on debates

---

29. See McKnight, *Colossians*, 187–92. Rather than the cross as a "first trigger" with another, "second and final trigger" to come, Christ's resurrection suggests that the eschatological trigger is past, the decisive battle is won, and the enduring afflictions reflect the death throes of defeated enemies.

about the history of Israelite religion vis-à-vis Old Testament texts. Instead, these debates are the occasion for relating the Creator-creation distinction to Christ's deity. Scholarly emphasis on Israel's inconsistent monolatry does not contradict the reliability of biblical history; indeed, Scripture narrates frequent idolatry and acknowledges the influence of surrounding polytheism. Whether the Old Testament simply prescribes monolatry (worship of one God) and assumes henotheism (acknowledgment of multiple deities) rather than advocating monotheism depends upon texts and contexts that must be left to specialist debate.[30] The focus here concerns the character of Second Temple Jewish monotheism as it brought Israel's Scriptures to bear on the ministry and reception of Jesus.

The recent historical trend toward "early high Christology" (hereafter EHC) has implications for the Creator-creature relation. Some versions of EHC champion a sharp distinction, in which the earliest Christians included Christ within the identity of YHWH—rendering to Jesus the worship due to Israel's Creator, Ruler, and Redeemer alone.[31] Such EHC countered "history of religion" accounts that relegated belief in Christ's deity to a later, even postbiblical, development. While some defenses of later or lower Christology continue to appear, at minimum EHC has been widely influential, and at maximum it has become an "emerging consensus."[32] Certain versions of EHC, however, retain developmental tendencies from the history of religion approaches. They blur the Creator-creature distinction, claiming that the worship of intermediary figures influenced early recognition of Jesus's divinity. Earlier, stauncher versions of EHC inform the exegesis elsewhere in this book, even as they raise dogmatic questions of their own. The present treatment focuses on softer, more developmental versions of EHC that raise dogmatic questions regarding the Creator-creature distinction.[33]

30. For a brief overview, see Larry W. Hurtado, "Monotheism," in *DTIB*, 519–21. See also Nathan MacDonald, *Deuteronomy and the Meaning of "Monotheism"*, 2nd ed., FZAW, II (Tübingen: Mohr Siebeck, 2012). But it is tempting to mention that "in the writings which, also according to modern critics, are of a later date and hold to a definite monotheism, the same expressions occur that we find in more ancient books: the Lord is God of gods and superior to all gods (Deut. 3:24; 4:7; 10:17; 29:26; 32:12, 16; 1 Kings 8:23; 2 Chron. 28:23; Jer. 22:9; Ps. 95:3; 97:9; etc.); cf. 1 Cor. 8:5ff.; 10:20)"; so Bavinck, *Reformed Dogmatics*, 2:32.

31. See especially Bauckham, *Jesus and the God of Israel*; Larry W. Hurtado, *Lord Jesus Christ: Devotion to Jesus in Earliest Christianity* (Grand Rapids: Eerdmans, 2003).

32. In the words of Crispin Fletcher-Louis, *Christological Origins: The Emerging Consensus and Beyond*, vol. 1 of *Jesus Monotheism* (Eugene, OR: Cascade, 2015).

33. The present discussion uses Fletcher-Louis's account to represent "developmental" EHC (my term). Among other accounts that offer constructive criticisms of stauncher versions from Bauckham and Hurtado are Chris Tilling, *Paul's Divine Christology*, WUNT, II (Tübingen: Mohr Siebeck, 2012); Wesley Hill, *Paul and the Trinity: Persons, Relations, and the Pauline Letters*

To survey a developmental case, we begin with a purported lack of initial Jewish opposition to Christ devotion, which arose only after Jesus's death and resurrection. On such an account, "christological monotheism" reflected in the New Testament likely had Jewish precedents, with "worship" of intermediary figures paving the way for unique "devotion" to Christ.[34] An alternative explanation attributes such devotion to powerful religious or visionary experiences. The alternative explanation, though, does not theologically preclude the possibility of idolatry—that such experiences involved human projection rather than divine revelation. Hence, for developmental EHC, the origins of belief in Jesus's deity may somehow lie in the incarnation itself, while pre-Christian Jewish traditions help with reconstructing its biblical legitimacy from a first-century theological perspective.[35] Among these proposed traditions are the Enochic Son of Man in *Similitudes of Enoch*, the ruler cult in Jewish messianism, and a story regarding worship of a glorious "divine" Adam.

Historical intricacies aside, our dogmatic interests involve the propriety of "a firm [Jewish] line of clear distinction between the one God and all other reality," despite occasional blurring in a few secondary texts.[36] Against such a sharp distinction, reflected in earlier and stauncher EHC accounts, others have appealed to Jewish texts involving divine creatures as creative agents, divine angels, and even divine human beings, along with worship of some of these divine agents.[37] In "exclusive inclusive monotheism," a developmental EHC model, "paradoxically . . . *precisely because he is absolutely distinguished from . . . the rest of reality, and free from all external constraint, . . . God is able to enter into and take on the nature*

(Grand Rapids: Eerdmans, 2015). Tilling proposes focusing divine Christology on distinctive soteriological relations between Jesus and us. Hill proposes focusing divine Christology on distinctive internal relations between Jesus and other divine persons. Both Tilling and Hill are hesitant about the language of "high" Christology. For another important volume containing a range of recent perspectives, see Matthew N. Novenson, ed., *Monotheism and Christology in Greco-Roman Antiquity*, NovTSup (Leiden: Brill, 2020). Among other items, it includes a summary of James McGrath's alternative to EHC, Hurtado's response to critics, and Bauckham's treatment of 1 Corinthians 8:6 and Colossians 1.

34. Fletcher-Louis, *Jesus Monotheism*, 1:137, 156. John 5 is treated as a late text, with ambiguity about whether the conflict it narrates actually happened.

35. E.g., Fletcher-Louis, *Jesus Monotheism*, 1:160. This appeal to the incarnation seems to focus on a wider principle of incarnation, not the christological teaching of Jesus himself while on earth. For a critique that Hurtado's account lacks the courage to trace EHC back to Jesus, see Chris Kugler, "New Testament Christology: A Critique of Hurtado's Influence," *BBR* 30, no. 3 (2020): 367–78.

36. Fletcher-Louis, *Jesus Monotheism*, 1:294–95.

37. See a fabulous new resource for studying such matters: Gregory R. Lanier, ed., *Corpus Christologicum: Texts and Translations for the Study of Jewish Messianism and Early Christology* (Peabody, MA: Hendrickson Academic, 2021).

and identity of that reality, even on occasion, taking that reality up into his very own self."[38] But such alternative models raise three issues for theological clarification.

The first clarification involves the *purported contrast* between divine self-revelation and a sharp Creator-creature distinction. The ensuing claim that "God is both able and willing, *of his own free choice*, to share himself with, to extend himself into or through, created entities or to take up such entities into his own life; that they might be—by his grace, power, and presence—what he is in his own intrinsic and indefeasible nature"[39] would be uncontroversial on some traditional interpretations— not necessarily inconsistent with staunch monotheism. To quote a very traditional account, "The most fundamental thing we come to in Christianity, the distinction between the world and God, is appreciated as not being the most fundamental thing after all, because one of the terms of the distinction, God, is more fundamental than the distinction itself."[40] In other words, the Creator-creature distinction is the servant, not the master, of the Creator's freedom for self-revelation. On other interpretations, of course, such a claim about participation could be problematic; its meaning needs clarification.

A second, related clarification involves the *distinguishable concepts* of the divine glory, identity, and nature. From Isaiah's juxtaposition of God's sharing no glory (42:8; 48:11) with giving *glory* to Israel (60:1–2), it may not follow that God's *identity* is shared with Israel.[41] Similarly, the prospect of "deification" may authorize the language of sharing the divine *nature* (2 Pet 1:4) without blurring the distinct divine *identity* vis-à-vis these humans.[42] So alternative models overreach when claiming that "the emerging consensus obscures the incarnational shape of the New Testament if, at the outset, it has decided that the relationship between God and the rest of reality must preclude God's delegation or sharing of his identity (with *the* incarnation in Jesus simply a one-off special case)."[43] This claim overreaches because traditional, conciliar Christology championed both the incarnation's uniqueness and its

---

38. Fletcher-Louis, *Jesus Monotheism*, 1:310. Punctuation (apart from ellipses) and italics are original.

39. Fletcher-Louis, *Jesus Monotheism*, 1:311. Again, punctuation and italics are original.

40. Robert Sokolowski, *The God of Faith and Reason: Foundations of Christian Theology* (Washington, DC: Catholic University of America Press, 1995), 33.

41. Contra Fletcher-Louis, *Jesus Monotheism*, 1:311.

42. Contra Fletcher-Louis, *Jesus Monotheism*, 1:312.

43. Fletcher-Louis, *Jesus Monotheism*, 1:315.

fulfillment of Old Testament anticipation involving certain forms of divine self-expression.[44]

A third clarification involves *the meaning of worship*. Developmental accounts claim that in certain Jewish texts "God is willing to share his identity or nature with another, even to the point that in *these* texts a worship of the *separate* figure (who is explicitly a *creature* in the case of the Adam story) is appropriate." In such texts, Adam or another "is not a second god" but "the image and likeness of the Creator himself": "*He is simply created to manifest God's presence*. And so we may say he is 'divine' and worthy of worship as such, in this very specific sense." Concerning such figures, "there *is* a cultic veneration of the 'divine' individual, but there is no sense of competition between that devotion and devotion to God. There is no worship of the creature *instead of the Creator*. In both cases there is a tight connection between God and the 'second' figure that eliminates any sense of a multiplication of divine identities."[45] These cases involve "worship" vocabulary and, although the Greek term may describe a gesture without "*actual worship*," there are instances that must be addressed—like angels prostrating themselves before Adam as God's visible or physical manifestation.[46]

Contra such developmental appeals, however, simply speaking of "worship" proves too much or too little. Too much: Adam is not treated as the Creator. Too little: it is historically consistent with a sharp Creator-creation distinction for creatures to be venerated in the worship of God. However debatable its propriety, such veneration is not equivalent to inclusion in the identity of YHWH—in the case of Jesus Christ, identifying him as the divine Son who participated in the very act of creation. Regarding the developmental model's occasional precedents, then, we

---

44. Partially coinciding (on its own terms) with developmental EHC is a trend toward speaking of "divine embodiment," which has now moved from Old Testament and patristic studies to the New Testament in the case of Brittany E. Wilson, *The Embodied God: Seeing the Divine in Luke-Acts and the Early Church* (Oxford: Oxford University Press, 2021). In brief, we can highlight that this aspect of biblical monotheism similarly puts careful definitions, extrabiblical contexts, and Scripture's coherence at stake. Definitions of *body* and *embodiment* vis-à-vis anthropomorphism and theophany need careful engagement; it is unclear why a fluidity of forms in revelatory events would be more consistent with enduring corporeality than immateriality. Extrabiblical contexts may contain more evidence of belief in divine corporeality than previously acknowledged by a mainstream tradition indebted to Platonism. But it takes another step to conclude that biblical texts themselves affirm divine corporeality, especially when (as Wilson acknowledges on p. 2, referring to Col 1:15; 1 Tim 1:17; Heb 11:27) certain passages clearly affirm divine invisibility. It seems difficult to reconcile divine corporeality (in the sense precluded by the Christian theological tradition) with Scripture's coherence and passages like John 4:24.

45. Italics original in Fletcher-Louis, *Jesus Monotheism*, 1:303–4.

46. Italics original in Fletcher-Louis, *Jesus Monotheism*, 1:269.

can agree that "it really is appropriate to give praise and glory and honor to the righteous *because this is what human beings were always made for.*"[47] Yet even this statement implicitly preserves the crucial distinction: the righteous human beings are praised not as the Creator but as those who fulfill the vocation they were made for.

These concerns notwithstanding, developmental accounts of EHC draw attention to historical nuances that may be theologically helpful—notably, the theme of royal priesthood. Biblical and postbiblical traditions avoid sharing divine glory with the king and the royal messiah, yet they sometimes allot the priest a share.[48] If Jesus understood himself to be leading a countertemple movement, indeed to be God's temple and Israel's long-awaited eschatological high priest, then "he aimed to make his movement the catalyst through which sacred space would be restored, idols vanquished and the Spirit made manifest."[49] This aim would be consistent with the divine imaging in Colossians 1: "By devoting themselves fully to the one true God and loving one another in accordance with this monotheistic commitment, Jesus and his followers sought to 'image' God as the renewed humanity who corporately embodied the Adamic Son of Man. . . . The bidirectional focus of the Jesus movement (from God to humanity and vice versa), implicit in the Christological titles and borne out by certain practices, was also meant to mark off this society as the human venue through which the transition to the eschatological temple would commence."[50]

Drawing together these threads, developmental accounts of EHC may chasten absolutist misunderstandings, but they should not blur the Creator-creature distinction of biblical monotheism. Jesus ultimately fulfilled the human vocations of several figures who uniquely represented Israel's God. Some precursors may have received veneration as representatives of Yhwh. No such figures, however, received worship in the sense that Christ did as God's Son, who is identified as sharing in the very work of creation. The incarnation is singular because of his unique embodiment of God's fullness. This Icon properly receives, not just occasions, worship—as the One, fully divine and perfectly human, to whom all other faithful image bearers of God are being conformed.

---

47. Italics original in Fletcher-Louis, *Jesus Monotheism*, 1:287.
48. Fletcher-Louis, *Jesus Monotheism*, 1:232.
49. Nicholas Perrin, *Jesus the Priest* (Grand Rapids: Baker Academic, 2018), 282. See also Nicholas Perrin, *Jesus the Temple* (Grand Rapids: Baker Academic, 2010), 189.
50. Perrin, *Jesus the Priest*, 283.

III. CHRISTOLOGICAL MEDIATION

To move beyond the crux of rightful worship, a christological Creator-creation distinction must also address the Son's integrative role in the cosmos. All things are somehow *in* him according to Colossians 1:17, entailing the need to address ontology with a grammar of creaturely participation in Christ. Similarly, Paul quotes a pagan poet in Acts 17:28, saying that in God "we live and move and have our being." While the former text makes a broad claim, the latter text focuses on human beings—arguing against idolatrous, impersonal representations of the Creator by identifying us as God's offspring. Together the two passages suggest universal creaturely and universally human forms of participation in God via Christ. They resist any sacred-secular dichotomy or ontological restriction of participation solely to redeemed human beings. Epistemologically, too, all the treasures of wisdom and knowledge are hidden in Christ (Col 2:3). Thus, God's Son is already Mediator by virtue of creation. Just as clearly, however, creaturely participation in Christ must have distinct contours and limits, given the specific union that members of Christ's body enjoy with their head, who is their Mediator with God by virtue of redemption (see chapter 9). Recent retrievals of Christian Platonism or sacramental ontology may not intend to marginalize Christ's redemptive mediation by magnifying his cosmic mediation. Nevertheless, five distinctions should inform a christological response to such proposals.

The first distinction concerns *redemption*: other creatures do not participate in the union with Christ that redeemed human beings enjoy. Scripture may not teach that no dogs go to heaven, but it does not insist that all dogs do so. In other words, although redemption will affect the entire cosmos, the reconciliation of human beings with God is its inaugurating reality and integral priority. Correspondingly, dogmatic reflection on the metaphysics of participation should prioritize soteriology as the Bible does.[51]

A second distinction concerns *filial union*: some human beings refuse to embrace God's saving love and thus do not participate in the distinctly

---

51. For a discussion that is cautiously open to the category of participation but champions divine perfection instead and commends the Reformed emphasis on locating participation within soteriology, see John Webster, "Perfection and Participation," in *The Analogy of Being: Invention of the Antichrist or the Wisdom of God?*, ed. Thomas Joseph White, OP (Grand Rapids: Eerdmans, 2011), 379–94.

filial union that redeemed people come to share with Christ. Being a child of God by grace means sharing in the communion with God that is uniquely Jesus's as God's Son by nature. Adoption involves a movement from outsider to insider—from slave to son. Without sufficient distinction between creation and redemption, nature and grace, or church and world, appeals to participation may be accompanied by departures from biblical accounts of sin and sacrifice.[52]

A third distinction concerns *forms of realism*: Platonism is a complex historical phenomenon, and it is not the only way of maintaining an appropriate connection between human concepts and the truth of divine revelation. Treating Christian Platonism as an aspect of orthodoxy would require a definition that is exceedingly broad and largely theological rather than historical. On one account, Christian Platonism means rejecting materialism, mechanism, nominalism, relativism, and skepticism—aspects of modernity that may indeed be laudable to avoid.[53] If a positive value lurks in these negations, realism—in the sense of having human concepts convey divine truth—would be the prime candidate. Yet appeals to Christian Platonism could involve an oversimplified rejection of modernity that fails to grapple with medieval Christendom's challenges. Meanwhile, canonizing a non-Christian epistemology, which theologians have variously appropriated and resisted, may hinder creative engagement with missional contexts. Language of participation and affirmation of realism should not obscure this evangelical challenge and opportunity: discerning the epistemological implications of Scripture's ontological commitments is a culturally embedded task that could generate a range of acceptable frameworks. Specifically christological possibilities should not be neglected. For instance, the Reformed affirmation of the Son's archetypal knowledge as God and ectypal knowledge of revelation as a faithful human being could celebrate Christ as the Logos without canonizing Platonism.[54] It is not clear that a particular theory of universal forms is necessary for affirming that all treasures of wisdom are hidden in Christ (Col 2:3).

---

52. E.g., although it repays careful engagement, Kathryn Tanner, *Christ the Key*, CIT (Cambridge: Cambridge University Press, 2010).

53. Thus appropriating the work of Lloyd Gerson is Craig A. Carter, *Interpreting Scripture with the Great Tradition: Recovering the Genius of Premodern Exegesis* (Grand Rapids: Baker Academic, 2018), 78–81. Carter also champions the call for sacramental ontology from Hans Boersma, *Heavenly Participation: The Weaving of a Sacramental Tapestry* (Grand Rapids: Eerdmans, 2011).

54. See briefly Richard A. Muller, *Prolegomena to Theology*, vol. 1 of *PRRD* (Grand Rapids: Baker Academic, 2003), 234–35.

A fourth distinction, which requires more extensive treatment, concerns *sacrament language*: although sacramental ontology has become closely aligned with Christian Platonism, there is no such language in Colossians 1. It is possible to address both creation's coherence in the divine Logos and even major aspects of redeemed participation in Christ without invoking this category. In the first instance, sacraments are rites. Applying the language generically to ontology risks confusion; if everything is sacred in this way, then arguably nothing is.[55] Indeed, the biblical justification for applying *sacrament* language to specific rites is complex, even when 1 Corinthians 10–11 is considered. That text links baptism and the Lord's Supper (10:2–4), also speaking of participation (10:16–21). In 11:17–34, the language of mystery is not used, but the spiritual import of participating (rightly or wrongly) in the Supper is emphasized. The eschatological, typological linkage between Israel's history and the church's rites (10:11) is consistent with the language of mystery used elsewhere (1 Cor 2:7; Eph 3:2–13). Given this complexity, it might be tempting to conclude that, since sacrament is a biblical category—but only indirectly so—there is corresponding freedom to speak of sacramental ontology. Of course, biblical language and theological concepts cannot correspond absolutely. In fact, there is freedom to speak of sacramental ontology if the underlying ideas are true and the concept wisely addresses contemporary contexts. However, since the participation language of 1 Corinthians 10–11 connotes worship and includes the possibility of false worship—participation with demons that arouses divine jealousy—referring to sacramental ontology risks confusion. Both the distinctive character of the sacraments and the dangers of false worship could be obscured. Perhaps not all participation is ontological, but Paul confronts false worship because ontically actual demonic relationships are established. If such participation is ontic but not always good, then once more speaking generally of "sacramental" ontology risks obscuring an important distinction.

As with the incarnation, the sacraments reflect God's provision via material goods—"the gifts of God for the people of God"—but again the significance of this argument must be qualified. It is wonderfully true

---

55. So Daniel J. Treier, *"Heavenly Participation: The Weaving of a Sacramental Tapestry*—A Review Essay," *CSR* 41, no. 1 (Fall 2011): 67–71. An earlier, fuller version of some material in this section appeared in Daniel J. Treier, "'Christian Platonism' and Christological Interpretation: A Response to Craig A. Carter, *Interpreting Scripture with the Great Tradition*," *Journal of Reformed Faith and Practice* 5, no. 3 (December 2020): 40–54.

that in Jesus Christ God assumed our human flesh. Likewise, in raising him from the dead God includes the material reality of this present cosmos in the promised redemption. Yet the sacraments' primary purpose is not to convey a principle about material goodness but to celebrate twofold participation in Christ's body: the grace of Jesus's real presence as we proclaim his death, and communion among churchly members of his resurrected body. Material things generally do not convey Christ's gracious presence or enable churchly communion in this specific way. "For everything God created is good"—true—but, as we go on to read, "nothing is to be rejected if it is received with thanksgiving, because it is consecrated by the word of God and prayer" (1 Tim 4:4–5). Material goods call for consecration; their participation in communicating God's gracious presence is not entirely automatic.[56]

The sacraments signal a more holistic and precise way of opposing a disenchanted universe by pointing to Christ's heavenly session as the ascended Lord. The terminology of an *enchanted* universe is ambiguous since Christian faith should not foster magic, superstition, or mistaken vulnerability to worldly powers.[57] At the same time, avoiding animism and affirming the distinct integrity of the material creation should not alter our appreciation for Christ's upholding of the cosmos and integration of various creatures into a coherent history. Hence there is no "secular" in the sense of a separate realm opposite the sacred. The current time remains secular only in the following sense: humanity does not yet fully acknowledge, and the cosmos does not yet fully enjoy, Christ's reign. Ephesians 1 and Colossians 1 highlight the important concept of the church as Christ's body in the *saeculum*. This prominent metaphor sanctifies our material existence as a primary vehicle of the risen Jesus's present mission. Regarding Christ's headship, "to acknowledge the divine life of the Word at work in Jesus is the foundation for thinking of the community of believers as bound together with him in a relation that is unlike any other. Because the life of the Word is—in virtue of being infinite and divine—different from the life of a bounded finite ego, it creates relations that are not just those of individual to individual."[58] The

---

56. Jeremy Mann highlighted the significance of this text for me.

57. In this regard, see the revisionist tale of early modernity in Jason Ä. Josephson-Storm, *The Myth of Disenchantment: Magic, Modernity, and the Birth of the Human Sciences* (Chicago: University of Chicago Press, 2017). These surrounding Augustinian reflections on secularity are influenced by Oliver O'Donovan's various works.

58. Rowan Williams, *Christ the Heart of Creation* (London: Bloomsbury Continuum, 2018), 249.

issues that sacramental ontology raises here, in the sphere of creation, will resurface in chapter 9, addressing the *totus Christus*, the "whole Christ," in the sphere of redemption.

For now, however, while sacramental ontology resonates with the goodness and ultimate purpose of the material creation, clarifying questions remain. How should mystery apply to the being of created things? Would their sacramental character consist in communicating *grace*—and if so, redemptive or "common" grace? Would not the former answer obscure the particularity, and the latter the primacy, of Word and sacrament? Alternatively, would the sacramental character of things consist in serving as *signs*—and if so, as specific parts of a medieval symbolic universe or general pointers to God's existence as Creator? Indeed, would such sacramental language basically reduce to conveying God's *presence*—and if so, in what sense apart from the church and its ministry?

Finally, again more extensively, a fifth distinction concerns the *biblical emphasis* to communicate concerning creaturely being—namely, praise. Those aspects of reenchantment that sacramental ontology rightly promotes could more precisely support a *doxological* ontology. The purpose for the christological mediation of God's revelatory presence is to elicit creation's praise. Human being has a priestly character; the being of other material goods should elicit our consecration—neither simply consumption nor enchantment.

The biblical-theological themes of temple and royal priesthood introduce this focus. The word pair of *cultivate* and *keep* from Genesis 2:15 applies later to the Israelites' relationship with God's Word and the priests' ministry at the tabernacle.[59] The human vocation of Genesis 1:28 involved extending divine presence throughout the cosmos. The language of being fruitful and multiplying applies later to the spread of the gospel, notably in passages like Acts 6:7 and 9:31—tying together the cultural and redemptive mandates of creation and new creation. The tending of Genesis 2 is an aspect of the ruling that Genesis 1 calls for. Yet the first human beings failed to protect the garden temple against incursion. Instead of representing the gracious God in whose image they were installed, they fell prey to temptation. They were expelled from

---

59. G. K. Beale, *The Temple and the Church's Mission: A Biblical Theology of the Dwelling Place of God*, NSBT (Downers Grove, IL: InterVarsity Press, 2004), 81. The following exposition summarizes aspects of Beale's work.

the sanctuary, required to reenter through divinely appointed means of grace. The Adamic commission did not cease but was reiterated in God's redemptive interaction with the patriarchs. In due course, Israel received sacred objects and rituals that bore witness regarding God's mighty acts.[60]

Passages like Psalm 19 epitomize the celebration of creation's witness: "The heavens declare the glory of God; the skies proclaim the work of his hands. Day after day they pour forth speech; night after night they reveal knowledge" (vv. 1–2). Of course, verse 3 acknowledges, the heavens do not literally utter words. Yet according to verse 4, "their voice goes out into all the earth, their words to the ends of the world." The focus of verses 7–14 upon God's law suggests continuity between this proclamation of divine glory via the cosmos and the display of divine wisdom in the redeemed community. As Leviticus 19:24 illustrates, the fruit of the earth epitomizes how nonhuman parts of creation participate in offerings of praise. David's recital in 1 Chronicles 16 urges not just Israel and all nations but even the heavens and earth, the sea and the fields and the trees, to enjoy praising YHWH (16:31–36). Of course, human persons uniquely—intentionally and verbally—praise God (e.g., Ps 30:9), our very purpose for being. For instance, God has prepared praise from infant mouths (Matt 21:16); they do not know what they are doing, but God is glorified even by the creation of what and who they are. Not just human acts but creaturely being is doxological. As we saw from Ephesians 1:6, 12, and 14, the praise of God's glory is history's ultimate end.

Consequently, although the Bible does not speak a systemic language of theoretical ontology, to understand creaturely being doxologically coheres with Scriptures concerning history's end, human beings' distinctive vocation, and nature's speech. Romans 1:18–32, especially verse 20, is consistent with this inference. Creation reveals the invisible God but focuses this unveiling on God's eternal power. Human hearts quickly idolize created things rather than worshiping the Creator. There is no suggestion that creaturely things comprise a symbolic universe to interpret or transcend. To the contrary, human beings suppress what creation's light makes visible—including what should be natural among creatures, in correspondence with proper recognition of the divine nature—clinging instead to darkness in their hearts. Ultimately, we need

---

60. See Beale, *Temple*, 117–21.

to know of God's judgment and saving righteousness (3:21), not a formal hierarchy of universals, due to our rebellion against the ontological and ethical order that our Creator has provided.

Accordingly, some Reformed theologians speak of covenantal ontology,[61] yet this appealing alternative is not wholly adequate. Notwithstanding its importance, covenant is a historical category. Even when lurking within the creation narratives, this category applies to relations and acts, not being as such. Applied to creation, covenant already anticipates Israel's salvation history. Even if the ethical focus of covenant should be anthropologically fundamental, the Bible also more broadly addresses the being of all creatures, tying their very existence to the Creator's glory. Doxological ontology supports covenantal distinction, along with appropriate continuity, (1) between human beings and other creatures: people can intend and verbalize God's praise, serving as priests for the rest of creation, even as they exist for God's praise before ever enacting it. Thus, doxological ontology likewise supports covenantal distinction, along with appropriate continuity, (2) between redeemed and unredeemed people: the redeemed can begin to intend and verbalize God's praise appropriately, even as the unredeemed exist for God's glory despite failing to represent God truly. Finally, doxological ontology supports creational distinction, along with appropriate continuity, (3) between Christ as God's true image and other divine image bearers: Jesus represents the Creator's character and reign without fail, even without remainder, in a manner to which other human beings shall be conformed (Rom 8:29) by redemption.

Covenantal theology prizes the truth that reality holds together *in* Jesus Christ, prioritizing his identity as the one Mediator between God and humanity. A Trinitarian account of this mediation celebrates the personal action of the Son and the Holy Spirit in creation and providence. In this way God sustains the integrity of the cosmos and restores the freedom of human beings to realize their priestly vocation

---

61. See especially chap. 1 of Michael S. Horton, *Lord and Servant: A Covenant Christology* (Louisville: Westminster John Knox, 2005). The "judicious integration of covenant and participation" would chasten the likes of not only Radical Orthodoxy (an influence upon sacramental ontology) but also antimetaphysical modern dogmatics; "theologies which reject inherited metaphysical systems and construct new theological ontologies are particularly ripe for overdetermination by metaphysics," according to Jared Michelson, "Covenantal History and Participatory Metaphysics: Formulating a Reformed Response to the Charge of Legal Fiction," *SJT* 71, no. 4 (2018): 410.

in Christ.[62] The acts and relationships that comprise earthly history lack the simple immediacy that fallen people tend to assume, in which individual persons directly interact with other human beings, physical entities, or perhaps social systems, as if that were all there is. Instead, whether people acknowledge the reality or not, all creaturely inter-actions are linked with God's Son as their Logos and proper end.[63] This precious truth has a larger context though: every human being must be adopted by redeeming grace to share in the filial relationship that the Son enjoys by nature. To be clear, doxological ontology does not surface as a middle way, a bland compromise between covenantal and sacramental ontologies. While learning from each, a doxological ontology addresses creaturely being with the biblical emphasis on praise. All creaturely being holds together in Christ, in an objective sense that should elicit praise (the sacramental emphasis); the praise of the redeemed, however, emerges from filial union with Christ whereby participation in God uniquely fulfills the purpose of human being (the covenantal emphasis).

In this doxological context, an aspect of Christ's mediation involves caring for and delighting in the nonhuman creation. The Logos epito-mizes the divine Wisdom of creation's original design. In him the cosmos and its history hold together through preserving grace after the fall. Incarnate in a human life, Jesus ate, drank, slept, and otherwise enjoyed material goods. He spent substantial amounts of time by himself in the natural world—not least the forty consecutive days of his testing, as well as occasions of itinerant homelessness. His teaching made extensive, attentive appeals to the animal, plant, and astral worlds. He provided material goods and holistic healing to many, sometimes using physical objects in doing so. He celebrated God's care for human beings in a comparative argument that built on God's care for birds and flowers.[64] Of course, he also cursed a fig tree and overturned tables. Perhaps the Augustinian distinction between "enjoying" God and "using" created

---

62. A tireless emphasis of Colin E. Gunton, *The Triune Creator: A Historical and Systematic Study*, Edinburgh Studies in Constructive Theology (Grand Rapids: Eerdmans, 1998). For a brief proposal regarding how we might understand humans' priestly "sacrifices" to God in continuity with creation and without contradicting Christ's unique work of redemption, see Colin E. Gunton, *Christ and Creation: The Didsbury Lectures* (Grand Rapids: Eerdmans, 1993), 118–21.

63. A tireless emphasis of Dietrich Bonhoeffer, *Ethics*, ed. Clifford J. Green, trans. Reinhard Krauss, Douglas W. Stott, and Charles C. West, DBWE 6 (Minneapolis: Fortress, 2005).

64. For brief implications from christological mediation for the arts, history, science, and ecology, see Treier, *Introducing Evangelical Theology*, 131–34.

goods can offer an analogy for relating human persons and the nonhuman creation: the point is not to encourage mere instrumentalism that minimizes nonhuman creaturely value apart from divine or human use. Instead, everything possesses something like penultimate dignity, having great value due to divine care and delight even as more ultimate value attaches to persons. Scriptures such as Psalm 104 celebrate clouds, winds, waters, mountains, valleys, birds, trees, grass, cattle, and so forth as praiseworthy divine works in their own right, yet they also celebrate their distinctive worth for sustaining human life and eliciting our praise. God receives glory from the being of all creatures, while desiring praise and fellowship from the intentional activity of human beings.

IV. IMAGE OF GOD

Thus, the significance of identifying Jesus Christ as the image of God has emerged through extended reflection upon Colossians 1. Proverbs 8:22–31 fostered early Christian identification of Jesus with the Creator's Wisdom and its personal expression in cosmic history. The reconciling work of the incarnate Son and his resurrection by the Holy Spirit enacted God's enduring commitment to the created order. However distorted its *direction* became by falling into sin and being subjected to a curse, the cosmos remains divinely beloved and good in its *structure*.[65] The Son's identity as the image means that the Wisdom by which God has eternally willed and temporally enacted creation, revelation, and redemption is personal. The universe's integrating principle is neither physical nor random. God's loving will, united in the communion of the Father and Son with the Spirit, holds creation together and holds it close to its Maker. Uniting human beings by grace with the One who enjoys filial divine communion by nature, the incarnation initiated the ultimate redemption of creation in a way that incorporates materiality, temporality, and sociality.

The image of God has been the fundamental concept of Christian theological anthropology for two millennia even though its precise meaning is mysterious. Despite appearing at the beginning, in Genesis 1:26–27, the concept is not overtly crucial for the rest of the Old Testament. The New Testament applies the language variously, albeit

---

65. To use a distinction articulated in Albert M. Wolters, *Creation Regained: Biblical Basics for a Reformational Worldview* (Grand Rapids: Eerdmans, 1985).

focusing on Jesus Christ. This biblical complexity has fostered three classes of views. Classic metaphysical and/or christological approaches focus on *reason* and/or *righteousness*, contemplating our distinction from other animals and unique relation to the divine Spirit (in Genesis) as well as the concept's New Testament development. The modern functional approach focuses on *royalty*, connecting the Genesis passage primarily to its ancient context, in which kings represented the authority of their lineage with temple statues that linked them with the gods. A more postmodern approach focuses on *relationship*, celebrating relatedness to God, relational distinction indicated by "male and female," and relationships with other creatures.[66] Each approach contributes insight yet faces criticism, primarily for privileging some context or portion of the biblical canon seemingly to the neglect of others. Perhaps a better, more encompassing pair of concepts, given Colossians 1 vis-à-vis the Old Testament, would be kingship and kinship: like ancient kings, the Creator installed representative images in the cosmic sanctuary; despite their rebellion, however, those who are in Christ may once again live as members of God's royal family.[67]

As Israel's idolatrous golden calf dramatized, human beings may not represent God according to their own ideas or initiative. That image was forbidden because it was false: God is mysteriously Spirit, not something physically majestic or culturally useful. The only physical image of God is the human being, who can hear, understand, speak, and embody the divine Word. Therefore, the image of God involves an identity or a vocation—God's earthly, embodied representation. Human beings convey only an image, not an exact replica, yet only we bear God's image. Now that we are fallen, we convey distorted images. While bearing God's image remains the basis of human life and dignity (Gen 5:1–3; 9:6–7; Jas 3:9), we are now caricatures—out of proportion regarding what God is like.[68]

---

66. For the broader overview behind the following paragraphs, see Treier, *Introducing Evangelical Theology*, 148–51.

67. On kinship see Catherine McDowell, "'In the Image of God He Created Them': How Genesis 1:26–27 Defines the Divine-Human Relationship and Why It Matters," in *The Image of God in an Image Driven Age: Explorations in Theological Anthropology*, ed. Beth Felker Jones and Jeffrey W. Barbeau (Downers Grove, IL: IVP Academic, 2016), 29–46. Other essays in that volume, while focused on cultural engagement, have christological implications.

68. Our image bearing is damaged but not destroyed. The strongest case for opposing such language—for referring to the image of God as undamaged—appears in John F. Kilner, *Dignity and Destiny: Humanity in the Image of God* (Grand Rapids: Eerdmans, 2015). Kilner is rightly concerned to maintain that all human beings have the *dignity* of being created to bear God's image and being held to that Christ-defined standard. By itself, however, this "standard" language

In Jesus Christ, the image already has been displayed not just accurately but as fully as possible. Numerous passages convey this basic idea, but the most direct *image* vocabulary appears in 2 Corinthians 4:4, Colossians 1:15, and Hebrews 1:3. In the first text, the gospel's light displays Christ's glory. In the second text, Christ's work of reconciliation fulfills the purpose of creation, over and in which the Son is God's preeminent representative (*prōtotokos*). In the third text, again creation and redemption hold together in the Son, who sustains all things as the exact representation of God's being. Encountering God's glory in Christ transforms us into his image (2 Cor. 3:18–4:6). Jesus Christ took humanity, including a body, into the divine life, so that he might enable us to see God's glory.

The aforementioned language of the *essential* and the *representative* image communicates the christological dimension of anthropology and the twin dimensions of Christ as our Mediator. *Image* essentially names the second person of the Godhead, the Son, as the focus of divine self-knowledge and self-communication. As we shall see in more detail later, the Son is the Logos, the Word that is internal to divine action and then becomes external in divine revelation. Thus *image* also representatively names the perfect human being who epitomizes God's loving character in action: revelation was initially given in the context of God's benevolent reign over creation but, given creaturely rebellion, is ultimately given in the context of redemptive reconciliation.

Accordingly, this chapter explored two dogmatic intersections between Christology and creation. First, maintaining a clear Creator-creature distinction is consistent with EHC. Second, maintaining such a distinction is consistent with creation's participation *in* Christ as the mediating Logos that holds the cosmos together. A more specific form of participation—filial union with God as Father, enabled by Jesus's Holy Spirit—pertains uniquely to redeemed human beings. Thus, the integration of all creation in Christ does not necessitate Platonic universal forms. The witness of all creation regarding God's glorious presence does not necessitate a sacramental ontology. Creaturely being is most biblically understood as doxological—already an occasion of, and always ordered to, the Creator's praise. Hence, *image of God* displays

---

may depersonalize image bearing and diminish its vocational prominence as a verbal concept. Obviously the image of Christ is undamaged, but our distorted representation seemingly should affect how we speak of the human *destiny* and the larger conceptual field.

the conceptual power of conciliar Christology: one person, fully divine and fully human. As the essential image, the Son is the fully divine Wisdom through whom God created. As the representative image, Jesus Christ is the fully human being who embodies the divine fullness in history, rescues other persons from bondage to sin and hostile powers, and reconciles the entire creation. Creation serves the end that the triune God eternally elected in Christ: communion.

CHAPTER 3

COVENANT AS THE MESSIAH

Luke 24:13–35

As epitomized in **Luke 24:13–35**, Jesus Christ is the **Messiah**, who fulfills God's **covenant** promises. *Recognition of the resurrected Lord is given as Christ makes himself present through Word and sacrament. The inaugurated fulfillment of the Old Testament's prophetic witness authorizes christological interpretation of its promises, patterns, and proclamation for God's covenant people, then and now.*

As we have seen, the biblical Christ's theodramatic ontology begins with the eternal *communion* of the Son and the Father in the Holy Spirit. This triune God elected the *creation* of the cosmos as a site for fellowship, ordaining that the cosmos would have a history. The structural principle of that history, and hence of God's self-revelation in Christ, is the *covenant*.

To expound the interface between covenant and Christology, this chapter begins with Luke 24:13–35, a famous text concerning Jesus's claim to fulfill the Old Testament's messianic promises. The second section unfolds the hermeneutical implications of this fulfillment for Christian interpretation of Israel's Scriptures. The third and fourth sections are doctrinally focused, unfolding the structure of the biblical covenants and the significance of the name Messiah for their inaugurated fulfillment.

I. MESSIAH RECOGNIZED IN LUKE 24:13–35

"When the set time had fully come," according to Galatians 4:4–5, "God sent his Son, born of a woman, born under the law, to redeem those under the law, that we might receive adoption to sonship." In the surrounding context, Paul addresses a crucial aspect of salvation history: the shift from the Torah to the Spirit as the primary form of covenant administration. There was, however, a prior challenge for recognizing the Messiah—namely, the shift from his immediate association with royal glory to acceptance of his sacrificial suffering. This initial challenge of recognition occasioned Luke 24, one of the most profound biblical treatments of preparation for the Messiah. Even in Luke's Gospel, which is oriented toward a Graeco-Roman context, Jesus's fulfillment of Israel's Scriptures remains integral to the narrative climax: "Then beginning with Moses and all the Prophets, he interpreted to them the things about himself in all the scriptures. . . . 'Were not our hearts burn within us while he was talking with us on the road, while he was opening the scriptures to us?'" (24:27, 32 NRSV).

Luke 24 narrates the paradigmatic struggle to recognize the risen Messiah in three movements. First, in Luke 24:1–12 God sends women, who were hard-to-believe messengers in that context, to announce the Messiah's resurrection. Second, in verses 13–35 Christ himself associates the resurrection with Old Testament Scripture, and Scripture with the Lord's Supper. Third, in verses 36–53 Christ sends his disciples as witnesses, initially within Jerusalem but eventually—as Acts, Luke's second volume, unfolds—to the ends of the earth. Our present focus rests upon the central encounter with the disciples on the road to Emmaus.

At this hinge of salvation history God's sovereignty—along with our inability to recognize the risen Christ apart from divine grace—becomes dramatically clear. The travelers gave Jesus what amounted to a police report, lacking not so much information as an adequate framework (v. 25).[1] Disciples had similar deficits of understanding on previous occasions, such as Peter's confession, the transfiguration, and Gethsemane.[2] Still, focusing on their inadequate framework does not illuminate the entire story. Recent translations of verses 16 and 31 reflect

---

1. Jean-Luc Marion, "They Recognized Him; And He Became Invisible to Them," *ModTheo* 18, no. 2 (April 2002): 146.
2. Marion, "They Recognized Him," 148.

the divine passive construction that was common in Second Temple Judaism: "They were kept [by God] from recognizing him"; "Their eyes were opened [by God] and they recognized him." God's self-revelation is sovereignly given.

This divine intervention prepares a paradigm for our instruction:

> The encounter of the two disciples with the risen Christ is framed by the references to their recognition (*epiginosko*) of him being withheld (v. 16) and given (v. 31). The verb *epiginosko* is consistently used in Luke–Acts for an act of identification, when there is an encounter with someone previously known whose present identity might not be immediately obvious. This is the basic issue in this resurrection narrative: the Jesus who is present is the Jesus the disciples had known previously, yet there is something different about him now—which makes recognition not a mere formality but rather a demanding engagement.[3]

The account suggests a broader analogy: "The recognition of the risen Jesus in an earthly presence, which is not described as abnormal in any respect other than in the difficulty of recognition, is analogous to the problem of scriptural interpretation, that is the recognition of the living God (through Jesus, in the Spirit) in a book whose language and content can be described and explained in the familiar categories of the humanities and social sciences."[4] The larger Lukan narrative suggests that the withholding and giving of this recognition is not arbitrarily mysterious but pedagogically purposeful, epitomizing how we are to recognize Christ in the Word and at the table.

Intriguingly, Luke 24 does not spell out a detailed interpretation of Israel's Scriptures, since in abstraction from Christ's presence the conceptual content would not unlock understanding. On the way to Emmaus, he taught by letting the disciples talk. They possessed the crucial detail when they mentioned three days (Luke 9:22), yet they missed the connection. The women brought back the message of Christ's resurrection, yet no one saw Jesus (24:24). John's Gospel also highlights Christ's presence when future disciples and the Samaritans asked Jesus to

---

3. R. W. L. Moberly, *The Bible, Theology, and Faith: A Study of Abraham and Jesus*, CSCD (Cambridge: Cambridge University Press, 2000), 46.

4. Moberly, *The Bible, Theology, and Faith*, 47. The following paragraph summarizes further points made by Marion, "They Recognized Him."

stay with them. Earlier in Luke's Gospel, Jesus asked if he might stay with Zacchaeus, whereas the disciples failed to stay with him in Gethsemane. On this occasion, Jesus fostered their faith by making himself present. With the blessing of the bread, the sign made the phenomenon visible. For Cleopas and his companion, just as for the eleven in 24:37, faith did not compensate for simple invisibility but instead made sight possible. Just when he became recognizable, however, Jesus removed his immediate presence, first from the Emmaus road and soon from the earth. We are not simply to gaze upon him but to show others who he is, even if the present world cannot contain the fullness of his glory.

The narrative of (1) *the journey* begins with (2) *Jesus's appearance* and (3) initial *interaction*.[5] We do not know how Jesus suddenly joined the travelers (v. 15). Given Luke's journey motif involving divine disclosure, this sudden presence with downcast (v. 17) disciples is paradigmatic: "Christ will be in the midst of . . . faithful fellow pilgrims and companions and will be everything that is necessary for them."[6] Jesus's feigned ignorance elicited their construal of his preresurrection identity (vv. 18–19). Ironically, Jesus recognized their confusion, whereas they did not recognize him whom they had known.[7] (4) *The disciples' summary* construed him as "a prophet, powerful in word and deed before God and all the people" (v. 19).[8] The crucifixion thwarted their hope for Israel's redemption (vv. 20–21). The disciples may have been downcast partly because Jesus did not meet their glorious, incomplete, and thus misleading expectations.[9]

Reference to the third day (v. 21) introduces the glory of the resurrection, anticipating (5) *the report* of the angelic vision (vv. 22–23).[10] Despite Jesus's prediction regarding the third day, this report amazed the disciples, who still could not grasp the narrative crux, that (6) *Jesus is alive* (v. 23b), even upon (5') *the report* of the empty tomb. Indeed, (4') *Jesus's own interpretation* did not elicit instantaneous recognition. The

---

5. For the inverted parallelism reflected in this outline, see Joel B. Green, *The Gospel of Luke*, NICNT (Grand Rapids: Eerdmans, 1997), 842.

6. Johann Baumgart ("Gospel on Easter Monday," in *Postilla*, 371v–372v) in Beth Kreitzer, ed., *Luke*, RCSNT 3 (Downers Grove, IL: IVP Academic, 2015), 483.

7. David Lyle Jeffrey, *Luke*, BTCB (Grand Rapids: Brazos, 2012), 284.

8. On the primacy of this category for perceptions of Jesus's itinerant ministry, see chap. 5 of Wright, *Jesus and the Victory of God*, 147–97.

9. Justo L. González, *Luke*, Belief (Louisville: Westminster John Knox, 2010), 277.

10. I. Howard Marshall, *The Gospel of Luke: A Commentary on the Greek Text*, NIGTC (Grand Rapids: Eerdmans, 1995), 895. The third day may also reflect Jewish beliefs regarding when the soul has left the body.

disciples were slow to believe the prophets (v. 25). Although they may have identified Jesus as a prophet, they foolishly failed to believe him. Of course, "Moses and all the Prophets" (v. 27) refers to Israel's Scriptures. Yet Jesus's prophetic authority reigned supreme, as he explained (*diermēneusen*, from *hermeneuō*) those Scriptures with reference to himself (vv. 26–27).

Again the ensuing (3') *interaction* involved Jesus feigning—departure this time (v. 28), as was socially expected (v. 29). He would depart soon enough, but he graciously stayed that he might (2') elicit *recognition before his disappearance* (v. 31): "He withdrew from them in the body, since he was held by them in faith. That indeed is why the Lord absented himself in the body from the whole church, and ascended into heaven, for the building up of faith."[11] The two disciples immediately pondered how compelling Jesus's explanation of the Scriptures had been (v. 32). Yet, although Jesus "opened" the Scriptures, their eyes were not "opened" by his explanation itself. A (1') *journey* back to Jerusalem ensued; Cleopas and his companion joined the roster of hard-to-believe messengers. Like the women "they received no particular commission,"[12] but their immediate return was appropriate: "The spoken Word and the enacted Sacrament are incomplete without witness; and witness itself involves both word and action."[13] Upon arrival, they learned that the assembly already possessed confirmation from the Lord's appearance to Simon (v. 34)—to which these two disciples added their journey.

The crucial moment of recognition involved the Lord's presence at the table (v. 30), specifically the breaking of the bread (v. 35). Jesus's actions are spelled out in ritual sequence: taking bread, giving thanks, breaking bread, and distributing it. The bread per se was not crucial; eating is not mentioned.[14] It is intriguing to speculate that Jesus's companions saw his nail-pierced hands as he served them.[15] His actions were reminiscent of the miraculous feeding in Luke 9:16, a context similarly preoccupied with recognition of Jesus's true identity as Messiah.[16] Breaking of the bread also anticipates the communal meals of Acts 2:42, 46. Many classic interpreters focused on the Eucharist, whereas some Reformation-era

---

11. Augustine (Sermon 235.4, in *WSA* 3, 7:42) in Arthur A. Just Jr., ed., *Luke*, ACCSNT 3 (Downers Grove, IL: InterVarsity Press, 2003), 382.
12. Green, *Luke*, 850.
13. González, *Luke*, 279.
14. Marshall, *Gospel of Luke*, 898.
15. Jeffrey, *Luke*, 286.
16. Green, *Luke*, 849.

and modern exegetes hear no sacramental overtones. Despite the lack of reference to the cup (taken after the Passover meal in 22:20), loud resonances with 22:17–19 make a sacramental allusion hard to avoid. Whereas the disciples failed to remember Jesus's anticipation of his resurrection, now the Eucharist will bring the distinctive recognition of his risen presence.

Consistent with his explanation of necessary suffering prior to expected glory, this recognition did not come from a glorious appearance. Jesus's explanation was complemented by the gift of his ongoing presence, received in the context of prayer and table fellowship.[17] The sacramental overtones echo the inclusive meal practices of Jesus's earthly ministry. Echoing Luke 16:31, the reference to Moses and the Prophets acknowledges their full authority: no one—even someone returning from the dead—could say anything to replace or "make somehow more palatable . . . the moral and spiritual challenge already present in Israel's scripture."[18] The Messiah's self-presentation does not supplant Israel's Scriptures but explains their anticipatory witness. The Scriptures, their interpretation, and the subsequent call to bear witness, much like the Messiah himself, are all divine gifts received by those who have been no faster to believe than anyone else.

The episode's christological import begins with the disciples' initial perception of Jesus as a powerful prophet. They hoped that he would be Israel's redeemer. Yet they misapprehended this prophet's predictions, and their hopes were dashed by his death. Their crucial oversight involved the suffering that must precede the Messiah's glory. In providing this explanation, Jesus took "Messiah" to his own lips. By withholding recognition until his explanation could be united with table fellowship, Jesus demonstrated his lordship in self-revelation and our ongoing need for his presence. Verse 34 reiterates his identity as Lord from verse 3 and ascribes to him agency in his resurrection and self-revelation: "The Lord has risen and has appeared to Simon." Resurrection is not just an event happening to Jesus's human body; resurrection is a divine act in which he inaugurated a new phase of his revelation as Lord.

While largely reiterating the thrust of verses 25–27, the explanation of the Scriptures in verses 44–47 adds texture. First, a threefold

---

17. On the complementarity of word and action, and the relation of the disciples' request to prayer, see Moberly, *Bible, Theology, and Faith*, 63.

18. Moberly, *Bible, Theology, and Faith*, 68.

canonical reference appears in verse 44: To the Law of Moses and the Prophets, the Psalms are added since they figure prominently in Luke's narrative of Christ's passion.[19] Second, another comprehensive claim is made: everything written about Jesus must be fulfilled. This claim involves comprehensive *fulfillment*, whereas the prior claim involved comprehensive *explanation*: Jesus explained everything that is said in all the Scriptures concerning himself. Neither case involves comprehensive *content*: not everything in the Scriptures must refer specifically to Jesus. Third, this understanding depends upon divine enablement; the repeated vocabulary of "opening" their minds (v. 45) suggests that Jesus's presence, not just teaching, is necessary. Fourth, in both cases the order is clear: suffering first, glory following. In verse 46, the entrance into glory is specified in terms of rising from the dead. Fifth, the Scriptures have an expansive thrust: repentance will be preached "in his name" (v. 47) throughout the world. This language anticipates Luke's second volume, notably Acts 2:38, while heightening the Lukan prominence of Isaiah 49:6: Israel's redemption leads to gentile inclusion. The disciples' dullness would again be manifest, however, when they failed to extend their witness beyond Jerusalem until God dispersed them via persecution.

The surrounding contexts have not only hermeneutical but also christological import. Verse 3 refers to "the Lord Jesus." By this point, if not much earlier, *Lord* signals his divinity.[20] Verses 5–6 refer to him as the "living" one, who predicted his resurrection. His typical self-appellation, Son of Man, appears in the remembered prediction of verse 7, which involves necessity (*dei*, "must"), although no specific Old Testament grounding is provided. Then, after the resurrection and the Emmaus encounter, the appearances in verses 36–53 emphasize both Jesus's transformation (given ongoing challenges of recognition, like the supposition that the disciples were seeing a ghost, along with his apparent entry by abnormal means) and enduring embodiment (showing his hands and feet, highlighting his flesh and bones, and eating). In addition to his humanity, the final narrated encounters underscore his deity—hinting at identification with YHWH in the "I AM" (*egō eimi*, translated as "It is I myself!") of verse 39, having revelatory authority in the ensuing verses, and blessing witnesses, who worshiped him.

---

19. Green, *Luke*, 856.

20. Arguing that Luke expects his audience to discern early on the mysterious divinity of the *Kyrios* is Caleb Friedeman, *The Revelation of the Messiah: The Christological Mystery of Luke 1–2 and Its Unveiling in Luke-Acts*, SNTSMS (Cambridge: Cambridge University Press, 2022).

Thus the fundamental theme of Luke 24 is the recognition of Jesus as Israel's risen Messiah. The initial messengers (vv. 1–12) were hard to believe, but the resurrection meant good news for faithful women, who were empowered as witnesses. The Messiah's self-presentation (vv. 13–35) incorporated other names—Jesus of Nazareth, Lord, and Son—while emphasizing *prophet* as a central aspect of his perceived and actual identity, both before and after the resurrection. In principle, recognizing the risen Messiah should have been possible for those who heard his predictions and understood Israel's Scriptures. In practice, however, expectations of royal glory occluded anticipation of messianic suffering. Recognizing Jesus therefore required a fresh explanation of Israel's Scriptures, accompanied by his life-giving presence. Such encounters initiated the sending of new messengers (vv. 36–53). Confident of his bodily resurrection and empowered by his Spirit, they proclaim God's offer of forgiveness in his name.

II. CHRISTOLOGICAL INTERPRETATION OF THE OLD TESTAMENT

Both the hermeneutical crux of Luke 24:25–27 and its reiteration in 24:44–47 assert that Jesus's messianic death and resurrection fulfilled prophetic necessity. Jesus initially used the generic language of speech. The prophets have "spoken" (v. 25). He explained "what was said in all the Scriptures concerning himself" (v. 27). Later he referred to "what is written" (vv. 44, 46), highlighting the Psalms' contribution within "the Scriptures" (v. 45). In the first case, "Did not the Messiah have to [*edei*] suffer . . ." (v. 26). In the second case, "Everything must be [*dei*] fulfilled" (v. 44). Yet this necessity could mislead us into overemphasizing a predictive approach to the Old Testament. As indicated by the inaccessible exposition of verse 27 and the broad summary of verses 46–47, the text does not identify explicitly and concretely fulfilled predictions.

Consequently, understanding Jesus's fulfillment of God's promises requires nuancing both hermeneutical *form* and theological *content*, in a two-way movement:

> It is important to recognize that the Gospels do not just take up a ready-made messianic expectation and apply it to Jesus. The fabric of reference to Scripture is very distinctive, featuring themes

(such as the suffering and death of the Messiah or his exaltation to God's heavenly throne) that were not commonly discerned in the OT by other Jews, while some messianic themes (such as military defeat of Israel's enemies) are ignored by the Gospels. The scriptural Christology of the Gospels has its roots in the distinctive ways in which Jesus himself discerned his identity and mission in the Scriptures and in the creative exegesis of Scripture in which early Christians engaged as a means of interpreting Jesus and his story.[21]

This two-way movement illuminates Old Testament promises, patterns, and proclamation.

A. Promises

The basis of both specific predictions and broader prophetic foretelling is divine revelation, putting God's character at stake. Prophecy and prediction are species of promise: God says what God will do directly and what God has willed to accomplish via creaturely agents. God initially promises a redeemer within the context of judgment, in the *Protoevangelium* of Genesis 3:15. "I will" statements count as a divine commitment, and the woman's "seed" anticipates the Abrahamic promise discussed in Galatians 3:15–18. The threefold content of the Abrahamic covenant (Gen 12:1–3) expands the initial promise to incorporate land, progeny, and blessing through a particular people. This promise unfolds further via Moses, David, and the Prophets.[22] Hence, "we may accept 'promise and fulfilment' as a key aspect of the relationship between the Testaments, without forgetting that there is more to the Old Testament than promise, and that the New Testament's fulfilment goes far beyond the expectations of the Old."[23]

Promise and fulfillment have broader and narrower ranges. The New Testament expresses fulfillment primarily with *plēroō* and secondarily with *teleō* or *teleioō*, as well as formulae like "it is written" (e.g., Matt 11:10; 26:31), "this is what was spoken by the prophet" (e.g., Acts 2:16), and "in accordance with the Scriptures" (e.g., 1 Cor 15:3–4). The

---

21. Richard J. Bauckham, "Christology," in *DJG*, 126. For a concise but thorough survey, see David W. Pao, "Old Testament in the Gospels," in *DJG*, 631–41.

22. David W. Baker, *Two Testaments, One Bible: A Study of the Theological Relationship between the Old and New Testaments*, rev. ed. (Downers Grove, IL: InterVarsity Press, 1991), 264. For definitions of these terms, see pp. 212–13.

23. Baker, *Two Testaments*, 265.

relevant passages could number well over one hundred.[24] While the frequency of these words and formulae conveys the broad importance of promise and fulfillment, closer examination of many passages discerns a narrower set of direct predictions or specific prophecies being fulfilled. For example, items in Matthew (such as Jesus's birth in Bethlehem in 2:5–6) could be viewed as fulfilling predictive prophecy (Mic 5:2). Although that example itself is complex, evangelical interpreters have typically recognized its fulfillment of expectations (even among teachers of the law; Matt 2:4–5) regarding the Messiah's birthplace.

As Isaiah 7:14 illustrates in the next chapter, some fulfillment involves multiple referents or stages. Israelites began returning to their land under Cyrus's reign, after the seventy years of exile anticipated by Jeremiah (Jer 29:10) and acknowledged by Daniel (Dan 9:2). This return was only partial; as reflected in Ezra and Nehemiah, its temple offered only a shadow of the previous splendor. In Jesus's day, much of Israel saw itself as still experiencing exile.[25] Fulfillment of God's promises in Jesus inaugurated the restoration of God's kingdom but did not establish the complete rest in the land that the prophets anticipated. Instead, this inauguration of the kingdom brought messianic suffering and, even after Jesus's resurrection, the destruction of the temple and another dispersal of the Jewish people.

The prophets' perspective was understandably limited, especially regarding the time and circumstances of fulfillment (1 Pet 1:10–12). A common illustration of this temporal ambiguity involves looking from sea level at multiple mountain peaks. When these stand in line with each other, onlookers may see only one peak, remaining unaware of both peaks behind the first one and valleys in between. This illustration is biblically fitting because many temporal mysteries in biblical prophecy concern Mount Zion and messianic fulfillment regarding the land of Israel.

B. Patterns

Multistage fulfillment of biblical promises aligns with the frequency of typological or figural exegesis in early Christian engagement with Israel's Scriptures. Types involve persons, institutions, and/or events.[26]

---

24. Baker, *Two Testaments*, 222–23.

25. See recent discussion in Scott, ed., *Exile*.

26. See definitions in Baker, *Two Testaments*; Richard M. Davidson, *Typology in Scripture: A Study of Hermeneutical Τύπος Structures* (Berrien Springs, MI: Andrews University Press, 1981);

Persons like Melchizedek, Moses, and David formed patterns that Jesus fulfilled as priest, prophet, and king. Institutions like the tabernacle and sacrificial system foreshadowed Christ's work. Events like the Exodus and the Noahic flood prefigured redemption and baptism. *Typos* vocabulary makes modest appearances in the New Testament, with the most hermeneutical relevance emerging in Romans 5:12–21, 1 Corinthians 10:1–13, Hebrews 8–9, and 1 Peter 3:18–22. If these passages epitomize the broader approach, then typological exegesis has several dimensions: a *historical* aspect within an earlier text is *prophetically* connected with a now-recognized moment of *eschatological* fulfillment in *Christ* that incorporates his body *the church*. Yet typological connections, even if the early Christians viewed them as prophetically anticipated in divine revelation, frequently remain subtle or merely implicit.

Distinctions between typology and allegory are contested. Early Christians often believed that Galatians 4:21–31, where Paul uses *allēgoroumena*, authorized allegorical exegesis. The motivations were apologetic and pedagogical: defending the new faith against Jewish objections and discerning spiritually fruitful meanings in seemingly problematic or opaque texts. Such exegesis usually intended to go beyond the original context without dismissing its historical significance. But debates emerged between the Alexandrian and Antiochene schools. Antiochenes perceived Alexandrians to approach the Old Testament ahistorically, in line with championing Christ's deity and personal unity. Recent scholarship, however, moderates the hermeneutical differences in those debates. Often Antiochenes still read allegorically, and Alexandrians still read historically.

The questionable orthodoxy of some Antiochene Christologies, along with the enduring influence of Origen, Augustine, and Gregory the Great, ensured that medieval exegesis incorporated a significant allegorical dimension. The "fourfold sense" involved the literal sense as foundational, along with three spiritual senses: the allegorical (corresponding to faith), the tropological (corresponding to love), and the

---

Leonhard Goppelt, *Typos: The Typological Interpretation of the Old Testament in the New* (Grand Rapids: Eerdmans, 1982). This section appropriates the summary in Daniel J. Treier, "Typology," in *DTIB*, 823–27. The events of Israel can include experiences, hopes, status, deliverance, disasters, and unbelief; see R. T. France, *Jesus and the Old Testament* (London: Tyndale, 1971), 75. Prominent christological types include Moses, Elijah-Elisha, David, the Son of Man, the Servant, the Righteous Sufferer, Adam-Christ, Jonah, the Rejected Stone, the High Priest, and sacrifice, plus the twelve tribes, the new covenant, and the temple regarding Jesus's disciples; see C. A. Evans and L. Novakovic, "Typology," in *DJG*, 986–90.

anagogical (corresponding to hope). A figure like Jerusalem could evoke them all—beginning with the literal city in history, then referencing the Christ-event there and/or the church (allegorically), the Christian soul (morally), and the New Jerusalem (eschatologically). Brief histories of biblical interpretation frequently align the Protestant Reformers with the literal, historical sense in anticipation of modernity. Those narratives, however, can be as overhasty as neat Alexandria-Antioch divisions. When the Reformers championed the literal sense, they extended trails already blazed by late medieval humanists. Although they decried allegorizing, some—notably Luther—periodically continued the practice. Perhaps they were opposing related Catholic doctrines as much as the practice itself.

Among modern biblical scholars, typological exegesis fell into disfavor, partly due to guilt by association with allegorizing and partly due to newfound emphasis upon historical particularity. At one end of a common scholarly spectrum, because early Christian exegesis often did not produce valid interpretations of the Old Testament's original meaning, it frequently does not even count as typological and should not be imitated. Any canonical legitimacy in the New Testament's allegorical interpretations comes only (1) *by virtue of inspiration*—requiring a distinction between the biblical doctrines and inappropriate hermeneutical methods that were sometimes used to support them. At the other end of that spectrum, similarly, early Christian readings are not seen as valid interpretations of the Old Testament's original meaning, but they often count as figural, with no significant distinction between typology and allegory. Thus figural exegesis may be legitimate (2) *by virtue of illumination*. Minimally, such thinkers defend the possibility of (2a) *sensus plenior*, a fuller divine sense within Scripture. More maximally, others believe that Christian readers should imitate the earlier practice of spiritual reading, even if such (2b) *lectio divina* uses the Jewish methods of the apostolic era.

The (1) inspiration-oriented approaches, which resonate with sectors of modern biblical scholarship, worry that figural exegesis violates historical canons of meaning; the (2) illumination-oriented approaches, which resonate with trends in patristics scholarship, minimize any distinction between typological and allegorical exegesis. Of course, these ends of a spectrum obscure complex possibilities in between. Nonetheless, critiquing overdrawn contrasts between Alexandria and Antioch, or allegory and typology—let alone the Reformation and its medieval precursors or modern successors—should not obliterate all distinctions, even if they remain fuzzy. Antiochenes and Alexandrians, not to mention Protestant Reformers and Roman Catholics, had meaningful disputes, even if they idealized in theory more disagreement than actual practice could bear. In its form of mimesis or representation of the world, typological exegesis seeks to preserve the narrative coherence between earlier and later referents, as in Christ our Passover lamb (1 Cor 5:7). Allegorical exegesis, in more fanciful moments anyway, suggests ahistorical, largely symbolic, connections instead, as in images from the Song of Songs applied to Christ or the church.[27]

If some distinction between typological and allegorical exegesis remains viable, then avoiding the polar ends of the current spectrum becomes vital. Rather than allowing apostolic typology only by virtue of biblical inspiration, or accepting even allegorical figuration by virtue of spiritual illumination, Christ authorizes some figural exegesis *by virtue of canonical expectation*. Earlier biblical persons, institutions, and events anticipate the ultimate fulfillment of God's promises in Christ and his church when the Old Testament's verbal sense is read within the context of the Christian Scriptures. If the church simply disregards modern historical canons that her theology helped to foster, then her appeals to the Scriptures will become implausible. If, alternatively, the church disregards figural exegesis, then her engagement with Israel's Scriptures will become unfruitful as she undercuts the roots of New Testament Christology. John Calvin epitomizes the stance that is needed: holding *both* that the Holy Spirit enables Christian recognition of figural meaning within the unified biblical story *and* that such recognition "is in no sense a material contribution on the part of the interpreter."[28]

Many typological readings would have been impossible to recognize until Christ's first advent and the outpouring of his Spirit. This epistemological reality does not entail a common criteriological shift, namely

---

27. Frances M. Young, *Biblical Exegesis and the Formation of Christian Culture* (Cambridge: Cambridge University Press, 1997). See also Iain Provan, *The Reformation and the Right Reading of Scripture* (Waco, TX: Baylor University Press, 2017), 98–105; Anthony C. Thiselton, *Hermeneutics: An Introduction* (Grand Rapids: Eerdmans, 2009), 84–87.

28. Frei, *Eclipse of Biblical Narrative*, 34. Frei's study was influential in restoring appreciation for premodern hermeneutics and promoting the *figural* terminology that is broader than some meanings of typology. On understandings of history in such debates, see John David Dawson, *Christian Figural Reading and the Fashioning of Identity* (Berkeley: University of California Press, 2002).

that spiritual experience offers the crucial warrant for such readings. By God's grace, experience may offer the context and the possibility for recognizing the warrant, which is God's mighty action in salvation history. Such mighty action manifests the reality and unity of the eternal divine plan. God acted providentially and redemptively in preparatory ways so that, Christ now having come, by his Spirit we may hear anew the fullness of what God has said in the Scriptures. If spiritual experience becomes the primary warrant for christological interpretation, however, then claims of fulfillment expand to obscure or even contradict the literal sense.[29]

An underdeveloped aspect of typological exegesis involves ethical application: "Traditionally expressed, one could perhaps say that typological tropology or tropological typology was the chief interpretative strategy for making the Bible contemporary, for absorbing one's own world into the world of the text."[30] Taking 1 Corinthians 10:1–13 as an example, Israel's story paradigmatically shapes the Christian pilgrimage and warns against idolatry; this figural move depends upon the ecclesiology of 10:1–4 and the eschatology of 10:11. Paul extrapolates from past to present divine action when articulating Israelite patterns that his audience should not emulate. God incorporates events within the Scriptures to encourage living in light of Christian hope (Rom 15:4). Biblical typology integrates the indicative with the imperative because in Christ we encounter both who God is for us and how we should respond to that covenant love. Reading Israel's Scriptures as testimony in this way "demands a self-involving response" and exerts "pressure" to accept a "commission" as Jesus's disciples.[31] The storied and prophetic aspects of Israel's Scriptures anticipate the climax of God's covenant love in Christ so that such interpretation is not arbitrary.[32] The church today finds herself fitting patterns from earlier generations of salvation history.

29. E.g., consider appeals to gentile inclusion at the Jerusalem Council in Acts 15 as a paradigm for the church's blessing of homosexual behavior. Among others who notice that this paradigm contradicts the literal sense is Carter, *Interpreting Scripture with the Great Tradition*, 21.

30. George A. Lindbeck, "Postcritical Canonical Interpretation: Three Modes of Retrieval," in *Theological Exegesis: Essays in Honor of Brevard S. Childs*, ed. Christopher Seitz and Kathryn Greene-McCreight (Grand Rapids: Eerdmans, 1999), 31.

31. Richard B. Hays, *Echoes of Scripture in the Gospels* (Waco, TX: Baylor University Press, 2016), 364–66. Hays offers numerous examples of the Gospels' figural reading of Israel's Scriptures.

32. N. T. Wright, *The Climax of the Covenant: Christ and the Law in Pauline Theology* (Minneapolis: Fortress, 1992), 264–65. See also comments regarding Hays's "reading backward" paradigm, along with Israel's responsibility for recognizing the scriptural priority of messianic suffering, in Provan, *Reformation and Right Reading*, 121–25.

Having previously referenced "the fullness of time" in Galatians 4:4, now it is appropriate to address Galatians 4:21–31. Paul's use of *allēgoreō*, despite his probable familiarity with Greek literary practices, is not simply tantamount to nonhistorical allegorizing. Referring to details of the Genesis narrative in the near context and relating the language of correspondence (4:25) to historical entities, Paul's approach is arguably typological or figural. As for the quotation of Isaiah 54:1 in Galatians 4:27, in its context of Isaiah 51:1–2 Sarah's barrenness is a prelude to the expansion of God's people: Sarah's children include all, even gentiles, who pursue God's righteousness. Eventually, Isaiah 64:10 associates Jerusalem with a curse, with desolation that evokes barrenness. Isaiah 54:1 comes immediately after the Suffering Servant passage, which was appropriated earlier in Galatians. Thus,

> Paul evidently expected the Galatians to see the connection between faith in the crucified Christ and incorporation into the numerous people who have the new Jerusalem as their mother. It is true that a direct correspondence between Sarah/Hagar and the sterile/married women of Isa. 54:1 does not work, but as various commentators have pointed out, Paul seems to refrain from actually mentioning Sarah in 4:25–26. The link between a sterile Sarah and a forsaken, cursed Jerusalem had previously been established by Isaiah; this background gives Paul the canonical authority to quote Isa. 54:1 within the context of the Genesis narrative. The point of the quotation, however, is to stress the link that believers enjoy not so much with Sarah precisely, but with the new, redeemed Jerusalem.[33]

On this basis, in Galatians 4:30 Paul modifies the LXX of Genesis 21:10 to treat Sarah's words as God's declaration, consistent with God's instruction to Abraham in Genesis 21:12. Such exegesis is undoubtedly creative, and it raises questions about supersessionism to which we return below. But such figural reading can be canonically regulated. Without minimizing the integrity of Israel's earlier interaction with God, figural exegesis recognizes patterns therein, reading the scriptural records of that covenant history from the perspective of eschatological fulfillment—as those "on whom the culmination of the ages has come" (1 Cor 10:11).

---

33. Moisés Silva, "Galatians," in *CNTOT*, 809. This paragraph largely summarizes Silva's discussion.

The Old Testament's Christian readers encounter patterns of divine action fulfilled in Christ as well as human responses found among God's people.

C. Proclamation

Since the appropriation of earlier *patterns* is prominent in the fulfillment of God's Old Testament *promises*, Christology refocuses the Christian *proclamation* of Israel's Scriptures. In some circles, progressive Christotelic hermeneutics and conservative Christocentric homiletics face a common critique, namely that they undermine the Old Testament's functional authority. In the former case, Christ as the end (the *telos*; Rom 10:4) of the Torah underwrites the historical and moral sifting of the Old Testament, especially its narratives—as if the teaching of some passages contradicts the God revealed in Jesus. In the latter case, passages like Luke 24 underwrite preachers' christological framing of every sermon, even from Israel's Scriptures. These hermeneutical disputes reflect long-term debates over biblical theology, not least between covenantal and dispensational approaches. The homiletical disputes reflect wider discussions about the nature and strategies of preaching, including not only hermeneutical debates but also ecclesiological differences.[34]

Without addressing every hermeneutical and homiletical question here, dogmatic Christology should at least clarify the basic effects upon Christian proclamation. Homiletically, moving from New Testament principles and examples to a theology of modern preaching is complex. Hermeneutically, many New Testament uses of the Old Testament do not focus on christological fulfillment but on doctrinal claims or moral appeals. Christologically, the proclamation of God's Word to God's people must account for the various *forms* of the Old Testament's prophetic witness regarding Jesus Christ along with the new *form* of covenant life that we enjoy *in* him through his indwelling Spirit.

First, then, (1) *Christocentric* is not a precise name for a specific approach but rather conveys a broader commitment to setting Old

---

34. E.g., a recent volume presents four views—redemptive-historic (or Christocentric, represented by Bryan Chapell), Christiconic (distinctly proposed by Abraham Kuruvilla), theocentric (represented by Kenneth Langley), and law/gospel (or Lutheran, represented by Paul Scott Wilson); see Scott M. Gibson and Matthew D. Kim, eds., *Homiletics and Hermeneutics: Four Views on Preaching Today* (Grand Rapids: Baker Academic, 2018). The respective ecclesiologies are Reformed, baptistic (two contributors), and Lutheran. The Reformed and Lutheran authors share classic Protestant tendencies from the magisterial Reformation, whereas the Christiconic and theocentric authors share baptistic tendencies.

Testament proclamation within redemptive history. Careful advocates do not actually claim that Jesus should be the center or climax of every sermon, at least in principle; the New Testament does not use the metaphor of Christ as the center in this exact way; and hermeneutics and homiletics are distinguishable. In the New Testament, Christ is the beginning or foundation and the end or climax. He is central in being the one Mediator between God and humanity, but the relationship of this motif to the Old Testament is complex. The substance of the new covenant was present in the Mosaic covenant by anticipation, not as its principle of administration. Thus, Jesus is central in being the biblical midpoint of history, but *redemptive-historical* is the apt concept for making this structural claim: the Messiah's arrival changes how God's people encounter the law and the gospel in Israel's Scriptures.[35]

Second, despite their insights, the non–Christocentric alternatives have limitations. A (2) Christiconic approach helpfully champions pericopes, units of discourse that contribute to larger structures of biblical theology. Yet these units may not be as objective and singular as the approach implies. Christologically, the approach focuses *icon* on Jesus's humanity in relation to the text's divine demand, perhaps one-sidedly emphasizing law over gospel. Conversely, a (3) Lutheran approach helpfully champions the early Protestant law-gospel framework. Nevertheless, its tendency to avoid the law's third use (for sanctification) one-sidedly emphasizes gospel over law, while these concepts may become abstractions that lose their christological density. A (4) theocentric approach helpfully corrects Christocentric aberrations. However, the same problems arise that affected the "center" motif above, and the approach of focusing on original author and audience does not provide redemptive-historical contours for how a given passage or sermon relates human life to divine grace now that the Messiah has come.

Therefore, third, these limitations underscore the Christ-centered insight that is operative within a redemptive-historical focus—and epitomized by the epistle to the Hebrews. The divine self-revelation within a biblical passage or presented by a sermon, whether emphasizing God's mighty deeds for us or royal demands upon us, has now been communicated in the final form of God's Son. This fulfillment may not require providing christological exposition within every sermon, and it certainly

---

35. See Oscar Cullmann, *Christ and Time: The Primitive Christian Conception of Time and History*, trans. Floyd Filson (London: SCM, 1951).

does not require finding Jesus on every biblical page. Yet the covenant people's hearing of God's voice must ultimately be *Christomorphic*—informed by how the gospel of Christ fulfills the anticipatory revelation of the Law and the Prophets. We encounter divine revelation, receive forgiving grace, draw near in prayer, and pursue holiness by virtue of this one Mediator. At least implicitly, the sermon's announcement of the good news and instruction in righteousness should reflect the *form* or structure of new covenant life in Jesus Christ, not least when the exposition comes from Israel's Scriptures. Christians serve the triune God of Israel, whose character and will have not changed. Even so, the ultimate revelation of YHWH's identity has now been given, altering the covenant's administration. Christomorphic covenant mediation *fulfills* the *Christoprophetic* promise of the Old Testament canon.

III. COVENANTS

These formal aspects of the Old Testament's christological interpretation—promises, patterns, and proclamation—cohere with two material aspects: the structural principle of covenants and substantive hope for the Messiah. The covenants, the present focus, are the principle of differentiated unity by which God's reign is administered until its redemptive consummation in Christ. This covenantal unity is centered in Christ himself, the climax of salvation history and the foundation of the church's ministry (1 Cor 3:10–15).[36] The covenant of grace has a unity of "substance" amid various forms of "administration."[37] This scriptural concept appropriates aspects of both covenants and testaments: both mutual acquiescence between parties, which characterizes the former, and the unilateral dimension of the latter vis-à-vis heirs.[38]

---

36. On Christ as the center of revelation vis-à-vis the *fundamentum fidei* (1 Cor 3:11), see Muller, *PRRD*, 1:416. On the neglect of covenants in recent theology, see Michael Allen, "Covenant in Recent Theology," in *Covenant Theology: Biblical, Theological, and Historical Perspectives*, ed. Guy Prentiss Waters, J. Nicholas Reid, and John R. Muether (Wheaton, IL: Crossway, 2020), 427–44.

37. Thus summarizing Calvin is Richard A. Muller, *The Triunity of God*, vol. 4 of *PRRD* (Grand Rapids: Baker Academic, 2003), 197.

38. Inheritance is pertinent since covenants in the ancient Near East (hereafter ANE) and the Bible are rooted in kinship relations. Hence, promissory aspects highlighting gracious divine initiative are never so unilateral that relational responses are not expected; thus Frank Moore Cross, "Kinship and Covenant in Ancient Israel," in *From Epic to Canon: History and Literature in Ancient Israel* (Baltimore: Johns Hopkins University Press, 1998), 3–21. For a rereading of Pauline theology that nuances how both gratuity and expected relationship are involved in the gospel, see John M. G. Barclay, *Paul and the Gift* (Grand Rapids: Eerdmans, 2015).

COVENANT AS THE MESSIAH

Hence, *covenant* in Scripture can refer to an immutable divine promise, an unbreakable divine ordinance, the resulting state of peace, the necessary human conduct, and the form of its administration.[39] Each form of covenant administration has shed distinctive light upon the coming of God's grace in Christ.

First, Reformed thought often refers to a *pactum salutis*, a covenant of peace or redemption between the Father, the Son, and the Holy Spirit. Psalm 2:7–8, "Thou art my Son, this day have I begotten thee," has been a supporting text.[40] The language of peace emerged from Zechariah 6:12–13, read as indicating harmony between God the Father and the Son as the priestly man.[41] Another text read in this way is Psalm 89, extended from its Davidic royal reference to typify Christ—especially since some of its language concerning exaltation (e.g., v. 27) and eternity (e.g., v. 36) seems to transcend David and his immediate descendants.[42] Although an eternal covenant can thus emerge inferentially, a double analogy and potential danger should qualify the concept. The double analogy involves a covenant being made between the eternal God and a temporal human figure, on one hand, and between the Trinitarian persons, on the other hand. In the former case, *covenant* is an analogy for an eternal, initially unilateral, divine promise. In the latter case, *covenant* is an analogy for a shared divine decision regarding undivided action *ad extra*; the triune God has only one will, not three.[43] Therein lies the potential danger: while all theological concepts involve analogies, with significant dissimilarity to the divine reality, the *pactum salutis* requires vigilance against undermining the unity of divine action. Even so, there seems to be a core biblical affirmation (perhaps especially in John's Gospel) of agreement between the Father and the Son to accomplish our redemption.[44]

Second, the covenant of redemption is often juxtaposed with an *Adamic covenant of works*: "an agreement between God and the human

39. Wilhelmus à Brakel, *God, Man, and Christ*, ed. Joel R. Beeke, trans. Bartel Elshout, vol. 1 of *The Christian's Reasonable Service* (Grand Rapids: Reformation Heritage, 1992), 428–29.

40. So Petrus van Mastricht, as summarized in Muller, *PRRD*, 4:110.

41. Muller, *PRRD*, 4:267.

42. Brakel, *The Christian's Reasonable Service*, 1:253.

43. Illustrating covenantal alertness to the danger of suggesting three divine wills, proposing that "the one divine will can be viewed from a twofold perspective" in light of personal distinctions, is Brakel, *The Christian's Reasonable Service*, 1:252. Incidentally, this page belies Barthian allegations that the Protestant orthodox ignored the "in Christ" of election.

44. See Guy M. Richard, "The Covenant of Redemption," in *Covenant Theology*, 45–57. The larger volume includes an annotated bibliography, surveying the history of scholarly debate.

race as represented in Adam, in which God promised eternal salvation upon condition of obedience, and threatened eternal death upon disobedience. Adam accepted both this promise and this condition."[45] The content of the law that obligated Adam, aside from the immediate prohibition regarding the tree, is typically associated with the Ten Commandments.[46] Hosea 6:7 is debated regarding the presence of a specific covenant with Adam or a more generic covenant with human beings.[47] As with the *pactum salutis*, the covenant of works is more inferential than explicit.[48] Traces of covenant in Eden involve analogies drawn backward from places like Deuteronomy and Hosea. Again the danger of category confusion arises. Scripture primarily deploys the analogy of a covenant for portraying redemption. Although the threat of death upon Adamic disobedience was real, the language of promise and salvation functions differently when related to a condition of obedience. Adam's hypothetical obedience would still have depended upon grace, even if the grace was creational rather than redemptive, and the outcome would have been life rather than salvation as such. Additional confusion arises from the language of works, which can become excessively focused on specific acts or deeds and haunted by Reformation-era controversies over merit. The concept of a covenant of works points legitimately to an initial, probationary test of obedience, distinct from the later covenantal administration of redemptive grace.[49] Yet alternative labels, like an Adamic covenant or covenant of life, at least provide reminders of created grace and warnings against mistaken connotations of a covenant of works.

Third, there is a progressive unity in the *covenant of grace* leading toward the Messiah's advent.[50] The foundational promise appeared in Genesis 3:15, having the immediate context of the human fall into sin.

---

45. Brakel, *The Christian's Reasonable Service*, 1:355 (original italics removed).

46. E.g., Brakel, *The Christian's Reasonable Service*, 1:359.

47. For a survey regarding Hosea 6:7, see Richard A. Muller, *Holy Scripture: The Cognitive Foundation of Theology*, 2nd ed., vol. 2 of *PRRD* (Grand Rapids: Baker Academic, 2003), 436–41. On arguments for Adam's acceptance of the covenant, see Brakel, *The Christian's Reasonable Service*, 1:365–66. On controversy over the possibility of the covenant's gradual abrogation, see Muller, *PRRD*, 1:206.

48. That is not necessarily problematic; for instance, *berith* does not appear in 2 Samuel 7 regarding the Davidic covenant, as noted by Stephen G. Myers, *God to Us: Covenant Theology in Scripture* (Grand Rapids: Reformation Heritage, 2021), 52.

49. For an intriguing, complex account of the test, see Nathan D. Shannon, *Absolute Person and Moral Experience: A Study in Neo-Calvinism*, T&T Clark Enquiries in Theological Ethics (London: T&T Clark, 2022).

50. As underscored in Brakel, *The Christian's Reasonable Service*, 1:452.

The ensuing covenants are characterized by the progressive administration of redemptive grace. As summarized in subsequent paragraphs, they develop features that prepare for the new covenant in Christ: the preservation of created life despite great wickedness; the promise of land, progeny, and blessing; a gracious pedagogy involving the divine law given through a particular nation; and the Davidic dynasty in which Jesus would fulfill his royal priesthood. Of course, divine grace preceded the fall in the initial blessing of creation. Yet the Bible frequently speaks of grace in specifically redemptive contexts, juxtaposed with law as a principle of covenant life (e.g., Rom 6:14). The Bible also speaks of apostasy in ways that recall humanity's original fall, suggesting that the latter was a covenantal breach of created blessing. So, again, *covenant of grace* communicates an important reality while being a potential misnomer. *Grace* characterizes the unity of the ensuing covenants in a way that goes beyond created grace, because here grace "means not simply or merely God's undeserved favor but God's favor to those who deserve disfavor."[51] Thus, the covenant of redemption, the triune God's eternal purpose of uniting all created things in Christ, is enacted historically—and thereby introduced as a covenant of redemptive grace after Adam and Eve's disobedience.

Fourth, turning to Scripture's explicitly named covenants, the *Noahic covenant* expressed God's commitment to preserve the earth for redemption, and the *Abrahamic covenant* spelled out three aspects of God's redemptive promise: land, progeny, and blessing. God's blessing of all nations began with a particular people, from whose land true worship would spread throughout the earth. This covenant anticipated God's redemptive self-revelation in Christ through the type of Abraham sacrificing his son Isaac and through the divine provision of a sacrifice in Isaac's stead. Abraham also anticipated the faithful covenant partnership of Jesus, who trusted the divine promise and obeyed the divine Word for the joy set before him. Correspondingly, this covenant underscored the gratuity of God's promise. God's call addressed Abraham outside the promised land, from an idolater forming a holy nation. As Paul highlighted (Gal 3:15–4:7; Rom 4, 9–11), this covenant's foundational character indicates that God planned all along for gentiles to join Abraham's family of faith.

Fifth, the *Mosaic covenant* prepared for Christ with the gracious

---

51. Ligon Duncan, foreword to *Covenant Theology*, 29.

pedagogy of divine law given through a particular nation and its offices. Through Moses, God particularized the redeemed people and instructed her communal life. The moral law explicated the love of God and neighbor that Jesus enjoined and epitomized. The civil law regulated Israel's national life in the promised land. The ceremonial law fore-shadowed Christ's once-for-all sacrifice, maintaining fellowship with God until the actual accomplishment of redemption.[52] This covenant also established offices that mediated God's authority. The anointed offices of priest, prophet, and eventually king anticipated the Messiah. While the Mosaic pedagogy protected the nation and prepared for the messianic offices, Israel's failure to keep this covenant dramatized the extent of the world's rebellion. Not only did humanity reject God's creational grace in pursuit of autonomy; even the covenant people rejected redeeming grace in persistent apostasy.

Sixth, the *Davidic covenant* promised the messianic king and related the priestly office to the temple rather than the tabernacle. Given David's desire to build the temple, God's promise to build a "house" for David (2 Samuel 7) had multiple resonances. Soon David's son Solomon epit-omized wisdom in all its ambiguity; wisdom's earthly paragon toppled in a way that atypically anticipated Jesus Christ, who would actually embody wisdom for us.[53] Kingship also affected the prophetic office. False prophets spoke "peace, peace" to itching ears in royal courts (e.g., Jer 6:14), whereas true prophets mediated the divine Word to which even kings remained subject (Deut 17:14–20). Hence Jesus both fulfilled messianic hopes for an ultimate Davidic son and unified in one person the distinct offices of priest, prophet, and king.

Seventh, Christ's inauguration of a *new covenant* established histor-ically the redemptive basis for the covenant of grace, pouring out the fullness of its blessings.[54] Jesus's faithful obedience fulfilled God's promise

---

52. Biblical scholars often reject this threefold distinction between moral, civil, and cere-monial law because no supporting literary structure appears within the Torah itself. However, "it is not pertinent to object that no such distinction among the laws is conceived of in the Old Testament itself, for that is precisely the point. The distinction arises as Christians ask how the Old Testament law can be read thoughtfully outside the social and religious context to which it first belonged"; so Oliver O'Donovan, *Resurrection and Moral Order: An Outline for Evangelical Ethics*, 2nd ed. (Grand Rapids: Eerdmans, 1994), 159–60.

53. See this reading of Ecclesiastes in Treier, *Proverbs and Ecclesiastes*.

54. For a summary that reflects the challenge of maintaining the covenant's substantial unity while respecting administrative differences between the old and the new, see Dolf te Velde, ed., *Disputations 1–23*, trans. Riemer A. Faber, vol. 1 of *Synopsis Purioris Theologiae: Synopsis of a Purer Theology: Latin Text and English Translation* (Leiden: Brill, 2014), 575–601. Highlighting the cov-enant's newness is Carl B. Hoch Jr., *All Things New: The Significance of Newness for Biblical Theology*

to rescue and rule the covenant people, while his once-for-all sacrifice secured the necessary atonement.[55] The Holy Spirit's regenerating and indwelling presence has become more focal, internalizing God's law and democratizing personal knowledge of God as a characteristic principle of life in this covenant. Thus, beyond more clearly revealing the covenant of grace, the new covenant climactically pours out its blessings, simultaneously accomplishing a faithful human response to grace and God's salvation-historical inclusion of the gentiles. Jesus has borne the covenant curse for Adamic and Israelite apostasy and has poured out God's Spirit. Consequently, Abrahamic faith can participate in the Messiah's faithfulness, anticipating through this Davidic ruler the promised blessing for all nations.

After the Holocaust, the fulfillment of God's covenants with Israel in Christ has understandably become more difficult to discuss. The Holocaust was not an isolated episode of anti-Semitism that could be cordoned off from the sinful history of Christian anti-Judaism. These horrors require Christians to address underlying issues, such as the relation between Jesus and Israel, the temple's relation to Jesus and his followers, the time and place of fulfillment for the land promises in Israel's Scriptures, the Torah's relation to Jesus and his Spirit, and the future for Jewish Israel in God's promised reign.[56] Denunciations of supersessionism are difficult to delimit in a way that honors Jewish concerns without precluding orthodox Christian claims.[57] Even so, a crucial distinction involves *fulfillment* rather than replacement: "God has not changed, but God has effected a change, as promised; the Law of Moses has not been renounced, but it has been rewritten on hearts, as promised; the need for forgiveness by sacrifice and holiness has not ended, but the death of Jesus has offered a new and permanent way into

---

(Grand Rapids: Baker, 1995). However, biblical contrasts between the older covenants and the new are relative, not absolute, as developed in Scott R. Swain, "New Covenant Theologies," in *Covenant Theology*, 551–69.

55. For an account of the Scriptures as "the covenant treaty of the new covenant Mediator" (p. 7), discerning Jesus's attitude regarding the Scriptures from his intentional obedience, see Matthew Barrett, *Canon, Covenant and Christology: Rethinking Jesus and the Scriptures of Israel*, NSBT (Downers Grove, IL: IVP Academic, 2020).

56. As chronicled, e.g., in David E. Holwerda, *Jesus and Israel: One Covenant or Two?* (Grand Rapids: Eerdmans, 1995).

57. According to a widespread definition, supersessionism teaches that "God chose the Jewish people after the fall of Adam in order to prepare the world for the coming of Jesus Christ, the Savior. After Christ came, however, the special role of the Jewish people came to an end and its place was taken by the church, the new Israel." See R. Kendall Soulen, *The God of Israel and Christian Theology* (Minneapolis: Augsburg Fortress, 1996), 1–2.

that state of forgiveness and holiness, as promised."[58] This new covenant is a distinctive form of administration, yet it has substantial unity with the grace God lavished on Israel for the world's sake. The new covenant is inaugurated but not yet consummated, and its consummation may involve forms of distinct blessing for Israel that do not undermine God's creation of one new humanity in Christ.

IV. MESSIAH

Three biblical offices—priest, prophet, and king—shared the feature of anointing. Jesus the Messiah, the Anointed One, has fulfilled all three as the sole Mediator between God and humanity (1 Tim 2:5). Chapter 7, which is focused on the Servant's earthly mission, expounds this threefold office; chapter 9, focused on his exaltation, expounds his identity as Mediator. In addition, three aspects are noteworthy regarding the Messiah's fulfillment of God's covenant.

First, both Old Testament teaching and Second Temple Jewish expectations focused messianic hopes upon *kingship*.[59] Beyond prophetic expressions of hope such as Zechariah 9–14, historical figures informed subsequent hopes for an ideal figure. YHWH sets moral and other parameters for Israelite kingship in additional passages like Deuteronomy 17:14–20; Judges 8:22–23; 1 Samuel 8–12; and 2 Samuel 6–7.

Second, both these parameters and prophetic hopes establish *God's kingship* as the ultimate context for faithful human rule. For instance, the conquest of Canaan may tempt us to exploit potential connections between Joshua and Jesus, with their names championing salvation, but Joshua does not treat its hero as a messianic figure—championing God's rule instead. Then, while Judges underscores the need for a human king, and Ruth traces divine providence leading to the Davidic dynasty, even that dynasty is qualified by 1–2 Samuel: (1) human kingship is subservient to God's as the ultimate hope of God's people; (2) the office of kingship is less important than the heart of the king; and (3) a greater David is awaited. Subsequent ideals in 1–2 Kings emerge via Solomon

---

58. Michael J. Gorman, *The Death of the Messiah and the Birth of the New Covenant: A (Not So) New Model of the Atonement* (Eugene, OR: Cascade, 2014), 72.

59. This summary and the next paragraph depend on Andrew T. Abernethy and Gregory Goswell, *God's Messiah in the Old Testament: Expectations of a Coming King* (Grand Rapids: Baker Academic, 2020). An earlier collection addresses important passages and perspectives: Philip E. Satterthwaite, Richard S. Hess, and Gordon J. Wenham, eds., *The Lord's Anointed: Interpretation of Old Testament Messianic Texts* (Grand Rapids: Baker, 1995).

and Josiah: in the former case, wisdom and zeal for the temple; in the latter case, adherence to the Torah.[60] Again, such ideals orient human kingship around God's, consistent with the Psalter and the Writings. While important passages in the Major Prophets, such as Isaiah 9:1–7; 11:1–10; 16:5; and 32:1, foretell a postexilic Davidic king, they support a larger aim, enacting the just rule of the divine King. The Book of the Twelve focuses hope for a Davidic king on enacting the justice of God's rule; Yhwh will bring the necessary deliverance. Consequently, reflecting Zechariah's focus upon Yhwh as universal King (14:9, 16), Matthew's account of the triumphal entry (21:1–11) presents Jesus as God, Messiah, and prophet, with Old Testament citations for each—even linking Zechariah 9:9 to Jesus's deity. These crucial trajectories toward the New Testament orient messiahship toward a Davidic king that would unify God's people in faithful worship and just ways. The heart of such a king would love God's Torah and God's temple.

Third, *early Christian exegesis* connected the Messiah's kingship with a previously neglected expectation of suffering.[61] The Davidic covenant of 2 Samuel 7 highlighted Christ's kingship, whereas the Psalms offered a primary lens for understanding his crucifixion. Isaiah depicted the faithful Servant who fulfilled both Israel's sacrificial vocation and God's promised return to rescue the covenant people. Gospel accounts of Jesus's death and resurrection highlight royal imagery in a manner consistent with previous messianic claims. Congruous with Luke 24, "Christian interpretation of the Scriptures arose from the recognition that Jesus was the expected Messiah *and* that he did not fit the picture. The lack of a pre-Christian Jewish concept of a suffering Messiah provides one of the first agenda items for the small circle of believers."[62]

More narrowly, then, early Christians appropriated traditional messianic passages, including Genesis 49:8–10; Numbers 24:17; 2 Samuel 7:10–14; Psalm 2; Isaiah 11; and Zechariah 6, which typically elicited

---

60. Adding Hezekiah as a second David, including trust in God's deliverance from the Assyrians, is Iain W. Provan, "The Messiah in the Books of Kings," in *The Lord's Anointed: Interpretation of Old Testament Messianic Texts*, ed. Philip E. Satterthwaite, Richard S. Hess, and Gordon J. Wenham (Grand Rapids: Baker, 1995), 77–79.

61. For a Messiah-focused approach to New Testament theology (including discussion of criteria on pp. 15–17), see Joshua W. Jipp, *The Messianic Theology of the New Testament* (Grand Rapids: Eerdmans, 2020).

62. Quoting p. 26 (italics original) in Donald Juel, *Messianic Exegesis: Christological Interpretation of the Old Testament in Early Christianity* (Philadelphia: Fortress, 1988), 24–26. Whereas many keep the Messiah and Suffering Servant profiles distinct until Jesus, a case can be made that "the King and the royal Servant are integrally related, if not identified"; see Richard Schultz, "The King in the Book of Isaiah," in *The Lord's Anointed*, 141.

royal expectations. Possibly fitting this category as well are Psalm 110, which pervades the New Testament to place the priestly Christ on the divine throne, and Daniel 7, which links Jesus's earthly self-designation *Son of Man* with the risen, reigning Christ. More broadly, other material that may have lacked a messianic history became important, including Genesis 22; Psalms 22; 31; 69; and Isaiah 53, along with verbal links like *seed* and *servant*.[63] Such material especially addresses Jesus's death: first suffering, glory to follow. Such material also highlights God's return to rescue and reign over the covenant people. Consequently, the fullness of messianic exegesis requires engaging Isaiah in future chapters: notably, Isaiah 7:14 and 9:6–7 regarding Christ's advent, Isaiah 61 regarding Christ's mission, and Isaiah 52:13–53:12 regarding Christ's passion.

The advent of Immanuel is the focus of the next chapter. This chapter has shown that recognition of the resurrected Jesus as Messiah is divinely given via Word and sacramental presence; christological interpretation of the Old Testament hears certain predictions and prophecies as divine promises, which justify the recognition of larger fulfillment patterns and Christomorphic proclamation; hence various covenants provide a dynamic unifying principle by which Israel's salvation history prepared for the Messiah.

---

63. Juel, *Messianic Exegesis*, 172.

CHAPTER 4

ADVENT AS IMMANUEL
Isaiah 7:14

As epitomized in **Isaiah 7:14**, the Old Testament anticipated the first **advent** of Jesus Christ as **Immanuel**, God with us, incarnate in a fully human life. *This incarnate state began with the Holy Spirit overshadowing Jesus's virginal conception in Mary. Returning God's redemptive presence to the covenant people, the eternal Son thus assumed a fully human nature and identified impeccably with humanity's fallen history.*

The present chapter brings together the eternal plan, the temporal stage, and the covenantal drama of the messianic Son. As the previous chapter explored, the Messiah's earthly career began to fulfill the promises of God's covenants with Israel. The preceding chapters located that covenant history inside an even larger drama: the Messiah is the Son of God who eternally enjoys communion with the Father in the Holy Spirit. This Son is the "spitting image" of God, through whom creation began, holds together, and will be fully united in joyful praise. The present chapter focuses on his first coming to earth as the incarnate God with us.

I. IMMANUEL ANTICIPATED IN ISAIAH 7:14

Isaiah distinctively anticipated this first advent. Through God's ultimate Servant, redemption would further reveal the identity of YHWH—the Sovereign Creator, before whom every knee will finally bow, who formed a saving covenant with Israel. Romans echoes Isaiah when Paul insists that he is not "ashamed" of the gospel (Rom 1:16; e.g., Isa 54:3–5), which reveals God's righteousness promoting faith (Rom

1:17). The Synoptic Gospels all begin with appeals to Isaiah (e.g., Matt 1:22–23; Mark 1:1–3; Luke 1:25, 31–32, 47–55). Isaiah 7:14 is a linchpin of this good news because of its early position in the book, its elaboration of Immanuel's birth, and its eventual focus on Christ's advent. The following exposition traces the context, the content, and the fulfillment of the sign to which this verse refers.

A. The Context

The context involves Ahaz, an unfaithful descendant of David who refused to believe that God would defend Judah. Instead, seeking help against a multinational threat (2 Kings 16), Ahaz disobediently pursued a foreign alliance. As a sign of God's judgment over Ahaz and Israel's eventual deliverance, Isaiah 7:14 promised a son named Immanuel, God with us. Previously, God told Ahaz, "If you do not stand firm in your faith, you will not stand at all" (Isa 7:9). Ahaz was not established in God's blessing because he did not trust God's promise. Rather than listening to God (7:7–9), he was misled by apparent signs of his time—fearing human forces instead (7:1–6). In a show of false piety Ahaz even refused YHWH's offer of a sign (7:10–12), rejecting God's patience (7:13). In Isaiah 7:14–17 God provides a sign that Ahaz did not ask for, a sign of impending judgment.

In the literary cotext, Isaiah 6 has narrated Isaiah's prophetic commission and anticipated the hard-hearted reception of his message. Indeed, the pattern of verses 9–10, in which God's people are "ever hearing, but never understanding . . . ever seeing, but never perceiving," will not apply to Isaiah alone. The parable of the sower (Matt 13:15; Mark 4:12; Luke 8:10) applied such expectations to Jesus's ministry (cf. John 12:40–41) before Paul applied them to his (Acts 28:26–27). The judgment anticipated in Isaiah 6:11–13a, though, is not without hope: as trees leave stumps when chopped down, so there will be a "holy seed" that remains as such a stump (v. 13b). Thus, Isaiah 6 has already begun to prepare for the multifaceted sign of Isaiah 7:14. That sign is introduced with Ahaz as the "first illustration of the hardening process" from Isaiah 6.[1]

In Isaiah 9, the subsequent context anticipates the victory of grace after the gloom of judgment. The chapter begins by proclaiming a future end to the humiliation of Zebulun and Naphtali, with honor to

---

1. Brevard S. Childs, *Isaiah: A Commentary*, OTL (Louisville: Westminster John Knox, 2000), 62.

come for "Galilee of the nations" (9:1). The ensuing poetry—beginning to shift in 9:2 from darkness to light, joy, and liberation—is fulfilled in Jesus's Galilean and gentile-embracing ministry, again according to Matthew (4:12–17). The distinction between light and darkness echoes God's original work of creation as well as a sharper contrast in an earlier work of redemption, the exodus from Egypt.[2] At the heart of this victorious shift, according to Isaiah 9:6–7, will be the birth of a son, who "will be called Wonderful Counselor, Mighty God, Everlasting Father, Prince of Peace." The verses are clearly messianic, involving an ideal, eschatological, Davidic monarch promised with "the zeal of the LORD Almighty."

Patristic commentators connected the government on the Messiah's shoulders with the cross that Jesus bore to Calvary. "Which king ever displayed the sign of his dominion upon his shoulder, and not in a crown upon his head or a scepter in his hand, or some mark of appropriate apparel? No, only the new king of the new ages, Christ Jesus, the king of new glory, has lifted up upon his shoulder his own dominion and majesty, which is the cross, so that from henceforth, as the previous prophecy stated, he reigned as Lord from the tree."[3] Obviously Isaiah's oracle did not foresee the cross directly. Given Isaiah 52:13–53:12, though, God's use of this metaphor anticipates the means by which Christ would establish his reign.

The names of the messianic Son are striking: "He is *born* as from human parentage and *given* as from God."[4] *Wonderful Counselor*: Unlike the clever but foolish Ahaz he has wisdom like God's.[5] *Everlasting Father*: "Probably the leading idea . . . is that his rule follows the pattern of divine fatherhood," with eternity applying to YHWH alone.[6] *Prince of*

---

2. Gregory the Theologian, *Oration* 38.1–4, SC 358:104–10, in *Isaiah: Interpreted by Early Christian and Medieval Commentators*, ed. Robert Louis Wilken, with Angela Russell Christman and Michael J. Hollerich, CB (Grand Rapids: Eerdmans, 2007), 124.

3. Tertullian, *Against Marcion* 3.19.1–3, SC 399:164–66, in Wilken, ed., *Isaiah*, 128. See also, e.g., Justin Martyr, *First Apology* 35, in ANF 1:174**, in Steven A. McKinion, *Isaiah 1–39*, ACCSOT 10 (Downers Grove, IL: InterVarsity Press, 2004), 71. And see John Calvin, *Commentary on the Prophet Isaiah*, vol. 1, trans. William Pringle, vol. 7 of *Calvin's Commentaries* (repr., Grand Rapids: Baker, 1993), 308.

4. J. Alec Motyer, *The Prophecy of Isaiah: An Introduction and Commentary* (Downers Grove, IL: InterVarsity Press, 1993), 102.

5. Isaiah 7 provides God's last word about Ahaz, who passes from the scene, as noted by Christopher R. Seitz, *Isaiah 1–39*, Int. (Louisville: Westminster John Knox, 1993), 68.

6. Motyer, *The Prophecy of Isaiah*, 102. This reference to divine fatherhood does not reach specifically Trinitarian doctrine; so Raymond C. Ortlund Jr., "The Deity of Christ and the Old Testament," in *The Deity of Christ*, ed. Christopher W. Morgan and Robert A. Peterson, TC (Wheaton, IL: Crossway, 2011), 50–52.

Peace: While peace ultimately comes from YHWH, echoes of Gideon and Solomon focus on the Messiah as a human ruler—with his reign containing no imperialistic bloodshed.[7] If the latter two names "note the conditions he will bring about," then "the first two elements match his earlier name of Immanuel," which should affect the interpretation of *Mighty God*. In 10:21 this name applies to YHWH: "Plainly, Isaiah means us to take seriously the *'ēl* component of this name as of Immanuel . . . [while] *Mighty* (*gibbôr*, 'warrior') caps the military references in verses 3–5."[8]

After Isaiah 9:7, long judgment sayings intervene regarding both God's people and Assyria before 10:20 returns to offering hope, which carries through Isaiah 11. A remnant will rely on YHWH, the Holy One of Israel—returning to the "Mighty God" (10:21). This hope of a remnant mitigates but does not remove the decree of destruction (10:22–23), signaling that God's people should not fear the Assyrians (10:24–25). In this context the motif of a burden and a yoke turns the Christian mind again to Jesus, whose yoke is easy and whose burden is light (Isa 10:26–27; Matt 11:28–30). Isaiah 11 inaugurates hope afresh with a shoot from the stump of Jesse, a fruitful branch from his roots (11:1) on whom the Spirit of the LORD will rest (11:2). The description of this Spirit-empowered ruler (11:3–5) clearly applies to a human Messiah, one who delights in the fear of YHWH.[9] Yet the earth's eschatological filling with the knowledge of YHWH (11:6–10) transcends merely human messiahship—for instance, in the agent's wise judgment (11:3) and punishing power (11:4). In that new exodus, YHWH regathers the remnant for which a highway is made (11:11–16; see 40:3).

Before the book turns to prophecies against Babylon and others, Isaiah 12 closes this section of anticipation. With "in that day you will say," 12:1 and 12:4 introduce eschatological songs of praise. Fundamentally these songs celebrate that YHWH has become the people's salvation (12:2). That is the context for understanding the sign's content.

---

7. Motyer, *Prophecy of Isaiah*, 103.

8. Thus, against treating *'ēl* as an adjective rather than a noun, see Motyer, *Prophecy of Isaiah*, 102. Seemingly conceding this grammatical point yet resisting the identification of the child with God (favoring "Hero Warrior" instead) is Joseph Blenkinsopp, *Isaiah 1–39: A New Translation with Introduction and Commentary*, AB (New York: Doubleday, 2000), 246, 250.

9. In this context, contra the widespread allegation that conciliar Logos Christologies ignored the Holy Spirit, see Cyril of Alexandria, *Commentary on Isaiah* 11:1–3, PG 70:309D–16B, in Wilken, ed., *Isaiah*, 136.

B. *The Sign*

Back in Isaiah 7:14, a sign commands our attention—"Behold!"—as "a special event, either ordinary or miraculous, that serves as a pledge by which to confirm the prophetic word."[10] The sign would have strengthened Judah's faith by demonstrating the reliable extent of God's promised protection, "whether in the deepest depths or the highest heights" (7:11). Now, however, the sign would demonstrate that Ahaz tested God's patience beyond its limit (7:13). The subjects involved in the sign are the "maiden" (7:14; a translation discussed below), her boy (7:15–16a), the land of the two dreaded kings (7:16b), and the LORD (7:17). To start with the latter, the following verses indicate that Assyria will be the LORD's instrument of judgment upon the house of Ahaz. In 7:16b, the land of the two dreaded kings is really the receiver rather than the active subject, for Aram and Israel "will be laid waste"—with YHWH implied as the ultimate agent of this destruction too. The focus on the boy in 7:15–16a concerns timing: the destruction of Aram and Israel will happen within a few years, before he reaches moral accountability.[11] The sign, then, does not consist primarily of the maiden. The name "God with us" (7:14)—in contrast with the looming judgment (7:17), as well as the shortsightedness of their fears (7:15–16)—points to what will be a future hope instead of a present reality.

Accordingly, the immediate context removes any conceptual necessity for the boy's conception to be wondrous. The initial words concerning the maiden in 7:14 could simply introduce the boy's theological name and the birth's geopolitical significance.[12] Admittedly, this claim contradicts the premodern Christian tradition, where many figures know that the Hebrew *'almâ* can mean "young woman" and would not require the LXX translation "virgin" (Greek *parthênos*). Yet such luminaries often insist, "For what wonderful thing did the Prophet say, if he spoke of *a young woman* who *conceived* through intercourse with a man?"[13] Relatedly, these interpreters insist that *Immanuel* cannot apply to a mere

---

10. Childs, *Isaiah*, 65.
11. An alternative possibility involves the boy reaching the age at which he could rule. That interpretation would gain credence if the sign involved Hezekiah, as argued by Seitz, *Isaiah 1–39*, 79.
12. As emphasized in helpful notes from my colleague Richard Schultz, the Hebrew *hareh* behind "will conceive" is an adjective and could simply be rendered "pregnant," while "and give birth to a son" comes from an adjectival participle. Modern translations are influenced by Matthew, which followed something like the LXX.
13. Calvin, *Isaiah*, 247.

man.[14] The classic, straightforwardly predictive approach, however, has not convincingly addressed how a prophecy about the Messiah fits the immediate context.[15]

Even so, nonmessianic identifications of the boy have their own difficulties. The first candidate opposed by classic interpreters is Hezekiah, Ahaz's son. He is never called Immanuel elsewhere, and neither are greater deliverers like Moses and Joshua; yet "God with us" apparently signifies more than an empowered human servant.[16] Highlighting an immediate Davidic heir would create tension with Ahaz's unbelief and the coming judgment. Admittedly, parallels to Hezekiah in Isaiah 36–39 are notable, especially the language of signs in 37:30, 38:7, and 38:22, coupled with the contrast between Hezekiah's and Ahaz's responses to the word of the LORD. Nevertheless, Hezekiah does not appear to fit chronologically,[17] and Isaiah makes clear that any peace in Hezekiah's time would be decidedly temporary.

A second candidate is Isaiah's son Maher-Shalal-Hash-Baz (8:1–4, in light of 7:3). Here Immanuel language recurs (8:8, 10), as does the language of signs (8:18). Yet this son's distinctive name is already crucial, while "Isaiah's wife at the time was no 'almâ and she did not call her son Immanuel!"[18] A variant of this approach treats Immanuel as another son of Isaiah, suggesting a parallel with Hosea's three children.[19] But the role played by this name and this birth vis-à-vis the surrounding narrative is unique.[20]

A third possibility involves an unnamed maiden, presumably known in the royal court, bearing a son whose imminent birth signals the looming defeat of Aram and Israel. By itself this possibility risks a "depressing anticlimax."[21] Depending on the interpretation of 7:15–16, even the imminent timing is complex, since Damascus fell to Assyria within

14. Calvin, *Isaiah*, 244–45.
15. Suggesting, for instance, that the divine decree Ahaz rejected ultimately promised the Messiah is Calvin, *Isaiah*, 245–46. By contrast, there was no pre-Christian messianic interpretation of Isaiah 7, according to Amy-Jill Levine and Marc Zvi Brettler, *The Bible with and without Jesus: How Jews and Christians Read the Same Stories Differently* (New York: HarperOne, 2020), 268–69. (Thanks to Andy Iversen for that source.)
16. Calvin, *Isaiah*, 248–49.
17. So John N. Oswalt, *The Book of Isaiah Chapters 1–39*, NICOT (Grand Rapids: Eerdmans, 1986), 212. Highlighting the parallels and valiantly attempting to address chronological problems via royal transitions or coregency is Seitz, *Isaiah 1–39*, 64–71.
18. Motyer, *Prophecy of Isaiah*, 86–87.
19. Blenkinsopp, *Isaiah 1–39*, 233.
20. Seitz, *Isaiah 1–39*, 62–63.
21. Motyer, *Prophecy of Isaiah*, 85.

three years, but Samaria only fell thirteen years later.[22] Such extended or ambiguous timing could weaken the sign's sufficiency as coming distinctly from YHWH. Although this third possibility may be most appropriate for handling the original context, the literary cotext traced above extends the sign in a messianic direction.

Hence there is "a tension between the immediate and the remote,"[23] along with ambiguity regarding whether the passage prophesies "weal or woe." Indeed, "the presence of a transcendent and holy God with us may well mean weal and woe together."[24] The sign's multifaceted reality should decrease contemporary confidence about identifying any immediate referent. The book of Isaiah already recontextualized the original speech act for God's people. Now Christians interpret the text many centuries later—at still another step removed from the initial setting. Even the historical situation was multifaceted, with the sign chosen by YHWH in Isaiah 7:14 presumably differing from what Ahaz was originally offered in 7:10–11.

Since a young, unmarried woman (*'almâ*) would almost axiomatically have been a virgin in that original context, disagreement is largely moot regarding whether the alternative *b^etûlâ* would have unambiguously signified a virgin.[25] Thus, the LXX translation of *'almâ* with *parthenos*, "virgin," is understandable; "while the prophet did not want to stress the virginity, neither did he wish to leave it aside."[26] Accordingly, "the English translation of the Hebrew by the AV as 'virgin' is misleading in too narrowly focusing on virginity rather than on sexual maturity. Conversely, the preferred modern translation of 'young woman' (NRSV) is too broad a rendering since it wrongly includes young wives."[27] "Maiden" conveys the appropriate connotations.

Ultimately, the sign anticipates the virginal conception of Jesus Christ, even if there was a proximate referent that is canonically obscure: "If a virgin overshadowed by God's Spirit should conceive and give birth, it would not only be a sign of God's presence with us. Better than that, it would be the reality of that experience. So Ahaz's sign

---

22. Motyer, *Prophecy of Isaiah*, 86.

23. Motyer, *Prophecy of Isaiah*, 87.

24. Oswalt, *Isaiah 1–39*, 208–9.

25. For an example labeling it "unambiguous," see Oswalt, *Isaiah 1–39*, 210. Some suggest that in passages like Genesis 24 it is "not specific" without other "qualifying words"; e.g., Motyer, *Prophecy of Isaiah*, 85.

26. Oswalt, *Isaiah 1–39*, 210.

27. Childs, *Isaiah*, 66.

must be rooted in its own time to have significance for that time, but it also must extend beyond that time and into a much more universal mode if its radical truth is to be any more than a vain hope. For such a twofold task 'almâ is admirably suited."[28] Until that fulfillment, the sign conveys a removal of God's protective presence from the covenant people. Under those circumstances, the "curds and honey" of Isaiah 7:15 indicate the poverty of an uncultivated diet.[29] Ironically, Assyria, the purported deliverer, is the agent of desolation (7:17). Having stumbled over YHWH (8:13–15), the people remain in darkness (8:22) until the dawning light of the promised Son (chap. 9) and the returning faith of a remnant (chap. 10). God's giving of a son echoes 7:14 in 9:6, establishing a trajectory toward a more ultimate fulfillment.[30]

C. The Fulfillment

Matthew stakes a claim regarding the sign's fulfillment amid exile's ongoing darkness. Isaiah's honey indirectly evokes the wilderness existence by which John the Baptizer, the messianic forerunner, identified with Israel's plight (Matt 3:4). His baptism enabled Jesus to do likewise (3:13–17). In Matthew 2 the events of Jesus's infancy—his birth in Bethlehem, flight to Egypt, and return from Nazareth—variously fulfilled Israel's Scriptures. Even earlier, the Gospel's stylized genealogy identified Jesus with the history of his people (1:1–17). In 1:18–25, the angelic annunciation to Joseph, Mary's bearing of Jesus, and his salvation

---

28. Oswalt, *Isaiah 1–39*, 211. Although helpful, Oswalt's discussion does not necessarily establish Maher-Shalal-Hash-Baz as "the most attractive option" for the initial referent—contra p. 213. Instead, any clarity about the initial referent is now lost—by divine design, given the planned fulfillment in the text's distant future.

29. "Thus the reason Immanu-el will eat curds and honey (vs. 15) is that this will be the only thing in the land to eat after the Assyrian triumph over Judah. . . . Isaiah's emphasis in the sign is *not* on the food that Immanu-el will eat, but on the events that will transpire *before* he begins eating that food (vs. 16)!" Emphasis original (replaced bold with italics) in John T. Willis, "The Meaning of Isaiah 7:14 and Its Application in Matthew 1:23," *Restoration Quarterly* 21 (1978): 9.

30. Suggesting that Isaiah 7–9–11 go beyond prophetic messianism is Daniel Schibler, "Messianism and Messianic Prophecy in Isaiah 1–12 and 28–33," in *The Lord's Anointed: Interpretation of Old Testament Messianic Texts*, ed. Philip E. Satterthwaite, Richard S. Hess, and Gordon J. Wenham (Grand Rapids: Baker, 1995), 87–104. Summarizing Isaiah's royal messianism with a more common distinction from the Suffering Servant and anointed messenger is Andrew T. Abernethy, *The Book of Isaiah and God's Kingdom: A Thematic-Theological Approach*, NSBT (Downers Grove, IL: IVP Academic, 2016), 169–70. Notably, this perspective does not connect Isaiah 7; 9; and 11 regarding one anticipated son. For commentaries moving in that direction (noticed by Auburn Powell and Luke Boone), see Paul House, *Isaiah, Vol. 1: A Mentor Commentary* (Ross-shire, UK: Christian Focus, 2018), 214–29; Gary V. Smith, *Isaiah 1–39*, NAC 15A (Nashville: B&H, 2007), 211–16.

of the people from their sins "took place to fulfill what the Lord had spoken by the prophet" (Matt 1:22) in Isaiah 7:14.

Fulfillment is a complex concept in Matthew's Gospel, encompassing far more than direct predictions.[31] Given this complexity and the canonical context of Isaiah 7, a predictive view of the sign's Matthean fulfillment is problematic and unnecessary. Evangelical scholars increasingly favor a typological view, according to which "Matthew sees in the passage a historical pattern that comes to climactic fulfillment with Jesus." In a sometimes overlapping multiple-fulfillment view, "the prophecy foresees not only a partial fulfillment in the days of Ahaz but also a climactic fulfillment in NT times."[32] When these views are distinguished, adherents of single-meaning, authorial-intention hermeneutics often favor the typological approach to avoid affirming *sensus plenior*, a fuller divine sense. Such hesitations are understandable. But Matthew frequently references "the prophet," as he does here, and the fulfillment involves "what the Lord had spoken." Hence Matthew himself apparently presents more than a clever *post facto* alignment of a recent event with an ancient motif: an angel anticipated the divinely orchestrated fulfillment of a promise. Other striking fulfillments may not involve direct prediction, but Matthew likely perceived *divine* orchestration and *communication* of a foreordained reality to which the Old Testament—and any precursor(s) in Israel's history—ultimately *referred*. Speaking of the promise's integrated preliminary and then ultimate fulfillment honors better the communicative intentions of both Matthew and Isaiah at the canonical level, and thus of God in both the initial context of Isaiah 7 and the eventual context of salvation history. While the original sign came quickly to indicate judgment, Isaiah's further dealings with Judah communicated a greater canonical sign, the coming of God's gracious Son.

Despite its excesses, patristic contemplation recognized that "because his birth was from a woman, it was human. Because she was a virgin, it was divine. He had neither a human father nor a divine mother."[33] The Savior's name, "because of which he is called 'God with us' by the prophet, signifies both natures of his one person."[34] Connecting Isaiah 7:14 with the governmental theme of 9:6 supported identifying Mary as

---

31. David L. Turner, *Matthew*, BECNT (Grand Rapids: Baker Academic, 2008), 19–25.

32. Quoting p. 70 within the helpful discussion from Turner, *Matthew*, 69–73.

33. Gregory of Nazianzus, *On the Son, Theological Oration* 3(29).19, in SC 250:218, in McKinion, ed., *Isaiah 1–39*, 10:62.

34. Bede, *Homilies on the Gospels* 1.5, in CS 110:47, in McKinion, ed., *Isaiah 1–39*, 10:63.

Theotokos: "If the baby born of the virgin is styled 'Mighty God,' then it is only with reason that the mother is called 'mother of God.' For the mother shares the honor of her offspring, and the Virgin is both mother of the Lord Christ as man and again is his servant as Lord and Creator and God."[35] Of course, compelling juxtapositions with Eve and other aspects of salvation history are often accompanied by unbiblical celebration of Mary's perpetual virginity.[36] On such occasions the church mistakenly shifted from celebrating divine initiative to denigrating aspects of humanity, notably female sexuality.

The Matthean fulfillment does not suggest that female passion was problematic or enduring virginity was necessary—quite the contrary on the plainest reading of Matthew 12:46–50. Nor is there any biblical suggestion that virginal conception provided a necessary mechanism for the Messiah to escape Adamic sin. The second Adam's sinlessness stems from the Holy Spirit overshadowing the eternal Son's assumption of a human nature. Otherwise, this Messiah identified fully with the human plight, as epitomized in Israel's exile, from which he rescued us by fulfilling all righteousness. The virginal conception signaled that the judgment involved in Isaiah 7:14 was ending and the promised light of God's saving presence was dawning anew. Virginal conception was fitting to convey YHWH's return: not absolutely necessary as a soteriological mechanism, only becoming contingently necessary to fulfill God's promise.

II. INCARNATION ANTICIPATED IN ISRAEL'S SCRIPTURES

Wrestling with Isaiah 7 has led to the suggestion that "the case for the expectation of a divine Messiah is strong in the Old Testament and was part of Jesus' understanding (*cf.* Mt. 22:41ff.). The title *Immanuel* is peculiar to Isaiah but the thought is part of the Davidic-Messianic fabric."[37] Whereas the previous chapter unfolded covenantal preparation that focused on the Messiah's humanity, the revelation of his deity may

35. Theodoret of Cyr, *Letter* 152, in NPNF 2 3:332**, in McKinion, ed., *Isaiah 1–39*, 10:73.
36. E.g., "And which would be more appropriate as the mother of Emmanuel, that is, *God with us*, a woman who had intercourse with a man and conceived by female passion, or a woman who was still chaste and pure and a virgin?" So Origen of Alexandria, *Against Celsus* 1.34–35, SC 132:168–172; trans. Henry Chadwick (Cambridge: Cambridge University Press, 1953), 33–35, slightly revised, in Wilken, ed., *Isaiah*, 100.
37. Motyer, *Prophecy of Isaiah*, 85.

be anticipated not only by texts like Psalm 45 but also by theophanies and intradivine dialogue in places like Psalm 110.[38]

A. Theophanies

Israel's Scriptures anticipate the incarnation indirectly. They prepare for Yhwh's fuller self-revelation to include salvation-historical drama in its reception. Intertestamental hopes varied, but a Davidic Messiah was fundamental in a way that shaped Christian typological herme-neutics. In God's providential preparation for Christ as prophet (greater than Moses), priest (greater than Levi), king (greater than David and Solomon), and sacrifice (greater than offerings at the sanctuary), such types do not directly require an incarnation but launch a trajectory toward something greater.[39] Thus, the expectation that Yhwh would return to redeem the covenant people was not yet clearly synthesized with hopes for a Davidic Messiah[40]—even if their Isaianic convergence becomes visible after the fact, fulfilling the promise of passages like Isaiah 35:3–4; 40:3–5; and 52:7.

Alternatively, the Old Testament anticipates the incarnation through Yhwh's general concomitance as well as more specific theophanies.[41] The God of Israel's anthropomorphic, anthropopathic, and anthropopraxic ways reflect this motif of being present and communicating with human beings.[42] God uses creaturely concepts, emotions, and actions in the service of self-revelation and covenant fellowship. Somehow, therefore, theophanies anticipate the incarnation; an encounter like Jacob's with the angel (Gen 32) can be treated as a direct encounter with God (Hos 12:3–5).[43] However, anthropomorphic theophanies involved a privileged few rather than the whole people, and theophanies for Israel apparently ended at Sinai, per their fearful request (Exod 20:18–19).[44] Occasions like Daniel 3, in the fiery furnace with Shadrach, Meshach, and Abednego,

---

38. On Psalms 45 and 110 see Ortlund, "Deity of Christ and the OT," 44–50. On Psalm 110 see also Swain, *Trinity and the Bible*, 59–81.

39. Graham A. Cole, *The God Who Became Human: A Biblical Theology of Incarnation*, NSBT (Downers Grove, IL: IVP Academic, 2013), 93–94.

40. Cole, *God Who Became Human*, 95.

41. For a Jewish scholar's general argument about openness to incarnation in Israel's Scriptures, see Michael Wyschogrod, "A Jewish Perspective on Incarnation," *ModTheo* 12, no. 2 (April 1996): 195–209. Such openness, though, poses important challenges regarding the church's dismissal of the Jewish people.

42. Cole, *God Who Became Human*, 23.

43. Cole, *God Who Became Human*, 56–57. Cole summarizes complex discussions about the angel of the Lord that do not lend themselves to confident conclusions.

44. Cole, *God Who Became Human*, 62.

may sometimes incorporate Christomorphic anticipation, yet they remain appearances, not preliminary incarnations.[45] Theophanies temporarily use creaturely forms to manifest divine glory. In the light of Jesus Christ, it is clearer how they point toward the incarnation, but they did not provide or promise what Isaiah 7:14 signaled. The incarnate Christ revealed divine glory in extended earthly action that came to its loving apex with a Roman cross and an empty tomb—unlike the Old Testament's mountaintop experiences.

B. Intradivine Dialogue

The incarnation's Old Testament anticipation, though, has recently been illuminated by rediscovering prosopological exegesis. This "person-centered reading of the Old Testament in the early church . . . contributed decisively to the development of the concept of the Trinity, since it was this way of reading that especially led to the consolidation of 'person' language to express the three-in-one mystery."[46] Standing behind the practice was the ancient strategy of *prosopopoeia*, or "character-making," in which rhetoricians "would employ in-character speeches as a persuasive technique," with dramas incorporating "dialogical shifts between speaking characters." Since authors did not always mark the use of this strategy explicitly, "ancient readers had to read with care in order to identify dialogical shifts—that is, they had to engage in prosopological exegesis," of which there is evidence beginning in the second century BC.[47] Applied to the Old Testament, this reading strategy effected a "foundational conceptual decision to privilege the 'person' metaphor in considering internal distinctions within the one God," suggesting "that the one God could successfully be read in the ancient Jewish Scripture as multiple 'persons.'" Accordingly, the earliest church depicted "the

---

45. So Calvin, quoted in Sidney Greidanus, *Preaching Christ from the Old Testament: A Contemporary Hermeneutical Method* (Grand Rapids: Eerdmans, 1999), 142. For an appeal to Angel of the Lord theophanies while mentioning Isaiah 9:6–7, see T. F. Torrance, *The Christian Doctrine of God: One Being, Three Persons* (Edinburgh: T&T Clark, 1996), 69–70. But for Augustinian caution about confusing Christophanies with the incarnate Son's visible mission, see Fred Sanders, *The Triune God*, NSD (Grand Rapids: Zondervan, 2016), 225–26. On p. 214 Sanders follows B. B. Warfield in saying that the Old Testament preparation for the incarnation is "richly furnished but dimly lit."

46. Matthew W. Bates, *The Birth of the Trinity: Jesus, God, and Spirit in New Testament and Early Christian Interpretations of the Old Testament* (Oxford: Oxford University Press, 2015), 7. Speaking of "prosoponic" exegesis while referencing prior patristics scholarship is Sanders, *Triune God*, 226–35.

47. Bates, *Birth of the Trinity*, 31. A fuller treatment of the historical background appears in chap. 4 of Matthew W. Bates, *The Hermeneutics of the Apostolic Proclamation: The Center of Paul's Method of Scriptural Interpretation* (Waco, TX: Baylor University Press, 2012).

interior divine life" not with "a static portrait" but rather in terms of "an unfolding story of mutual esteem, voiced praise, collaborative strategizing, and self-sacrificial love."[48]

For an example of such exegesis, consider the cry of dereliction in Psalm 22. The earliest Christians did not interpret "My God, my God, why have you forsaken me?" in modern terms, involving "a genuine separation of Jesus and the Father." Instead, "Jesus had inhabited a foreordained theodramatic script authored by the Spirit," a revelatory anthropomorphism—God forsaking the man on the cross: "Indeed, as the Son gave voice to the scripted words, those words captured his true emotions perfectly, as the fully human Son was in the process of being abandoned unto death and perhaps even felt himself really (ontologically) forsaken by the Father, even though the Son had confidence that the reality was otherwise, that the Father would . . . ultimately rescue and vindicate him on the other side of his suffering."[49]

Another crucial text that the New Testament reads prosopologically is Psalm 110. Hebrews reads verse 4 in terms of the Father anointing the Son as a Melchizedekian priest.[50] Jesus himself read verse 1 in terms of the Father anointing the Son as the Messiah. In Matthew 22:41–46, Jesus responded to the Pharisees' testing with a puzzler of his own: Whose son is the Messiah? The prosopological answer comes when David, speaking by the Holy Spirit, calls him "Lord" in Psalm 110:1. The Messiah must be more than a descendant of David, since he is greater than his human ancestor. The Messiah's sonship is not just Davidic but divine.

Such exegesis—with its retrospective component—presupposes the divine authorship and narrative unity of Israel's Scriptures. Of course, it would be inappropriate to assign a personal divine role within a biblical dialogue based on a textual corruption or a serious mistranslation. Nevertheless, critical controls can articulate the validity and regulate the application of this approach.[51] Its early prominence challenges historical hypotheses that question Christ's preexistence, relegating his divine sonship to a later, post-resurrection retrojection.[52] Instead, the Old Testament anticipated the incarnation of God's Son in a fitting

---

48. Bates, *Birth of the Trinity*, 40.
49. Bates, *Birth of the Trinity*, 134.
50. On prosopological exegesis in Hebrews, see Madison N. Pierce, *Divine Discourse in the Epistle to the Hebrews: The Recontextualization of Spoken Quotations of Scripture*, SNTSMS (Cambridge: Cambridge University Press, 2020).
51. Bates, *Birth of the Trinity*, 190–201.
52. Bates, *Birth of the Trinity*, 204.

manner—neither prematurely narrating nor predicting his advent so specifically as to remove the drama of human response. In the mystery of God's plan, it was necessary for the Messiah to suffer—and thus to be culpably rejected. The shape of redemptive history itself entailed the indirect revelatory anticipation of the incarnation. Consequently, Israel's Scriptures anticipated the incarnation with theophanies, with the intradivine dialogue that prosopological exegesis can hear as such, and with the promise signaled by Isaiah 7:14 given its surrounding context.

III. THE VIRGINAL CONCEPTION

Although Scripture only makes it explicit in Matthew and Luke, Jesus's virginal conception is an integral element of creedal orthodoxy. However, aside from debates about the fulfillment of Isaiah 7:14, the virginal conception faces three primary objections in the modern era. First, some object that the "virgin birth" (to use popular nomenclature) reflects an isolated or competing tradition rather than early Christian orthodoxy. Second, some object that the virgin birth precludes the incarnate Son's full humanity. Third, some object that the virgin birth represses embodiment, especially female sexuality. Hence the virgin birth is a frequent barometer of modern christological winds. Addressing these pressures can enhance our appreciation of its theological significance and even its neglected significance for the historical Jesus.

A. Modern Objections

First, the *integrity of the biblical witness*. Many believe that the New Testament contains contradictory depictions of Jesus's origins, with the virginal conception in Luke and probably Matthew serving as a "minority report."[53] Supposedly, these depictions bear marks of literary creativity, perhaps heightened from dramatic Old Testament birth narratives, to an extent that mitigates straightforward historical claims.[54] Minimally, earlier New Testament witnesses like Mark and Paul are silent on the matter, diminishing its significance for early Christian orthodoxy. More maximally, divine preexistence and virginal conception are treated as

---

53. See Andrew T. Lincoln, *Born of a Virgin? Reconceiving Jesus in the Bible, Tradition, and Theology* (Grand Rapids: Eerdmans, 2013), especially 39. For a response that informs the surrounding paragraphs, see Daniel J. Treier, "Virgin Territory?," *ProEccl* 23, no. 4 (Fall 2014): 373–79.

54. As noted responsibly, e.g., in Frederick Dale Bruner, *The Christbook: Matthew 1–12*, rev. ed, vol. 1 of *Matthew: A Commentary* (Grand Rapids: Eerdmans, 2004), 35–36.

contradictory,[55] and some witnesses outside Matthew and Luke are taken to treat Joseph as Jesus's biological father.[56] Purportedly, Jesus's Davidic lineage would have required legal adoption by Joseph if there were a virgin birth.[57]

In response, to begin with, such claims about biblical diversity rest on a tradition-historical approach that is inconsistent with the classically Christian understanding of Scripture. Beyond resisting premature theological harmonization, the developmental assumptions of this approach problematically isolate particular biblical accounts, whereas "the early church's careful attempts to protect Matthew's and Luke's teaching in both the church's canonical and creedal formulations also deserve our respect."[58] Responding more inductively, (1) the silence of other early New Testament proclamation may involve tact, with a crucified Messiah being scandalous enough already (and most fundamental); (2) Joseph is not mentioned by Mark or Paul, who may obliquely hint at a virgin birth ("son of Mary," Mark 6:3; "born of a woman," Gal 4:4); (3) the silence in the occasional, generally short, catholic epistles is unsurprising; (4) John 1:13 may be "casting a side glance" at Jesus's virgin birth while speaking of believers' new birth; and (5) "the great *differences* . . . between Matthew's and Luke's Christmas stories make *their narrow agreement on Jesus' virginal conception* the more striking."[59] In fact, "are not *two* independent literary sources for a doctrine usually impressive to historical research?"[60] The "Seed of the Woman" in Genesis 3:15, even if only suggestively, makes the virginal conception seem fitting.[61]

Second, the *integrity of Jesus's humanity*. Whereas ancient anthropologies had Mary providing the fullness of Christ's humanity—the virginal

---

55. As discussed in Bruner, *Matthew*, 1:36.
56. As advocated thoroughly in Lincoln, *Born of a Virgin?*
57. So, e.g., Kyle Roberts, *A Complicated Pregnancy: Whether Mary Was a Virgin and Why It Matters*, Theology for the People (Minneapolis: Fortress, 2017), 69.
58. Bruner, *Matthew*, 1:35.
59. Italics original from Bruner, *Matthew*, 1:38–39. The relative paucity of New Testament references could reflect caution about evoking pagan parallels. For their important differences, though, see Hans Schwarz, *Christology* (Grand Rapids: Eerdmans, 1998), 239. Isaiah 7:14 lacks prior messianic interpretation that might have generated the idea. So C. E. B. Cranfield, "Some Reflections on the Subject of the Virgin Birth," *SJT* 41 (1988): 181, 186–87. Given the convenience of Joseph's Davidic descent, early Christians lacked incentive to invent a supernatural alternative, as noted by Markus Bockmuehl, *This Jesus: Martyr, Lord, Messiah* (Downers Grove, IL: InterVarsity Press, 1994), 31. Later emergence of the virgin birth may also reflect the evangelists' or Mary's discretion while she remained alive; so Pope Benedict XVI, *Jesus of Nazareth: The Infancy Narratives*, trans. Philip J. Whitmore (New York: Image, 2012), 16, 53.
60. Bruner, *Matthew*, 1:41.
61. Referring to Matthew Henry for this point is Bruner, *Matthew*, 1:41.

conception *resisting* docetic tendencies—modern genetics requires a male Y chromosome for Jesus to be fully human. Supposedly, orthodoxy should jettison the virginal conception to avoid making Christ "less than" human or a different kind of being. Some even suggest that the orthodox doctrine "conflicts with the logic of the incarnation, the very basis of the gospel itself"—associating at least many adherents with "a gnostic view of Jesus"![62]

In response, however, precisely because of differences between ancient anthropologies and modern genetics, no one should assume that a divinely provided Y chromosome precludes the Son *becoming* flesh by *assuming* a fully human nature. Otherwise we risk implying that persons with chromosomal abnormalities are not fully human.[63] After all, Adam was fully human without exactly the same origins as his progeny; even nonliteral interpretations of Genesis can posit a distinctive beginning for the human image of God. Traditionally, the anhypostatic character of the Son's humanity—that it is not independently personal but becomes so only in the Logos who assumed it—resists tying its fullness to its origination.[64] The Son's personal assumption of humanity gave life to *this* individual. To sustain the objection here while remaining orthodox, critics of the virgin birth would need to show how, with a complete human being from the very genetic beginning, they could avoid a sophisticated form of adoptionism. At minimum, there is good reason not to accept this incomplete humanity objection *prima facie*.

Third, *implications for embodiment and gender.* Feminist theologians raise concerns on principle—for instance, about valorizing Mary as hardworking yet passive. They also raise concerns about practice—for instance, about proclaiming equal personhood yet stereotypically associating women with certain tasks or sexual temptation. It is easier to affirm in principle that God is not gendered than to achieve consistency with that affirmation in practice.[65] Not coincidentally, theology tends to be

---

62. The latter suggestion comes from Roberts, *Complicated Pregnancy*, 183–85. The distinction in the previous sentence appears, e.g., on p. 73.

63. As noted by Marc Cortez.

64. This point holds despite complexities regarding "anhypostatic" and "enhypostatic" terminology, highlighted in chap. 3 of Oliver D. Crisp, *Divinity and Humanity: The Incarnation Reconsidered*, CIT (Cambridge: Cambridge University Press, 2007).

65. See, e.g., Ann Loades, "On Mary: Constructive Ambivalence?," *The Way* 34, no. 2 (April 1994): 138–46.

dominated by divine fatherhood while neglecting human motherhood.[66] As a further corollary, "Mary's motherhood returns to its hiding place, while conventional theological traditions of Marian devotion and Mary as the exemplary believer come to the fore."[67] In this hiding place, Mary's virgin motherhood tends to be construed one-sidedly, either positively or negatively obscuring its vulnerability. Orthodox dogmas or debates about oppression take over.[68] A broader feminist concern is that the virginal conception reflects distaste for embodiment and suppresses the messiness of birth.[69]

In response, evangelical Christology should certainly remove cultural stumbling blocks where possible. More than a symbol with which theologians may creatively work, however, the virgin birth comprises historical testimony with which believers must responsibly wrestle.[70] At stake is a God-given sign of the incarnation, a promise fulfilled for us and our salvation—even if the church's understanding has sometimes been inadequate. Given evangelical Christology's commitment to both the Bible's historical veracity and its final authority, it should be possible to embrace the virgin birth while reforming interpretations of its significance.

B. Christological Significance

Consistent with ecumenical orthodoxy, the virginal conception commits evangelical Christology to honoring Mary as *Theotokos*, God-bearer—recognizing that God included a woman vitally in the incarnation. Even in having the unique opportunity to publish her baby's God-given name, Mary occupied "the place of a herald, . . . [with] no earthly father to perform that office."[71] Mary is also a reminder that the focus of calling God *Father* is not masculine gender but familial love. In her magnificent song as well as treasured Gospel memories, she speaks prophetically, comforting the afflicted and

---

66. Cristina Grenholm, "Mary Among Stereotypes and Dogmas: A Feminist Critique and Reinterpretation of the Patriarchal Cornerstone of Motherhood," *Journal of the European Society of Women in Theological Research* 15 (2007): 22.

67. Grenholm, "Mary Among Stereotypes," 26.

68. Grenholm, "Mary Among Stereotypes," 29–33.

69. For another theological survey, see chap. 4 of Roberts, *Complicated Pregnancy*.

70. Some stories that critics substitute for the virgin birth are historically bizarre, the domino effects on other doctrines are often significant, and alternative "certainties" can be as breathtaking as those of fundamentalists; so Bruner, *Matthew*, 1:42–43.

71. Calvin, *Isaiah*, 248.

afflicting comfortable oppressors.[72] Such an evangelical Christology can honor both Mary and marriage: upholding the plain sense of Matthew's Gospel regarding Mary's conjugal life with Joseph respects the divine choice of a betrothed and then married, rather than perpetually virginal, *Theotokos*.[73] A healthy evangelical Christology honors Mary as the Bible does, avoiding pagan syncretism and championing Christ Jesus as our one Mediator.[74]

The virginal conception also has implications for the historical Jesus's self-understanding that have been pervasively neglected in modern scholarship. Whether heard directly from Joseph and Mary or John the Baptizer, or discerned indirectly from scandalous rumors, the incarnate Son's knowledge of his extraordinary birth would explain the nearly pervasive Isaianic background for New Testament Christology. This background makes better sense as the early heart of Jesus's self-understanding than as a late ecclesial invention. Mystery notwithstanding, the virginal conception signaled that the God-man should recognize himself as the promised Servant of Yʜᴡʜ, accept rejection and atoning death, and expect resurrection by which he would renew Israel and reach the gentiles. Once he understood his strange beginning vis-à-vis Isaiah 7:14, Isaiah 40–66 could naturally follow. How the incarnate Son experienced his self-identity in his divine nature is obviously beyond our ken. Yet the Isaianic sign of Immanuel makes sense of how he could have recognized his divine identity *even in his human nature, as a student of Scripture.*

Having addressed Christology's intersection with creation (chapter 2) and the covenant of grace (chapter 3), we now address its dogmatic intersection with the fall. Immanuel assumed the fullness of our human condition, such as it is, yet without sin (Heb 4:15)—being

72. These points are summarized in Amy Peeler, "Protestants Need to Talk More About Mary," *Didaktikos: Journal of Theological Education* 3, no. 3 (November 2019): 12–13.

73. Related to "Quiet Joseph" and "Mother Mary," see this point highlighted in Bruner, *Matthew*, 1:50.

74. For staunch opposition to pagan goddess veneration and identification of Mary as intercessor, see Aída Besançon Spencer, "From Artemis to Mary: Misplaced Veneration versus True Worship of Jesus in the Latino/a Context," in *Jesus without Borders: Christology in the Majority World*, ed. Gene L. Green, Stephen T. Pardue, and K. K. Yeo, MWT (Grand Rapids: Eerdmans, 2014), 123–40. Chalcedonian opposition to Nestorianism makes *Theotokos* an "essential constituent of a properly non-dualist Christology," as asserted by Aaron Riches, *Ecce Homo: On the Divine Unity of Christ*, Interventions (Grand Rapids: Eerdmans, 2016), 17. But Riches's ensuing language of "Mary's co-redemptive role" (p. 246) is misleading and needless. Global Christologies also highlight the virginal conception's significance vis-à-vis Islam, as noted in V.-M. Kärkkäinen, J. Levison, and P. Pope-Levison, "Christology," in *GDT*, 175.

"born of a woman, born under the law" (Gal 4:4), even with the messiness that tempted the church to render Mary's condition immaculate. The virginal conception did not denigrate embodiment but signaled that the Holy Spirit would overshadow Jesus's human life to be "God with us."[75]

IV. FULL HUMANITY

In affirming his full humanity, debates over the incarnate Son's impeccability now focus upon whether he assumed a fallen human nature.[76] Eschewing Mary's immaculate conception while embracing the virginal conception, evangelical Christology increasingly stresses Jesus's full humanity; in well-known patristic words, "what is not assumed is not healed." The fallenness debate has emerged in the context of modern assumptions about what such full humanity means.[77]

Since Barth was an influential champion of the fallen nature view, this debate revisits the dilemma over metaphysical and actualistic ontologies. Twentieth-century debates between Thomistic scholasticism and Hegelian tendencies energized by Barth suggest that Christology might be "the key to the logic of createdness and finitude in theology."[78] Indeed, "the conclusion of the Council of Chalcedon in 451, that we must see in the life of Jesus a complete and unqualified divine agency and a complete and unqualified human reality, physical and mental, is not an unnecessarily complicated elaboration of simple biblical teaching; it is no more than a statement of the duality and tension that pervade every page of the New Testament and that lie behind the practice of Christian prayer."[79] This biblical and Chalcedonian duality

---

75. On the "Christocentricity of the Spirit," see Bruner, *Matthew*, 1:26–28.

76. A helpful survey is Kelly Kapic, "The Son's Assumption of a Human Nature: A Call for Clarity," *IJST* 3 (2001): 154–66. Also surveying the issues, while defending the Son's impeccability, is chap. 6 of Oliver D. Crisp, *God Incarnate: Explorations in Christology* (New York: T&T Clark, 2009).

77. Tracing the modern contrast via Barth versus Thomas Aquinas, as well as championing Christ's sinlessness in terms of representative humanity, is Katherine Sonderegger, "The Sinlessness of Christ," in *Theological Theology: Essays in Honour of John Webster*, ed. R. David Nelson, Darren Sarisky, and Justin Stratis (London: Bloomsbury T&T Clark, 2015), 267–75. For a Catholic argument that Mary's immaculate conception did not preclude her enduring, like Jesus, the "exterior effects of original sin," see Thomas G. Weinandy, *In the Likeness of Sinful Flesh: An Essay on the Humanity of Christ* (Edinburgh: T&T Clark, 1993), 153–56. In that account, though, the redemptive purpose of the (supposed) gift of being immaculate is unclear.

78. Williams, *Christ the Heart of Creation*, 124.

79. Rowan Williams, "Christology," in *The Vocation of Anglican Theology*, ed. Ralph McMichael (London: SCM, 2014), 90.

entails both that the divine Christ was a sinless human being and that he was sent "in the likeness of sinful flesh" (Rom 8:3) in order to be "tempted in every way, just as we are" (Heb 4:15) and to "be sin for us" (2 Cor 5:21).

Unfortunately, the fallen nature debate often confuses the metaphysical and actualistic approaches rather than using them dialectically. Human *nature* invokes a metaphysical category, best reserved for dealing with a *kind essence*: human being as a created kind distinct from other animals, inanimate objects, plants, angels, and so on. In that sense, human nature characterized Adam and Eve both before and after the fall. Whatever their ontological import, the fall and the resulting curse did not metaphysically destroy humanity as a distinct kind of being. Speaking of fallen humanity invokes a historical category best reserved for dealing with existential conditions. When identifying Jesus as *homoousios* with us, Chalcedon does not speak explicitly of pre- or postlapsarian humanity. That conciliar modesty makes it possible to affirm an unfallen human nature (as a kind essence) without denying Christ's full identification with our fallen condition (as an existential situation).[80]

This distinction sheds light on a broader consensus as well as frequent sources of confusion. On one hand, with only occasional exceptions, fallen nature advocates and detractors both agree that Christ was sinless.[81] On the other hand, traditionalist advocates of an unfallen human nature often agree that Christ did not straightforwardly assume prelapsarian flesh. Instead, they "see the Virgin Birth as signalling divine initiative to preserve Christ from fallenness, understood as sinfulness. . . . [F]lesh fallen in his mother was *restored* in her Son to an unfallen, that is, sinless, state."[82] Hence the crucial disagreements concern how to speak of our fallen condition with respect to created humanity and Christ's sinlessness on one side yet guilt-bearing corruption and Christ's genuine temptation on the other.[83] Among further complications is the patristic

---

80. In the words of the Westminster Confession of Faith 8.2, he assumed "all the essential properties" and "common infirmities" of humanity, "yet without sin."

81. As emphasized (p. 3 et passim) in E. Jerome Van Kuiken, *Christ's Humanity in Current and Ancient Controversy: Fallen or Not?* (London: T&T Clark International, 2017).

82. Emphasis original in Van Kuiken, *Christ's Humanity*, 89.

83. For a summary of Barth's complex fallen nature position, which epitomizes the issues at stake (including denial that Jesus committed personal sin alongside unguarded statements about Jesus needing repentance and Heb 5:2–3 applying to him), see Robert B. Price, "Barth on the Incarnation," in *The Wiley Blackwell Companion to Karl Barth: Barth and Dogmatics*, ed. George Hunsinger and Keith L. Johnson (London: Wiley-Blackwell, 2020), 139. Donald Macleod

tendency to speak of humanity as a collective entity in a sense—distinct from a kind essence—that many modern theologians eschew. Given the complexities involved, ironically both sides appeal to some of the same patristic sources.[84] A patristic consensus held "that Adam's fall into sin put humankind under the dominion of Satan, death and disordered desires which incline towards sin," frequently speaking of "corruption" regarding this postlapsarian state of humanity, including Christ's. This language "has led some modern readers to conclude that the fathers saw Christ's humanity as *morally* corrupt. In fact, though, the early church typically used this term to describe *physical* corruption, the 'decay' to which material bodies are prone."[85]

Three delimitations help to articulate Christ's unfallen identification with the fallen human condition. First, *the Spirit's sanctification accompanies the Son's assumption of human flesh.* The fallen nature position emphasizes that these are logically distinct, whereas a traditional position emphasizes that they form one contemporaneous divine act.[86] Given immediate sanctification, the Son assumed humanity "from" (*a quo*; via Mary), but not "of" or "to" (*ad quem*), a fallen nature.[87] When the term *fallen* focuses corporately on the Son embracing humanity's postlapsarian conditions of physical weakness, cultural contingency, and judicial death, this adjective could be cause for rejoicing. Focused individually, though, speaking of Jesus's *fallen* humanity risks negating created nature or implicating him in wayward desire. Then the adjective becomes unhelpfully confusing at best. Second, *Jesus's sinlessness*

problematizes fallen nature arguments from Barth and others that appeal to Christ's human solidarity, since they could likewise entail that Jesus must sin—as noted in Van Kuiken, *Christ's Humanity*, 88.

84. Van Kuiken, *Christ's Humanity*, 90. For another illustration of the complexity, Van Kuiken (pp. 72, 75) notes the influence of Hugh Ross Mackintosh yet shows that T. F. Torrance, his Scottish successor, is mistaken in claiming Mackintosh for the fallen nature position. Torrance claimed that losing the patristic emphasis on Christ's identification with fallen "humanity" correlated with the emergence of Mary's immaculate conception and a forensic, extrinsic soteriology; see, e.g., T. F. Torrance, *The Mediation of Christ* (Grand Rapids: Eerdmans, 1984), 49–50. Yet, however astute its diagnosis of pastoral ills, this grand theological narrative is historically problematic.

85. Van Kuiken, *Christ's Humanity*, 91–92.

86. Michael Allen, *The Christ's Faith: A Dogmatic Account*, SST (London: T&T Clark, 2011), 130.

87. Michael Allen, "Christ," in *The T&T Clark Companion to the Doctrine of Sin*, ed. Keith Johnson and David Lauber, Bloomsbury Companions (London: T&T Clark, 2018), 464. A problem for the fallen nature view is its association with Edward Irving, who denied Christ's sinlessness. Adherents of the unfallen nature view rightly maintain the classic Protestant conviction that any alienation of the will from God is sinful. Therefore, the unfallen nature view is fundamentally correct that the Spirit's sanctifying work began immediately at Jesus's conception, deepening his perfection rather than allowing for potential disobedience.

focuses upon the complete love of God and self-giving love of neighbor.[88] For instance, he touched the unclean leper and the hemorrhaging woman. By virtue of his deity, he could authoritatively interpret or apparently overrule the Torah so that such actions would not violate God's covenant. In his humanity, he discerned and fulfilled the Torah's true intent regarding justice, mercy, and faithfulness.[89] Apparent violations did not violate the underlying twofold law of love (Matt 22:36–40). Third, *accepting our guilt per se would be different than suffering its effects.*[90] To anticipate implications for Christ's passion, some legal-fiction accounts of atonement are problematic: Jesus identified with sinners to bear the deadly effects of our guilt, but God did not falsely charge him with committing our disobedient actions.

With these delimitations in place, *corruption* and *temptation* can take proper christological positions. The incarnate Son assumed humanity's postlapsarian physical corruption while the sanctifying Spirit immediately prevented any acquisition of attendant moral corruption. Accordingly, regarding temptation, the Messiah could face every type of circumstantial test without having any existential deviation from the divine will. Thus the incarnate Son was an impeccable person, by virtue of both his full deity and his fully Spirit-bearing humanity. The multivalence of *peirazō*—which can mean testing and temptation—is instructive in passages like Hebrews 4:15 and James 1:1–18. God does not tempt people in a way that is responsible for their inclination toward sin; God tests people with circumstances that should prove their faith and improve their perseverance. As these circumstances present tests externally, human beings are responsible for internal temptations that result.

The relation between physical corruption and postlapsarian passions can clarify the incarnate Son's holy experience of human desire. By God's design we are dependent and desiring creatures, provided with

---

88. Williams, "Christology," 77–90.

89. I owe these reflections to initial conversation with Jon Laansma and later conversations with Ty Kieser and Greg Lee. If some recent scholars are correct that Jesus upheld the Torah's purity codes, then there might be less of an apparent challenge to his sinlessness here. See Matthew Thiessen, *Jesus and the Forces of Death: The Gospels' Portrayal of Ritual Impurity within First-Century Judaism* (Grand Rapids: Baker Academic, 2020). For another brief discussion of Jesus's potential complicity with social sin, see chapter 7.

90. E.g., Calvin's view was "that Christ suffered only the *effects* of God's wrath; the Father was never displeased with the Son"; so Van Kuiken, *Christ's Humanity*, 70n57.

goods it is proper to seek and use. However, the fall cursed us with a fear of scarcity in the face of mortal corruption. This fear transforms legitimate desires for satisfying physical needs and enjoying created goods into disordered passions. The incarnate Son faced the full range of such mortal circumstances, yet with faith rather than disordered fear. He experienced the dependence involved in the human life cycle, hunger, thirst, fatigue, misunderstanding family members, relative homelessness, ill-conceived popularity, fickle rejection, unreliable friends and followers, celibacy, grief, betrayal, subjection to unjust powers—and all that before the horrors of crucifixion. Thus, he faced to the uttermost a human drama of decisions to embrace the divine will, as Gethsemane testifies. This drama involved no deliberation between sinful and holy inclinations, only dealing with appropriately natural desires, such as the avoidance of death, in relation to his God-given vocation.

Hence the incarnate Son fully identified with our created nature and our fallen history, but as the second Adam he was not powerless in sharing our plight. His is the full humanity for which we were made and in which we will gloriously and eternally participate. The virginal conception bears eloquent witness to the divine act of the Word becoming flesh, with the origin of Jesus's humanity inevitably remaining distinct from ours. Via the Father's initiative and the Spirit's overshadowing, the virginal conception announced God's fresh visitation (Isa 40:3–11; 59:21; 61:1–3). With God nothing is impossible (Luke 1:37), not even a virginal conception that joined divine initiative and a faithful human response in God's full identification with our broken humanity. From conception to the completion of his mission, Jesus received the *communicatio gratiarum*: the communication of the Holy Spirit's gracious empowerment. Inability to sin did not make the incarnate Son less authentically human, for someday our humanity will become sinless like his (1 John 3:1–3). Meanwhile he suffered our panoply of temptations (Heb 4:14–16), and his obedience, though inevitable, was genuinely voluntary.[91]

---

91. Theological debates aside, on philosophically mistaken concepts of "libertarian" freedom see Harry G. Frankfurt, "Freedom of the Will and the Concept of a Person," *Journal of Philosophy* 68 (1971): 5–20. Moral responsibility pertains even when a person cannot do otherwise.

V. IMMANUEL

Just as with *image of God*, so too is *Immanuel* a title rather than a proper name. In the immediate context of Matthew 1:18–25, Immanuel's proper name is Jesus (vv. 18, 21). *Immanuel* speaks powerfully to the name Jesus's dual significance:

> Jesus will not be a god—or even God—*disguised* as a human being and walking around Palestine. . . . The grist or surface of every Gospel paragraph is entirely human; the gist or depth of every paragraph is excitingly divine. Jesus is a *human Jew*—this is what his name *says*: "Joshua"; Jesus is also the *divine Lord*—this is what his name *means*: "God Saves." Only when Jesus is seen through this dual optic does the gospel of Jesus finally make sense. And Matthew, perhaps intentionally, begins to grind the lens of this dual optic of true humanity and true divinity already in the initial chapter of his Gospel, a lens that will be polished still more in John's Gospel and brought to a sheen in the Creeds.[92]

In its salvation-historical context of multiple fulfillment, *Immanuel* indicates that Christ's first advent is YHWH's return, to dwell redemptively with the covenant people. It would not convey the same love if in sending Christ YHWH simply sent someone else.[93] This theme recurs variously in Matthew's Gospel, climactically in Jesus's promise to be "with" the disciples always as they undertake his Great Commission (28:18–20).[94]

The advent of God's incarnate Son embraces all creatures great and small, as Mary's integral participation attests:

> Here is a meeting made of hidden joys
> Of lightenings cloistered in a narrow place
> From quiet hearts the sudden flame of praise
> And in the womb the quickening kick of grace.
> Two women on the very edge of things
> Unnoticed and unknown to men of power
> But in their flesh the hidden Spirit sings

---

92. Bruner, *Matthew*, 1:30.
93. N. T. Wright, "The Biblical Formation of a Doctrine of Christ," in *Who Do You Say That I Am? Christology and the Church*, ed. Donald Armstrong (Grand Rapids: Eerdmans, 1999), 59.
94. Turner, *Matthew*, 73.

And in their lives the buds of blessing flower.
And Mary stands with all we call 'too young',
Elizabeth with all called 'past their prime'
They sing today for all the great unsung
Women who turned eternity to time
Favoured of heaven, outcast on the earth
Prophets who bring the best in us to birth.[95]

95. "The Visitation," used with the author's permission from Malcolm Guite, *Sounding the Seasons: Seventy Sonnets for the Christian Year* (London: Canterbury, 2012).

CHAPTER 5

REVELATION AS THE WORD

John 1:1–18

As epitomized in **John 1:1–18,** Jesus Christ is the **Word,** whose incarnation is God's ultimate self-**revelation**. *As the first six ecumenical councils recognized, the hypostatic union of full deity and full humanity in this Logos was essential for the triune God's redemptive love to illuminate us. Contra the seventh ecumenical council (787), though, the uniqueness of this incarnate Word requires continuing iconoclastic obedience to the second commandment. From revelatory alignment with Trinitarian missions there comes theological support for* filioque *regarding the Spirit's procession.*

It is no accident that our opening chapters study the beginnings of two New Testament books. First things first, Ephesians 1 and Colossians 1 laud the eternal Son's communion with the Father and agency in creation as the divine image. The fall, however, brought the next two chapters down to earth: Luke 24 and Isaiah 7 address the Messiah's advent as the fulfillment of God's Old Testament promises. Turning to John 1, this fifth chapter contemplates another New Testament beginning. With the incarnation actualized, not just anticipated, the previous themes converge: John 1 contemplates the eternal Son's communion with the Father and agency in creation as the Word. John 1 also celebrates what Israel's Scriptures anticipated, that is, God's redemptive dwelling among us. Thus, John 1 crystallizes the previous studies of the Son's eternal heights and connects them with the incarnation's earthly depth. From

Immanuel's advent—the beginning of YHWH's redemptive return to the covenant people—our focus now shifts to the incarnation as an ongoing state.

The present chapter treats the revelatory reality of the incarnation in four sections. After first expounding the Word's incarnate glory in John 1:1–18, secondly the chapter elaborates the Logos Christology that shaped the early ecumenical councils: (1) heresies that catalyzed its development, (2) the crucial orthodox concept of the hypostatic union, and (3) challenges concerning its legacy. Then a third section engages the iconoclastic controversy, where Christology intersects forcefully with the nature of revelation. Fourth, a concluding exposition of *Word* summarizes the concept of incarnation and the Trinitarian nature of our saving illumination by the Logos, supporting the Spirit's procession from the Father "and the Son," *filioque.*

I. INCARNATE GLORY IN JOHN 1:1–18

John 1:1–18 presents a three-part prologue to John's Gospel. In verses 1–5 the Word is introduced, both identified with and distinguished from God (*Theos*). In verses 6–13 the world is illuminated by the Word, who is not only the agent of creation but also the advent of redemption. In verses 14–18 the Word becomes incarnate, not only redeeming vulnerable human flesh but thereby revealing the glorious fullness of divine grace and truth.

A. The Word Introduced (John 1:1–5)

The first five verses of John's prologue introduce the Logos: "In the beginning was the Word," alluding to Genesis 1:1.[1] Whatever else may intersect with John's Logos, its bedrock context is the Old Testament theology of God's creative Word of Wisdom. Unlike Genesis, John's beginning is followed by agent depiction rather than narration, by existence rather than action vocabulary. Moses begins to narrate creation; John, "my illiterate, unschooled fisherman is freed from the centuries, freed from time," to reveal the eternal Creator.[2] *Logos* is challenging to translate, but *Word* is the dominant candidate for good reason. *Reason*

---

1. *Logos* is italicized when referring to the Greek term in John 1, but otherwise Anglicized.
2. Hilary of Poitiers, *On the Trinity* 2.13, 15–17, *CCSL* 62: 50–54, in Bryan A. Stewart and Michael A. Thomas, eds., *John: Interpreted by Early Christian and Medieval Commentators*, CB (Grand Rapids: Eerdmans, 2018), 20.

may represent the Hellenistic context, but John's Gospel presents the Logos in terms of internal personal relations and then external incarnate expression. *Speech* is a candidate from the Christian tradition, reflecting the multiplicity of words in rational discourse while grappling with Greek and Latin equivalents.[3] But that term could reify a generic phenomenon apart from specific occasions of discourse. *Word*, with its history of associations, conveys the singularity of the infinite, eternal, rational, personal divine discourse—and the components with which human language can participate therein. Astonishingly, this Logos is also the dynamic unifier of God's creative, commanding, communicative acts—from "Let there be . . ." and "God saw that it was good" to "Thou shalt . . ."

Logos and *Theos* are both distinguished and identified. Distinguished in that the Word was "with"—"toward" and so "at home with" or "close to"—God.[4] Identified in that the final clause applies existence vocabulary (*hēn*, "was") a third time, to identify the Word as God. The alternative, Arian interpretations from Jehovah's Witnesses and others are red herrings for several reasons. In the second clause, the definite article appears before *God* (*ton Theon*) within a prepositional phrase that uniquely relates the Son and the Father, despite their distinction. In the third clause, lack of the definite article before *God* is appropriate for acknowledging the Father and Spirit, despite the focus on identifying the Word as God. Although coming first in the emphatic Greek order, *God* is not the subject of the clause. Instead, the *Word* is the subject, with *God* as the predicate. *Theos* is more than an impersonal adjective such as *divine*, as John clarifies once verse 18 relates Father and Son explicitly.[5] This eternal intimacy is emphasized in verse 2 ("*He was with God in the beginning*"). The beginning (*archē*) itself can be a title for Christ, as in Colossians 1:18. Granted its temporal character, here the word evokes "the root of the universe" along with "the beginning of history":[6]

---

3. See, e.g., the response to Erasmus in John Calvin, *Commentary on the Holy Gospel of Jesus Christ according to John*, trans. William Pringle, vol. 17 of *Calvin's Commentaries* (repr., Grand Rapids: Baker, 1993), 28. For the contrary excerpt from Erasmus, see Craig S. Farmer, ed., *John 1–12*, RCSNT 4 (Downers Grove, IL: IVP Academic, 2014), 9–10.

4. J. Ramsey Michaels, *The Gospel of John*, NICNT (Grand Rapids: Eerdmans, 2010), 47n6. For an argument favoring "toward" rather than the traditional "with," see Christopher S. Atkins, "Rethinking John 1:1: The Word Was Godward," *NovT* 63 (2021): 44–62. The christological judgments of this chapter are the same in either case.

5. On John 1:1 identifying Jesus as more than "a god" or generically divine, see Andreas J. Köstenberger, "The Deity of Christ in John's Gospel," in *The Deity of Christ*, ed. Christopher W. Morgan and Robert A. Peterson, TC (Wheaton, IL: Crossway, 2011), 99–100.

6. Leon Morris, *The Gospel according to John*, NICNT (Grand Rapids: Eerdmans, 1989), 73.

> Though you came from the mouth of God,
> Born as his Word on earth below,
> Yet as his Wisdom you lived
> Forever in the Father's heart.[7]

Indeed, the Logos is the eternal agent of God's creative work. In verse 3, John begins to narrate divine action: "As soon as the Word has been introduced, 'was' gives way to 'came' or 'came to be' (*egeneto*), a verb conspicuous in the LXX of the Genesis account."[8] Genesis also reverberates in other terms, including *life* (v. 4), *light* (v. 4), and *darkness* (v. 5).[9] Since the Logos participates in the creation of "all things," and "nothing" was made without him, he cannot be merely a creature.[10] In verses 2–3, "so that no one might suppose the Godhead of the Son to be inferior," John "immediately added the characteristics of genuine Godhead . . . and attributed to him the office of Creator."[11]

In verse 4 the Word's work shifts from creation to providential preservation.[12] Verb tenses, although not primarily time-oriented, reflect the shift, from things that "were made" (aorist, focusing on creation as a completed act) earlier in verse 3 to "has been made" (perfect, acknowledging continued existence) at the end.[13] John connects and contrasts created things with life and light that originate in the uncreated Logos. Eventually John's Gospel defines life in terms of Jesus Christ and the salvation he brings (e.g., 11:25–26), but here the reference is probably general since the new birth does not appear until later.

Given the light's universal reach yet the world's ongoing darkness, verse 5 introduces the need for redemption. Its second phrase could refer to a lack of understanding, but that theme is articulated emphatically later (3:19–21). Taking the verb in terms of conflict instead ("has not overcome it") leads naturally into the succeeding verses, introducing the mixed reception of John the Baptizer and Jesus, while

---

7. Prudentius, Hymns for Every Day II, A Hymn for Christmas Day, in FC 43:78–80*, in Joel C. Elowsky, ed., *John 1–10*, ACCSNT 4a (Downers Grove, IL: IVP Academic, 2006), 19. The rest of the poem narrates creation, preservation, incarnation, and redemption.

8. Michaels, *John*, 51.

9. Morris, *John*, 73.

10. So Augustine of Hippo, *On the Trinity* 1.9, WSA I/5: 70–71, slightly revised, in Stewart and Thomas, eds., *John*, 30.

11. John Chrysostom, *Homilies on the Gospel of John* 4.1, 3 in NPNF 1 14.16–18**, in Elowsky, ed., *John 1–10*, 17.

12. Calvin, *John*, 31.

13. Morris, *John*, 80.

matching the term's other use in 12:35.[14] Light aptly signals divine splendor: "However many thousands of things a light illuminates, its own brightness is not diminished."[15] Church fathers commonly appeal to the analogy of the sun and its rays for the eternal Son's shining forth from the Father.[16]

B. *The World Illuminated (John 1:6–13)*

Verse 6 moves from broader illumination to the specific witness of John the Baptizer. Modern readers may not find John compelling, but multiple New Testament texts indicate that early Christians did. Like the Word, the Baptizer was sent from God; unlike the Word, he was merely a human witness.[17] Beginning in verse 19, John resists being identified as the Messiah, recognizing himself to be the forerunner of YHWH's return to Zion. John 3:22–36 reiterates this contrast with the memorable aphorism of verse 30: "He must become greater; I must become less."

Beyond conveying the Baptizer's witness, this section's christological significance is twofold. First, the Baptizer's ministry highlights the world's failure to recognize the Mediator of creation (v. 10). *World* is multivalent, sometimes denoting the cosmos yet other times designating the human population that the Creator loves or the culture(s) opposed to God and lost in darkness. This darkness is likely epitomized in Israel's failure to receive her Messiah (v. 11).[18] Consequently, the illumination of verses 4–5, 9 is general, tied to the creation and preservation of human beings as rational creatures, who participate in the Logos that they may radiate God's love. The incarnation has shined the Creator's

---

14. Raymond E. Brown, *The Gospel according to John*, 2nd ed., AB (New Haven, CT: Yale University Press, 1986), 8. If 8:3 and 8:4 are original, their uses of the term support this interpretation.

15. John Chrysostom, *Homily* 5.3–4 *on John*, PG 59:57–58, in Stewart and Thomas, eds., *John*, 31.

16. E.g., John Chrysostom, *Homily* 2.4; 3.2–4; 4.1–2 *on John*, PG 59, 34–35, 39–41, 47–48, and Cyril of Alexandria, *Commentary on John* 1.1, 2–3, in Pusey 1, 18–19, 24, 31–32, in Stewart and Thomas, eds., *John*, 23, 27.

17. John the Baptizer typifies Israel's vocation as Jesus's forerunner, as noted by L. S. Thornton, *Revelation and the Modern World*, vol. 1 of *The Form of a Servant* (London: Dacre, 1950), 243.

18. As for the incarnation appearing before 1:14, perhaps "this concise sketch of salvation history, which in four strophes moves to the decisive point, the incarnation, anticipates as a type the activity and fate of the incarnate Word within this movement. John loves such ambivalences"; so Martin Hengel, "The Prologue of the Gospel of John as the Gateway to Christological Truth," in *The Gospel of John and Christian Theology*, ed. Richard Bauckham and Carl Mosser (Grand Rapids: Eerdmans, 2008), 282.

light into history, despite the resistance of human culture. Second, this light has had saving effects (v. 12).[19] Believers have been adopted as God's children by grace, coming to know the One who is God's Son by nature (v. 13). Accordingly, the Baptizer's ministry can be paradigmatic for these beloved brothers and sisters: he has been sent by God to testify concerning the light of life in Christ, who is the ultimate eyewitness of divine glory.

C. The Word Incarnate (John 1:14–18)

With "the Word became flesh" (v. 14), the incarnation becomes explicit. The Baptizer's witness and the Light's arrival have advanced the implicit narrative from creation, fall, and preservation to the crucial moment. Now the Light *is* the Logos, not just "in" him, and scandalously this Word became flesh, that is, "came into the world *as* flesh, or *in* flesh."[20] *Flesh* connotes more than embodiment—scandalous as that would already be—because Scripture uses the term to speak "contemptuously" of humanity.[21] God remembers that we are but flesh (Ps 78:39), frail and temporary like grass (Isa 40:6–8). While our finitude is natural, our current mortality is not—paying the wages of sin so that assuming flesh identifies Immanuel with our fallen condition.[22] Even so, like "a king who kindly and genuinely converses with a poor beggar," the Word "in no way dishonors himself" but rather "makes the beggar famous and admired by all."[23]

Evoking the tabernacle with "made his dwelling among us" reinforced by the nearby reference to "glory," John introduces his sanctuary Christology.[24] Soon Jesus refers to his body as God's temple (2:19). Glory occupies the boundary between ontology and epistemology— the radiance of God's being in our sight. The tabernacle and temple

---

19. On language that could hint at the virginal conception, see Morris, *John*, 100.

20. Italics original in Michaels, *John*, 77.

21. Calvin, *John*, 45.

22. Solidarity in *sarx* supports the "theology of the universal gospel" highlighted in Carlos Raúl Sosa Siliezar, *Savior of the World: A Theology of the Universal Gospel* (Waco, TX: Baylor University Press, 2019), 11, 42. This universal thrust undergirds John's supposed sectarianism. Addressing "supersessionism" vis-à-vis Jesus's *Jewish* flesh is Angus Paddison, "Christology and Jewish–Christian Understanding: Reading the Fourth Gospel as Scripture," in *Christology and Scripture: Interdisciplinary Perspectives*, ed. Andrew T. Lincoln and Angus Paddison (New York: T&T Clark, 2008), 41–57.

23. John Chrysostom, *Homily 11.1–2 on John*, PG 59: 79, 80, in Stewart and Thomas, ed., *John*, 36.

24. See Paul M. Hoskins, *Jesus as the Fulfillment of the Temple in the Gospel of John*, Paternoster Biblical Monographs (Waynesboro, GA: Paternoster, 2006).

localized but did not limit God's presence. They were sites at which people encountered God via glorious manifestations and ritual practices. Likewise, Jesus's body localized encounters with but did not limit God the Son's earthly presence. With the cross standing at the ironic apex of this revelatory history (e.g., 12:20–36), new ritual practices became profoundly appropriate.

The Son's manifestation of divine glory focuses upon faithful love. Still in 1:14, *monogenēs*, "one and only," probably reflects both his deity and his humanity.[25] As noted in chapter 1, eternal generation is an appropriate dogmatic entailment whether or not "only begotten" is the best translation. "Grace and truth" allude to Exodus 34:6, which characterizes Yhwh as "compassionate and gracious . . . slow to anger, abounding in love and faithfulness." In Exodus 33, Moses impossibly asked to see God's glory; God hid Moses in the cleft of the rock for just a glimpse. While John's "grace and truth" only corresponds partially to the LXX rendering of "love and faithfulness," a connection remains likely. John's ensuing comparison between Jesus and Moses does not contrast bad and good, but lesser and greater, or preparatory and ultimate. The Torah gave proper instruction regarding Yhwh's gracious character, but its human mediator, Moses, could barely glimpse the divine glory. Now "we all"—the believing community, joined and represented by the Baptizer—have seen that glory: beyond a single, heavily restricted, encounter, the Messiah has embodied God's covenant love.

Verse 18 collates the prologue's Logos theology, preparing for the Son's revelatory mission to commence. The Mosaic contrast has been sketched: "No one has ever seen God." An ensuing text-critical question concerns whether John speaks of "the one and only Son" or "the one and only God." The latter has solid attestation, and the former may be the likelier result of a scribal change. Either way, the identification of this One with God is repeated from 1:1–2, and the transition has been made from Logos to Son. The divine Son is "in closest relationship with" the Father—the metaphor of being "at the Father's side" or "bosom" poetically glossing the intimacy of 1:2. Having become flesh, he will "make known" God. As John's Gospel proceeds, the

---

25. So Andreas J. Köstenberger and Scott R. Swain, *Father, Son and Spirit: The Trinity and John's Gospel*, NSBT (Downers Grove, IL: IVP Academic, 2008), 77.

Son's words and works reflect his union with the Father.[26] The verb *make known* can be used for "setting forth a narrative," as the two disciples did in Luke 24:35 regarding their Emmaus road encounter.[27] The ensuing narrative, setting forth the revelation of divine glory, focuses upon Jesus as Israel's Messiah and the heavenly Father's Son. The Gospel's christological climax involves faith in the risen Jesus as Lord and God (20:28), Messiah and Son of God (20:31). Yet, in the earlier narrative crux of John 5:19–26, Jesus already and insistently identifies himself as the divine Son.

As the incarnate Logos accomplishes his mission in John's Gospel, he fulfills Israel's Scriptures as the Lamb of God (1:29) and the Light of Life (8:12). John's theology of glory is, in Luther's famous terms, a theology of the cross. From beginning to end and along the way (e.g., 8:28), the Gospel's account of divine self-revelation evokes Isaiah's theme of abasement and exaltation.[28] Despite the disappearance of *Logos* after the prologue, John's Gospel is full of Jesus's divine speech.[29] Consistent with eternal preexistence, John celebrates the incarnate Son's omniscient foreknowledge (e.g., 2:23–25). "I AM" sayings buttress this identification as YHWH. Aside from fulfillment-oriented introductions like "I am the bread of life," several *egō eimi* sayings are "absolute": 4:26; 6:20; 8:24, 28, 58; 13:19; 18:5, 6, 8. Purported backgrounds for these sayings should not displace John's testimony regarding Jesus's self-attestation, but they highlight connections to Isaiah.[30] Like the Isaianic Servant, the incarnate Son both identified with and intervened in the people's plight; similarly, the incarnate Son was both identified with and sent from the God of Israel. The Logos and "I AM" sayings in John evoke the giving of the

---

26. Thus connaturality is a crucial emphasis in St. Athanasius, "Four Discourses Against the Arians," in *Athanasius: Select Works and Letters*, ed. Philip Schaff and Henry Wace, NPNF2 4 (repr., Peabody, MA: Hendrickson, 2004), 303–447.

27. Morris, *John*, 114.

28. See R. W. L. Moberly, "Isaiah and Jesus: How Might the Old Testament Inform Contemporary Christology," in *Seeking the Identity of Jesus: A Pilgrimage*, ed. Beverly Roberts Gaventa and Richard B. Hays (Grand Rapids: Eerdmans, 2008), 232–48.

29. See the first half of Robert H. Gundry, *Jesus the Word according to John the Sectarian: A Paleofundamentalist Manifesto for Contemporary Evangelicalism, Especially Its Elites, in North America* (Grand Rapids: Eerdmans, 2002).

30. As ancient biographies containing theologically remembered tradition, the Gospels may not provide the *ipsissima verba*—exact words—from specific incidents. But if they do not provide the *ipsissima vox*—Jesus's authentic voice—then the sheep are not hearing their risen Shepherd. Hence John's witness presents Jesus eliciting charges of blasphemy for identifying himself as YHWH incarnate. On John's Christology vis-à-vis Isaiah's monotheism see, among other sources, Richard Bauckham, "Monotheism and Christology in the Gospel of John," in *Contours of Christology in the New Testament*, ed. Richard N. Longenecker (Grand Rapids: Eerdmans, 2005), 148–66.

divine Name in Exodus 3:14 along with the combination of divine preexistence and eschatological ultimacy that characterize YHWH in passages like Isaiah 43:10 and 46:4. The Lamb in whose name we trust for salvation (John 1:12, et passim) has shined the Light of divine glory among us (as John 17 emphasizes).[31]

This Johannine soteriology of illumination undergirds conciliar Logos Christology. Classic exegetes collocate the Logos with the Son as the Father's image: "For words are images of things that are thought; they are rays, a kind of image of light, or as he is called, *apaugasma*."[32] *Apaugasma* appears in a related passage, Hebrews's exordium (1:1–4), along with the term *hypostasis* ("person"). Both Hebrews and John connect the eternal Son's illuminating and sustaining agency with his redemptive and revelatory mission: "No one has ever seen God" (John 1:18), yet "blessed are the pure in heart, for they will see God" (Matt 5:8).[33] As the Way and the Life, this Light is the Incarnate Truth— redemptive revelation that reacquaints us with God's love personally.[34] Involving a divine economy that moves from creation to consummation, "illumination is a participation in the Son's knowledge of the Father by the power of the Holy Spirit."[35] The patristic emphasis upon being God's children—for us by grace, for the Word by nature—owes a unique debt to John's Christology.[36]

II. CONCILIAR LOGOS CHRISTOLOGY

Together *advent* and *revelation* elicit "the doctrine of the Incarnation . . . an attempt at conceptual expansion of the church's

---

31. See Grant Macaskill, "Christology, Divine Aseity, and the I Am Sayings in the Fourth Gospel," *JTI* 12, no. 2 (2018): 217–41.

32. Caspar Cruciger, Commentary on John 1:1, in *In Evangelium Iohannis*, 5–8, in Elowsky, ed., *John 1–10*, 8–9. On the patristic association of *image* and *Word*, see treatment of the Son as *intellectus* by the early Augustine in Lewis Ayres, *Augustine and the Trinity* (Cambridge: Cambridge University Press, 2010). See also Luigi Gioia, OSB, *The Theological Epistemology of Augustine's De Trinitate*, OTM (Oxford: Oxford University Press, 2008), 267–69.

33. Augustine makes this connection in Tractates on the Gospel of John, in NPNF 1 7:23–24**, in Elowsky, ed., *John 1–10*, 54.

34. On "Incarnate Truth," see Katherine Sonderegger, "The Humility of the Son of God," in *Christology, Ancient and Modern: Explorations in Constructive Dogmatics*, ed. Oliver D. Crisp and Fred Sanders (Grand Rapids: Zondervan, 2013), 60–73.

35. Ike Miller, *Seeing by the Light: Illumination in Augustine's and Barth's Readings of John*, SCDS (Downers Grove, IL: IVP Academic, 2020), 5 (original italics removed).

36. "John thus provided many of the answers to, as well as the questions leading up to, these great debates and was used by *both sides* of many arguments!" So Paul N. Anderson, "On Guessing Points and Naming Stars: Epistemological Origins of John's Christological Tensions," in *The Gospel of John and Christian Theology*, 315.

confession that Jesus Christ is Lord."[37] John 1 is historically and theo-logically fundamental: "Every mainstream theologian whose work survives from this [patristic] period begins from the assumption that discourse about Jesus should take place within the framework of the Prologue to the Gospel of John, Jn 1.1–18."[38] Since those who do not learn from history may be doomed to repeat it, exposition of the councils' Logos Christology is a fitting extension of the preceding biblical exegesis—beginning with heresies that catalyzed conciliar Christology, proceeding to its crucial concept of the hypostatic union, and concluding with its contested legacy.

A. The Catalyst: Heresies

Orthodox Christology affirms that Jesus Christ is (1) fully divine, (2) fully human, and (3) one person; six major heresies elicited these ecumenical affirmations. The hypostatic union means that two natures, divine and human, are fully united in this one Mediator between God and humanity. God's Son was already, eternally, a divine person "before" assuming human nature in time.

The following narrative, while theologically stylized, acknowledges changing contours in patristics scholarship.[39] Although older, systematic, textbook narration anachronistically obscures historical development, what are now delimited as major heresies became providential occasions for identifying Scripture's christological teaching.[40] The ecumenical creeds do not exhaust the identity of Jesus Christ; they establish ortho-dox boundaries within which the church faithfully worships and fully proclaims the good news. These boundaries invite theological contem-plation and contextualization of the christological mystery. The early rejection of Ebionism and Docetism established two essential commit-ments: Christ's *deity* and genuine *humanity*. The rejection of Arianism

37. "Incarnation," from Webster, *Word and Church*, 115 (original italics removed).
38. Sara Parvis, "Christology in the Early Arian Controversy: The Exegetical War," in *Christology and Scripture: Interdisciplinary Perspectives*, 121.
39. See both panoramic comments on pp. 31–32 and the larger contribution of Lewis Ayres, *Nicaea and Its Legacy: An Approach to Fourth-Century Trinitarian Theology* (Oxford: Oxford University Press, 2004). Ayres's concerns about modern systematic theology (chap. 16) weigh heavily on this chapter's aspirations for historical nuance. Without some streamlining, however, it would be impossible to teach conciliar Christology or to appropriate that tradition for Protestant dogmatics. Some nuancing appears in Ayres, *Augustine and the Trinity*, 7–9.
40. Downstream from the councils' christological systematization, we can scarcely under-stand the issues as they initially faced them, suggests Bernard Lonergan, *The Way to Nicea: The Dialectical Development of Trinitarian Theology*, trans. Conn O'Donovan (Philadelphia: Westminster, 1976), 137.

at Nicaea (325) and eventually at Constantinople (381), along with the rejection of Apollinarianism, clarified those essential commitments: Jesus's *full* deity and humanity. Then the rejection of Nestorianism and Eutychianism at Chalcedon (451) secured the integrity of those two commitments by adding a third: the *hypostatic union* of these fully divine and fully human natures in the one person of God the Son, Jesus Christ our Lord.

1. Ebionism

Ebionism evoked the church's affirmation of Christ's preexistent deity. As with several of these eventual heresies, our direct sources are sketchy. Ebionites probably emerged from Jewish Christianity, perhaps the Judaizers whom Paul opposed. The Ebionite Jesus was a unique human being, born of two human parents. He was a messianic "prophet like Moses," but if he was labeled "son of God," it was only on account of his obedience—consistent with some ascetic tendencies. Ebionism has often been narrated as the first in a series of adoptionist Christologies, but that family label is misleading.[41] This early Jewish Christology arose in the late first or early second century and scarcely outlasted the third. Its mainstream presence withered with the church's Hellenization, and so it was not focally condemned by a council but opposed by later writers. We do not know whether the Ebionites had access to texts like John 1:1–18; their movement may be "the exception that proves the rule" regarding its fundamental significance.[42]

2. Docetism

Conversely, docetic views evoked the church's affirmation of Christ's genuine humanity. *Docetism* labels an early family of heresies holding that Jesus only appeared to be human. Platonic dualism influenced the surrounding context: matter seemed to be evil or deficient in being, so that deity could not be united to a body, which would involve change and suffering. Gnostic versions, wanting to break free of the world through a spark of illumination, related Jesus to a mythological redeemer

---

41. Jeremiah Coogan, "Rethinking Adoptionism: An Argument for Dismantling a Dubious Category," *SJT*, forthcoming. Coogan shows that the category is anachronistic, reading the early centuries in light of fourth-century conclusions, and confusing, relating views that somehow acknowledge Christ's divinity to those that never do.

42. On the role of St. Irenaeus (c. 130–c. 202, after Ebionism was established) in establishing the influence of John's Gospel, see Hengel, "Prologue of John," 266.

figure. If such a redeemer walked on earth, his body could only be phantom, whereas for orthodox Christianity redemption includes the body—freeing whole persons and the cosmos from the curse of sin rather than materiality.[43] For those like Cerinthus (in the latter part of the first century), the divine aspect, "Christ," came upon Jesus at baptism, using him to appear until the crucifixion, when it left—never having been genuinely united to the human. Others like Marcion (c. 85–c. 160) suggested that Christ only appeared to be human. For them, Jesus's body was ghostly.

Again historical knowledge is limited regarding John's earliest influence, but, as orthodoxy recognized, Johannine theology opposes Gnostic assumptions and docetic Christology. The Word becomes real, not just apparent, flesh. However strong Johannine dualism may be along the way, John's Gospel consistently incorporates physical things into its narrative of Jesus's redemptive mission. Then Jesus dies a bloody death on the cross before tangibly engaging his disciples and eating food after his resurrection. Tertullian (c. 155–c. 220), a key opponent of Gnosticism, opposed patripassianism, the idea that God directly (as Father) suffered on the cross. Since the deity could not die on the cross, distinct divine persons and the Son's real humanity had to be affirmed—for God to remain alive, so to speak, amid genuinely redemptive suffering. Related to patripassianism was monarchianism, which treated God in terms of one monarch (the Father). Heretical monarchianism treated the Son and the Spirit as mere appearances (so the modalism of Sabellius, condemned early in the third century) or at least denied them equality with the one God. Along with Tertullian, Irenaeus played a key role in emerging orthodoxy. Against Gnostic redeemer myths, he emphasized a rule of faith tied to salvation history, passed down from the apostles. This *regula fidei* committed the church to reading Old and New Testament Scriptures together, telling one story of one God of Israel. For Irenaeus, this story involved recapitulation: Jesus faithfully reliving and reversing humanity's fallen history. Rather than providing an escape from the drama of earthly life, the divine Redeemer completed the story by rewriting a second human act himself.

---

43. Aloys Grillmeier, SJ, *From the Apostolic Age to Chalcedon (451)*, trans. John Bowden, vol. 1 of *Christ in Christian Tradition* (Atlanta: John Knox, 1975), 83. Although the dating and nature of Gnosticism involve some debate, the christological weight of the rule of faith supports continuing to use that term, as do many scholars.

3. Arianism

Arianism, the archetypal heresy, evoked the church's affirmation of Christ's full deity.[44] Yet Arianism outgrew its namesake, whose exact views and influence are debated. Arianism denied the Son's self-existence and, accordingly, eternity: "There was a time when he was not," that is, he was "begotten timelessly" as the first creature, through whom God initiated the rest of creation and its history. Arianism treated the Son as a mediating, semi- or quasi-divine creature. Arianism was willing to call him the Son of God but did not associate full deity with that title. A (mis)reading of Colossians 1:15 can epitomize the Arian position, relegating the Son to being "the firstborn over all creation" in a chronological sense.

Orthodoxy took long years to emerge and gain a decisive victory. The first Council of Nicaea in 325 created a brief creed that rejected Arius's position. Debate centered around the term *homoousios*, saying that the Son is of the same being or essence as the Father. Arianism was willing to say that the Son is *homoiousios*, similar to the Father but still created and subordinate. Apparently, Arianism shared the wider Hellenistic commitment to protect God's transcendence, keeping the deity from getting hands dirty with the world.[45] By treating the Son as a mediating creature, Arianism could keep God indirectly related to creation. Although this position was rejected in 325, its defense of one transcendent God, the ebb and flow of imperial allegiances, and ecclesiastical politics periodically favored Arianism throughout the fourth century. St. Athanasius (c. 296–373), a young observer at the Nicene council in 325, soon became Bishop of Alexandria and Arianism's chief opponent, but he was embroiled in conflict and exiled from his bishopric on five occasions.

Like most of early Christianity, Athanasius championed *theosis*, in which salvation involves deification or divinization: human participation

---

44. For "archetypal," see Maurice Wiles, *Archetypal Heresy: Arianism through the Centuries* (Oxford: Clarendon, 1996). Many scholars now see "Arianism" as a somewhat artificial construct.

45. Among the sources that have rewritten the story of the Arian controversy referenced in his subtitle are R. P. C. Hanson, *The Search for the Christian Doctrine of God: The Arian Controversy, 318–381* (Edinburgh: T&T Clark, 1988); Rowan Williams, *Arius: Heresy and Tradition*, rev. ed. (Grand Rapids: Eerdmans, 2002). Both see Arius as an early, extreme, and thus minor, figure vis-à-vis what orthodoxy later dubbed *Arianism*. Williams emphasizes Arius's cosmological focus on divine transcendence. Hanson emphasizes a soteriological implication from Arian Christology's acknowledgment of a human body but not a human soul: Arianism acknowledged divine transcendence and Christ's redemptive suffering by having the Logos suffer without being the deity himself.

in the divine nature (2 Pet 1:4). "For he was incarnate that we might be made gods."[46] God must communicate the divine life in an ontologically immediate way that makes human participation possible. If Jesus Christ is not God incarnate, then humans cannot receive the essence of salvation: communion with God. Athanasius also underscored life: if human beings became subject to death by virtue of the fall, then salvation must involve the divine life triumphing over death in the Son's resurrection.[47] More directly connected to John 1, Athanasius distinguished between the *agennētos* ("unbegotten") Father and the *agenētos* ("uncreated") Son.[48] The Father and the Son are distinct persons: the Father generates the Son, and the Son is generated. But this generation is eternal, contra the Arian view. The Logos is the Son of God by nature, whereas humans become God's children by adoptive grace.

Wrestling with Arianism clarified the logic of Christian salvation and worship. Its defeat was not a triumph of Hellenization but the recognition of biblical orthodoxy.[49] If Arianism were correct, then there could be a hidden God behind the love apparently revealed in Jesus Christ. Thus Arianism had humanity reaching toward God through a quasi-divine intermediary rather than personally encountering God's saving initiative.[50] And if Arianism were correct, then worshiping Jesus would violate the Creator-creature distinction; the Bible allows for no third kind of being. Ironically, by attempting to protect divine transcendence, Arianism fell into idolatry.

---

46. See, e.g., St. Athanasius, *On the Incarnation*, trans. John Behr, PP 44a (New York: St. Vladimir's Seminary, 2011), 167.

47. Thus Athanasius's soteriology focused on human irrationality and mortality, as summarized by Frances M. Young, *From Nicaea to Chalcedon: A Guide to the Literature and Its Background* (Philadelphia: Fortress, 1983), 70.

48. See Grillmeier, *Christ in Christian Tradition*, 1:267. F. C. Conybeare claimed, "If Athanasius had not had the Fourth Gospel to draw texts from, Arius would never have been confuted," but T. E. Pollard responded, "If Arius had not had the Fourth Gospel to draw texts from, he would not have needed confuting"—quoted in Behr, *Way to Nicaea*, 70.

49. Hanson, *Search*, 870. As he concludes on pp. 874–75, the church wrestled since the second century with the coherence between monotheism and the worship of Jesus; ultimately, Athanasius insisted on the immediacy of God healing us in Christ. Origen's complex legacy, along with earlier Logos Christologies of mediation, affected both Arians and Nicaeans, as emphasized by Behr, *Way to Nicaea*, 206 et passim.

50. See Colin E. Gunton, "And in One Lord, Jesus Christ . . . Begotten, Not Made," in *Nicene Christianity: A Future for a New Ecumenism*, ed. Christopher R. Seitz (Grand Rapids: Brazos, 2001), 35–48; Alan Torrance, "Being of One Substance with the Father," in *Nicene Christianity*, 49–61. Scholars draw the historical contrasts between Arianism and pro-Nicene orthodoxy variously, but they agree regarding a soteriological difference. Drawing the fundamental contrast between Trinitarian "unity of being" and mere "unity of will" (summarized on pp. 30–31, with soteriological implications highlighted here) is Khaled Anatolios, *Retrieving Nicaea: The Development and Meaning of Trinitarian Doctrine* (Grand Rapids: Baker Academic, 2011).

4. Apollinarianism

In Arianism's wake, Apollinarianism evoked the church's affirmation of Christ's full humanity. At long last, in 381 the Council of Constantinople reaffirmed the decision of Nicaea from 325, officially vanquishing Arianism, as the Niceno-Constantinopolitan Creed insisted on the Son's full deity. The church also wrestled, however, with the fullness of the incarnate Son's humanity. Docetic Christologies were already heretical. But Apollinarians continued the Alexandrian focus upon the union of the Logos with human flesh. They diminished the Son's full humanity by having the Logos replace what would otherwise have been the human mind or spirit.

Broadly speaking, Apollinarianism was a form of monophysitism, a one-nature (-*physis*) Christology emphasizing the Word become flesh. Given Alexandria's dominant anthropology, the divine Logos could serve as the life-giving principle normally provided by the *nous*, the rational soul.[51] Emphasizing the Logos's intimate union with the human body would secure the incarnate Son's personal unity. Yet Apollinarianism went beyond promoting *mia physis*—one nature—in that largely orthodox way. Determined to preserve the unity of the incarnate Christ's thinking and willing, it overreacted against an emerging focus on Jesus's full, distinct humanity. Its monophysite Christology would avoid not only a division of the Son's person but also corruption from a sinful human spirit. Like Arianism, Apollinarianism protected the deity from direct contact with a defective aspect of creation—but in the opposite way, denying the Son's full humanity rather than full deity.

Apollinarianism's key opponents were the Cappadocian fathers St. Basil of Caesarea (330–379), St. Gregory of Nazianzus (329–390), and Basil's brother St. Gregory of Nyssa (c. 335–c. 395). From earlier roots they revived the formula, "What is not assumed is not healed" (*quod non est assumptum non est sanatum*). If the Redeemer does not assume full humanity, an aspect is left irredeemable, being treated as essentially corrupt. Hence Apollinarianism was condemned, beginning in 362 at Alexandria and decisively in 381 at Constantinople. Admittedly, Apollinarius contributed to upholding the Son's deity and personal

---

51. Variations on this theme apparently characterized both Arians and Athanasius. Apollinarius either maintained a trichotomist distinction between body, soul, and spirit or used the terms with contextual imprecision, according to Young, *From Nicaea to Chalcedon*, 189.

unity.[52] Yet the church gradually recognized that salvation was at stake not only in the Son's full deity but also in his full humanity. In becoming flesh, the Word accepted more than mere embodiment; he assumed postlapsarian humanity's fallen condition, sin excepted.

5. Nestorianism and Eutychianism

Although by 381 orthodoxy affirmed the Son's full deity and full humanity, Nestorianism and Eutychianism evoked the church's affirmation of his personal unity. The focus on two natures raised fresh challenges of articulating their relationship; certain misunderstandings jeopardized the genuine affirmation of one nature or the other. Imagine Christologies being poured into a funnel. The widest denial of Christ's deity was Ebionism, the narrower denial Arianism. The widest denial of the incarnate Son's humanity was Docetism, the narrower denial Apollinarianism. Constantinople reduced the width of potential errors considerably. Still, subtler errors persisted on each side: Arianism's successor was Nestorianism; Apollinarianism's monophysite successor was Eutychianism.

Nestorianism implicitly denied Christ's full deity by distinguishing the natures too sharply, virtually as two persons. As Archbishop of Constantinople, Nestorius (c. 386–450) was asked to rule about calling Mary the *Theotokos* (God-bearer). He rejected the title, worrying that it led to Arianism (treating the Son only as Mary's child, a creature) or else Apollinarianism (treating the Son as not completely human). Nestorianism was thereby perceived as teaching that Mary gave birth to a man who became an instrument of the deity. As we saw previously, *Theotokos* has biblical support: "'Blessed are you among women, and blessed is the child you will bear! But why am I so favored, that *the mother of my Lord* should come to me?'" (Luke 1:42–43; emphasis added). The title is especially pertinent when the Greek *Kyrios* ("my Lord") renders the Hebrew *Adonai* ("my Lord"), which Jews used as a reverent substitute to avoid verbalizing the divine name YHWH. In denying *Theotokos* to Mary, Nestorius lost the Son's personal unity by overemphasizing the distinction between the two natures. Refusing to identify the one born of Mary as "God" made the two natures seem to be two persons: the Logos adopting Jesus. Put differently, the union of

---

52. E.g., he was influential regarding the term *hypostasis*; so Grillmeier, *Christ in Christian Tradition*, 1:337.

the natures would only be moral, not essential—as if God is in Christ, but Christ is not God.

Saint Cyril of Alexandria (c. 376–444) vigorously opposed Nestorius, who was condemned at Ephesus in 431. Afterward, some supporters thought that Cyril conceded too much to the emphasis on full humanity in the principle "what is not assumed is not healed." Hence another form of monophysitism arose from Eutyches (c. 380–c. 456). Now the Son's one nature had to be both divine and human, since Apollinarianism had been ruled heretical. The Eutychian solution involved one hybrid nature, a *tertium quid* (third thing) fusing divinity and humanity. Facing condemnation, Eutyches pleaded his case to St. Leo I (the Great), Bishop of Rome (c. 400–461). In response, Leo's "Tome" drew from Cyril of Alexandria and Tertullian to frame a consensus position. The result influenced the Definition at the Council of Chalcedon (451), where both Nestorius and Eutyches were condemned. According to Chalcedon, the two natures are united in the one person (*hypostasis*)—hypostatic union— yet they remain distinct: deity and humanity may not be confused, even when they come into intimate personal union in the Son. In Johannine terms, Nestorianism lost the preexisting personal unity of the Word, antecedent to the incarnation; Eutychianism lost the integrity of the flesh that the Word assumed.

B. The Crucial Concept: The Hypostatic Union

The Chalcedonian Definition articulates the hypostatic union by establishing boundaries: "one and the same Christ, Son, Lord, only-begotten, acknowledged in two natures which undergo no confusion, no change, no division, no separation; at no point was the difference between the natures taken away through the union, but rather the property of both natures is preserved and comes together into a single person and a single subsistent being."[53] Thereby Chalcedon ruled out both Nestorianism ("one and the same Christ . . . no division, no separation") and the Eutychian overreaction ("in two natures which undergo no confusion, no change"). By the middle of the fifth century, then, despite its "dogmatic minimalism" conciliar Christology staked three essential claims: the Son's full deity, full humanity, and personal unity.[54]

---

53. "Council of Chalcedon—451," in *Nicaea I to Lateran V*, vol. 1 of *Decrees of the Ecumenical Councils*, ed. Norman P. Tanner, SJ (London: Sheed & Ward, 1990), 86–87.

54. On "dogmatic minimalism," see Oliver D. Crisp, "Desiderata for Models of the Hypostatic Union," in *Christology, Ancient and Modern: Explorations in Constructive Dogmatics*, ed.

1. The Double *Homoousios*

These claims entailed three major concepts: the double *homoousios*, divine personhood, and dyothelitism. Johannine Logos Christology eventually generated the Niceno-Constantinopolitan acknowledgment of the incarnate Son as *homoousios* with God the Father. Hence this first entailment began to emerge long before Chalcedon, focused on Christ's deity. The Chalcedonian Definition proceeded to affirm that the incarnate Son was *homoousios* not only with God but also with humanity, except for sin. This double *homoousios* articulates the integrity of the two natures: full deity, full humanity—body and soul.

2. Divine Personhood

Accompanying the double *homoousios* is the incarnate Son's personal unity, asymmetrically rooted in his eternal deity. The *communicatio idiomatum*, the communication of the two natures' properties, articulates the operative principle of this personal unity, but the Son was already a divine person before the incarnation. Whereas the modern West approaches personhood psychologically, the classic tradition addressed his personhood ontologically. Thus, the incarnate Son's full humanity does not entail the experience of a *psyche* exactly like ours or the grounding of personhood in human personality. To articulate this asymmetry, some Chalcedonians soon spoke of Christ's human nature as *anhypostatic*, that is, without human personhood prior to assumption by the Logos, and *enhypostatic*, that is, becoming fully personal in that assumption. Because conciliar Christology confesses a hypostatic union without addressing psychological experience, affirming two distinct natures need not entail Nestorianism, despite evoking modern concerns.[55]

Oliver D. Crisp and Fred Sanders (Grand Rapids: Zondervan, 2013), 27. Suggesting an analogy with indirect claims made by "riddles" is Sarah Coakley, "What Does Chalcedon Solve and What Does It Not? Some Reflections on the Meaning and Status of the Chalcedonian 'Definition,'" in *The Incarnation: An Interdisciplinary Symposium on the Incarnation of the Son of God*, ed. Stephen T. Davis, Daniel Kendall, SJ, and Gerald O'Collins, SJ (Oxford: Oxford University Press, 2002), 143–63. For a reminder that Chalcedon's four "negatives" point like a fingerpost in "positive directions," see G. C. Berkouwer, *The Person of Christ*, trans. John Vriend, Studies in Dogmatics (Grand Rapids: Eerdmans, 1954), 92.

55. Making this point vis-à-vis the Reformed tradition, which is often accused of Nestorian tendencies, is Stephen R. Holmes, "Reformed Varieties of the *Communicatio Idiomatum*," in *The Person of Christ*, ed. Stephen R. Holmes and Murray A. Rae (London: T&T Clark, 2005), 86.

3. Dyothelitism

Eventually the necessity of dyothelitism—affirmation of Christ's two wills, divine and human—became apparent. Ongoing controversy included an Eastern tendency to discount Cyril's influence over the Chalcedonian Definition.[56] Worrying that Chalcedon did not preserve the incarnation's single subject, some promoted monophysite alternatives. The Second Council of Constantinople in 553 upheld the Chalcedonian Definition while ardently opposing Nestorianism.[57] Subsequently, some champions of Christ's single subjectivity avoided monophysitism but still refused to speak of distinctly divine and human wills. Their monothelitism (one will, *thelēma*) held that Christ had only one principle of operation. Thanks to the advocacy of Maximus the Confessor (c. 580–662), for which he suffered greatly, monothelitism was condemned at the Third Council of Constantinople (680–681). Among other arguments, Jesus's prayer in Gethsemane (Matt 26:36–46) was crucial: unless both the divine will and the Messiah's human obedience were involved, the resulting passion could not accomplish our salvation. Dyothelitism associates will with nature: in a Trinitarian context, the one divine essence entails one perichoretic will, exercised in the three persons' undivided external operations like creation and salvation; in a christological context, two natures entail two wills, with the actions of Jesus Christ counting as both divine and human— whatever the nature(s) or principle(s) of operation from which they emerge.

C. A Contested Legacy

Despite the providential enhancement of the church's biblical understanding through the gradual exclusion of heresies, the conciliar legacy

---

56. Three of the Definition's four adverbs came substantially from Cyril and the fourth emphasized his claim about the inseparability of Christ's two natures; so John A. McGuckin, *Saint Cyril of Alexandria and the Christological Controversy: Its History, Theology, and Texts* (Crestwood, NY: St. Vladimir's Seminary, 2004), 239. For monophysite texts and a sketch of their historical context, see Iain R. Torrance, *Christology After Chalcedon: Severus of Antioch and Sergius the Monophysite* (repr., Eugene, OR: Wipf & Stock, 1998).

57. On this council's contribution and anhypostatic/enhypostatic terminology, see Fred Sanders, "Introduction to Christology: Chalcedonian Categories for the Gospel Narrative," in *Jesus in Trinitarian Perspective: An Intermediate Christology*, ed. Fred Sanders and Klaus Issler (Nashville: B&H Academic, 2007), 26, 30. Recent critiques of that terminology do "not disturb the dogmatic point which the language is intended to express," according to "Jesus in Modernity," in Webster, *Word and Church*, 168n45.

remains contested. Nicene Trinitarianism emerged from Johannine Logos Christology once an ensuing tendency toward ontological subordination of the Son and the Spirit was corrected. Even among adherents of Nicene Trinitarianism, however, Chalcedon's legacy faces political, philosophical, and psychological challenges. Brief summaries of these challenges follow here, along with preliminary responses upon which the next chapter will build.

1. Political Challenges

First, political challenges surround Chalcedon, both before and after. Before: The story of councils and noncouncils after Nicaea is awash with imperial meddling and imperious bishops. After: The East's mixed reception raises questions about how fully ecumenical Chalcedon was and whether full subscription to its language is required for orthodoxy.[58] Contemporary global Christologies are also concerned about the valorization of emperors that accompanied not only the conversion of Constantine but also the creedal confession of Jesus's divine lordship.[59]

In addressing these challenges, Protestants should maintain that, on one hand, Chalcedon is *only* ministerial: Scripture's final authority positions the council as a "historically situated event with flawed human participants who were not biblically, theologically, or epistemologically perfect, neutral, objective automatons."[60] On the other hand, Chalcedon is *genuinely* ministerial: without church councils we more "easily get lost in the tall grass of our subjective experience and our cultural predilections," including trends in modern biblical scholarship.[61] Accordingly, evangelical churches affirm an essentially Chalcedonian Christology, even as it is important to address politically compromised aspects of its legacy. Meanwhile, the status of monophysite or other separated

---

58. For a readable account, see Donald Fairbairn and Ryan M. Reeves, *The Story of Creeds and Confessions: Tracing the Development of the Christian Faith* (Grand Rapids: Baker Academic, 2019).

59. E.g., regarding Eusebius's valorization of Constantine, see Young, *From Nicaea to Chalcedon*, 14. For even evangelical theologians in the global South raising political concerns regarding conciliar orthodoxy, see, e.g., C. René Padilla, "Toward a Contextual Christology from Latin America," in *Conflict and Context: Hermeneutics in the Americas*, ed. Mark Lau Branson and C. René Padilla (Grand Rapids: Eerdmans, 1986), 81–91. The volume also helpfully contains dialogue with Emilio Antonio Nuñez, Douglas Webster, and John Howard Yoder.

60. Stephen J. Nichols, "The Deity of Christ Today," in *The Deity of Christ*, ed. Christopher W. Morgan and Robert A. Peterson, TC (Wheaton, IL: Crossway, 2011), 36.

61. The quotation is from Nichols, "Deity of Christ Today," 36. The *ministerial* adjective is a frequent suggestion of Kevin Vanhoozer, e.g., in "Christology in the West: Conversations in Europe and North America," in *Jesus without Borders: Christology in the Majority World*, ed. Gene L. Green, Stephen T. Pardue, and K. K. Yeo, MWT (Grand Rapids: Eerdmans, 2014), 32–33.

communions such as the Oriental Orthodox may be left to the discernment of Eastern churches and ultimately the judgment of God, perhaps with optimism that these groups share essentially conciliar judgments despite non-Chalcedonian concepts. Such optimism probably accompanies contemporary evangelical tolerance for philosophical rehabilitation of monophysite proposals. But intellectual tolerance should not foster confessional permissiveness. Together cautious forbearance and confessional discipline are needed to reflect healthy Protestant convictions about conciliar providence.

2. Philosophical Challenges

Similarly, philosophical challenges confront conciliar Christology from two directions—loosely speaking, from both pre-Enlightenment and pro-Enlightenment perspectives. Insofar as modern analytic philosophy and recent analytic theology retain traditional metaphysics, they reflect a pre-Enlightenment project. Their christological preoccupations involve sound premises and valid arguments that assess the clarity and coherence of creedal formulae. Insofar as sectors of modern theology respond to German idealism and Barth's legacy, they reflect post-Enlightenment suspicion of conciliar metaphysical language. Their christological preoccupations involve the dynamism of biblical narrative, worrying about domestication of the incarnation's divine self-revelation. Sometimes, despite different reasoning, analytic and antimetaphysical perspectives coalesce in their suspicions that Chalcedon is unfaithful to Nicaea and Constantinople, that Chalcedon's aftermath reveals its inadequacies, and thus that Chalcedon is either too minimalist (providing no theoretical coherence) or too metaphysical (neglecting Israel's story while nullifying the incarnation with traditional divine attributes).[62]

In addressing these challenges, evangelical Christology should make a reasoned appeal to mystery.[63] The incarnation should remain

---

62. For postmetaphysical theologians illustrating such philosophically inflected appraisals of Chalcedon, see, e.g., Robert W. Jenson, "Christ in the Trinity: *Communicatio Idiomatum*," in *The Person of Christ*, 61–69; Bruce L. McCormack, "The Person of Christ," in *Mapping Modern Theology: A Thematic and Historical Introduction*, ed. Kelly M. Kapic and Bruce L. McCormack (Grand Rapids: Baker Academic, 2012), 149–73.

63. In Gabriel Marcel's well-known distinction, modern alienation tempts us to approach "mysteries" (which should elicit theological contemplation and ecumenical cooperation) as "problems" (which elicit attempts at scientific "explanation"). For an analytic theologian's concession that conciliar Christology requires appealing to mystery, see Timothy Pawl, *In Defense of Conciliar Christology: A Philosophical Essay*, OSAT (Oxford: Oxford University Press, 2016), 88–91. Although Pawl is right that such appeals are sometimes unsatisfactory, analytic zeal for conceptual clarity can eventually obscure truth or generate trivialities (e.g., the so-called "no

mysterious given its singularity, restraining speculation due to limits upon theology's analogical resources: a unique event can appeal to nothing more than modest analogies. Philosophical analysis can occasionally provide clarifying insight. Rather than posing technical defeaters, however, philosophical challenges frequently press material objections from contextually limited perspectives, as the next section illustrates with modern psychological interests.

3. Psychological Challenges

Modernity's new preoccupation with human agents and historical contexts generated quests for Jesus's self-understanding and objections to his full deity if that entailed perfections like impassibility. Pro-Enlightenment theologians championed the creative genius of the human spirit. This celebration of the ego, combined with critiques of traditional metaphysics, reoriented concepts of human personhood, seemingly requiring that Chalcedon's ontological affirmation of Christ's full humanity be supplemented with a psychological account of his personality development. Not coincidentally, an exemplary Jesus from the Synoptic Gospels became more fashionable than the Lord of Pauline theology, let alone the Johannine Logos. Moreover, it seemed impossible for the Chalcedonian Christ to remain a single subject if he were fully human and fully God—with axioms like divine impassibility being embraced (uncritically, it is alleged) from Hellenistic philosophy.

In addressing these challenges, the next chapter returns to early high Christology and, contra most kenotic proposals, reaffirms the *extra Calvinisticum*. While being cautious about the extent of appropriate speculation regarding Christ's self-understanding, a Reformed Christology can both maintain classically orthodox affirmations and narrate Jesus's faithful human development. As for divine impassibility, the church gradually rejected three ways of reducing its apparent tension with the incarnation, affirming, (1) contra Docetism, Christ's genuine suffering; (2) contra Arianism, Christ's undiminished deity; and (3) contra Nestorianism, a single subject of Christ's divine actions and human suffering:

---

person" problem). For an earlier caution about "mystery" that focuses on maintaining contact with ordinary language, see Steven T. Katz, "The Language and Logic of 'Mystery' in Christology," in *Christ, Faith and History: Cambridge Studies in Christology*, ed. S. W. Sykes and J. P. Clayton (Cambridge: Cambridge University Press, 1972), 239–61.

It is crucial, therefore, to differentiate between that which the Word undergoes in his own nature and the experiences that can only be attributed to the Word by virtue of his appropriation of the human nature. . . . The Word who is above suffering in his own nature suffered by appropriating human nature and obtained victory over suffering. The celebration of this paradox in the creeds and hymns is the crowning achievement of a distinctly Christian account of divine involvement, an account for which no school of philosophy may take credit.[64]

4. Patristic Consensus

Beyond appealing to providence, acknowledging mystery, and accounting for varied expectations regarding personhood, addressing challenges to Chalcedon's legacy requires attending to recent patristic scholarship, which highlights a genuine christological consensus that emerged from Scripture and was expressed at the ecumenical councils.[65] In terms of ecumenical reception or christological explanation, Chalcedon may seem less like a solution than a definition of the problem.[66] But perhaps ecumenical delimitation of the mystery underlying Christian salvation and worship was the "solution" that was needed.

In the Nicene period, debates over the logic of monotheism and the nature of divine mediation—with frequent references to the divine image—were crucial. Such mediation involved knowing God, not just knowing about God, combining functional and ontic concerns.[67] For

---

64. Quoting p. 175 from the summary of Paul L. Gavrilyuk, *The Suffering of the Impassible God: The Dialectics of Patristic Thought*, OECS (Oxford: Oxford University Press, 2004), 172–75. For the account that he lauds, see St. Cyril of Alexandria, *On the Unity of Christ*, trans. John Anthony McGuckin (Crestwood, NY: St. Vladimir's Seminary, 2000).

65. Admittedly a nonspecialist, the present author finds the soundings taken below—coupled with the work of figures cited elsewhere—to represent strong scholarly trends. Among possible exceptions regarding Chalcedon's Cyrilline consensus would be Christopher A. Beeley, *The Unity of Christ: Continuity and Conflict in Patristic Tradition* (New Haven, CT: Yale University Press, 2012). But see the critical review in Michel René Barnes, "On *The Unity of Christ* by Christopher A. Beeley," *Nova et Vetera* 14, no. 1 (2016): 331–41. For an account narrating Chalcedon as a "bold but, in the end, not entirely successful attempt to reconcile divergent historical voices," with its later importance "distorted and unintelligible if it is detached from its place in a much longer, more complex narrative," see Brian E. Daley, SJ, *God Visible: Patristic Christology Reconsidered* (Oxford: Oxford University Press, 2018), viii. Daley's plausible suggestion on p. 201 that Chalcedon's symmetry may have obscured its affirmation of Christ's single subjectivity does not necessarily gainsay its Cyrilline character.

66. Young, *From Nicaea to Chalcedon*, 178.

67. Jon M. Robertson, *Christ as Mediator: A Study of the Theologies of Eusebius of Caesarea, Marcellus of Ancyra, and Athanasius of Alexandria*, OTM (Oxford: Oxford University Press, 2007), 6. Daley's *God Visible* also underscores the saving epiphany of Christ himself as a unifying thread throughout patristic Christology.

soteriological reasons, Athanasius championed God's immediacy and a correspondingly inclusive monotheism that replaced external mediation language with references to the eternal Word.[68] Granted that revisionary scholarship complicates the profile of Arianism, still that group was "united, at the very least, in the desire to 'exclude' the Son from the identity and 'essence' of the one true God."[69] By contrast, pro-Nicene orthodoxy identified the incarnate Son with the eternal Word that mediated God's redemptive self-revelation.

Surrounding Chalcedon, then, a consensus reasserted itself regarding christological grace that establishes divine-human communion.[70] For Nestorianism, Christ was the "uniquely graced man," providing an "anthropological" grace. For Cyril of Alexandria, however, grace was christological, "the sharing of divine communion" involving God's own Son. Chalcedon was fundamentally Cyrilline. Undoubtedly there was political chaos, and terminological developments added confusion.[71] That said, Chalcedon was assuming the condemnation of Nestorius and focused on opposing Eutychianism. That focus explains how Chalcedon's Cyrilline commitments could coincide with the two-natures emphasis that provoked some of Cyril's supporters. Like other formulae of the period, Chalcedon structurally repeats that Christ is "the same one," underscoring the single subjectivity of the incarnate Logos.[72] This Cyrilline consensus focused on communion, not just connection, with God: consequently, the "double birth" of the Logos as eternally begotten and then incarnate would be required for deliverance from the mortal corruption to which sin has subjected humanity.[73]

Highlighting this patristic consensus puts conciliar challenges in a new light. Politically, as problematic as they were, both heretical provocations and imperial power could be instruments by which divine providence led church councils to build a christological foundation. Philosophically, as modest as the councils were, their minimalism could foster theological contemplation while focusing christological unity on a soteriological

68. Robertson, *Christ as Mediator*, 136, 214–16.

69. Robertson, *Christ as Mediator*, 230.

70. As introduced, e.g., by Donald Fairbairn, *Grace and Christology in the Early Church*, OECS (Oxford: Oxford University Press, 2003), 3.

71. For identification of various groups around Nicaea, see Fairbairn and Reeves, *Story of Creeds*, 67. For charting of four key terms related to Chalcedon, see pp. 86–87.

72. Fairbairn, *Grace and Christology*, 220–21. Cyril's "one and the same" language appears as early as Irenaeus; see Behr, *Way to Nicaea*, 124–25.

73. Fairbairn, *Grace and Christology*, 223.

consensus. Psychologically, as understandably curious as they are, modern believers should acknowledge their assumptions about personhood and personality. The councils' ontological focus appropriately demarcates both freedom for exploration and limits upon speculative explanations. Poetry and paradox have their properly biblical and liturgical places.[74] Moreover, as already suggested in chapter 4 and explored further in the next chapter, it is possible to account for Jesus's human recognition of his divine sonship by attending to the virginal conception. In sum, much of this chapter establishes the need for Christology to be *Nicene* in order to be *Johannine*; recent patristic scholarship reestablishes the need for Christology to be *Chalcedonian* in order to be Nicene.

III. THE ICONOCLASTIC CONTROVERSY

In 787 the Second Council of Nicaea, the seventh council recognized by both East and West, appealed to the incarnation when embracing icons.[75] This appeal impinges upon the relationship between Christology and revelation, as well as the classically Reformed inclination toward iconoclasm. At Nicaea II, iconodules victoriously defended the use of icons by appealing to Christ's sanctification of flesh as a vehicle of revelation. Since God assumed a human face in Jesus, iconodules found it appropriate for creaturely forms to share in the divine glory they represent. Hence icons may not be "worshiped" (*latria*), but they may be "venerated" (*dulia*)—as vehicles for worshiping the otherwise invisible God.[76] Iconodules worship Christ as a divine person, not his human nature per se, but they maintain that dissociating worship from his physical form would be Nestorian. Whereas icons became especially important within Eastern Christianity, they also influenced the Catholic West. Both sometimes underscored Christ's deity to the neglect of his full

---

74. For this emphasis and powerful examples, see Edward T. Oakes, SJ, *Infinity Dwindled to Infancy: A Catholic and Evangelical Christology* (Grand Rapids: Eerdmans, 2011).

75. For brief Protestant narration that is sympathetic to the council, see Fairbairn and Reeves, *Story of Creeds*, 153–58. See also Aidan Nichols, OP, "Image Christology in the Age of the Second Council of Nicaea," in *The Oxford Handbook of Christology*, ed. Francesca Aran Murphy (Oxford: Oxford University Press, 2015), 169–82.

76. Protestant orthodox divines highlight iconodules' inconsistency regarding this distinction, claiming that Roman Catholicism tolerated internal disagreement. See, e.g., Francis Turretin, *Institutes of Elenctic Theology*, ed. James T. Dennison Jr., trans. George Musgrave Giger (Phillipsburg, NJ: P&R, 1994), 2:52–53, 60. Noting that the devil's temptation of Christ only required (idolatrous) "service" is William Perkins, *A Warning Against Idolatry of the Last Times (1601)*, ed. Shawn D. Wright, The Works of William Perkins 7 (Grand Rapids: Reformation Heritage, 2018), 687.

humanity, yet medieval Roman Christianity still gave mystical attention to Jesus's suffering, even in gory detail.[77]

Protestant assessment of Nicaea II's *authority* should include four factors. First, Scripture alone is God's final authority over faith and practice. Respect for ecumenical creeds' ministerial authority values their consensus identifications of Scripture's fundamental dogmas, without conceding their infallibility. Second, Nicaea II is last and arguably least among the ecumenical councils, the reception of which became increasingly complicated from Chalcedon onward. Third, relatedly, the christological scope of Nicaea II is minimal. Most of its twenty-two canons focus on property and priesthood; how many iconodules embrace its worries over men and women eating together? The canons of previous councils were also wide-ranging and variously received, but they followed overtly christological dogma. Hence Protestants may plausibly deem Nicaea II to lack the dogmatic import of the previous six councils. Put differently, Nicaea II appeals briefly to the incarnation for a practical judgment rather than asserting a directly christological judgment. Fourth, a clear decision about the council's authority is necessary: Nicaea II makes conscience-binding claims. The council suspends all clergy who teach otherwise and excommunicates all laypersons who think otherwise. Iconoclasts are not permitted simply to leave others' consciences accountable to God while maintaining their own view. Rather, the council anathematizes anyone who does not "salute such representations as standing for the Lord and his saints."[78]

Ensuing assessment of Nicaea II's implied christological *argument* favors iconoclasm for several reasons. Admittedly, iconodule arguments from John of Damascus and others are more expansive than Nicaea II or this necessarily brief response can portray. But, first, the second of the Ten Commandments is emphatic in both its comprehensiveness (not worshiping any graven image) and its consequences.[79] Second,

---

77. For an overview of such medieval piety that addresses intercessory and erotic dimensions, see Rowan Williams, "A History of Faith in Jesus," in *The Cambridge Companion to Jesus*, ed. Markus Bockmuehl (Cambridge: Cambridge University Press, 2001), 220–36. For depictions of Christ's suffering, see Alison Milbank, "Seeing Double: The Crucified Christ in Western Mediaeval Art," in *The Oxford Handbook of Christology*, 215–32.

78. "Second Council of Nicaea—787," in *Nicaea I to Lateran V*, vol. 1 of *Decrees of the Ecumenical Councils*, 137.

79. In God's providence, I write this section hours after the death of J. I. Packer, from whom I first encountered iconoclasm. He highlighted this emphatic quality, and the underlying rationale of jealousy for divine glory as well as the priority of the divine Word, in Packer, *Knowing God*, 43–51.

pedagogical arguments (from visual representation of God in Christ, to address illiteracy and the like) do not authorize a redemptive-historical shift in which the incarnation nullifies the second commandment's import.[80] Third, the distinction between *latria* and *dulia* is contested (as noted above), while being incoherently applied to Mary and the saints along with Christ.[81] Fourth, purported biblical support and patristic precedents for icons are inapplicable or nonexistent.[82] Fifth, the allegation that iconoclasm is docetic is unpersuasive since the Reformed tradition has celebrated Christ's humanity so vociferously as to face regular accusations of Nestorianism. Hence, sixth, although the incarnation underscores that human beings are made for beatific vision, iconoclasm remains necessary in the current era.[83] Suppose we grant that sometimes Reformed iconoclasm pays insufficient attention to the incarnation, whereas an authentic image of Christ is ontologically possible: we still lack sufficient knowledge of Jesus's actual features, and the uniqueness of his person precludes the artistic use of generic human features. Consequently, "seeing" God in Christ remains an eschatological hope, a desire deferred. Currently, fellowship with God in Christ depends upon the indwelling Holy Spirit eliciting our response to God as Father through the Word of grace.

The second commandment's concrete application lies beyond our purview here, but iconoclasm is pertinent to the Christology of divine revelation. The incarnation does not set aside biblical proscriptions

---

80. Contra the structure of the argument from Nicaea II's leading advocate, John of Damascus, "Exposition of the Orthodox Faith," in *Hilary of Poitiers, John of Damascus*, ed. Philip Schaff and Henry Wace, *NPNF2* 9 (repr., Peabody, MA: Hendrickson, 2004), 88. Ancient Israelites were at least as illiterate as Christians in the Graeco-Roman context.

81. Again, contra John of Damascus: Christ's humanity is hypostatically united to God whereas Mary (or the wood of the cross) is not, so that "honour rendered" to an image must pass over to a "prototype" differently. "Where indeed has God instituted the relative worship of latria, whose proximate object is the creature and remote object God? Were not the calf-worshipping Israelites of old (and so the pagans themselves) ready to encrust their idolatry with the same distinction?" So Turretin, *Institutes of Elenctic Theology*, 2:57.

82. On the lack of ancient icons and of biblical worship regarding the temple, the brazen serpent, and the like, see, e.g., Turretin, *Institutes of Elenctic Theology*, 2:57–61. Treating the brazen serpent as a sacrament instead is Wilhelmus à Brakel, *The Law, Christian Graces, and the Lord's Prayer*, ed. Joel R. Beeke, trans. Bartel Elshout, vol. 3 of *The Christian's Reasonable Service* (Grand Rapids: Reformation Heritage, 1994), 110.

83. So David VanDrunen, "Iconoclasm, Incarnation and Eschatology: Toward a Catholic Understanding of the Reformed Doctrine of the 'Second' Commandment," *IJST* 6, no. 2 (2004): 130–47. VanDrunen helpfully summarizes key iconoclast arguments. He rightly acknowledges that beatific vision will involve sight in ways that might qualify the common Reformed emphasis upon the Word. However, he may not acknowledge clearly enough that "seeing God" has a necessarily metaphorical sense.

of visibly representing God for the sake of devotion.[84] The incarnation reaffirms the created goodness of the material cosmos; just so, the second commandment does not proscribe artistic participation but only circumscribes certain uses of images. During his earthly sojourn, some first-century people saw Jesus's face. Given the Son's enduring incarnation, we anticipate a tangible aspect of the beatific vision. But the visual form of this Jewish man did not convey YHWH's essential features. To say otherwise would jeopardize the universal solidarity of the incarnation, which transcends the sharing of physical characteristics and is vital for redemption (Heb 2:5–18). Underscoring this universal human solidarity may be especially meaningful for women and other marginalized persons, without diminishing Israel's privilege as the covenant people through whom the Messiah came.[85] Iconoclasm honors the human particularities with which the incarnation involved such solidarity—acknowledging that we do not know what Jesus really looked like, thus avoiding distorted conformity with our own cultural images. Not just feminist but also liberationist concerns are legitimately addressed: Is caesaropapism a merely accidental feature of the iconoclast controversy and the iconodule victory? Instead, the Son's human flesh illuminated us with God's redemptive and filial love, as now proclaimed in the biblical Word and the visible words of the sacraments.

IV. WORD

Although neither Jesus's self-designation nor a frequent christological title, *Logos* is John's unique way of introducing the eternal Son before narrating his incarnation. Logos also synthesizes broader patterns, integrating passages like Hebrews 1:1–4 and motifs such as image or Wisdom with the Creator's self-expression in the Old Testament. Speaking of the Word identifies Immanuel's first advent as God's definitive self-revelation, with "becoming flesh" birthing

---

84. Nor should we attach John of Damascus's distinction between the spirit and the letter of the commandment to the inevitability of our image-making—contra Chris E. W. Green, *All Things Beautiful: An Aesthetic Christology* (Waco, TX: Baylor University Press, 2021), 22. Otherwise Green's book offers interesting reflections, as does Natalie Carnes, *Image and Presence: A Christological Reflection on Iconoclasm and Iconophilia*, Encountering Traditions (Stanford, CA: Stanford University Press, 2018). But the latter uses *iconoclasm* as a category apart from the second commandment.

85. Part of the problem, of course, is that iconic representations of Jesus have typically reflected Byzantine or German or other cultural contexts far more than his first-century heritage.

incarnation as a dogmatic concept. Hence this chapter's examination of the ecumenical councils reflects the profound influence of the Johannine prologue. Speaking of the Word interweaves the incarnation with John's Trinitarian theology, including the life-giving illumination of the Holy Spirit.

A. Incarnation

From the root metaphor of incarnation, being enfleshed, comes the christological concept of assuming full humanity. Since the Logos even assumed embodiment, this ultimate divine self-revelation incorporates all aspects of human life. The incarnation is a state with a beginning ("became"), a mortal human body ("flesh"), a history ("made his dwelling among us"), and revelatory significance ("the Word" communicating the "grace and truth" of God).[86] The incarnation is an event in time, whatever the nature of divine eternity. The Logos cannot simply be *ensarkos*, in flesh, eternally; there must be a "prior" Logos *asarkos*, without flesh, to fit the incarnation's narrative shape—as a temporal happening lovingly willed in the divine decree, not to mention having its earthly climax in the ascension. The "preexistent" Logos is not already *incarnatus* (incarnate) but *incarnandus* (electing, sent by the Father and enabled by the Spirit to become incarnate in time), eternally making room for eventful fellowship with us.

Incarnation is not uniquely Johannine in an isolated sense. Concepts are the bridge from the root metaphors in words and phrases to regular habits of thought and speech regarding objects and ideas. Parallels between John 1:1–18 and passages like Philippians 2:5–11, despite Philippians' lack of *flesh* language, support the broader doctrinal concept of incarnation. Such passages share a pattern of descent and ascent. Indeed, Paul speaks christologically of flesh in Romans 8:3: "For what the law was powerless to do because it was weakened by the flesh, God did by sending his own Son in the likeness of sinful flesh to be a sin offering." The incarnate Word epitomizes the decree encapsulated in the eternal Son (Eph 1:3–14), the wisdom expressed in

---

86. This paragraph draws from Daniel J. Treier, "Incarnation," in *Christian Dogmatics: Reformed Theology for the Church Catholic*, ed. Michael Allen and Scott R. Swain (Grand Rapids: Baker Academic, 2016), 217–18. Probably it is more precise to say "he was made man" rather than "he became human," since the former phrasing better combines the particular and the universal while resisting mythological transformation; so Colin E. Gunton, *The Christian Faith: An Introduction to Christian Doctrine* (Oxford: Blackwell, 2002), 97–98. Given cultural complications, the present work generally uses the biblical idiom of becoming flesh.

the true image (Col 1:15–29), the covenant fulfilled in Israel's Messiah (Luke 24:13–35), and the divine presence returning in Immanuel's birth (Isa 7:14).

B. Trinitarian Illumination

The Word is one of the pressure points in Israel's Scriptures that anticipated the revelation of God's triune identity.[87] Incarnation and Trinity go together, uniting God's being and act in love: "Christ never comes alone. The coming of Christ always occurs in the Spirit and always relates us in the Spirit through the Son to God the Father."[88] John 1 abundantly supports the conciliar *homoousios*—the Son's essential sameness with the Father. Simultaneously, *homoousios* implies relational distinction; we do not refer to "being of the same essence" with oneself.[89] Such relational distinction is evident in "with God" from John 1:2, the ensuing *light* motifs, and John's frequent *mission* language. The Johannine missions—the Son becoming incarnate, the Spirit overshadowing him and indwelling us—reveal the personal processions of generation and spiration: "God's unity and salvation history's unity mirror each other in a precisely Trinitarian way."[90]

This Johannine mirroring of Trinitarian processions and missions aligns theologically with the *filioque* clause that was added to the Nicene Creed, according to which the Holy Spirit proceeds "from the Father *and the Son*." Granted, the West's unilateral insertion of this clause was ecclesiastically problematic, in light of which "through the Son" has virtue as a potential compromise. Brief christological comments cannot do justice to the *filioque*'s dogmatic complexities. Nonetheless, John's Trinitarian theology of revelation makes Jesus's breathing out of God's Spirit another aspect of his divine life-giving.[91] The *filioque* is the processional impetus (ontologically) and corollary (epistemologically)

---

87. C. Kavin Rowe, "Biblical Pressure and Trinitarian Hermeneutics," *ProEccl* 11, no. 3 (2002): 295–312. On the intentional divine economy for "revelation" of this "mystery," see Sanders, *Triune God*, 37, 43–45, 105–6, 209–10. Scripture, especially John's Gospel, provides "(1) raw material, (2) patterns of reflection on it, and (3) pressure" so that a "doctrine" of the Trinity is "in" the Bible, even without technical concepts (pp. 187–88).

88. Christoph Schwöbel, "Christ For Us—Yesterday and Today: A Response to 'The Person of Christ,'" in *The Person of Christ*, 186.

89. As, e.g., Basil notes, according to T. F. Torrance, *The Trinitarian Faith* (repr., Edinburgh: T&T Clark, 1995), 125.

90. Sanders, *Triune God*, 178. On the dangers of using *immanent* and *economic* Trinity language for this claim, see pp. 144–48.

91. Marianne Meye Thompson, *The God of the Gospel of John* (Grand Rapids: Eerdmans, 2001), 146, 186–87.

of this filial mission. It does not entail two principles of origin for the Spirit any more than Trinitarian creation entails three *principia*.[92] As for the ensuing charge that the West depersonalizes the Spirit, Johannine Trinitarianism credits the Advocate with completing the circle of God's life-giving revelation, guiding the church back to the words of the Logos and forward to even greater works in his name. John 15:26 reflects both the Spirit's communicative agency and the respective collaboration of the Father and Son. Given the divine persons' ontological equality and distinct revelatory missions, Johannine Trinitarianism authorizes an inference regarding the processions: the Father gives to the Son not only to have life in himself (5:26) but also to participate in the Spirit's going forth. *Word* and *Son* complement each other: *Son* names a distinct person, begotten of the Father and sharing in the divine being; *Word* emphasizes identification and unity, naming the Son in terms of both the divine thought and its expression; *image* holds these two names together. Given the scandalously personal nature of the Logos by which God is revealed, it is no surprise that the Spirit is personal *as* the gift of love between Father and Son. This bond does not depersonalize the Spirit but specifies the agency being exercised, along with its corresponding origin.

In John's Gospel, then, the mutual love of Father and Son in the Spirit is the unconditioned wellspring from which God shines the light of created and redeemed life upon us. The Old Testament does not take for granted the privilege of knowing God, whose ways—if not for divine self-revelation—would be well-nigh inscrutable.[93] The Johannine Jesus does not reveal altogether new characteristics of Israel's God but visibly embodies Yнwн's saving love. Thus, far from ignoring Israel's Scriptures, conciliar Logos Christology celebrates their fulfillment in the incarnation of the Word. Through the indwelling Spirit of this Word, we come to enjoy the filial communion with God for which we were made.

---

92. Bavinck, *Reformed Dogmatics*, 2:316.
93. Thompson, *God of the Gospel*, 102–3.

CHAPTER 6

HUMILIATION OF THE LORD AS SERVANT

Philippians 2:5–11

As epitomized in **Philippians 2:5–11**, Jesus Christ is the Lord whose **humiliation** as **Servant** revealed the glory of God's love in rendering the ultimate human obedience. *His twofold earthly state intertwined humiliation with exaltation while also involving the redemptive sequence of suffering followed by glory. Contra kenotic Christologies, a classically Reformed account of the* communicatio idiomatum *addresses Christ's presence by affirming the* extra carnem, *Christ's knowledge by acknowledging his pilgrim faith, and Christ's power by articulating theandric agency.*

Philippians 2:5–11 was prominent alongside John 1:1–18 in the formation of the ecumenical creeds. Yet this renowned passage—or at least its kenotic vocabulary of self-emptying—has become emblematic of modern challenges to conciliar Christology. The present chapter begins with modest exposition of this key passage, which has garnered mountains of scholarly discussion.[1] Following this exposition comes a classically Reformed response to the political, philosophical, and psychological challenges introduced in the previous chapter. The first aspect of this dogmatic response involves the *status duplex*, the twofold state of humiliation and exaltation, as an active articulation of conciliar two-natures Christology that parallels Philippians 2:5–11. A second aspect involves

---

1. Its significance is suggested by the title of Ralph P. Martin and Brian J. Dodd, eds., *Where Christology Began: Essays on Philippians 2* (Louisville: Westminster John Knox, 1998).

the *communicatio idiomatum*, the sharing of divine and human properties in the person of the incarnate Son, which has implications for Christ's presence, knowledge, and power. After advancing a contemporary version of a classically Reformed view, the chapter concludes with a summary of Servant and Lord as christological names.

I. EXALTED HUMILITY IN PHILIPPIANS 2:5–11

The fundamental purpose of Philippians 2:5–11 is to exalt Christlike humility. The preceding verses, 2:1–4, lead into this theme. Paul appeals to blessings enjoyed by those who are in Christ (v. 1) as the basis of unity (v. 2). To be thus likeminded, the Philippians must reject selfish ambition (v. 3a) and embrace humility (v. 3b), prioritizing the interests of others (v. 4). The ensuing exhortation in 2:5 governs the passage. The imperative *phroneite* ("have the same mindset") calls for an attitude or purpose, not just an ideology. The appropriate mindset is *en Christoi Iesou* ("as Christ Jesus"), which could refer to the Philippians' union with Christ but more likely refers to his example.[2] This mindset is to be *en humin*, which could refer personally ("in you") but may also have a corporate dimension ("among you"). To fulfill the calling of 2:1–4, each Christian must adopt this mindset, but ultimately the community needs to do so together.

Whether composed or quoted by Paul, the "hymn" in 2:6–11 is significant evidence of an early incarnational Christology. If the hymn was composed by Paul, then he expressed a high Christology, entailing divine preexistence, at least by the early 60s AD. In that case the hymn primarily supports the call for humility by explicating Christ's example and its exalted end. If, instead, the hymn was quoted by Paul, then a high Christology circulated even earlier, while the hymn's original purpose could be distinct from its present use. A well-known proposal to the latter effect construes the hymn in soteriological rather than hortatory terms—as celebrating Christ's saving work rather than calling us to imitate him. Although the historical reconstruction remains subject to

---

2. The syntax is elliptical. If the verb to supply in the second half of the verse repeats *phroneō*, then the point is the former: think as you think in Christ, similar to 1:27. So John M. G. Barclay, "Kenosis and the Drama of Salvation in Philippians 2," in *Kenosis: The Self-Emptying of Christ in Scripture and Theology*, ed. Paul T. Nimmo and Keith L. Johnson (Grand Rapids: Eerdmans, 2022), 21n32. On such questions, see the commentaries for more standard views.

speculative debate, at minimum the scholarly trend is to notice the hymn's remarkable fit with the surrounding passage.[3] Christologically, the text begins with a descending arc that parallels John 1:1–18, and it factors prominently in discussions of the early high Christology introduced in chapter 2 of the present book. Among the ensuing historical proposals, the hymn may provide evidence of early (1) devotion to Christ, with which subsequent language of a divine nature correlated.[4] Or the larger passage may provide evidence for early recognition of (2) Jesus's inclusion within the unique divine identity, from which formalized devotion sprang.[5] Sympathetic critics have suggested an alternative focus upon (3) relations that nevertheless support an incarnational reading—the relations of Christ Jesus within the Godhead and with those who are redeemed in him.[6] For dogmatic purposes, these historical proposals offer multiple lines of evidence for a theology of incarnation even if early Christology's exact development remains inaccessible.

The relative pronoun "who" at the start of 2:6 makes its antecedent, "Christ Jesus" (2:5), the agent throughout 2:6–8. First, he did not "consider" something in a particular way (2:6)—juxtaposed with the same verb in 2:3, where Paul calls upon the Philippians to "value" others above themselves. Second, he "made himself nothing" (2:7). Third, he "humbled" himself (2:8)—an echo of the related noun in 2:3.[7] The epitome of this humiliation is indisputable: death on a cross, which was not only gruesome but also criminally shameful. Given the related adverbial participle, "becoming obedient" indicates the manner in which Christ humiliated himself. This crux of the earthly story (2:8) has climactic results (2:9–11). The prior actions (2:6–7), though, require additional probing.

The first action, the mindset taken in 2:6, has a direct object, an object complement, and an attendant circumstance that are ontologically revealing. The direct object is the infinitive phrase "equality with God."[8]

3. On Ernst Käsemann's soteriological focus, hesitation about the category "hymn," and the need to interpret the material as Pauline, see, e.g., Gordon D. Fee, *Paul's Letter to the Philippians*, NICNT (Grand Rapids: Eerdmans, 1995), 192–97.

4. So Hurtado, *Lord Jesus Christ*.

5. So Bauckham, *Jesus and the God of Israel*.

6. So, respectively, Hill, *Paul and the Trinity*; Tilling, *Paul's Divine Christology*.

7. Suggesting that *humiliate* better conveys this action's social context is Joseph H. Hellerman, *Philippians*, EGGNT (Nashville: B&H Academic, 2015), 116.

8. Lacking space to engage them in detail, this exposition does not depend on judgments about the revisionary proposals of Crispin Fletcher-Louis, "'The Being That Is in a Manner Equal with God' (Phil. 2:6c): A Self-Transforming, Incarnational, Divine Ontology," *JTS* 71, no. 2 (2020); Barclay, "Kenosis," 15–16. They highlight the adverbial form of *isa*, with implications

Given who and what God is, such equality cannot properly belong to anyone else. In the Roman context, however, similar language sometimes applied to human rulers. Concerning the related object complement, the anarthrous *harpagmon* ("used to his own advantage"), the crucial question is whether it indicates prior possession (*res rapta* in Latin, "holding onto something already obtained") or not (*res rapienda*, "taking something to oneself"). Most contemporary scholarship accepts the possibility or even the propriety of the former: Christ did not view equality with God, which was already (and thus eternally) his, as something to hold onto.[9] Hence the attendant circumstance with which the verse begins, "being in very nature God," communicates his divine identity. But the translation of *morphē* as "nature" is disputed. The various possibilities reflect not only lexical evidence but also scholars' assumptions about the required threshold for ontological implications.[10] The term certainly focuses upon rank and its social perception. Given the immediate context, however, this "form" reveals an essential reality—rather than something merely external, let alone misleading. The parallel use in verse 7 ("the very nature [form] of a servant") clearly conveys genuine, not docetic, humanity.

The ensuing question concerns how "being in very nature God" relates to Christ's mindset. Traditionally the relationship has been interpreted concessively (*although* he was God), contrasting his action with our expectations about divine glory. Recently, however, some have interpreted the relationship causally (*since* he was God), construing his action as our proper expectation about God's self-giving love.[11] Yet the traditional, concessive interpretation still commends itself. The "but" at the start of 2:7 underscores a contrast: together the unexpected emptying (2:7) and the humiliating descent (completed in 2:8) go beyond

for *harpagmon*. But a long history of alternative interpretation raises questions about whether the grammar has the requisite implications they advocate; in any case they do not contradict an incarnational interpretation.

9. R. W. Hoover's influential work to this effect is extensively defended in Wright, *Climax of the Covenant*, 62–90. For positive interpretation of *harpagmos* besides Hoover, see Schröter, "Präexistenter Sohn," 121. For other recent discussion, see Lidija Novakovic, *Philippians: A Handbook on the Greek Text* (Waco, TX: Baylor University Press, 2020), 49–50.

10. Dennis W. Jowers, "The Meaning of μορφῇ in Philippians 2:6–7," *JETS* 49, no. 4 (December 2006): 739–66.

11. See, e.g., discussion of "although" also meaning "because" in Michael J. Gorman, *Inhabiting the Cruciform God: Kenosis, Justification, and Theosis in Paul's Narrative Soteriology* (Grand Rapids: Eerdmans, 2009), 16–29. For anticipation of this trend see, e.g., Barth, *CD* IV/1:133, 193. As theologically illuminating as these discussions are, their claims may not hold semantically.

grammatical juxtaposition; they confound prior theological expectations. A glorious right to universal allegiance is associated with God (2:9–11). Thus, here Paul emphasizes counterintuitive imitation of Christ, who refused the dictum that rank has its privileges.

The second action, the self-emptying of 2:7, is glossed by "taking the form of a servant," which indicates the manner or means of the *kenōsis*. The verb operates metaphorically, without specifying of what he emptied himself. The pronoun *heauton* in "made himself nothing" is no more ontological than *morphē*, and probably less so: focus rests on the identity rather than the essence of Christ Jesus, especially given the surrounding emphasis upon status. The glosses "being made in human likeness" and "being found in appearance as a man" (vv. 7–8) pile up words focused on visibility. The conciliar tradition correctly highlights that this *kenōsis* involves incarnational addition—taking up human slavery that hides divine glory—rather than ontological subtraction. Apparent passivity ensues: having been found in human likeness. Usually, these aorist participles would specify time antecedent to the main verb; here it is possible that self-emptying speaks of the incarnation generally, while "taking," "being made," and "being found" focus antecedently on its beginning. The initiative taken by Christ consisted in becoming subject to a lowly status and merely human perception.

The third action, the humiliation of 2:8, raises the question of whether Paul is already alluding to the Servant Songs of Isaiah, even prior to their appearance in 2:9–11. On one hand, Isaiah in the LXX contains a different word for servant (*pais*) than 2:7 (*doulos*), which connotes a slave. Emphasis in Philippians rests on the lowly, obedient state that Christ assumed. Hence any Isaianic echo lacks the verbal correspondence that would build exegetical confidence. On the other hand, thematic resonances with Isaiah 52:13–53:12 are several: the servant will be *exalted* (52:13); many were appalled at his disfigured *appearance* (52:14); kings' *mouths* were silenced because of him (52:15); yet he had been held in low *esteem* (53:2–3); and then it was the Lord's will for him to *suffer* vicariously (53:4–12). The Isaiah pericope also mentions the Servant's *understanding* at its beginning (52:13) and end (53:11), resonating with Paul's celebration of Christ's mindset. At minimum, a common story arc characterizes both passages: humiliating descent unto death and victorious ascent unto life. This arc's transition at Philippians 2:9, "therefore," echoes a similar transition at Isaiah 53:12.[12] Accordingly, the humiliation of obedience unto crucifixion in Philippians 2:8 may already identify Christ with the Isaianic Servant.

The ensuing exaltation in Philippians 2:9–11 alludes to Isaiah 45:23–25, including Jesus within the identity of Yhwh. The "name above every name" that God gives (Phil 2:9) is uttered by the *I* and *me* of Isaiah 45, "the Lord" apart from whom there is no God and Savior (Isa 45:21) and in whom—alone—there is deliverance (Isa 45:24–25). The promised bowing of every knee and confessing of every tongue before Yhwh will happen "at the name of Jesus" (Phil 2:10). This identification does not make Jesus the name above every name, which is Lord (*Kyrios*), but his exaltation (2:11) involves a new event beyond simply returning to preexistent glory.[13] As its LXX equivalent, *Kyrios* strengthens the identification with Yhwh, and this eschatological confession redounds to the glory of God the Father (consistent with texts like 1 Cor 15:24–28). Since Isaiah anticipates Yhwh's climactic *revelation* through the Servant's eschatological redemption of Israel, the confession of Jesus as Lord is not an utter novum. There is no fundamental change in Yhwh, which would be unthinkable for one of Scripture's most monotheistic passages. There is, however, a new element in this fulfillment: the exaltation of the God-*man*, incorporating Jesus's name into the world's acknowledgment of God's glory. The Servant has received his promised "portion among the great" (Isa 53:12) in an unanticipated form. Consequently, the passage's *ethical purpose* has a *soteriological basis*: we imitate Christ's mindset not because our virtue of humility will have its parallel reward but because we will participate in his eschatological glorification. Our obedience is an outworking of God's present empowerment and our eschatological salvation (Phil 2:12–13).[14]

Objections to an incarnational reading of Philippians 2:5–11 are not compelling. First, *morphē* language cannot primarily refer to the

---

12. Interestingly, the Hebrew verb for "poured out" (his life unto death) in Isaiah 53:12 is translated elsewhere with the Greek *kenoō*, as noted by Barclay, "Kenosis," 16n23.

13. On Yhwh/*Kyrios* texts' application to Jesus, see David B. Capes, *The Divine Christ: Paul, the Lord Jesus, and the Scriptures of Israel*, ASBT (Grand Rapids: Baker Academic, 2018).

14. Construing the hymn as soteriological and the passage as either ethical or soteriological depending on the hymn's composition speculatively creates a false dichotomy. Theological agendas sometimes tempt scholars to minimize the ethical thrust. Apart from the hymn per se, for a convincing case that the passage has a strong soteriological element, see Barclay, "Kenosis." Whether or not Philippians 2 is "first and foremost about soteriology" (p. 8), Barclay is right that Philippians 2:9–11 does not simply reveal who the Christ of 2:6–8 really was but results from what he accomplished, and such a result is incommensurable with a merely parallel, earthly reward for our humility (p. 11).

image of God, as if an implicit Adam Christology precludes apparent references to Christ's divine preexistence.[15] Despite several words for appearances, *eikōn*—the LXX word for "image" in Genesis 1:26–27—is absent, whereas Colossians 1:15 uses exactly that term to evoke creation. Although *en homoiōmati* in Philippians 2:7 matches the LXX term for "likeness" in Genesis 1:26, here Christ is in *human*, not divine, likeness. Referring to Adamic humanity rather than preexistent divinity would weaken Paul's call for humility: rather than Christ emptying himself of rightful privilege by prioritizing others, the Adamic alternative would have him not grasping what he never possessed.[16] Second, conceptual resonances with John 1:1–18 are strong even without verbal parallels. With *Theos* language that is both connected to and distinct from Christ, the passages convey similar judgments about his condescension, its fulfillment of Isaiah, and its protagonist's identity.[17] Correspondingly, to mediate between verbal differences and similar judgments, both overlapping and distinct concepts are needed: It is appropriate to speak of incarnational Christology and divine identity in both passages while acknowledging their different motifs.

Christ Jesus is the named subject of the action, but this detail should not be overinterpreted in debates about a Logos *asarkos*. *Christos* is the dominant identifier throughout Philippians 1 and the beginning of Philippians 2. To some degree Philippians 2:5 echoes the "in Christ" focus of the preceding material. This phrasing offers his human example for imitation, whereas speaking of the eternal Son would have required a considerable shift, made the call for imitation more indirect, and complicated the reference to Jesus in 2:10. Even so, his identity as Son

---

15. For an appeal to Adam Christology as an alternative to incarnational Christology, see James D. G. Dunn, *Christology in the Making: A New Testament Inquiry into the Origins of the Doctrine of the Incarnation*, 2nd ed. (Grand Rapids: Eerdmans, 1996), 114–17. Few contemporary exegetes follow Dunn, although some allow for Adam Christology secondarily. See the refutation of Dunn (within a wider treatment of Christ's divine preexistence) in Fee, *Pauline Christology*, 390–93.

16. A point made, e.g., in Douglas McCready, *He Came Down from Heaven: The Preexistence of Christ and the Christian Faith* (Downers Grove, IL: InterVarsity Press, 2005), 79–80.

17. The concepts/judgments distinction emerges in the critique of Dunn's approach by David S. Yeago, "The New Testament and the Nicene Dogma: A Contribution to the Recovery of Theological Exegesis," *ProEccl* 3 (1994): 152–64. Detailing the paucity of engagement with Yeago's essay in exegetical commentaries, while surveying responses to Dunn, is Daniel J. Treier, "Christology and Commentaries: Examining and Enhancing Theological Exegesis," in *On the Writing of New Testament Commentaries: Festschrift for Grant R. Osborne on the Occasion of His Seventieth Birthday*, ed. Stanley E. Porter and Eckhard J. Schnabel (Leiden: Brill, 2012), 299–316. For a constructive critique of Yeago, which underscores the new aspect of the exaltation in Philippians 2:9–11, see Darren Sarisky, "Judgments in Scripture and the Creed: Reflections on Identity and Difference," *ModTheo* 37, no. 3 (July 2021): 703–20.

is not altogether absent, being implied by the climactic reference to the glory of God the Father in 2:11 (echoing the introduction in 1:2). Given these factors that make Christ Jesus the natural subject, there is no need to infer any mysterious ontological claim like preexistent humanity or denial of a Logos *asarkos*. To use conciliar language, the God-man is "one and the same" with the eternal Son; Paul can loosely refer to his human name and earthly vocation without projecting them metaphysically backward into eternity. We now bow at the name of Jesus and confess him as Lord when we associate with Christ both the *kenōsis* and the glory in Philippians 2:5–11.

II. THE *STATUS DUPLEX*

Philippians 2 is a *locus classicus* for the *status duplex* of Jesus Christ, his twofold state of humiliation and exaltation. In traditional form, the states are sequential, matching Philippians 2:6–8 and 9–11: first humiliation, then exaltation. Strictly speaking, their subject is the incarnate Logos, not simply the divine Son or the human nature. *Kenōsis* is distinct from humiliation: *kenōsis* (or *exinanitio*) involves the eternal Son's assumption of human nature and thus "denotes the slave-form of Christ's whole life," whereas humiliation encompasses *kenōsis* but adds the incarnate Son's obedience unto death.[18] Hence the two states narratively coincide with the two natures: for our redemption the eternal Son assumed a human nature and, while incarnate on earth, veiled his divine glory by rendering obedience and enduring crucifixion.[19] Subsequently, he was exalted in his resurrection, ascension, and heavenly session. This exaltation went beyond a return to prior glory; now the God-man has made the divine glory more public and incorporates humanity in the divine reign. Consequently, in the

---

18. Heinrich Heppe, *Reformed Dogmatics*, ed. Ernst Bizer, trans. G. T. Thomson (repr., Eugene, OR: Wipf & Stock, 2007), 488–89. In fact, "the incarnation as such, without any further qualification, always was and remains an act of condescending goodness but not, strictly speaking, a step in the state of humiliation. It became this as a result of the fact that it was an *incarnation*, the assumption of a weak human nature"; so Herman Bavinck, *Sin and Salvation in Christ*, ed. John Bolt, trans. John Vriend, vol. 3 of *Reformed Dogmatics* (Grand Rapids: Baker Academic, 2006), 310. The *imago Dei* indicates that it would not be humiliating (even if it is profoundly loving) for God to assume created humanity as such.

19. This veiling did not preclude moments of glory, whether reserved for the disciples or revealed to the multitudes, as underscored in Berkouwer, *Person of Christ*, 346–51. Dangers of overemphasizing Christ's "incognito" form include denying biblical miracles or denigrating the adequacy of divine revelation and diminishing human accountability for unbelief.

sequential account humiliation focuses on the priestly office whereas exaltation focuses on the kingly office.

Barth's actualistic Christology, however, treats the two states dialectically rather than sequentially, speaking of "two sides or directions or forms of that which took place in Jesus Christ for the reconciliation of man with God."[20] The one side identifies Jesus Christ as "the Lord who became servant," involving "the obedience of the Son of God"; the other speaks of "the servant who became Lord" and "the exaltation of the Son of Man." The associated patterns of dialectical inversion throughout *Church Dogmatics* IV are breathtaking: an aspect associated with humanity (like obedience) is predicated of the incarnate Son as divinely named, then the reverse, and finally these realities are integrated in one person. Though far from abandoning the hypostatic union, Barth contrasts "describing a being in the particular form of a state" with "the twofold action of Jesus Christ, the actuality of His work: His one work, which cannot be divided into different stages or periods of His existence, but which fills out and constitutes His existence in this twofold form."[21]

This revisionary proposal offers supplemental insight: a strictly sequential view does not communicate the ironies of divine self-revelation that are conveyed in John's Gospel and elsewhere. The Son was lifted up and glorified on the cross (e.g., John 12:23–36)—the epitome of his humiliation in Philippians 2:6–8. Thus, more generally, his human flesh unveiled the extent of God's love even as it hid aspects of divine glory. "Where and when is He not both humiliated and exalted, already exalted in His humiliation, and humiliated in His exaltation?"[22] The traditional "exaltation-after-humiliation" model can foster a misleading separation of the (priestly) crucifixion from Christ's (prophetic) proclamation and (royal) inauguration of God's kingdom. Exaltation happened *in* humiliation as well.[23]

Yet the critique of the sequential tradition overreaches. Passages like Philippians 2:5–11 apply *humiliation* vocabulary to a narrative sequence. As we saw in chapter 3, parallel concepts like suffering and glory have a fulfillment sequence. Whereas Barth famously said that historical critics

---

20. Barth, *CD IV/1*, 133.
21. Barth, *CD IV/1*, 133.
22. Barth, *CD IV/1*, 133.
23. See Jeremy R. Treat, *The Crucified King: Atonement and Kingdom in Biblical and Systematic Theology* (Grand Rapids: Zondervan, 2014), 155–65.

were not critical enough,[24] here dialectical theologians are not dialectical enough. It is strange but true that a solely actualistic view removes the action from the two states while perhaps focusing too separately on the divine and human natures. The dialectical "humiliation of God" and "exaltation of man"[25] load all of salvation history's action onto the incarnation or even the divine election behind it. However debatable its contours, Barth's "thought displays a general tendency to absorb every 'before' and 'after' into an eternal decision in which God not only elects Christ together with all of humanity but in this act determines his own being."[26] The humiliation of Jesus Christ is not simply the humiliation of God but primarily the obedience and vicarious death of the God-man. Indeed, these actions happen *in* or *by virtue of* his human nature, even if they belong to the unique Son of God. Accordingly, the exaltation goes beyond the revelation of, and return to, prior divine glory. In passages like Philippians 2:9–11, the new exaltation of the Son's humanity happens *through* (thus *after*, not just *in*) humiliation.[27]

Beyond having both sequential and dialectical aspects, the two-fold state raises the question of how to associate humility with God. Classically, as St. Augustine (354–430) illustrates, affirmations of divine humility concerned God *pro nobis* ("for us") rather than *in se* ("in himself"). Although not merely predicated of the Son, humility was not clearly predicated of the immanent Trinity. By contrast, Barth again champions the bold modern alternative, in which "God is humble and . . . this humility consists of eternal, inter-trinitarian obedience."[28] In the crucial move, "the structure of the economic works mirrors the immanent being of God without qualification outside the event of revelation itself."[29] The ensuing challenge involves avoiding radical voluntarism or three wills in God. Hence others commend an account of divine humility as "God's presence in strength for the sake of his creation" rather than "mere lowliness" or intradivine obedience.[30] Similarly,

24. Karl Barth, "The Preface to the Second Edition," in *The Epistle to the Romans*, trans. Edwyn C. Hoskyns (Oxford: Oxford University Press, 1968), 8.

25. Barth, *CD IV/1*, 134.

26. Michael Horton, *Justification*, vol. 2, NSD (Grand Rapids: Zondervan, 2018), 28.

27. Again, see Treat, *Crucified King*, 155–65.

28. Quoting from a larger account involving these representative figures: Matthew A. Wilcoxen, *Divine Humility: God's Morally Perfect Being* (Waco, TX: Baylor University Press, 2019), 182. "Barth is not saying that humility is a divine perfection, equally descriptive of Father and Son and Spirit. Rather, humility describes the Son's eternal relation to the Father"; so Price, "Barth on the Incarnation," 140.

29. Wilcoxen, *Divine Humility*, 183.

30. Katherine Sonderegger's account, as summarized in Wilcoxen, *Divine Humility*, 184.

other studies of humility as a virtue have critiqued its equation with lowliness, incorporating empowerment.[31]

It is questionable, though, whether we should speak of such humility—reinterpreted as magnanimity—as an immanent divine perfection. As an intra-Trinitarian perfection, divine love certainly incorporates humility, the willingness to serve freely without return and without immediate regard for status, within its economic expression. Insofar as humility retains associations with condescension, though, such magnanimity assumes creaturely dependence or redemptive need, thus being inappropriate to characterize immanent divine perfection per se. Not every distinction between God *pro nobis* and God *in se* generates inappropriate tension over a hidden God. Speaking immanently of divine humility might still be more confusing than illuminating, making it harder to echo the rhetorical emphases of Philippians 2:5–11. There humility (or, more pointedly, humiliation) articulates both the Son's kenotic self-giving in the incarnation and its extension in his human obedience unto death—with these actions, however, expressing divine love in a manner that God's immanent glory renders unexpected.[32]

III. THE *COMMUNICATIO IDIOMATUM*

The church articulates the mystery of the hypostatic union in terms of the *communicatio idiomatum* or "communication of attributes": the personal sharing of the properties of the divine and human natures so that they may be predicated of the single subject Jesus Christ.[33] As a crucial example, consider the reference in Acts 20:28 to "the church of

---

31. E.g., Stephen T. Pardue, *The Mind of Christ: Humility and the Intellect in Early Christian Theology*, SST (London: T&T Clark, 2013).

32. So, although Grant Macaskill highlights the biblical association of humility vocabulary with God in terms of positional lowering, it labels God's "willingness to serve those who have no capacity to return his gift"—quoting p. 248 from the overview of his larger book in "Christian Scriptures and the Formation of Intellectual Humility," *Journal of Psychology and Theology* 46, no. 4 (2018): 243–52. This "willingness" is an economic expression of the glory of divine love.

33. Presumably because of differing Lutheran and Calvinist interpretations, many theological dictionaries and christological texts lack a formal definition, offering only a parenthetical gloss or a historical sketch of disputed components. *Exchange* appears in the standard gloss of John Behr, *The Nicene Faith, Part 2: One of the Holy Trinity*, vol. 2 of *Formation of Christian Theology* (Crestwood, NY: St. Vladimir's Seminary, 2004). But that term could imply passing properties between the natures, so *personal sharing* is more amenable to a classically Reformed approach. Initially, the *communicatio* involved "somewhat shocking turns of phrase . . . predicating human experiences directly of God the Word and divine qualities directly of the man Jesus"—with its greatest scandal concerning Christ's passion. So Brian E. Daley, SJ, "Antioch and Alexandria: Christology as Reflection on God's Presence in History," in *The Oxford Handbook of Christology*, 132.

God, which he bought with his own blood." Redemption is attributed to God acting in Christ, who could only shed blood by virtue of his humanity, not his deity.[34]

Protestant theology generated distinct debates over this venerable concept. In the Reformation era, Lutherans and Calvinists debated Christ's presence in the Eucharist and, correspondingly, the so-called *extra Calvinisticum*: the Calvinist affirmation that the incarnate Lord retained divine omnipresence beyond (*extra*) the confines of his flesh rather than (as Lutherans held) sharing ubiquity with his human nature. Some early modern Lutheran, then Anglican, and eventually Reformed theologians began to propose kenotic Christologies, which generated debates focused on Christ's knowledge. More recently, so-called Spirit Christologies crystallized the preceding debates with respect to Christ's power. Since the conceptual issues and cultural pressures are interrelated, the following sections will address these three christological debates in distinct turns. A cumulative account of the *communicatio* will gradually emerge: (1) affirming the incarnate Son's presence *extra carnem*, beyond his flesh; (2) accounting for *kenōsis*, including Jesus's pilgrim faith, without adopting a kenotic emptying of his divine knowledge; and (3) articulating Christ's theandric agency as both omnipotent God and Spirit-empowered man.

A. Christ's Presence: Affirming the Extra Carnem

The *extra Calvinisticum* is the derogatory Lutheran name for the Reformed *extra carnem* doctrine that "the eternal Son of God, during his incarnate life on earth, was not enclosed by or limited to the physical body of Jesus Christ but continued to uphold the universe by virtue of maintaining a form of presence beyond or outside Jesus' physical body."[35] Although pre-Reformation circumstances may not have provoked this exact formulation, affirmation of the Son's ongoing omnipresence beyond Christ's flesh characterized the classic tradition—so much so that this *extra carnem* has been called the *extra catholicum*.[36] Its catholic embrace coincides with speaking, from a temporal perspective, of a prior

---

34. For additional examples like eternal existence and birth or omnipotence and weariness, see Stephen J. Wellum, *God the Son Incarnate: The Doctrine of Christ*, FET (Wheaton, IL: Crossway, 2016), 438.

35. James R. Gordon, *The Holy One in Our Midst: An Essay on the Flesh of Christ*, ES (Minneapolis: Fortress, 2016), 1.

36. See E. David Willis, *Calvin's Catholic Christology: The Function of the So-Called Extra Calvinisticum in Calvin's Theology* (Leiden: Brill, 1966).

Logos *asarkos*. John's temple Christology offers an analogy: as YHWH dwelt in the tabernacle and temple "while remaining free in sovereign immensity, so also did the eternal Word assume flesh—concrete spatial and material existence—while remaining unhindered in his immense presence."[37]

Lutheran worries about the Calvinist *extra* are fundamentally two. First, the *extra* precludes a particular account of Christ's real presence in the Lord's Supper. Those intricacies await a future chapter. Second, the *extra* emphasizes the distinction between the incarnate Son's two natures, in a fashion perceived as risking Nestorianism. The Lutheran theology of the cross so keenly identifies the crucified Jesus with the exalted Lord that Reformed vigilance about the risen Christ's bodily location seems to separate, not just distinguish, his divine and human natures. If some earlier Lutherans were willing to risk a monophysite, premature intrusion of the earthly Jesus's humanity into heaven—to maintain its assumed union with the omnipresent Word—eventually some modern Lutherans birthed kenotic Christology by reversing the direction. Instead of the divine nature communicating exalted properties such as ubiquity to the human nature, somehow the human nature communicated its limited properties to the divine.

Efforts to understand divine presence grapple with God's spiritual transcendence of the spatial location of physical particles. Hence, like all analogies, christological appeals to the temple are inexact: the person, not just the body, of Jesus Christ is the new temple, and his human nature does not have the independent existence that characterized Israel's tabernacle and temple.[38] Speaking merely of the Son's indwelling a human body would be Nestorian. The Son's omnipresence involves both "immensity" as an immanent perfection of the divine being and "ubiquity" as its economic expression. Immensity involves "the free, gratuitous, non-necessary character of God's relation to space."[39] Ubiquity involves "God's entire and constant presence in and to all things, the ceaseless and sovereign lordship in which the Most High, who is without measure or limit, inclines to be present to his creation and so holds and renews it in life."[40] God's omnipresence is an essential perfection that involves an economic inclination for fellowship. The Son's incarnation

---

37. Gordon, *Holy One in Our Midst*, 135.
38. Gordon, *Holy One in Our Midst*, 147–48.
39. Webster, "The Immensity and Ubiquity of God," in *Confessing God*, 94.
40. Webster, "Immensity and Ubiquity of God," 99.

enacts that inclination in a singular way yet without jeopardy to the essential property.

Consequently, although philosophical analysis may favor models involving action at a distance rather than occupancy in space,[41] Christian theology must articulate the relational nearness that *presence* implies. The relevant Scriptures, like "Where can I flee from your presence?" (Ps 139:7), emphasize that God establishes and maintains intimate forms of relational engagement, especially with human beings. Surely the marvel of the incarnation has God uniquely dwelling among us in a way that incorporates both newfound nearness and enduring sovereignty. In terms of occupancy, the incarnate Logos is wholly, yet not entirely, present at every spatial point—both inside and outside Christ's physically located humanity—without any Nestorian bifurcation of his two natures.[42] The *extra carnem* neither divides Christ within himself nor distances him from us but only delineates the constant integrity of the Creator's being vis-à-vis creatures.

B. *Christ's Knowledge: Accounting for* Kenōsis

The historical origins of kenotic Christologies reflect preoccupation with Christ's knowledge, where they place the strongest conceptual pressure upon traditional views. In the early modern environment that incubated them, the initial proposals attempted to rescue—not simply reject—conciliar Christology. Lutherans like Gottfried Thomasius (1802–1875) worried about incompatibility between the single-subject Christology prized by their tradition and the emerging emphasis on Jesus's self-consciousness. Thomasius proposed distinguishing between immanent and relative divine attributes. The former—notably divine love—the incarnate Son retained as essential to being God. Of the latter—notably the *omni-* attributes—Christ could empty himself without losing his divine identity because (on this account) they define God in juxtaposition with creatures: as unlimited in presence, knowledge, power, and so forth. This proposed distinction regarding divine attributes has won few if any adherents, but even prominent critics like I. A. Dorner

---

41. James M. Arcadi, *An Incarnational Model of the Eucharist*, CIT (Cambridge: Cambridge University Press, 2018), 86.

42. In terms of the analytic distinction between entension and pertension, the divine Son "remains entended, wholly existent at every place, while Christ's physical body is spatially circumscribed and pertends the area in which it exists"; so Gordon, *Holy One in Our Midst*, 196. The classic *totus* versus *totum* distinction is reflected in the *wholly* versus *entirely* language.

(1809–1884) shared the broader commitment to account for the incarnate Christ's developing self-consciousness.[43] Subsequent British kenoticists may not have been as preoccupied with Jesus's psychological development, whether they reflected Anglican reveling in the incarnation's mysterious beauty and earthiness, pietistic wonder at the paradoxes of Christ's passion, or perhaps both.[44] Historical particularities, however, seemed to be incompatible with the Son's divine perfection. Omnipresence, omniscience, and omnipotence could all be viewed in terms of exhaustive powers whose possession was incompatible with full humanity. As kenotic approaches matured, they migrated from proposing flatly that the Son (ontologically) emptied himself of divine attributes to suggesting more ambiguously that he was (functionally) restricted in the awareness or use of such powers. Hence, again, Christ's knowledge became the crux of the issue—once awareness of divine perfection seemed incompatible with the inherent development of a human *psyche*.

Today modified kenotic Christologies may offer philosophically viable accounts of the incarnation, but they still pose theological problems.[45] Suppose, for the sake of argument, that a kenotic account can maintain the earthly Jesus's full deity and thus remain orthodox—in the sense of being "biblical" anyway—despite departing from conciliar metaphysics. Nevertheless, four problems would linger. First, kenotic accounts have

43. Space limitations prevent detailed historical discussion. Key texts appear in Claude Welch, ed., *God and Incarnation in Mid-Nineteenth Century German Theology: Thomasius, Dorner, Biedermann*, trans. Claude Welch, A Library of Protestant Thought (New York: Oxford University Press, 1965). As noted in the general introduction on p. 8, this concentration on Christ's consciousness "more generally reflect[ed] the notion of personality as centering in self-consciousness, and in turn the question of the relation of modern concepts of personality to the traditional language of *persona* and *substantia* in both Christological and trinitarian doctrine."

44. Already in 1738 the hymn "And Can It Be?" from Charles Wesley (1707–88) marveled that Christ "emptied himself of all but love." Later figures like P. T. Forsyth (1848–1921) were influenced by both Anglicans like Charles Gore (1853–1932) and crucicentric pietism.

45. Though quite diverse, a key collection representing "modified" kenoticism is C. Stephen Evans, ed., *Exploring Kenotic Christology: The Self-Emptying of God* (Oxford: Oxford University Press, 2006). It displays the theological problems mentioned above in various chapters. Admittedly, defining social Trinitarianism is difficult, and there are reasons to worry when a traditionalist backlash generates the denial of intra-Trinitarian love—on which see chap. 5 in Thomas H. McCall, *Analytic Christology and the Theological Interpretation of the New Testament*, OSAT (Oxford: Oxford University Press, 2021). Yet some accounts are so strongly social that they warrant traditionalist concerns over tritheism, while rejection of inseparable operations is apparently essential for kenoticism. This issue was recognized by early critics; see, e.g., I. A. Dorner, "System of Christian Doctrine Part II: Special Doctrines: The Doctrine of Christ," in *God and Incarnation in Mid-Nineteenth Century Theology*, 237. Social Trinitarianism was already referenced at least as early as chap. 6 in D. M. Baillie, *God Was in Christ: An Essay on Incarnation and Atonement* (New York: Scribner's, 1948). On the neglected significance of Constantinople III (680–81), with its conciliar affirmation of numerically one divine essence, inseparable operations, and so forth, see Scott M. Williams, "Discovery of the Sixth Ecumenical Council's Trinitarian Theology: Historical, Ecclesial, and Theological Implications," *Journal of Analytic Theology* 10 (2022): 332–62.

not satisfactorily addressed the distinction between Christ's earthly and glorified humanity. Does the ascended Jesus remain limited, with glorification merely rewarding human obedience? Or was the incarnate Son's limitation temporary, necessary on earth for reasons that no longer obtain in heaven? The former approach insists on *kenōsis* at the cost of permanently restricting the Son's divine perfection; the latter approach acknowledges his glorified perfection at the risk of special pleading about the earthly necessity of *kenōsis*. Second, kenotic accounts abandon traditional versions of divine perfections. God's essential immutability changes to loving moral constancy, and perfections like omnipotence gain an exception clause that risks special pleading ("unless God chooses to become kenotically incarnate").[46] Third, kenotic accounts, at least until recently, have reflected masculine assumptions about power, vulnerability, and condescension.[47] Fourth, a kenotic account requires strongly social Trinitarianism. Minimally, the redefinition of inseparable Trinitarian operations *ad extra* complicates Christian monotheism; maximally, a trajectory heads toward kenotic panentheism.

Despite these problems, kenoticism has remained attractive due to theological intuitions, historical assumptions, and biblical passages that need to be addressed.[48] The theological intuitions cluster around modernity's newfound interest in human self-consciousness: Western Protestants frequently struggle to imagine how Christ could be fully human while knowing himself to be God, or fully divine while undergoing ego development, or a unified person while possessing both divine and human self-understanding. The historical assumptions cluster around modernity's quests for the earthly Jesus in his first-century context: the many contributions of such critical scholarship are accompanied by assumptions about how Jesus could have understood himself and his mission. The next chapter will reengage YHWH's eschatological return to Israel, the importance of which "early high Christology" has recently recovered, regarding its impact on Christ's self-understanding. With respect to these theological intuitions and historical assumptions, however, a crucial point already surfaced in a previous chapter: the

---

46. Granted, some divine attributes like impassibility are quite controversial apart from the incarnation, so this problem will not concern everyone equally.

47. As demonstrated by Coakley, "*Kenōsis* and Subversion."

48. For another example of its attraction to evangelicals, see the appreciative overview in John G. Stackhouse Jr., "Jesus Christ," in *The Oxford Handbook of Evangelical Theology*, ed. Gerald R. McDermott (New York: Oxford University Press, 2010), 146–58.

fulfillment of hopes informed by Isaiah 7:14, 9:6–7, and beyond made it possible for the human Jesus, aware of his virginal conception, to understand himself as included within the identity and eschatological revelation of YHWH.

As for specific biblical passages like Mark 13:30–32, their *prima facie* kenoticist readings are unnecessary but should give way to *partitive exegesis*: distinguishing "between what Scripture says of Christ as divine and what it says of him as human."[49] In his human nature, Christ was ignorant, and sometimes traditional worthies strained biblical exegesis to say otherwise. For instance, they misinterpreted Mark's statement of the Son's ignorance as merely indicating that he would not reveal knowledge to others.[50] Yet it would be just as unconvincing to speak flatly of the Son's kenotic ignorance. The surrounding verses, not to mention the rest of Mark's Gospel, complicate the picture. In verse 30 Jesus reflects definitive knowledge related to the eschatological future, and in verse 31 he claims divine authority for his words. His statement in verse 32 serves the exhortation to "Watch!" by conveying knowledge of what the Son of Man joins fellow Israelites in not knowing. There is no impropriety in acknowledging his human ignorance here since "if Christ, as man, did not know the last day, that does not any more derogate from his Divine nature than to have been mortal," which was also necessary for him in discharging his office as Mediator.[51] Of course, in response to kenoticist arguments regarding Chalcedon's lurking Nestorianism, it is true that *knowing* applies to the person and not just one nature or the other.[52] The same is true more broadly of the *choosing* and *acting* associated with two wills. Natures must not be reified and treated as persons. However, nature and person relate closely because natures characterize the essential traits of entities, in this case persons. Speaking of a human nature identifies a characteristic principle of personal agency. For the incarnation, the point is neither that *natures as such* are agents nor that two persons are involved; instead, the one person uniquely enacts two

49. Behr, *Nicene Faith*, vol. 2, part 2, 476. For an introduction to partitive exegesis in the context of Athanasius, see John Behr, *The Nicene Faith*, part 1, *True God of True God*, vol. 2 of *Formation of Christian Theology* (Crestwood, NY: St. Vladimir's Seminary, 2004), 208–15.

50. For sample excerpts, see Thomas C. Oden and Christopher A. Hall, eds., *Mark*, ACCSNT 2 (Downers Grove, IL: InterVarsity Press, 1998), 190–95. For a short survey, see William C. Placher, *Mark*, Belief (Louisville: Westminster John Knox, 2010), 192–94.

51. John Calvin, *Commentary on a Harmony of the Evangelists, Matthew, Mark, and Luke*, vol. 3, trans. William Pringle, Calvin's Commentaries 17 (repr., Grand Rapids: Baker, 1993), 154.

52. E.g., this critique is expressed against Gregory Nazianzus's partitive interpretation by Placher, *Mark*, 193.

patterns of operation. Some biblical texts attribute acts to Jesus Christ that have one or the other nature as a principle of agency; as with the crucifixion in the earlier example of Acts 20:28, so too the ignorance in Mark 13:30–32.

Correspondingly, the incarnate Christ's human development, including the exercise of pilgrim faith, can be properly acknowledged apart from kenoticism. Protestants should cautiously break with the classic view that Jesus possessed the beatific vision throughout his earthly life. Admittedly, to quote a contemporary Thomistic account, "in the very structure of personal being, ontology is more fundamental than consciousness."[53] According to the ensuing argument, though, Jesus's human nature required immediate knowledge of God and thus of his own deity for "safeguarding the unity of his personal agency in and through the duality of his two wills"—via evidential certitude regarding the divine will alongside a restriction of natural vulnerability regarding its mode of exercise. In this way, Christ's obedience and prayer would have been human manifestations of his divine identity, of his filial relationship with the Father in the Spirit.[54] Against this argument, however, human obedience springs from faith, which is not sight.[55] To the claim that Jesus's impeccability would require "unimpeded perception" of God,[56] we can partially concede that his faith's knowledge of divine grace and his moral responsibilities must have been firm. Even so, faith's view of the divine plan is not transparent and comprehensive. When the present book has suggested how, as an interpreter of Isaiah, Jesus could have grown to understand his inclusion within the identity of YHWH, such growth in wisdom (Luke 2:40–52) manifests pilgrim faith; Christ was a wayfarer in more than bodily stature. Indeed, this active obedience is a gift of the gospel, whereby humanity is perfected in a historical rather than punctiliar fashion. Immediate possession of the beatific vision throughout his earthly incarnation would nullify the reward involved in

53. Thomas Joseph White, OP, *The Incarnate Lord: A Thomistic Study in Christology* (Washington, DC: Catholic University of America Press, 2015), 237. White's chap. 5 offers an important defense of the beatific vision view.

54. White, *Incarnate Lord*, 238–39. On p. 246, White distinguishes between the beatific vision as filial in mode (deemed essential for personal unity in Christ's activity, contra Nestorianism) and fully human in nature (given Christ's created intellect and will, contra monophysitism). The language of *evidential certitude* appears throughout. On natural vulnerability, see pp. 270–73. For clarification of the Spirit's role in Thomas's account, see Dominic Legge, OP, *The Trinitarian Christology of St Thomas Aquinas* (Oxford: Oxford University Press, 2017), 173–82.

55. See especially chap. 2, which briefly discusses relevant biblical texts, in Allen, *Christ's Faith*.

56. McFarland, *Word Made Flesh*, 134.

Christ's exaltation, rendering moot the necessity of bodily resurrection and glorifying transformation.[57] The Holy Spirit empowered Jesus and protected him from sin while testifying inwardly to his Father's filial love, but the earthly Christ did not immediately enjoy the eschatological vindication and fullness of resurrected glory that characterize the beatific vision. He grew in the human depth of his filial communion with the Father, and he grappled faithfully with the drama of his vocation.[58]

Once both kenotic and beatific vision accounts are excluded, the ensuing decisions concern "two minds" and *krypsis*. In assuming a human nature, the Son added a noetic and volitional structure to the eternal cognitive and causal powers that he possessed in union with God the Father and the Spirit. Put nonmetaphysically, along with his enacted choices the incarnate Logos's thinking must count as both divine and human. God is necessarily good; in responding sinlessly to temptation (e.g., Heb 4:15), Jesus's human mind and will must have relative integrity to choose the good freely.[59] Thus speaking of two minds can contribute clarity and even possible analogies: in the present case, extending dyothelite commitments to account for Christ's humanity more fully.[60] However, this modern, metaphysical affirmation comes at a potentially misleading cost: contemporary people often identify the human mind with the physical brain while lacking appreciation for apophatic aspects of language about God. Hence speaking of two minds risks bifurcating Christ's single subjectivity. Alternatively, the frequent labeling of *paradox* as a traditional alternative to kenoticism can also be misleading. The tradition did not really embrace paradox, at least when the word is interpreted strictly as involving actual contradiction. Conciliar Christology acknowledged mystery and may not have addressed modern questions, but that

---

57. Allen, *Christ's Faith*, 59–68.

58. For several essays disagreeing with White's beatific vision view from a Catholic perspective, see Thomas G. Weinandy, OFM, Cap., *Jesus: Essays in Christology* (Ave Maria, FL: Sapientia, 2014). Pages 280–82 offer the intriguing argument that the question of whether the earthly Jesus had the beatific vision is Nestorian because beatific vision assumes objective contemplation with ontological distinction. To the reframed question of whether he "was humanly aware of himself as Son," Weinandy answers yes. The proposal here is that it is not Nestorian to narrate increasing depth in Jesus's human perception of his filial identity.

59. Thomas V. Morris, *The Logic of God Incarnate* (Ithaca, NY: Cornell University Press, 1986), 149–62.

60. Morris's analogies for accessing relations between multiple minds could have modest value, especially given his delimitation of their dissimilarities. On artificial intelligence, dream states, mental strata, and multiple personalities or the like, see Morris, *Logic of God Incarnate*, 104–7. Still, despite Morris's care regarding the multiple personalities analogy, the proposal seems unwise. For additional concerns, see Wellum, *God the Son Incarnate*, 452.

neither entails contradiction nor precludes all two-minds accounts.[61] As for nonkenotic appeals to *krypsis*—the earthly hiddenness of Christ's divine perfections—they too carry misleading connotations. The earlier Lutheran understanding of those hidden perfections differs from recent analytic proposals.[62] Accordingly, *krypsis* may convey a thematic aspect of the *communicatio*, but it should not name the fundamental approach.

To draw these threads together, a classically Reformed Christology renders a kenotic account unnecessary and theologically untenable: "In the context of God's self-determination, kenosis should not be understood as a divesting of divine properties, but as the sovereign realization of divine love: Thus kenosis becomes plerosis (fulfillment; cf. Col 2:9f.)."[63] Kenotic Christologies place their strongest pressure upon traditional views of the incarnate Son's knowledge, due to modernity's historical and psychological interests. Yet they depend on problematic distinctions between Christ's earthly and glorified humanity, denials of traditional divine perfections, masculine notions of power, and strongly social Trinitarianism. Kenoticism is unnecessary to account for Christ's faithful pilgrimage, especially if human self-understanding of his deity grew vis-à-vis Isaianic fulfillment. As an extension of dyothelite orthodoxy, it may be appropriate to speak cautiously of two minds in Christ, addressing biblical passages like Mark 13:30–32 through partitive exegesis. The first two steps in this account of the *communicatio* proceeded in historical order: first the initial Protestant controversy over Christ's

---

61. An earlier essay critiqued both two-minds and some traditional accounts amid hesitating about metaphysical projects and prioritizing Cyrilline single-subject Christology: Treier, "Incarnation," 236–41. Its basic commitments remain operative here, but it may have overreached when alleging certain Nestorian connotations in accounts it critiqued. Notwithstanding the newness of questions about Jesus's self-understanding, a careful two-minds account may be an appropriate extension of dyothelitism.

62. Lutheranism needed the divine properties' communication to the human nature to be hidden. A contemporary *kryptic* proposal that treats Christ's divine knowledge as preconscious, limiting his earthly ministry to operating with human knowledge, is effectively a new version of functional kenoticism; see Andrew Ter Ern Loke, *A Kryptic Model of the Incarnation* (London: Routledge, 2014). Another account has the Word restricting the human nature's access to divine properties, but without the Word restricting the exercise of such properties; so Crisp, *Divinity and Humanity*, 147–53. It is unclear whether such *krypsis* implies a distinct state that (unnecessarily) goes beyond a classically Reformed *communicatio*, in which limited knowledge may periodically come to the fore as a principle of agency in the God-man, without hiddenness pervasively characterizing him.

63. My translation of John Webster, "Kenotische Christologie," in *Die Religion in Geschichte und Gegenwart: Handworterbuch für Theologie und Religionswissenschaft*, ed. Hans Dieter Betz et al., vol. 4 (Tübingen: Mohr Siebeck, 2006), 931. Even as he juxtaposes the self-emptying with the fullness of deity dwelling in Christ's bodily form, Webster rightly concedes that "kenotic Christologies present an important protest against the neglect of Christ's humanity and against an uncorrected theism."

presence; then modernity's kenotic contentions over Christ's knowledge. Now the third step involves the contemporary challenge of articulating Christ's theandric agency.

C. Christ's Power: Articulating Theandric Agency

Theandric agency surfaced while addressing Christ's omnipresence and omniscience, but contemporary dyothelitism can go further. Affirming the *extra Calvinisticum* already invoked omnipotence because God's presence includes the sovereign capacity for action across spatial distance. Accounting for *kenōsis* also introduced partitive exegesis, especially regarding Christ's knowledge. Now, having entailed dyothelitism, conciliar Christology requires articulating theandric agency—to acknowledge Jesus Christ as a single subject while addressing modern concerns. On Palestine's dusty paths, Jesus had to act as the faithful *human* covenant partner that God called Adam and Israel to be; simultaneously, Gethsemane and Golgotha comprised the apex of *God's* loving action for our salvation. Such action *ad extra* indivisibly involves all three persons of the Godhead. The *extra carnem* is essential for confessing this unity, maintaining the incarnate Son's responsive oneness with the Father in the mutual love of the Holy Spirit. Dyothelitism is essential because God alone saves, and what is not assumed would remain unhealed. Additional elements help with articulating this theandric agency: an instrumental human nature, reduplicative propositions, and partitive exegesis.

First, an instrumental human nature. As a single subject, Christ acted "authoritatively as God and instrumentally as a human being."[64] Instrumentality honors the asymmetry in the incarnation—the Son being without human personhood (anhypostatic) in advance, only becoming a human person once he assumed concrete (enhypostatic) humanity in Jesus.[65] Speaking of Christ's human nature as instrumental

---

64. A summary quote from J. David Moser, "Tools for Interpreting Christ's Saving Mysteries in Scripture: Aquinas on Reduplicative Propositions in Christology," *SJT* 73, no. 4 (November 2020): 285–94.

65. In metaphysical terms, Christology should probably be compositional, thus concretist and three-part: (1) the divine Logos assumed a human nature as a unified entity comprised of a (2) body and (3) soul, not just an abstract set of properties. For a summary, see Arcadi, *An Incarnational Model of the Eucharist*, 154–65. More extensively, see Oliver D. Crisp, *The Word Enfleshed: Exploring the Person and Work of Christ* (Grand Rapids: Baker Academic, 2016). Such metaphysical inquiries, though, elicit questions (e.g., those itemized by Crisp on pp. 102–5) that may be unhelpful, including the so-called no-person problem, in which the Christ who wept over Lazarus is not "identical with" the person of the Son. Here theologians may be content with plainer biblical and traditional appeals to both mystery and common sense. Notwithstanding technical notions of identity, the Son has clearly "identified with" his human nature in the closest

does not violate Kantian strictures against treating human beings as mere means to ends because there is no human person apart from the divine Son's assumption of a human nature. Conversely, speaking of Christ's human nature as instrumental does not entail his immediate possession of the beatific vision. As the ultimate means of not only divine self-revelation but also human redemption, the incarnation elicited Jesus's free embrace of his ensuing humiliation as human and not just divine. An instrumental human nature does not depersonalize Christ because the ends at stake require the means of *personal* action, both divine and human. Human personal action is finite, issuing from faith rather than sight until the eschaton.

Second, reduplicative propositions. Christ is a single agent, yet he has, and acts by virtue of, dual principles of agency—with a sharing of operations (*communicatio operationum*) emerging from the *communicatio idiomatum*. As the Third Council of Constantinople (680–81) concluded while drawing from Pope Leo the Great's *Tome to Flavian*, Jesus had not only two natural wills but also two energies. These energies are not personal subjects: abstract terms regarding the two natures cannot properly be subjects of action statements regarding Christ. For instance, instead of "the divine nature became incarnate" or "the human nature died," it is "the Son" who became incarnate and died for our salvation. Reduplicative statements, however, like "(he was, e.g., omniscient) according to his divine nature" or "insofar as he is human (he could be, e.g., ignorant)," provide the qualifying nuances for articulating theandric agency.[66]

Third, partitive exegesis (as introduced above). Some biblical texts depict Christ's action with respect to one nature or the other. Granted, there is a danger of Nestorian bifurcation between the natures, losing the Son's unity as a single subject, when metaphysical terms are reified after Chalcedon.[67] A catalog of contemporary alternatives presses that

---

possible manner. Without the incarnation, Christ's human nature would not be personal, and the no-person problem would be moot. In any case, compositional Christology supports holistic dualism against emergent materialism: the Son assumed a human body and soul. See John W. Cooper, *Body, Soul, and Life Everlasting: Biblical Anthropology and the Monism-Dualism Debate* (Grand Rapids: Eerdmans, 2000).

66. See further (cited by Moser) Allan Bäck, *On Reduplication: Logical Theories of Qualification* (Leiden: Brill, 1996). For a defense of this broader approach, see Ty Kieser, "Theandric and Triune: John Owen and a Case for Classically Reformed Christological Agency" (PhD diss., Wheaton, IL, Wheaton College Graduate School, 2020).

67. Williams, *Christ the Heart of Creation*, 116–17. Tellingly, though, Arianism rejected partitive exegesis, as noted by Hanson, *Search*, 108.

charge against accounts of theandric agency that emerge from partitive exegesis. This catalog would obviously begin with kenotic alternatives. The next chapter addresses another alternative, Spirit Christologies, which often attribute Christ's actions largely or even exclusively to his humanity. Here it remains to address how partitive exegesis relates to still another trend: appealing to the noncompetitive relationship between divine and human action.[68]

A recent proposal for "Chalcedonianism without reserve" extends this noncompetitive principle so far that it conflicts with the traditional partitive approach. The phrase *without reserve* claims that Catholic, Orthodox, and Reformation Christologies "fail to follow through fully on the implications" of Chalcedon, so that "although in the majority tradition Jesus' full humanity is formally affirmed, it is not viewed as integral to his identity, since it is only where his humanity is overshadowed by the power of his divinity that God is revealed."[69] By contrast, "fundamental to a Chalcedonianism without reserve is the principle that because the divine nature is inherently invisible and so not capable of perception (1 Tim 1:17; cf. Col 1:15; 1 John 4:12), when we look at Jesus, what we see is his humanity only. It follows that no aspect of that which we perceive in Jesus—his miracles, his faith, his obedience, or anything else—can be equated with his divinity; all are fully and exclusively human, and thus created, realities."[70] Apparently this version of the noncompetitive principle identifies the agency underlying Christ's biblical actions wholly with his Spirit-empowered humanity. An appeal is made to Luther's exhortation that we should disregard everything except Christ's humanity, while consistently distinguishing between the who or whom (the divine Word) and the what (created Jewish flesh) that humans perceive in the incarnation.[71]

The wider concern is that the traditional partitive approach marginalizes Christ's humanity due to idolatrous perceptions of his deity.[72] For

---

68. Recent articulations reflect the creative engagement with Thomas Aquinas in Kathryn Tanner, *God and Creation in Christian Theology: Tyranny or Empowerment?* (Minneapolis: Fortress, 1988).

69. McFarland, *Word Made Flesh*, 3.

70. McFarland, *Word Made Flesh*, 6.

71. McFarland, *Word Made Flesh*, 6–7. For a fairly standard reading of Luther's innovative legacy, see Johannes Zachhuber, *Luther's Christological Legacy: Christocentrism and the Chalcedonian Tradition* (Milwaukee: Marquette University Press, 2017). But for a more traditionalist Luther, see David J. Luy, *Dominus Mortus: Martin Luther on the Incorruptibility of God in Christ* (Minneapolis: Fortress, 2014).

72. Noticing McFarland's shared tendencies with Aaron Riches and Rowan Williams is Kirsten Sanders, "The Logic of Chalcedon and the Burning Bush," online, *The Henry Center,*

instance, Leo's *Tome* speaks of Jesus's deity "shining forth with miracles" even as his humanity "succumbs to injuries"—a contrast allegedly confusing *what* is at work (divine power) with *who*, so that some aspects of Jesus's humanity become more aligned with deity than others.[73] Of course, avoiding idolatry and attending to Christ's humanity are vital dogmatic concerns. Likewise, an account of divine revelation in the incarnation must acknowledge God's material invisibility and avoid "the implication that deity and humanity take turns acting throughout the life of Jesus."[74]

Three factors, however, still favor a classically Reformed account. First, clarity is needed about the sense(s) in which human perception is at stake. If perceiving Jesus involves only "created substance" and "nothing that is divine" due to divine incorporeality, then that sense of the claim is widely embraced and seemingly trivial. If the claim means that human beings only encounter deity through Jesus's flesh and not nakedly otherwise, again that sense is traditionally uncontroversial. Even Lutherans may worry, though, about stronger senses of the claim—entirely disallowing phenomenal manifestation of deity in Christ—wondering "whether the life of Christ as we encounter it within the event horizon of finite history includes features which suggest the enactment of divine predicates."[75] Second, concern is appropriate over minimizing a Logos *asarkos* and rejecting the *extra Calvinisticum*; the "rejection of a 'distinct' activity of the Word seems once again to conflate the two activities/energies of the incarnate Christ," even if the worrisome conflation comes from the opposite (human) direction than the traditional (divine) tendency.[76] In other words, such modern Christologies reflect monophysite assumptions about single-subject

Trinity Evangelical Divinity School, October 30, 2020, https://henrycenter.tiu.edu/2020/10/perceiving-the-word-made-flesh. Registering a similar concern regarding Williams's book, that "the stricture on Divine intervention in the world has severely constrained the Presence of the Divine Nature in the earthly Christ," is Katherine Sonderegger, "Christ as Infinite and Finite: Rowan Williams' *Christ the Heart of Creation*," *ProEccl* 30, no. 1 (February 2021): 98–113.

73. As summarized in Ian A. McFarland, "Perceiving the Word Made Flesh," online, *The Henry Center, Trinity Evangelical Divinity School*, October 30, 2020, https://henrycenter.tiu.edu/2020/10/perceiving-the-word-made-flesh.

74. David J. Luy, "Chalcedonian Christology and the Partitive Impulse," online, *The Henry Center, Trinity Evangelical Divinity School*, October 30, 2020, https://henrycenter.tiu.edu/2020/10/perceiving-the-word-made-flesh.

75. So (the Lutheran) Luy, "Chalcedonian Christology and the Partitive Impulse."

76. R. Lucas Stamps, "Perception, Incarnation, and the Flesh of Christ," online, *The Henry Center, Trinity Evangelical Divinity School*, October 30, 2020, https://henrycenter.tiu.edu/2020/10/perceiving-the-word-made-flesh.

agency, albeit from the human rather than the divine side.[77] Third, clarity is needed about the limits of human perception vis-à-vis the need for faith.[78] Granted the importance of focusing on *who* Christ is, divine simplicity precludes separating the *what* of the divine nature from revelatory encounters with the Word. Hence, despite the impossibility of finitely "seeing" the infinite qualitative distinction between God and humanity, faith cannot perceive the mystery of Christ as the divine Word without somehow encountering transcendent divine action that embodies God's perfection.[79]

Contemplating Scripture passages like Mark 4:35–41 supports partitive exegesis that recognizes Jesus's divine agency. Miracles have evidentiary significance for Jesus's uniqueness (e.g., John 10:38), yet they establish continuity between Christ and his Spirit-filled followers (e.g., John 14:12). Strictly speaking, no miracle made Christ empirically identifiable, as his rejection attests; miracles could only serve as evidence in a cumulative self-disclosure of the God of Israel.[80] Even so, occasions like Jesus's stilling of the storm evoked the question, "Who is this? Even the wind and the waves obey him!" (Mark 4:41). Admittedly, the focus is on who he is—with no directly visible divine power. Still, there is no attribution of the miracle to the Spirit's empowerment, and emphasis rests upon transcendent fullness rather than kenotic humility.[81] The same

77. Here space prevents adequate engagement with McCormack, *Humility of the Eternal Son.* Aside from concern over divine impassibility, his proposal is driven by purported incompatibility between the Son's full humanity and a Cyrilline single-subject Christology. In treating any instrumental account of human nature as infringing upon the self-activated obedience that he deems necessary for full humanity, McCormack univocally redefines *subject* in modern psychological terms. His proposed kenosis involves ontological receptivity whereby the triune God eternally determines that the Son, the second mode of divine being, would be incarnate and suffer as Jesus of Nazareth.

78. Questions about the import of faith in post-Chalcedonian Christology surface in D. Blair Smith, "Perceiving Christ in Faith," online, *The Henry Center, Trinity Evangelical Divinity School,* October 30, 2020, https://henrycenter.tiu.edu/2020/10/perceiving-the-word-made-flesh.

79. McFarland recognizes that his position "provides no empirical means for distinguishing a Jesus who is merely *empowered* by God (as any human being might be) from a Jesus who *is* God," so he appeals to the contrast between faith and sight; see Ian A. McFarland, "Perceiving the Word Made Flesh: A Rejoinder," online, *The Henry Center, Trinity Evangelical Divinity School,* October 30, 2020, https://henrycenter.tiu.edu/2020/10/perceiving-the-word-made-flesh. He uses *empirical* language multiple times; if that alone is the point, then rejection of the *extra* might be extraneous, and the ensuing disagreement might be minimal.

80. As suggested by McFarland.

81. Contra attempts at limiting this act to an empowered Davidic king exercising special powers, à la Psalm 89:23–27, e.g., in J. R. Daniel Kirk, *A Man Attested by God: The Human Jesus of the Synoptic Gospels* (Grand Rapids: Eerdmans, 2016), 433–44. First, Psalm 107 may be operative, pointing to Jesus's deity; so Simon J. Gathercole, *The Preexistent Son: Recovering the Christologies of Matthew, Mark, and Luke* (Grand Rapids: Eerdmans, 2006), 61–63. Second, already in Israel's Scriptures the anticipated Messiah may be divine and not just Davidic; see a measured assessment

who that goes to the cross operates by virtue of, or according to, the *what* of the Creator. This God's revelation in Israel's Scriptures conditioned the disciples' awestruck inference from Jesus's power over wind and waves, despite the exact implication remaining unstated. Divine and human agency operate on noncompetitive planes, yet they are also asymmetrical. Partitive exegesis does the most justice to both the cross and biblical encounters with a divinely powerful Jesus.

To summarize, the preceding account of the *communicatio idiomatum* has responded extensively to philosophical and psychological challenges for conciliar Christology. First, this account affirms Christ's divine presence *extra carnem*—ubiquitous, beyond human flesh, as the sovereign Lord. Second, given dyothelitism, this account acknowledges Christ's pilgrim experience of human knowledge without adopting a kenotic Christology, whether ontological or functional, with *kenōsis* instead humbling the divine person through assuming a human nature. Third, this account addresses Christ's power by articulating theandric agency via an instrumental human nature, reduplicative propositions, and partitive exegesis. The philosophical challenges noticed along the way frequently consist of psychological concerns—modernity's perceived tension between Jesus's unity as a personal subject and the possibility of his self-understanding as the God-man who possessed certain powers. Beyond expounding classically Reformed categories, this account has incorporated a historical suggestion: in his humanity Jesus could recognize his deity because of his virginal conception, which pointed to his identity as Immanuel and his vocation as the Servant of YHWH.

To the preceding argument, finally, this account adds a theological reminder: Christ's divine perfection, although fully actualized, does not entail the extension of supernatural powers in every act. The "pure act" that characterizes the perfection of God's power transcends human conceptions of presence and agency, operating on a distinct plane. Christ's incarnate actions counted as divine even when they did not extend beyond limited human capacities. When Jesus performed healings as a human being empowered by the Holy Spirit, these were divine works of the God-man even without drawing upon his extraordinary powers. Besides, traditional Trinitarianism would not ascribe supernatural empowerment to the Spirit in any divisible abstraction from the divine

---

in Markus Zehnder, "The Question of the 'Divine Status' of the Davidic Messiah," *BBR* 30, no. 4 (2020): 485–514.

essence and agency shared by the Son. By the same principle the incarnate Son's knowledge, whether of self or others, was neither exhausted by the operation of a physical brain nor isolated from ongoing communion with the Father in the Spirit. Perhaps our conceptions of omniscient wisdom contain assumptions that exacerbate its perceived tensions with developing human self-understanding and finite knowledge. Human beings construe knowledge in terms of quantitative possession (how much?) and focal attention (to what?), but the noncompetitive nature of divine and human agency must extend even to the Son's self-understanding. He could possess omniscient wisdom yet, while incarnate, focus earthly attention in ways that would often—maybe ordinarily—employ no supernatural extension of his powers, fostering the genuine experience of human development with partial knowledge. Of course, even this suggested nuance reflects a human perspective, deploying limited powers with which we cannot comprehend God's perfect wisdom or the singular reality of the incarnation.

IV. SERVANT AND LORD

With the previous two chapters, this chapter has formed a triptych depicting the earthly inauguration of our Lord's incarnation. From a prior perspective, Isaiah 7:14 epitomizes the Old Testament's anticipation of Immanuel's advent—Yhwh returning to be redemptively present with the covenant people. From an internal perspective, John 1:1–18 epitomizes the incarnation's revelation of the Logos—the Word illuminating us with God's saving love. Now, from a subsequent perspective, Philippians 2:5–11 epitomizes the New Testament's exaltation of the humiliation of God's Servant—the God-man giving up divine privilege and going obediently to the cross, glorifying the extent of God's love for sinful humanity.

Servant is the identity that leads from the incarnation's beginning into Christ's earthly mission and eventual exaltation, connecting the promised revelation of Yhwh with the redemption of the covenant people.

In the OT Israel is frequently addressed as God's "servant (*'ebhedh*)" (e.g., Isa 41:8). But from among his people God calls a number of individuals to be his servants, entrusted with a special task. God acts in a special way through these chosen servants: Moses supremely, but also through prophets, priests, kings, and wise persons. The failure of each of these categories generates expectations of a future servant; the NT proclaims how Jesus fulfills and transcends each of these categories. . . .

The OT also knows of a suffering servant of God, particularly in the Psalms and in Isa 40–55, a servant who suffers for the sins of others but who will ultimately be vindicated. The NT links the figure of the Suffering Servant with that of the Messiah and sees his death on the cross as an atonement for the sins of the world, and his resurrection and ascension as the vindication of God's servant.[82]

The biblical richness of *servant*, especially in Isaiah, leads to our crucial passage. With Isaiah's eschatological monotheism appropriated in Philippians 2:9–11, the Suffering Servant is at least anticipated in Philippians 2:6–8.

The additional context of Graeco-Roman slavery underscores the political implications of Christ's humiliation as *doulos*. Not only did the divine Son humble himself in becoming incarnate; before obediently suffering a horrific death, he even became like a slave, enduring betrayal, injustice, poverty, shame, and slander in solidarity with the oppressed. Thus, Christ's identity as the Servant further addresses the political challenge, identified in the previous chapter, of problematic associations between Jesus's deity and imperial power.[83] The high Christology of Philippians 2:5–11 does not bless emperors' pretensions. Christ's exaltation only baptizes earthly authority as a submissive witness to the triumph of his self-giving love.[84]

Political implications also accompany *Lord*, Christ's other significant

82. Charles H. H. Scobie, *The Ways of Our God: An Approach to Biblical Theology* (Grand Rapids: Eerdmans, 2003), 96. Scobie treats God's servant as one of the four overarching themes of biblical theology. See also the exposition in Robert Letham, *The Message of the Person of Christ*, BST (Downers Grove, IL: InterVarsity Press, 2013), 63–78.

83. E.g., on a triumphalist turn in art and liturgical parallels with the imperial court, see Justo L. González, *From the Beginnings to the Council of Chalcedon*, vol. 1 of *A History of Christian Thought* (Nashville: Abingdon, 1987), 261–62. On their integration, see further Justo L. González, *The Early Church to the Dawn of the Reformation*, vol. 1 of *The Story of Christianity* (New York: Harper One, 2010), 143–46.

84. Earthly rulers bear this witness occasionally by tempering judgment with mercy, reflecting Christ's exercise of authority; more often they bear this witness by having their office point objectively to his kingship, under which theirs has been temporarily reauthorized with a limited scope. So Oliver O'Donovan, *The Desire of the Nations: Rediscovering the Roots of Political Theology* (Cambridge: Cambridge University Press, 1996).

name in Philippians 2:5–11. Not every occurrence of *Kyrios* includes Jesus in the identity of Yʜwʜ or implies a contrast with Roman emperors' use of the term. Nevertheless, texts like 1 Corinthians 8:4–6 join our current passage in thus identifying Jesus Christ as Lord. The gospel narrative of Luke-Acts also does so, with the resurrection vindicating Jesus's identity as Messiah and Lord (Acts 2:36). This vindication does not delay Jesus's identification with Yʜwʜ until the resurrection; the Gospels already depict John the Baptizer as preparing the way for this Lord to fulfill hopes of Yʜwʜ's return throughout his earthly ministry (e.g., Luke 3:6). Counterimperial claims need not be overt or primary to be present: with Israel's God redemptively present once more, rulers of raging nations are put on notice. The church's initial, fundamental confession, "Jesus is Lord" (Rom 10:9–10; 1 Cor 12:3), testifies about the vindication of the risen Servant, who "will see his offspring" (Isa 53:10).

Together *Servant* and *Lord* proclaim the good news of Yʜwʜ's redemptive return to Israel. The surrounding context of Isaiah 45:20–23, to which Philippians 2:9–11 alludes, anticipates that the Servant will more fully reveal the sovereign Creator as Redeemer—by fulfilling the vocation at which Israel representatively failed. Thus conciliar Christology is fundamental to worship and salvation. Worship: Jesus Christ has been exalted as Loʀᴅ, and "the law of prayer is the law of faith," so the church's praise entailed confessing his deity. Salvation: Yʜwʜ alone saves, yet "what is not assumed is not healed," so the eternal Son assumed our humanity as the Suffering Servant.

CHAPTER 7

MISSION AS JESUS OF NAZARETH, THE SAVIOR

Luke 4:14–30

As epitomized in **Luke 4:14–30**, Jesus of Nazareth is the **Savior**, whose earthly **mission** inaugurated God's kingdom in person. *Uniquely anointed with the Holy Spirit, Jesus represented humanity as the perfectly faithful Israelite before God; fulfilled the threefold office of prophet, priest, and king; and proclaimed forgiveness, healing, and liberation in word and deed.*

Having gazed intently at the triptych of advent, revelation, and humiliation, we turn to the earthly mission of the incarnate Savior. Four Gospels tell this story at length, so any one passage can only begin to epitomize it. Luke 4:14–30, though, distinctively narrates Jesus's initial public offering: there Jesus inaugurates his ministry and identifies his mission as the fulfillment of Isaiah's hopes. Other Gospel texts fill out the picture: retrospectively, Luke 24 regarding the risen Messiah's fulfillment of God's covenants with Israel; prospectively, Matthew 1 and John 1 regarding the incarnation's advent; and, climactically in the next chapter, Mark 10 regarding the Suffering Servant's atoning passion. Concerning the heart of Jesus's earthly mission, though, Luke 4 offers the paradigmatic portrait, revealing its *catalyst*—the Holy Spirit; its *core*—the threefold office of prophet, priest, and king; and its *consequences*—forgiveness, healing, and liberation that enact God's reign.

I. MINISTRY ANNOUNCED IN LUKE 4:14–30

In Luke 4, Jesus's self-presentation follows his temptation and is followed by a mixture of mighty works and popular rejection. The temptation narrative in Luke 4:1–13 characterizes Jesus as "full of the Holy Spirit," who leads him into the wilderness (4:1). Jesus's forty days of testing by the devil faithfully recapitulate Israel's forty years of being tested by God (Deut 8:2) and testing God (Deut 6:16), thus undergoing judgment for unbelief. Although Jesus is hungry and receives neither manna nor quail, he does not grumble, nor does he give in to the devil's bargain. He responds as Israel should have, relying on God's Word. He overcomes not only the flesh but also the world and the devil, refusing to serve the latter or to rule the former prematurely. This victory strategically qualifies Israel's personal representative to take his mission public. The victory is won, as it must be, in his Spirit-filled humanity. Yet perhaps there is also a hint of his deity: when Jesus refers to worshiping "the Lord your God" alone (v. 8, quoting Deut 6:13), he quotes the prohibition of Deuteronomy 6:16 against putting "the Lord your God" to the test. This faithful one who refuses to test God may also be, through *double entendre*, telling Satan to stop testing *him*, the Son of God.

In the aftermath of Jesus's announcement, exorcisms and healings inaugurate Isaiah's fulfillment in Capernaum, adopted as the mission's home base. In Luke 4:31–37, Jesus sets the oppressed free, exorcising a demon who recognizes this Holy One of God. The passage emphasizes the authoritative divine Word. Jesus teaches on the Sabbath (v. 31), amazes people with the authority of his words (v. 32), commands the demon (v. 35), again amazes people with authoritative words (v. 36), and generates buzz throughout the region (v. 37). In Luke 4:38–44, Jesus frees people from various illnesses. When Jesus heals Simon's mother-in-law, he rebukes her fever (vv. 38–39). Other healings he accomplishes by laying on hands (v. 40), but the narrative returns to exorcisms via rebuke (v. 41), with demons acknowledging Jesus as the Son of God although being forbidden to identify him as the Messiah. After time in solitary prayer (v. 42), Jesus is found, but he departs, reiterating his focus on proclaiming the good news of God's kingdom, thus fulfilling the purpose for which he was sent (vv. 43–44).

The central account announcing Jesus's mission has an overview that relocates him (Luke 4:14–15), followed by a broadly chiastic structure (Luke 4:16–30): (1) arrival (v. 16); (2) exposition and reaction (vv. 17–22); (2') another exposition and reaction (vv. 23–29); (1') departure (v. 30). The overview reemphasizes the Holy Spirit, in whose power Jesus returns to Galilee (v. 14). His fame is already spreading (vv. 14–15), so the overview tacitly acknowledges Luke's programmatic use of the succeeding narrative.[1] Elsewhere, praise (v. 15) is reserved for God (e.g., 17:15–16), so this favorable opinion says more than people realize. Going specifically to Nazareth, Jesus identifies faithfully with his people, customarily going to the synagogue (v. 16). Upon receiving the scroll, Jesus chooses the passage: he actively found Isaiah 61 (v. 17).[2]

The anointed figure of Isaiah 61:1–2 was anticipated by the preceding chapters (58–60) and the Servant Songs. The preceding chapters promise Zion's enjoyment of God's salvation, which must come from God because among the people there is no justice (59:1–16). God's own righteousness will redeem those who repent, giving them the divine Spirit (59:17–21). The Servant Songs are introduced by anointing with God's Spirit (42:1) and indicate that the Servant is sent by Yhwh (48:16). Also paralleled in Luke 4:18 are the opening of blind eyes and the release of prisoners (Isa 42:7). From Luke 4:19, the year of the Lord's favor evokes Isaiah 49:8. Hence the anointed figure embodies Yhwh's redeeming presence along with a proper response: "to set the oppressed free" (Luke 4:18) collates Isaiah 61:1–2 with 58:6, specifying the fasting that God truly desires.[3] Anticipating Zion's glorious salvation with an extended call for repentance, Isaiah 58 confronts the performance of religious duty that does not overcome injustice with love. By contrast, the anointed figure embodies the redemptive righteousness proper to Yhwh's servant.

Luke 4:18–19 evokes an eschatological year of Jubilee. Admittedly, "the year of the Lord's favor" and eschatological understandings of Isaiah

1. Luke's distinctive placement of the account is intentional; so Darrell L. Bock, *Luke 1:1–9:50*, BECNT (Grand Rapids: Baker Academic, 1994), 398.

2. "In some ways, this is the most important text in Isaiah for understanding Luke's portrayal of Jesus," according to Ben Witherington III, *Isaiah Old and New: Exegesis, Intertextuality, and Hermeneutics* (Minneapolis: Fortress, 2017), 302. On synagogues, see Jordan Ryan, *The Role of the Synagogue in the Aims of Jesus* (Minneapolis: Fortress, 2017).

3. Omitting "to heal the brokenhearted" does not diminish healing, given the phrase regarding the blind—although that phrase follows the LXX rather than the Masoretic Hebrew text (hereafter MT). Omission of the final phrase from Isaiah 61:2 probably highlights "favor," which appears again in Luke 4:24. So David W. Pao and Eckhard J. Schnabel, "Luke," in *CNTOT*, 288–89.

61 may not evoke the Jubilee in particular. Plus the immediacy of "today" (Luke 4:21) is counterbalanced by Jesus's hometown rejection (4:24–30) in contrast with gentile inclusion. Still, the *release* vocabulary in Isaiah 61:1 recalls Leviticus 25, and "the Jubilee connection does highlight the social, economic, and political impact of the arrival of the eschatological era. As in Isa. 61 (and 40–55), this Jubilee theme is one among many that contribute to the wider prophetic paradigm of the second exodus."[4] Passages like Luke 7:22, along with other appearances of the poor, the blind, and release in Luke–Acts, make the eschatological reversal of impoverished fortunes programmatic for Luke's gospel narrative.

Not to be lost in the background of Isaiah and the Jubilee is Luke's focus: Jesus himself. First-person pronouns make this focus emphatic.[5] In Isaiah's portrayal this anointed one is prophetic: his mission repeatedly involves proclamation. Associated with the ultimate Servant by this point in Isaiah, this prophet both proclaims YHWH's redeeming righteousness and embodies righteousness for the redeemed. Beyond prophet and Servant, Jesus is also the coming Davidic king. The Dead Sea Scrolls contain messianic readings of Isaiah 61:1–2, and Luke's preceding narrative of Jesus's baptism (3:22) has evoked the royal installation of Psalm 2 (as well as Isaiah 42).[6] Thus, Jesus does not just proclaim good news of liberation, healing, and the Lord's favor; he begins freeing the oppressed, as he soon demonstrates (e.g., Luke 4:31–37).

Jesus's sending realizes the purpose of his anointing. A single infinitive follows the indicative *anointed*, identifying the Messiah's mission "to proclaim good news to the poor." The multiple infinitives following *sent* explicate this mission more fully: (1) "to proclaim freedom for the prisoners and recovery of sight for the blind"; (2) "to set the oppressed free"; (3) "to proclaim the year of the Lord's favor." There is obvious emphasis upon proclamation, as the repetition of *kērussō* suggests. The initial "proclaim good news," although having the different root *euangelizomai*, supports this emphasis. Intriguingly, the second item repeats the emphasis upon sending with *apostellō*: "to send the oppressed into" release

---

4. Pao and Schnabel, "Luke," 290. The next sentence summarizes a claim from pp. 288–90. Jesus embodied and taught a social ethics that resonates with the Jubilee paradigm, as influentially argued (however complex the author's legacy) by John Howard Yoder, *The Politics of Jesus: Vicit Agnus Noster*, 2nd ed. (Grand Rapids: Eerdmans, 1994).

5. Green, *Luke*, 210.

6. Somewhat contra, e.g., the non-Davidic reading in Joseph A. Fitzmyer, *The Gospel according to Luke I-IX: Introduction, Translation, and Notes*, AB (Garden City, NY: Doubleday, 1981), 529. For a messianic reading of Isaiah 61:1–2 in the Dead Sea Scrolls, see 4Q521.

or forgiveness. As ensuing narratives reinforce, Jesus not only preaches; he delivers. More than a prophet, he is the messianic king.

The drama of Luke 4:20–22 involves the complex fulfillment of Isaiah's prophecy.[7] Luke focuses all eyes on Jesus (v. 20) with immediacy: "Today . . ." (v. 21). This announcement itself is part of the fulfillment ("in your hearing"). They have heard the proclaimer proclaim himself. They testify of him and marvel at the grace of his words (v. 22), which bring good news indeed. The perfect tense of the fulfillment (*peplērōtai*) supports its inaugurated character. Yet the text also signals that comprehensive eschatological fulfillment is not immediate. The hearers do not understand who Jesus really is. They domesticate him with the rhetorical question, "Isn't this Joseph's son?"—ironically indicating that they cannot identify his Father or recognize his relation to the divine Spirit.

When Jesus confronts this lack of understanding in Luke 4:23–29, his hometown goes beyond failing to honor him. Whereas Satan tried to get Jesus to jump off a building, the crowd tries to throw him off a cliff.[8] Hence Jesus fulfills the typical pattern of a rejected prophet, as anticipated by Elijah and Elisha (mentioned here) along with Isaiah (lurking in the background). On another hill Jesus will face a rugged cross. But for the moment, his divinely orchestrated journey spares him from the mob (4:30).

This programmatic text signals the integral character of Jesus's mission. His actions and words contain a "revolutionary ferment," even if, "in the final analysis, every revolution is a human attempt to create here and now the perfect society that God has promised to create at the end of the present age."[9] Thus eschatological nuance, regarding inauguration rather than immediate realization of God's kingdom, gives no quarter to quietism: "Seen from this perspective, the Jesus of certain evangelicals says: 'I am not King yet, except in a spiritualized sense. Later, however, I will come back, and then I will fulfill the previous definition: with a throne, sword, territory, soldiers, and everything.'"[10] That is not the

---

7. For a reading in terms of Trinitarian prosopological fulfillment, noting patristic precursors, see Bates, *Birth of the Trinity*, 94–95.

8. Jeremy Lundgren highlighted this connection for me.

9. C. René Padilla, "Revolution and Revelation," p. 77, cited in J. Samuel Escobar, *In Search of Christ in Latin America: From Colonial Image to Liberating Savior* (Downers Grove, IL: IVP Academic, 2019), 170.

10. John Howard Yoder, "La expectativa mesiánica del reino y su carácter central para una adecuada hermenéutica contemporánea," p. 110, in Padilla, *El reino de Dios y América Latina*, p. 104, cited in Escobar, *In Search of Christ*, 207.

Jesus of Luke 4:14–30. Yet Jesus's mission call is "not to oppose the official [governmental powers'] myths with other secular myths, but to point out the judgment of God with respect to all attempts to build the kingdom of God."[11] The church participates in Jesus's ongoing mission when his followers bear witness to God's reign in words, deeds, and forms of cultural presence that are empowered by his Holy Spirit.

II. SPIRIT CHRISTOLOGY

Given Jesus's proclamation, "the Spirit of the Lord is on me," the emergence of Spirit Christology is both helpful and potentially confusing. The meaning of this recent terminology is highly variable. For some, Spirit Christology is an alternative that should replace conciliar Logos Christology; for others, although they affirm ecumenical dogmas, Spirit Christology should be the primary emphasis; for still others, Spirit Christology offers a complementary perspective.[12] Advocates often appeal to precursors, whether among church fathers or figures like John Owen (1616–83). But some of these appeals are overinflated, accompanied by narratives of the Spirit's neglect that assume contested pneumatological claims. In any case, speaking of Spirit Christology is nearly tautologous: the Messiah is the Anointed One, with the Spirit as the empowering divine presence that the oil signifies.[13] Where Spirit Christology is helpful, its insights recover what should already be integral to biblical *Christ*ology.

In economic relation to the Son, the Father sent the Spirit in two

---

11. CLADE II, *América Latina y la evangelización en los años 80* (Mexico City: Fraternidad Teológica Latinoamericana, 1979), p. 230, cited in Escobar, *In Search of Christ*, 277.

12. The terminology appeared at least as early as the 1950s; see, e.g., Thornton, *Form of a Servant*, 1:287; Tillich, *Systematic Theology*, vol. 3. A common example of the first category is Roger Haight, SJ, "The Case for Spirit Christology," *JTS* 53 (1992): 257–87. Seemingly fitting the second is Myk Habets, "Spirit Christology: The Future of Christology?," in *Third Article Theology: A Pneumatological Dogmatics*, ed. Myk Habets (Minneapolis: Fortress, 2016), 207–32. For a well-intended proposal that nevertheless risks Nestorianism, see John McIntyre, *The Shape of Christology: Studies in the Doctrine of the Person of Christ*, 2nd ed. (Edinburgh: T&T Clark, 1998). Using *complementary* language is Leopoldo A. Sánchez M., *Receiver, Bearer, and Giver of God's Spirit: Jesus' Life in the Spirit as a Lens for Theology and Life* (Eugene, OR: Pickwick, 2015).

13. E.g., associating the Spirit with God's empowering presence, the anointed king prayed, "Do not cast me from your presence or take your Holy Spirit from me" (Ps 51:11). On this association in the New Testament, see Gordon D. Fee, *God's Empowering Presence: The Holy Spirit in the Letters of Paul* (Peabody, MA: Hendrickson, 1994). Of course, *spirit* in Old Testament contexts has associations with breath, wind, and the like, which usually convey divine energy without directly implicating a divine person (albeit with a couple of personal hints); see further Jack Levison, *A Boundless God: The Spirit according to the Old Testament* (Grand Rapids: Baker Academic, 2020).

basic stages. Having been anointed at his baptism, the incarnate Christ began uniquely *bearing* the Spirit during his public ministry. Once he accomplished his earthly mission and ascended to heaven, the Son participated in *bestowing* the Spirit upon all flesh as Pentecost's proximate agent (John 14:15–18, 26; 15:26; 16:7–15; 20:21–23; Acts 1:4–5, 8; 2:33), baptizing with the Spirit and fire (Matt 3:11, 16).[14] Accordingly, to trace the incarnate Son's Spirit-baptized and Spirit-baptizing ministry involves examining (1) his inseparable divine operations with the Spirit, (2) his active human obedience overshadowed by the Spirit, and eventually (3) his Spirit-empowered, healing, and liberating mediation of God's kingdom.

A. Inseparable Operations

In examining the incarnate Son's inseparable operations with the Father and the Spirit, we return to early high Christology (EHC), relate it to early high pneumatology, and then reflect on implications of "the Spirit" for personal agency. Previous chapters already traced extensive evidence for Christ's deity: eternal sonship (Eph 1:3–14); participation in creation (Col 1:15–29); divine, not just Davidic, messiahship (Isa 7:14); incarnation as the Logos (John 1:1–18); and identification as LORD (Phil 2:5–11). In addition to John 1:1–18, other texts identify him as "God" (*Theos*): John 20:28; Romans 9:5; Titus 2:13; 2 Peter 1:1; and Hebrews 1:8–9.[15] John's incarnational Christology is not a late aberration but intensifies a widespread conviction.

Notwithstanding their focus on narrating Jesus's Spirit-empowered earthly mission, the Synoptic Gospels share this conviction. Despite the influence of EHC, however, many still claim that Matthew, Mark, and Luke treat Jesus as an "idealized human figure" only.[16] They reject the claim that certain "ascriptions, actions, or attributes" uniquely incorporated Jesus within YHWH's identity. When alternative accounts advocate a "high, human Christology," they surface scholarly inconsistency about

---

14. Three stages could be elaborated, as in Sánchez M., *Receiver, Bearer, and Giver.* But for economy's sake, receiving fits within bearing. For a christological proposal that highlights Matthew 3:11, see Frank D. Macchia, *Jesus the Spirit Baptizer: Christology in Light of Pentecost* (Grand Rapids: Eerdmans, 2018).

15. On *Theos* see Harris, *Jesus as God.* On Hebrews see R. B. Jamieson, *The Paradox of Sonship: Christology in the Epistle to the Hebrews*, SCDS (Downers Grove, IL: IVP Academic, 2021).

16. Larry Hurtado's work cleared a new path, but it was preceded by too many works to list, from pioneers like Oscar Cullmann, Martin Hengel, Richard Longenecker, I. Howard Marshall, and C. F. D. Moule. This paragraph's non-EHC quotations come from Kirk, *Man Attested by God*, 4, 12, 19, 24–25.

whether *high* and *divine* Christology are equated. Of course, responding to EHC critics here is constrained by scholarly competence, spatial limitations, and theological generalizations. There is no denying that the cognitive environment of biblical texts can be relevant, and alternative paradigms may not be mutually exclusive. Hence EHC critics remind us that the Gospels often narrate the relationship between God and Jesus along with Father and Son; the hermeneutical focus of passages like Luke 24 rests on the human Messiah; and when construing the divine identity, Judaism had more operational variety than the religious category of monotheism might suggest.[17]

Unfortunately, much scholarship on the Gospels minimizes Jesus's possible deity to maximize his full humanity.[18] Among the ensuing problems, first, these scholars treat passages like Isaiah 9:6–7 with historical-critical assumptions in which the text cannot speak prophetically of Christ as God despite the apparent suggestion of the words.[19] Second, EHC critics highlight the supposed frequency of Jewish texts depicting idealized humans (or other creatures) as sharing in God's sovereignty. However, EHC arguments go further, appealing specifically to Yhwh's unique sovereignty over all creatures, represented by a cosmic heavenly throne—sovereignty whose possession incorporates Jesus within the Creator's divine identity.[20] Similar considerations apply to bowing and worship, as noted above in chapter 2. Third, EHC critics lack adequate caution in appeals to debated Jewish texts, which may well be postbiblical. Fourth, protestations about not denying divine Christology elsewhere seem curious. It is historically odd to expect that the Synoptic Gospels would present (only) an idealized human Christology in utter distinction from Pauline and other contemporaneous (or earlier!) biblical texts.

Matthew 28:18–20 can join Mark 4:35–41 in illustrating EHC evidence from the Synoptic Gospels. Mark 4:35–41 goes beyond having

---

17. On p. 36 Kirk recognizes affinities between his project and Fletcher-Louis's (see chapter 2 above).

18. For earlier cautions against focusing on Christ more than God see, e.g., James D. G. Dunn, "Christology as an Aspect of Theology," in *The Future of Christology: Essays in Honor of Leander E. Keck*, ed. Abraham J. Malherbe and Wayne A. Meeks (Minneapolis: Fortress, 1993), 202–12.

19. E.g., Kirk, *Man Attested by God*, 105–6.

20. To summarize Richard Bauckham, "Is 'High Human Christology' Sufficient? A Critical Response to J. R. Daniel Kirk's *A Man Attested by God*," *BBR* 27, no. 4 (2017): 503–25. Surveying related issues (including James McGrath's work) is Matthew N. Novenson, introduction to *Monotheism and Christology in Greco-Roman Antiquity*, ed. Matthew N. Novenson, NovTSup (Leiden: Brill, 2020), 1–8. The same volume contains EHC defenses from Hurtado and others.

YHWH set the king's hand over the sea (Ps 89:25).[21] The remainder of the psalm complicates this paean to the king by complaining that God has apparently renounced covenant promises to David's heirs. The beginning complicates the purported background too by insisting that no one is like YHWH, not least in ruling over the raging sea. Markan emphasis upon Jesus's powerful *word* calming the storm favors more than just idealized humanity. In Psalm 89 God does the speaking, and the king dependently calls upon God as Father. "What kind of man is this?" may not convey creedal Logos Christology, but with limited categories the disciples contemplate more than an idealized human being. At the end of Matthew's Gospel, Jesus claims "all authority in heaven and on earth," beyond what was envisioned for Adam and David. The ensuing worship is not just bowing down to a superior; Jesus is included within the identity of YHWH. Matthew uses *proskuneō* to convey this inclusion, buttressed by the inclusio of "God with us" and "I will be with you always."[22] Since (the church has traditionally believed) Matthew's baptismal formula faithfully represents Jesus's authority, the gospel concludes with his claim to proto-Trinitarian sharing of the divine Name.

Thus the Synoptic Gospels provide the narratives that an incarnational Christology would have us expect.[23] Exorcisms signal the intervention of God's eschatological rule; miracles bring new creation, following the eschatological Elijah; forgiveness and judgment sayings claim divine authority; Jesus's words are juxtaposed with Torah while reconstituting Israel's twelve around himself and claiming present, earthly authority (in contrast with other mediatorial figures); Jesus has a uniquely intimate, reciprocal, and revelatory relationship with the Father.[24] It is historically advantageous for these signals of divine identity to reflect Jesus's self-understanding. Otherwise, explanatory gaps must be filled with the early

---

21. So Kirk, *Man Attested by God*, 433–36.

22. On Matthew 28:18–20, mentioning 14:22–33, see Bauckham, "Response to Kirk," 517–22. On *proskunein* see C. F. D. Moule, *The Origin of Christology* (Cambridge: Cambridge University Press, 1977), 175–76.

23. Bauckham, "Response to Kirk," 516.

24. As summarized in Sigurd Grindheim, *God's Equal: What Can We Know about Jesus' Self-Understanding in the Synoptic Gospels?*, LNTS (London: T&T Clark, 2011), 39, 59, 76, 100, 115, 123, 167, 188. Regarding items like forgiveness, critics respond that "anything the Gospel writers depict Jesus's followers as doing cannot be a deed by which they intend to signal, in and of itself, that Jesus is divine"; so Kirk, *Man Attested by God*, 483. But Christ may have uniquely introduced and authoritatively delegated these items.

church's Hellenizing creativity or modern developmental schemes.[25] Accordingly, the preceding "Yнwн's equal" arguments identify Christ as the "preexistent Son" and place his purposeful "I have come . . ." sayings in a distinctive light. Their indication of his divine preexistence has *prima facie* plausibility. Alternative interpretations, like prophetic or messianic humanity, are unsustainable. The closest, angelic parallels are inadequate to capture contextual factors in passages like Mark 10:32–45, where the Son of Man tells why he has come.[26] Preexistence-oriented readings involve a cumulative case: the historical plausibility of coherent development between the Synoptic Gospels, their precursor Paul, and their successor John outweighs attempts to explain away EHC item by item. Because the Synoptic Gospels are the biblical locus for understanding Jesus's earthly mission, their witness to his preexistent divine identity is vital.

Along with reflecting divine preexistence and the Father's initiative, though, the incarnate Son's mission relied on the Holy Spirit's empowerment. Biblical associations of *spirit* with divine power are indisputable, whereas the Spirit's personhood can seem indistinct. Yet proto-Trinitarian formulae go beyond Matthew 28:18–20 to include epistolary examples like 2 Corinthians 13:14. The narrative of Ananias and Sapphira in Acts 5 confronts lying "to the Holy Spirit," suggesting the communicative agency of personhood. A Trinitarian reading of Revelation 1–3 aligns the Spirit's revelatory work with its anticipation in John 14–17.[27] Prosopological exegesis also helped early Christians to recognize the Spirit's divine personhood.[28] Indeed, the Spirit's communicative agency was operative in the traditioning processes that were necessary for the church's Trinitarian understanding.

Such historical development addresses the apparent conundrum of whether finding conciliar orthodoxy in Scripture itself would "render the next several centuries of theological development all but

25. Grindheim, *God's Equal*, 219–21. For a narrative reading of *Kyrios* in Luke along the lines of divine identity Christology, see C. Kavin Rowe, *Early Narrative Christology: The Lord in the Gospel of Luke* (Grand Rapids: Baker Academic, 2009).

26. So Gathercole, *Preexistent Son*. For a strident review, see James D. G. Dunn, "Review of Simon Gathercole, *The Pre-Existent Son: Recovering the Christologies of Matthew, Mark, and Luke* (Grand Rapids: Eerdmans, 2006)," *RBL*, April 2007. Even if Dunn highlights lingering challenges, however, his (largely rhetorical) questions take much for granted—e.g., when dismissing Psalm 110's use in Mark 12:35–37.

27. So Brandon D. Smith, *The Trinity in the Book of Revelation: Seeing Father, Son, and Holy Spirit in John's Apocalypse*, SCDS (Downers Grove, IL: IVP Academic, 2022).

28. See Kyle R. Hughes, *The Trinitarian Testimony of the Spirit: Prosopological Exegesis and the Development of Pre-Nicene Pneumatology* (Leiden: Brill, 2018).

incomprehensible."[29] Instead, prosopological exegesis contributes one rationale for expecting such theological development. Another rationale involves the gradual distribution and complex identification of the biblical canon. Still another rationale is hermeneutical: determinate textual meaning includes theological implications that are not immediately recognizable. If Jesus understood himself to be included in the unique identity of YHWH and communicated that understanding through apostolic witnesses, neither the underlying theology nor its implications for worship would necessarily be clear all at once.

Accordingly, the Son's theandric mission comprised an inseparable Trinitarian operation. To begin with, "How then can he who gives the Spirit not be God? . . . He received it as man, he poured it out as God."[30] A divine mission involves a personal procession and a created effect.[31] Divine operations inseparably enact the triune God's essential powers, perhaps with appropriated reflections of personal processions.[32] Given inseparable *operations* we can say, "God became incarnate." The Son's *mission* in the incarnation, though, was both a divine operation and an "extension of the mode of existence of a divine person to incorporate a created reality."[33] Given the personal distinctions and missions involved, we can also say, "The Son became incarnate," "The incarnate Son was the unique earthly bearer of the Spirit," and "The risen, ascended Son was the One through whom the Father bestowed the Spirit." The Spirit has corresponding missions that commenced with Christ's baptism and Pentecost, newly indwelling and empowering Jesus and his followers.[34] Although the Spirit played a distinct role in the economy of the incarnation, that operation did not make the Spirit the agent of the incarnate Son's actions, who is Jesus Christ, even if the Spirit enabled the Son to live humanly in the Father's filial love.

The concept of a person's *spirit* should inform the pneumatology of the theandric Son's mission. The spirit is the inward impetus, the

---

29. So Fredriksen, "How High?," 317.

30. St. Augustine, *The Trinity*, ed. John E. Rotelle, OSA, trans. Edmund Hill, OP (Hyde Park, NY: New City, 1991), 431–32 (15.46).

31. Adonis Vidu, *The Same God Who Works All Things: Inseparable Operations in Trinitarian Theology* (Grand Rapids: Eerdmans, 2021), 175.

32. Vidu, *Same God*, 100.

33. Vidu, *Same God*, 73.

34. Vidu, *Same God*, 263. Vidu differs from the previous chapter, however, by affirming Christ's possession of the *visio Dei* throughout progressive deification (p. 273), and perhaps by insisting that in the theandric Christ all of God's activity is "carried out through natural means" (p. 207).

animating principle, behind thoughts and actions (1 Cor 2:11). In addition to holiness, God's Spirit is associated with love and freedom, giving life in its fullness since "love will characterize us when we are truly free to be ourselves (see Rom. 6–8; 12–15; 1 Cor. 12–14)."[35] For the incarnate Son, this concept runs bidirectionally: the Holy Spirit is not only "of God" but also "of Christ" (Rom 8:9). The Spirit is both the incarnate Son's loving animation to know God as Father (the Spirit "of God" in him) and his disciples' similar impetus (the Spirit "of Christ" in them; Rom 8:14–16). The incarnate Son's filial impetus involved the communication of grace to his human nature along with the Trinitarian intersubjectivity of his divine nature. Amid profound mystery, not only do distinct processions accompany inseparable operations, but the Spirit's name also identifies the Son's personal animation to embrace the Father's love. This animation, appropriated to the Spirit by processional naming, is economically realized in distinct missions with respect to the incarnate Son and his disciples.

B. Active Obedience

In the context of inseparable Trinitarian operations, Spirit Christology highlights active human obedience as an integral component of the Son's earthly mission. Space permitting, every moment of Christ's life could be narrated from this perspective: he is the second Adam and the faithful Israelite who fulfilled God's covenantal requirements, not just another intermediary like Moses or David. Climactically, he offered heroic obedience on the cross, but here we follow the major movements from birth and boyhood through baptism and temptation into public ministry.

1. Birth and Youth

The Holy Spirit overshadowed not only Jesus's virginal conception but also his early growth in human wisdom (Luke 2:40, 52). Eight days after his birth, his circumcision and offering already aligned him with Israel under the Torah, reflecting his parents' faithfulness and God's constant grace (Luke 2:21–40).[36] His precocious presence at the temple (Luke 2:41–52) deepened understanding of God as his Father, with no disrespect to Joseph and Mary. Their offering upon his birth and his

---

35. Daniel J. Treier, *Introducing Evangelical Theology* (Grand Rapids: Baker Academic, 2019), 277.

36. H. Orton Wiley, *Christian Theology*, vol. 2 (Kansas City: Beacon Hill, 1952), 148–50.

upbringing as a carpenter's son reflected relative poverty.[37] Solidarity with the needy persisted as he later ministered with no place to lay his head (Luke 9:58).

2. Baptism and Temptation

After Jesus's humble birth and graced youth, the Spirit led him into baptism and temptation as he launched his public ministry.[38] In solidarity with Israel as she faced divine judgment (Matt 3:7–12), he was baptized "to fulfill all righteousness" (Matt 3:13–15). At that moment the Father's voice and the Spirit's manifestation as a dove lauded the beloved Son for whom Israel hoped.[39] The Synoptic Gospels all narrate the temptation on the heels of this baptism. As isolating as the temptation may have been, its faithful recapitulation of Israel's failed test was a vital qualification for Christ's redemptive mission. The temptation revealed Jesus's scriptural fidelity as he refused premature enjoyment of divine rule apart from the cross.

3. Public Ministry

The Spirit evoked filial devotion and empowered mighty works throughout Jesus's public ministry.[40] Its offices and effects are traced in subsequent sections. The element of persistent obedience should not be neglected: "'My food . . . is to do the will of him who sent me and to finish his work" (John 4:34); "My Father is always at his work to this very day, and I too am working" (John 5:17; see further vv. 18–30, 36–38). This active obedience encompassed more than behavioral conformity to God's law. Christ was fully obedient in prayerful thoughts

---

37. Astonishingly, the helpful second edition of *Dictionary of Jesus and the Gospels* (cited elsewhere) contains not even an index entry on Joseph!

38. This framework appears in Gerald F. Hawthorne, *The Presence and the Power: The Significance of the Holy Spirit in the Life and Ministry of Jesus* (Dallas: Word, 1991). Unfortunately, despite contributing biblical evidence for pneumatological Christology, Hawthorne did not realize that a kenotic account is unnecessary and a dyothelite account is viable (see pp. 208, 213). See also, e.g., the worry about Jesus "cheating" with divine powers in Mark L. Strauss, "Jesus and the Spirit in Biblical and Theological Perspective: Messianic Empowering, Saving Wisdom, and the Limits of Biblical Theology," in *The Spirit and Christ in the New Testament and Christian Theology: Essays in Honor of Max Turner*, ed. I. Howard Marshall, Volker Rabens, and Cornelis Bennema (Grand Rapids, 2012), 283–84.

39. On the baptism and several other events discussed here, see the relevant chapters in Darrell L. Bock and Robert L. Webb, eds., *Key Events in the Life of the Historical Jesus: A Collaborative Exploration of Context and Coherence* (Grand Rapids: Eerdmans, 2010).

40. For a compact survey and an account of historical criteria, see the introduction and Robert L. Webb, "The Historical Enterprise and Historical Jesus Research," in *Key Events in the Life of the Historical Jesus: A Collaborative Exploration of Context and Coherence*, ed. Darrell L. Bock and Robert L. Webb (Grand Rapids: Eerdmans, 2009), 9–93.

along with public words and deeds, not merely obeying from the heart but leaving nothing of God's will undone. Jesus loved God with his entire being and his neighbor as himself. In solidarity with Israel and thereby the world, he assumed the weakness and bore the consequences of our fallen condition, becoming subject to physical death. Yet this solidarity involved no complicity with the sinners he represented or powers he defeated.[41]

Hence active obedience comprises a vital aspect of redemption, despite potential confusion vis-à-vis the contrasting passive obedience of the crucifixion. Christ's self-giving love on the cross was far from passive (John 15:13). When his mission required enduring injustice (Acts 2:23), he willingly laid down his life (John 10:18; Heb 12:2). Indeed, martyrdom was Jesus's climactic moment of obedience (Phil 2:6–8), as Gethsemane dramatized (Luke 22:42). Spirit Christology must speak to both sides of that dyothelite drama: the inseparable operations of the Father and the Son whom he sent, and the filial human obedience of Jesus Christ.

III. THE *MUNUS TRIPLEX*

As Messiah, God's Anointed One, the incarnate Son of God fulfilled three primary offices in a united, ultimate way.[42] This *munus triplex* or "threefold office" emerged from the anointings previously given to prophets, priests, and kings.[43] This framework not only integrates the

---

41. Suprapersonal sin can be social, involving agency ascribed to institutions or societies, and structural, involving downward causality from social institutions to persons. So Daniel K. Finn, "What Is a Sinful Social Structure?," *TS* 77, no. 1 (2016): 136–64. Cited in Daniel Lee Hill and Ty Kieser, "Social Sin and the Sinless Savior: Delineating Supra-Personal Sin in Continuity with Conciliar Christology," *ModTheo* 38, no. 3 (July 2022): 568–91. Hill and Kieser recognize that conciliar Christology and atonement require Christ to be socially sinless. Consequently, finite human existence in a sinful society does not establish culpability, which requires defective volition. Jesus participated in a sinful society ("what is not assumed . . ."—but it was!) without defective volition (". . . would not be healed"—but it has been!). Jesus could not address every surrounding injustice, and he may have (righteously) occasioned distress for some people. Christology must distinguish a redemptive Jesus from the rest of humanity with particular excellences, as noted by S. W. Sykes, "The Theology of the Humanity of Christ," in *Christ, Faith and History: Cambridge Studies in Christology*, ed. S. W. Sykes and J. P. Clayton (Cambridge: Cambridge University Press, 1972), 66.

42. Portions of this section and the next are adapted from chap. 9 of Treier, *Introducing Evangelical Theology*.

43. The following account summarizes key aspects from Geoffrey Wainwright, *For Our Salvation: Two Approaches to the Work of Christ* (Grand Rapids: Eerdmans, 1997). As a Methodist, Wainwright shows that the *munus triplex* predates (e.g., in Thomas Aquinas) and transcends (e.g., in John Wesley) the Reformed tradition.

Old and New Testaments; it also helps those who are now in Christ to understand their redeemed identity. As a royal priesthood (1 Pet 2:9), the church declares the praises of one Mediator (1 Tim 2:5) through whom needy sinners receive divine mercy.[44] Thanks to anointing with the Holy Spirit, this threefold office fits "the church's liturgical experience of Christ as 'object of worship,' 'mediator in worship,' and 'pattern for worship.'"[45] The Spirit who anointed Jesus in an ultimate sense now anoints the body of Christ in a participatory sense (e.g., 1 John 2:27).

As Prophet, Christ is the revelatory Mediator, representing God to humanity, addressing our ignorance. Beyond Isaiah 61:1–2, primary passages include Matthew 17:5, with the beloved Son of Matthew 3:17 being gloriously transfigured; John 4:25, with the Samaritan woman expecting the Messiah's clear teaching; and Hebrews 1:1–2, with the Son embodying the climactic divine Word in a long series of prophetic words. The church has received a prophetic ministry (Joel 2:28; Acts 2:17–21), so that "the messengers of Christ find themselves anticipated by the One who sends them, not in such a way as to render their mission unnecessary but rather to make it awaited."[46] When the church overemphasizes this prophetic office, however, a focus on teaching generates moralism and/or rationalism.[47]

As Priest, Jesus is the redemptive Mediator, representing humanity before God, offering himself vicariously, addressing our enmity. Primary passages include Psalm 110:4, with Melchizedek typifying an eternal priesthood. In citations of this psalm (Heb 5:6; 7:15) and in other passages (e.g., 4:14–16; 7:28–8:2), Hebrews celebrates this priestly ministry, as do depictions of Jesus as the Lamb of God (e.g., John 1:29). Baptism anoints believers into royal priesthood, with several texts (e.g., 2 Cor 5:17–21; Heb 10:19–25; 1 Pet 2:5, 9–10; Rev 1:6) applying such concepts to the church's identity. The church mysteriously, although not redemptively, participates in Christ's suffering (Col 1:24). When the church overemphasizes this office, however, a focus on spiritual sacrifice generates pietism and/or mysticism.

---

44. John Wesley relates the offices to sinners' respective needs in *Explanatory Notes on the New Testament*, regarding Matthew 1:16, as quoted in Wainwright, *For Our Salvation*, 108.

45. Wainwright, *For Our Salvation*, 118–19. This framework structures the Christology in Geoffrey Wainwright, *Doxology: The Praise of God in Worship, Doctrine, and Life: A Systematic Theology* (New York: Oxford University Press, 1980).

46. Wainwright, *For Our Salvation*, 132.

47. Thus citing W. A. Visser't Hooft, *The Kingship of Christ*, p. 17, is Wainwright, *For Our Salvation*, 174–75.

As King, Jesus Christ mediates divine rule as both God and man, addressing our bondage.[48] The Mediator initiates our participation in God's reign over the cosmos (e.g., Ps 89:35–37; Eph 1:22–23; Phil 2:9–11). When the church overemphasizes this office, however, a focus on righteous rule generates utopianism and/or apocalypticism, as Christians either passively wait for, or heroically attempt to usher in, the fullness of God's kingdom. Far from being triumphalist, the Messiah's revelation of divine glory ensured earthly suffering: no crown before or without the cross. The cross brings freedom from sin and a paradoxical form of "slavery" to God through serving our neighbors—the true freedom of love.[49]

Each office highlights facets of a unified christological reality. Christ the Prophet proclaims truth, eliciting faith. Christ the Priest gives life, eliciting love. Christ the King leads the way, eliciting hope. Modern people may not be familiar with prophets, priests, and kings, but they still seek gurus, find experts, and follow celebrities. Jesus exercises these offices in both humiliation and exaltation. Prophet and Priest continue to characterize his ministry after the resurrection, as our ascended Lord. King already began to characterize his ministry prior to the resurrection, as the personal bearer of God's Spirit. Although Christ exercised these offices in his humanity, his deity gave them depth and scope, uniting in person what was formerly separate in principle.

The *munus triplex* has faced modern challenges. Biblical scholarship tends to associate kingship and priesthood over against prophecy, to align the former two but not the latter with anointing, and to minimize Jesus's unique combination of the offices in one person.[50] Anointing, we are told, was not required of prophets. Whereas the eschatological prophet's anointing is evident in Isaiah 61:1 and the New Testament, the royal and priestly anointings are different, scarcely being mentioned in the New Testament. The prophetic office was the only one that Jesus exercised during his earthly ministry. Even then he did not display the prophetic inspiration characteristic of the Old Testament office, whereas in Israel teaching was under the priestly purview. The traditional application of

---

48. On royal priesthood see Uche Anizor and Hank Voss, *Representing Christ: A Vision for the Priesthood of All Believers* (Downers Grove, IL: IVP Academic, 2016), plus their technical works.

49. Martin Luther, *Freedom of a Christian*, from *LW*, 31:344, cited in relation to Romans 13:8 and 1 Corinthians 9:19 by Wainwright, *For Our Salvation*, 158–59.

50. On the historical reality that priests were Israel's primary teachers and prophets had a more interruptive ministry of the Word, see chap. 5 of Uche Anizor, *Kings and Priests: Scripture's Theological Account of Its Readers* (Eugene, OR: Pickwick, 2014).

all three offices to Jesus, then, transcends his historical humanity and trades upon a conciliar understanding of the God–man.[51]

These challenges, though, illuminate the framework's theological contribution. Davidic kingship is indisputably associated with Jesus's messiahship: naturally, Jesus did not exercise the traditional office during his earthly ministry; instead, he anticipated accession to the Davidic throne in a new, ultimate way. Neither did Jesus exercise the traditional office of Levitical priest, as Hebrews underscores; however, he became both sacrifice and priest in a new, ultimate way. Jesus may have understood himself as the eschatological high priest who would reconstitute a faithful remnant of Israel.[52] In that case Davidic exceptions regarding priestly functions (e.g., 1 Sam 21:6, highlighted in Matt 12:6) could prove the rule—anticipating Jesus's messianic combination of the offices that finally realized Exodus 19:6: "You will be for me a kingdom of priests and a holy nation." As for prophet, again Jesus was not literally anointed, and he may not have experienced (or needed!) ecstatic inspiration. But he was received as a prophet by the populace; he spoke truth to religious and political powers; and he foretold the future. The Gospels present him as a new, ultimate Davidic king, Adamic priest, and Mosaic servant, thus fulfilling the promise of Deuteronomy 18:15. Consequently, the threefold office celebrates the ultimate unification of these mediating offices in the incarnate Son, the human bearer of the Holy Spirit who makes known God the Father. This new wine burst the skins (Luke 5:37–39).

IV. GOD'S FORGIVING, HEALING, AND LIBERATING REIGN

Thus empowered by the Spirit to fulfill his threefold office, the incarnate Son mediated the eschatological invasion of God's forgiving, healing, and liberating reign. Christ's kingship is unlike what people expect. Earthly kings lord it over others, accumulating wealth and enjoying privilege at their expense. Bureaucracies become preoccupied with status and systems rather than service. By contrast, in proclaiming God's reign Jesus emphasized his lowly status, service of others, and

---

51. See, e.g., Wolfhart Pannenberg, *Jesus—God and Man*, trans. Lewis L. Wilkins and Duane A. Priebe, 2nd ed. (Philadelphia: Westminster, 1977), 212–25.

52. Thus making a proposal that notices the Davidic exceptions mentioned in the next sentence is Perrin, *Jesus the Priest*.

eventual martyrdom (Mark 10:35–45). Jesus's ministry addressed the full range of human needs, not just forgiveness, which traditional atonement theologies emphasize, but also healing and liberation that restore justice. Integral to shalom, such justice brings "the flourishing that results from the right ordering of power."[53]

Healing—the "restoration of wholeness (Ps. 41:3), making well whether physically, mentally, or spiritually"[54]—was integral to Jesus's mission.[55] When John the Baptizer sent messengers from prison wondering about Jesus's messiahship, they were told to report the healings and exorcisms they had seen (Luke 7:18–23), using the language of Isaiah 29:18–19 and 35:5–6 as well as 61:1–2. These healings brought temporary liberation from death's power, signaling eventual liberation in the fullness of God's kingdom. Healing and salvation are intertwined, metaphorically and beyond: "By his wounds we are healed" (Isa 53:5). The frequent manner of Jesus's healings, eliciting faith, "did not treat the sick as mere passive recipients . . . [but] made their experience part of their relationship with God."[56] Healings signaled the inauguration of God's kingdom in person.

Jesus's mission charter references healing along with liberation— release from bondage, restoration of justice—for prisoners and the oppressed. Such prophetic, poetic passages do not strictly identify beneficiaries so much as celebrate widespread hope. The announcement of Isaiah's fulfillment in Luke 4 is followed by an exorcism (4:31–37) and numerous healings (4:38–44). These forms of liberation are surrounded by others: healing and forgiving a paralyzed man (5:17–26), liberating him from sin and guilt; eating with tax collectors and sinners, liberating them from social rejection (5:27–32); challenging expectations about fasting, liberating people from merely external religion (5:33–39). Jesus honored women, establishing Mary and others as trustworthy witnesses to his liberating work (1:46–56; 24:1–12). Occasionally Jesus liberated followers from physical threats, suggesting that eventually he will reconcile human relationships with not only God and each other but also

53. Bethany Hanke Hoang and Kristen Deede Johnson, *The Justice Calling: Where Passion Meets Perseverance* (Grand Rapids: Brazos, 2016), 40.

54. Paul G. Chappell, "Heal, Healing," in *EDT*, 368–69.

55. On the complexity of Jesus as healer in African Christology, see chap. 5 of Timothy C. Tennent, *Theology in the Context of World Christianity: How the Global Church Is Influencing the Way We Think about and Discuss Theology* (Grand Rapids: Zondervan, 2007).

56. Richard Bauckham, *Jesus: A Very Short Introduction* (Oxford: Oxford University Press, 2011), 43. Note, e.g., Mark 6:5–6.

the cosmos. Of course, Jesus did not lead a political revolution against the Romans. Yet his followers shook up the entire world (Acts 17:6), challenging oppression with God's grace in Christ.[57]

Christ's ministry of reconciliation was liberating, addressing social structures and systemic evil as well as personal sin. For instance, Jesus endured a "lynching" like Black people faced in the American South.[58] He faced mob violence that relied on the tacit support and overt misuse of government power. This mob violence substituted prejudice for truth in a frenzy of scapegoating. Christ's willingness to undergo such injustice reflects God's solidarity with the oppressed, who are constantly vulnerable and have their dignity diminished by pervasive fear. From still another angle, the crucified Jesus endured sexual humiliation that put him in solidarity with numerous victims throughout history, especially though not exclusively women.[59] These and other liberation-focused approaches may not account for the fullness of biblical material on atonement; sometimes they may not affirm conciliar Christology. But they highlight integral aspects of Christ's redemptive suffering that are frequently neglected.[60] They underscore that Jesus was crucified because of how he lived.[61]

Consequently, Jesus demonstrated God's "preferential option" for the poor.[62] This concept typically does not claim that God loves people more or less based on income. Instead, God loves in ways that are tailored for our needs; sometimes a parent seemingly favors a vulnerable child.[63]

---

57. On Jewish purity regulations, see the recent argument of Thiessen, *Jesus and the Forces*. Apparently interpreters have misunderstood "leprosy" texts and overemphasized Jewish legal unanimity opposite Jesus's supposed break with its traditions, while the unifying concern over ritual impurity involved death. Yet not all of Thiessen's readings are equally convincing, and his thesis may run into complications with gentile inclusion elsewhere in the New Testament. On political effects vis-à-vis the Roman empire, see C. Kavin Rowe, *World Upside Down: Reading Acts in the Graeco-Roman Age* (New York: Oxford University Press, 2009).

58. James H. Cone, *The Cross and the Lynching Tree* (Maryknoll, NY: Orbis, 2011).

59. See the recent work of Erin Heim, with links available at https://www.pastortheologians .com/podcasthomepage/2021/10/11/sexual-violence-metoo-and-the-crucifixion.

60. Thus calling for an "evangelical liberation theology" is Craig L. Blomberg, "'Your Faith Has Made You Whole': The Evangelical Liberation Theology of Jesus," in *Jesus of Nazareth: Lord and Christ: Essays on the Historical Jesus and New Testament Christology*, ed. Joel B. Green and Max Turner (Grand Rapids: Eerdmans, 1994), 75–93.

61. Latin American evangelicals frequently reiterated this understanding of Jesus; to trace their influence, see David C. Kirkpatrick, *A Gospel for the Poor: Global Social Christianity and the Latin American Left* (Philadelphia: University of Pennsylvania Press, 2019).

62. In Luke the poor is not just an economic category but incorporates "outsiders"; so Joel B. Green, "Good News to Whom? Jesus and the 'Poor' in the Gospel of Luke," in *Jesus of Nazareth: Lord and Christ*, 59–74.

63. I owe this framing to Gerardo Corpeño (who references Roberto Guizveta, *Caminemos con Jesus*), through whose PhD dissertation I encountered much Lukan and liberation theology

There is also correlation, though not inevitable causation, between material poverty and spiritual riches. In his Sermon on the Mount, Jesus called the "poor in spirit" blessed (Matt 5:3). He chastened any dependence upon earthly realities—whether Jewish descent, physical wealth, or anything else—for security. The Father's loving care enables seeking first God's kingdom and relying ultimately on nothing else. The rich have a harder time doing so, as the young ruler illustrates (Luke 18:18–30). God's providential care extends to all creatures (Matt 6:25–34) without contradicting the human responsibility to represent divine love and wise stewardship throughout the cosmos.[64]

Accordingly, Jesus pursued liberation in tandem with reconciliation while living as a faithful Israelite:[65] "How different might have been the story of the last two thousand years on this planet grown old from suffering if the link between Jesus and Israel had never been severed!"[66] Severing this link left the church with a sociopolitical legacy that includes imperial collaboration, colonialism, patriarchy, racism, and slavery. Of course, some conflict was unsurprising since Jesus aspired to reform

beyond what is cited here. Where evangelical Christology must depart from liberation theology largely involves its denials—rather than its affirmations of anthropological, not just ecclesiastical, concerns; a utopian, not just factual, dimension; critical, not just dogmatic, reflection; a social, not just personal, orientation; and pursuit of orthopraxis, not just orthodoxy. Ranking the former items over the latter risks false dichotomies, allowing an unbiblical Christology "from below" to set the agenda, as in Leonardo Boff, *Jesus Christ Liberator: A Critical Christology for Our Time* (Maryknoll, NY: Orbis, 1978). Even so, reminders that "the whole Christ liberates" have been necessary; see, e.g., Edgardo Colón-Emeric, "Jesus Was Born in Guatemala: Toward a Latinx Wesleyan Christology," in *Methodist Christology: From the Wesleys to the Twenty-First Century*, ed. Jason E. Vickers and Jerome Van Kuiken (Nashville: Wesley's Foundery, 2020), 155–56. For wrestling with the inadequate compassion of traditional Protestant Christology (which tends to have Christ suffering for, but not with, us), see Richard J. Mouw and Douglas A. Sweeney, *The Suffering and Victorious Christ: Toward a More Compassionate Christology* (Grand Rapids: Baker Academic, 2013).

64. A recent feminist proposal expands the creedal *homoousion* to incorporate all of creation within the being assumed by the incarnate Christ; so Rebecca L. Copeland, *Created Being: Expanding Creedal Christology* (Waco, TX: Baylor University Press, 2020). Although they can provoke churchly repentance for sinful anthropocentrism, such "deep incarnation" proposals are inconsistent with the focus of Holy Scripture on Jesus's solidarity with humanity.

65. A virtue of Moltmann's Spirit Christology is close attention to neglected moments of Christ's life—e.g., "Acceptance of the Outcasts–the Raising Up of the Humiliated" garnering multiple pages. See Jürgen Moltmann, *The Way of Jesus Christ: Christology in Messianic Dimensions*, trans. Margaret Kohl (Minneapolis: Fortress, 1993), 112–16. On the theological ambiguities of reconciliation perhaps hindering liberation, see O. Ernesto Valiente, *Liberation through Reconciliation: Jon Sobrino's Christological Spirituality* (New York: Fordham University Press, 2016), 10–11, 25.

66. Howard Thurman, *Jesus and the Disinherited* (Boston: Beacon, 1976), 6. For extensive historical-theological outworking of this claim, engaging figures like Immanuel Kant (1724–1804) in one case and European colonialism on the other, see J. Kameron Carter, *Race: A Theological Account* (New York: Oxford University Press, 2008); Jennings, *Christian Imagination*. However, *Jewish* is not an uncomplicated category for Jesus, as discussed in Kayko Driedger Hesslein, *Dual Citizenship: Two-Natures Christologies and the Jewish Jesus* (London: Bloomsbury, 2015).

Israel's life as God's people.[67] The universal scope of his reconciling ministry is apparent from outreach to the marginalized—whether sinners like tax collectors and prostitutes, regions like Galilee, unclean peoples like gentiles, or women in general—not least in table fellowship.[68] Such outreach was not condescending but empowering, partly due to Jesus's solidarity with "the least of these," including his migrant status, both forced and voluntary.[69] In a narrower sense reconciliation focuses on atonement; only gracious reconciliation between God and humanity provides the secure love with which to pursue earthly justice in faith and hope.[70] Then creaturely reconciliation follows from Jesus's merciful recapitulation of human existence before God.[71]

Since God's kingdom contains multiple senses and stages,[72] Christians discern varying parameters for currently seeking physical healing and political liberation along with divine forgiveness. The Gospels emphasize Jesus's proclamation with personal presence, powerful deeds, and authoritative words. How and when his followers will experience healing and liberation "between the times" is naturally debatable. But Jesus certainly

---

67. Suggesting that "the divergent reactions to Jesus . . . flow not from his incidental characteristics but from the central features of his life, teaching, and actions," is Michael J. McClymond, *Familiar Stranger: An Introduction to Jesus of Nazareth* (Grand Rapids: Eerdmans, 2004), 138. In a sense Israel is "the raw nerve in Christian theology," per the title of chap. 9 in Cornelis van der Kooi and Gijsbert van den Brink, *Christian Dogmatics: An Introduction*, trans. Reinder Bruinsma and James D. Bratt (Grand Rapids: Eerdmans, 2017). For an Arabic perspective on Jesus's identity, see Ghassan Khalaf, "Jesus and Judaism: His Identity and Relationship to Judaism," in *Arabic Christian Theology: A Contemporary Global Evangelical Perspective*, ed. Andrea Zaki Stephanous (Grand Rapids: Zondervan, 2019), 89–210.

68. Eating even appears among "Jesus's Works" in the Christology "from below" of Dan R. Stiver, *Life Together in the Way of Jesus Christ: An Introduction to Christian Theology* (Waco, TX: Baylor University Press, 2009). Episodes like Jesus's encounter with the Syro-Phoenician woman (Mark 7:24–30) are sometimes evoked as contradicting his reconciling ministry. Once cultural expectations are accounted for, however, in the context of this doubly marginalized gentile woman, "this pericope marks the further opening of the door rather than an attempt to swing it shut again," according to R. T. France, *The Gospel of Mark*, NIGTC (Grand Rapids: Eerdmans, 2002), 296. The Gospels' narration depicts Christ as a master teacher, eliciting the woman's exemplary faith. See further Bauckham, *Jesus*, 54.

69. Christopher M. Hays and Milton Acosta, "Jesus as Missional Migrant: Latin American Christologies, the New Testament Witness, and Twenty-First Century Migration," in *Who Do You Say I Am? On the Humanity of Jesus*, ed. George Kalantzis, David B. Capes, and Ty Kieser (Eugene, OR: Cascade, 2020), 158–77.

70. This claim appears in an Anabaptist and liberationist fashion by Antonio González, *The Gospel of Faith and Justice*, trans. Joseph Owens (Maryknoll, NY: Orbis, 2005). Whether or not his broad application of Matthew 25:31–46 is correct, he shows how historic churches' "Constantinian" situations have attenuated the passage's liberating impact.

71. On Jesus's "decision not to turn Rome into an enemy—even as a child living under the thumb of an empire," see Esau McCaulley, "Toward a Black Anthropology and Social Ethic: Why the Humanity and Jewishness of Jesus Matters," in *Who Do You Say I Am? On the Humanity of Jesus*, 156.

72. Handily summarized in Carson, *Jesus the Son of God*, 50–53.

proclaimed holistic good news, relating the forgiveness of sins and the reconciliation of relationships to the healing of bodies and liberation from oppression.

V. JESUS OF NAZARETH, THE SAVIOR

In the words of one introductory title, "Even His Name Means Salvation"![73] God instructed Joseph and Mary to use the name Jesus in light of its Hebrew meaning, "Yahweh saves" (Matt 1:21). The same passage names him Immanuel, God with us (Matt 1:23): he brings salvation in person. The name Jesus both indicates a particular human being and identifies him with the divine name of Savior, whereas eventually Christ also became a name that goes beyond entitling him as Messiah.[74] His hometown, Nazareth, remains marginal except for two enigmatic statements (Matt 2:23; John 1:46) that attach its theological significance to him rather than the reverse.[75] Once Jesus encountered the mixed reaction detailed at the start of this chapter, he moved to Capernaum.[76]

The gospel "lives" do not psychologize Jesus; they characterize him indirectly by narrating actions and relationships. This fully human person ate, drank, grew, slept, traveled, and worked. He healed disease and exorcised demons; he also worked wonders that generated food or otherwise demonstrated cosmic power. He taught in parables and with authority. He called twelve followers and accumulated a host of others. The number twelve suggests regathering Israel around himself; the prominence of women within a nearby circle suggests an inclusive reframing of communal membership. Jesus had close friends with whom he feasted and at whose death he wept. Yet he also ate with disreputable people, eliciting accusations of gluttony and drunkenness. There were enemies to love too: he suffered ultimate betrayal from one disciple, abandonment from others, fickleness from crowds, and rejection from

---

73. William C. Placher, *Jesus the Savior: The Meaning of Jesus Christ for Christian Faith* (Louisville: Westminster John Knox, 2001).

74. Acts reflects this development; see further Michael F. Bird, *Jesus Is the Christ: The Messianic Testimony of the Gospels* (Downers Grove, IL: IVP Academic, 2012).

75. John 1 underscores its relative obscurity apart from Jesus. Matthew 2 makes either a typological connection to Samson as a Nazirite, or a wordplay with *neṣer* ("shoot, branch"; Isa 11:1), or both. See Nicholas G. Piotrowski, "Nazarene," in *DJG*, 624–25.

76. On these villages, including Capernaum's larger size and connections to Peter, see Rainer Riesner, "Archeology and Geography," in *DJG*, 44–59.

his hometown. Along the way he faced confrontations with religious leaders before imperial callousness resulted in unjust crucifixion.

For all of Jesus's cleverness and courage, the Gospels' narrative arc most fundamentally characterizes him in terms of compassionate humility.[77] If ancient biographies characterized a hero's life in terms of his death, then his words from the cross, "Father, forgive them, for they do not know what they are doing" (Luke 23:34), speak volumes. The naming of Jerusalem's sin is clear, yet so is compassion, not without exasperation (e.g., 23:28–31), regarding humanity's violent rejection of God's reign. Earlier indications of such compassion include Matthew 9:36 ("When he saw the crowds, he had compassion on them, because they were harassed and helpless, like sheep without a shepherd") and 11:29 ("I am gentle and humble in heart, and you will find rest for your souls"). Compassion goes beyond pity, committing to solidarity with and action on behalf of the suffering other(s).[78] Jesus's gentleness did not involve being a "meek and mild" milquetoast but having a humble self-appraisal from which loving agency springs. When he became angry, for instance in dealing with disciples or cleansing the temple, he lost no control to arbitrary feelings; he enacted moral judgments.[79] Jesus certainly confronted idolatry and injustice, but he did not engage evil as a power that must be overcome with superior force.[80] He compassionately overcame the usurpers of God's good creation with evangelical truth. Undoubtedly his compassionate humility sprang from filial communion with God the Father by the Holy Spirit, in which he participated humanly by prioritizing the practice of prayer.[81]

Thus this chapter has finished contemplating the heart of Jesus's earthly mission as Savior. Luke 4:14–30 is a programmatic text, proclaiming the arrival of God's reign in Jesus as the good news Isaiah foretold. The catalyst of his mission was the Holy Spirit. Yet Spirit Christology highlights not only the incarnate Son's active human obedience but also

---

77. So Dane Ortlund, *Gentle and Lowly: The Heart of Christ for Sinners and Sufferers* (Wheaton, IL: Crossway, 2020).

78. On compassion's distinction from pity, see Oliver Davies, *A Theology of Compassion: Metaphysics of Difference and the Renewal of Tradition* (Grand Rapids: Eerdmans, 2003).

79. See Benjamin Breckinridge Warfield, "The Emotional Life of Our Lord," in *The Person and Work of Christ*, ed. Samuel G. Craig (Philadelphia: Presbyterian and Reformed, 1950), 93–145. On p. 122 Warfield mentions "the paradox that true mercy is no less the product of anger than of pity," distinguishing divine mercy from mere tolerance.

80. Henri Blocher, *Songs of the Servant: Isaiah's Good News* (repr., Vancouver: Regent College, 2005), 78.

81. On this neglected topic see chap. 6 of Bockmuehl, *This Jesus: Martyr, Lord, Messiah*.

his missional agency within the inseparable operations of the Blessed Trinity. The core structure of his mission involved the threefold office of prophet, priest, and king. The consequences of his mission included the forgiveness, healing, and liberation that inaugurated God's eschatological reign. The mission's protagonist, Jesus of Nazareth, has enacted God's saving promises by bearing God's Spirit and embodying God's presence, bringing God's mercy to bear on a broken world.

CHAPTER 8

PASSION AS THE SON OF MAN

Mark 10:32–45 [Isaiah 52:13–53:12]

As epitomized in **Mark 10:32–45** (with **Isaiah 52:13–53:12** in the background), Jesus Christ is the **Son of Man**, whose **passion** was the once-for-all act of atonement through which God redeemed us. *Amid an array of biblical metaphors, penal substitution is the central concept that clarifies how Jesus's crucifixion bore away sin's deadly consequences. The extent of Christ's sinless identification with fallen humanity is evident in his body's burial and his soul's descent to the dead. Yet as Son of Man he also attained our eschatological triumph.*

According to the Gospels, Jesus's most frequent self-designation was the Son of Man, yet its historical and theological significance remains contested. Son of Man connects with both Jesus's earthly mission and his heavenly session, anticipating eschatological consummation. It comes to the forefront, though, in crucial texts regarding his passion. The self-sacrifice that characterized Jesus's earthly mission led to the cross, and in the mystery of God's plan the cross led ultimately to the crown. Accordingly, in John 12:23 Jesus anticipated his death with the words, "The hour has come for the Son of Man to be glorified," and in John 12:34 the crowd responded, "How can you say, 'The Son of Man must be lifted up'?" In the passage that introduces the current chapter, Mark 10:32–45, Jesus first uses the designation when he predicts being delivered over to death by the religious and imperial establishment (v. 33); later he uses it when he characterizes the purpose of his mission (v. 45).

Consequently, the present chapter begins with Mark 10:32–45 and ends with Son of Man as the name that can encapsulate Jesus's passion. As the Mark passage integrates the passion in a fundamental way with the rest of Jesus's life, it evokes Isaiah 52:13–53:12 (hereafter "Isaiah 53"), the crucial Old Testament passage about the Suffering Servant. On that foundation this chapter builds a broader account of the passion's *accomplishment*: Christ's ministry of atonement. And after discerning the implications "for us" of the creedal phrases, "He suffered under Pontius Pilate, was crucified, died, and was buried," the chapter turns to the subsequent phrase, "He descended into hell." This reference to the passion's *aftermath* underscores the extraordinary extent of Christ's self-sacrificing love.

I. SACRIFICIAL RANSOM IN MARK 10:32–45 (ISAIAH 52:13–53:12)

Mark 10:32–45 follows typically poignant words from Jesus with two additional conversations (vv. 32–34; vv. 35–45). In preceding verses (vv. 17–31), Jesus encountered a rich young ruler who was so attached to possessions that he was unwilling to follow Jesus. Upon hearing of the difficulty that rich people face in entering God's kingdom, the disciples were scandalized; their assumption was that riches manifested God's blessing rather than a spiritual obstacle. On their behalf Peter asked what benefit they would eventually receive from leaving everything to follow Jesus. The closing words of Jesus's reply were, "But many who are first will be last, and the last first" (v. 31). In an ensuing conversation on the way to Jerusalem, Jesus prepares astonished, fearful disciples for his death (vv. 32–34). Another subsequent conversation is prompted by disciples who, with brazen interest in prominent positions, reflect persistent failure to understand Jesus's teaching (vv. 35–45).

In the first conversation (vv. 32–34), Jesus addresses the twelve as an inner circle, apprising them of what will happen to him. The prediction is thorough: not just being killed and resurrected three days later, but a litany of preceding steps: pagan condemnation, mockery, spitting, and flogging. There is repetition from prior parallels, including 9:31, but "having been killed" drops out since "with so much emphasis on maltreatment . . . a second reference to being killed would be otiose."[1] Each element—even Jesus's knowledge, a unique property of YHWH from Isaiah 40 and following—appears in the "'blueprint' for the suffering of the Isaianic servant."[2]

In the second conversation (vv. 35–45), Jesus intervenes to correct the disciples. As usual, the Markan drama both implies a critique of misunderstanding and issues a call to discipleship. At the Gospel's midpoint (8:22–26), the disciples have gained only a fuzzy glimpse; they need full restoration to see clearly. So James and John recognize Jesus as their "teacher" (10:35) who will enjoy royal, eschatological "glory" (v. 37). But wanting honored seats, they do not know what they are asking and cannot accomplish what Jesus will (v. 38). They will drink the cup and receive the baptism of suffering, perhaps even martyrdom (v. 39).[3] But honored seats in God's kingdom have already been assigned (v. 40). Again Mark's Christology both deflects ultimate glory to God as Father and distinguishes Jesus as speaking with unique knowledge.[4] Nor does the drama end there. The other disciples become indignant with James and John (v. 41)—jealous not for Jesus's honor but for their own. Taking advantage of a teachable moment (vv. 42–45), Jesus calls them together, knowing of their indignation despite its private expression. He contrasts pagan rulers' power with the only form of greatness to which his disciples should aspire: being servants (*diakonoi*), even slaves (*douloi*), of all.

In that context, Mark 10:45 offers a vital statement of Jesus's redemptive mission, a climactic conclusion to the Gospel's central section. As we shall see, the name Son of Man has associations with divine glory yet connotes solidarity with humanity. "Did not come" suggests his divine preexistence and intentional mission. The ensuing contrast confronts the

---

1. Robert H. Gundry, *Mark: A Commentary on His Apology for the Cross* (Grand Rapids: Eerdmans, 1993), 572. On p. 575 Gundry suggests that the general verb (rather than "crucify") strengthens the authenticity of this prediction.

2. France, *Mark*, 413. For a chart of elements in the Markan prediction passages, see William L. Lane, *The Gospel of Mark*, NICNT (Grand Rapids: Eerdmans, 1974), 375. This foreknowledge limits the appropriate inferences to draw from Jesus's limited knowledge in 13:30–32.

3. Drinking the cup points minimally to a shared fate, maximally to divine judgment. Suggesting that the disciples' cup references suffering but not judgment is Pheme Perkins, "The Gospel of Mark," in *NIB*, 8:653.

4. On deflection, see Elizabeth Struthers Malbon, "The Christology of Mark's Gospel: Narrative Christology and the Markan Jesus," in *Who Do You Say That I Am? Essays on Christology*, ed. Mark Allan Powell and David R. Bauer (Louisville: Westminster John Knox, 1999), 33–48. Rendering v. 40 as emphasizing supernatural knowledge—"is not mine to give *except* [that it is mine to give] to those for whom it has been prepared" (with emphasis added)—is Gundry, *Mark*, 577–78.

disciples with the counterexample of their teacher, whose servanthood they are to imitate. He came "to give his life as a ransom for many." Notwithstanding possible martyrdom for some disciples, this phrase indicates the Son of Man's unique vocation.

Mark 10:45 evokes Isaiah 53, with "many" echoing the "many (nations)" aghast at the Servant (52:14–15) and the "many" whose sin he bears (53:11–12).[5] Isaiah 53's influence transcended Jesus's passion, affecting his entire ministry.[6] Here, though, the Servant Songs led Jesus to the cross as the climax of his earthly vocation. For present purposes, Isaiah 53 provides (1) God's perspective on the mysterious Servant (52:13–15), (2) human perspectives on the Servant (53:1–10), and (3) God's climactic perspective on the vindicated Servant (53:11–12). This structure reflects the shifting pronouns that identify the speaker(s), theologically anticipating the contrast of Mark 8:33 between God's and merely human perspectives.[7]

First, the opening stanza (52:13–15) introduces *God's perspective on the mysterious Servant*.[8] He will act wisely and eventually be exalted (52:13, 15), but his humiliating appearance appalls many (52:14). Although other Servant Songs (at least Isaiah 42) may refer corporately to Israel, here the Servant is an individual whom Israel initially rejects—indicating a vicarious role on behalf of, not given to, Israel.[9] Yet the Servant's wise action will effect wisdom in others ("they will understand," 52:15; cf. Dan 12:3).[10] That effect builds a bridge between Isaiah 49–52, which

---

5. Summarizing differences between Isaiah 53 and Mark 10:45, influenced by efforts from C. K. Barrett and Morna Hooker to break their linkage, is Gundry, *Mark*, 591–92. Suggesting that Mark 10:45, despite no verbal echo of the Servant, still connects to Isaiah 53 is France, *Mark*, 420. Noticing Isaiah 53 as a test case differentiating "premodern" from modern exegesis is Carter, *Interpreting Scripture with the Great Tradition*. Highlighting Mark's Isaianic context, with the Gospel answering the prayer of Isaiah 63:19–64:4 that the heavens would open and Yhwh would descend, is Hays, *Echoes in the Gospels*, 18.

6. Jeannine K. Brown, "Jesus's Messiah as Isaiah's Servant of the Lord: New Testament Explorations," *JETS* 53, no. 1 (March 2020): 58, 67.

7. Andrew T. Abernethy, *Discovering Isaiah: Content, Interpretation, Reception* (London: SPCK, 2021), 122–31. In this Servant song Yhwh, not the prophet, is the first-person speaker, as highlighted by Richard E. Averbeck, "Christian Interpretations of Isaiah 53," in *The Gospel according to Isaiah 53: Encountering the Suffering Servant in Jewish and Christian Theology*, ed. Darrell L. Bock and Mitch Glaser (Grand Rapids: Kregel, 2012), 59–60.

8. So Motyer, *Prophecy of Isaiah*, 423–24.

9. As noted by Walter C. Kaiser Jr., "The Identity and Mission of the 'Servant of the Lord,'" in *The Gospel according to Isaiah 53*, 87–107. On "sprinkle" or "startle" in Isaiah 52:15, see Motyer, *Prophecy of Isaiah*, 425–26. Relating the verb to anointing ("spatter") is John Goldingay and David Payne, *Isaiah 40–55*, ICC (London: T&T Clark, 2006), 294–95. Apparently the Servant will accomplish a priestly, purifying act.

10. George A. F. Knight, *Servant Theology: A Commentary on the Book of Isaiah 40–55*, ITC (Edinburgh: Handsel, 1984), 165.

anticipates salvation, and Isaiah 54–55, which invites participation in salvation.[11] The Servant will be "lifted up" and "highly exalted," language normally used of God, while the "many" indicates virtually all.[12] From God's perspective, the Servant represents YHWH with widely redemptive consequences.

Second, 53:1–10 depicts the Servant's suffering from *human perspectives*. The focus of the second stanza, 53:1–3, is upon his rejection; verse 1 assumes that few have embraced the prophetic revelation of the Lord's redemptive might. The description in verse 2a recalls "the Messianic imagery of 4:2, the 'holy seed' imagery of 6:13 and the royal imagery of 10:33–11:1."[13] Yet the description in verse 2b indicates no natural human attraction, and in verse 3 the Servant is despised by many.[14]

The third stanza (53:4–6) reflects a redeemed perspective on the suffering. Verse 4 indicates that the Servant willingly bore what people mistook as divine punishment. "Stricken" evokes Leviticus; 61 out of its 78 Old Testament uses appear in Leviticus 13–14.[15] The subsequent realization in Isaiah 53:5 is that the sins for which the Servant was "pierced" and "crushed" were ours—in exchange for which we receive peace and healing. Verse 6 summarizes our helpless waywardness—like lost sheep—making explicit what passive verbs in verses 4b–5 leave implicit: the Servant's vicarious suffering is at YHWH's initiative. Both the Servant (v. 4) and YHWH (v. 6) have chosen this sacrifice. Intriguingly, the pronoun *hu'* ("he") appears unnecessarily in verses 4–5, perhaps echoing the "I am he" of YHWH in Isaiah 43:10, 13: "This portrait of the Servant comprises two elements, that of a very human Israel, and that of 'God *in* Israel.'"[16]

The fourth stanza, beginning in Isaiah 53:7, underscores the extent of this vicarious suffering: to the death. The Servant's "mouth" frames verses 7–9, with the Lord's "hand" connecting verse 10 to the Lord's arm in verse 1. Like sheep, the Servant is silent as he is led to the

---

11. The Servant has explicit identification with Israel from Isaiah 40 until 49:3 (41:8–9; 44:1–2, 21; 45:4; 48:20)—after which the Servant ministers to Israel (e.g., 49:5).

12. The phrase is used only in Isaiah, and in 6:1, 33:10, and 57:15 it refers to YHWH; so John N. Oswalt, *The Book of Isaiah Chapters 40–66*, NICOT (Grand Rapids: Eerdmans, 1998), 378.

13. Goldingay and Payne, *Isaiah 40–55*, 279–80.

14. Noting the one/many contrast is Motyer, *Prophecy of Isaiah*, 428. Highlighting potential references to what we now see in terms of disability is Jeremy Schipper, *Disability and Isaiah's Suffering Servant*, Biblical Refigurations (Oxford: Oxford University Press, 2011). This language, however, is not so comprehensive that the passage should be reinterpreted to eliminate a sacrificial death.

15. Averbeck, "Christian Interpretations of Isaiah 53," 54.

16. Knight, *Servant Theology*, 171.

slaughter (v. 7), yet he goes actively. Verse 8 reinforces the isolation: no beneficiaries protest the Servant's seizure and death. The divine punishment assumed in verse 4 reappears in verse 8, but not as the people thought. Verse 9 juxtaposes the Servant's burial with his blamelessness, being guilty of neither violence nor deceit, whether in external acts or internal states expressed by the mouth (which epitomized Isaiah's guilt in 6:5). The verse's first half is difficult, but the core mystery involves how a criminal could receive a rich man's burial. Fulfillment in Jesus offers an answer.

Third, returning climactically to YHWH'S perspective on the vindicated Servant, a fifth and final stanza offers both a hopeful epilogue and a fuller explanation for the Servant's death. There is overlap with 52:13–15 ("many" and initial hope for exaltation) and 53:4–6 (reinterpretation of the humiliation and death). Hence 53:10 reiterates that YHWH willed the Servant's suffering and reassures us that YHWH wills for the Servant to prosper. Upon the mystery of how the Servant could "see his offspring and prolong his days," Jesus's resurrection sheds the awaited light.[17] Isaiah 53:11 also repeats "life," anticipating that the Servant's knowledge and righteousness (characteristics that Isaiah associates with YHWH) will bring righteousness to "many" even as he bears their iniquities.[18] Isaiah 57:14–21 indicates that exile did not elicit repentance (57:17), but peace and healing will come from YHWH personally (57:18–19)—except for those who persist in wickedness (57:20–21). By implication YHWH will guide many toward the necessary change of heart (57:18). As Isaiah 53:12 concludes, whether the many and the strong are the portion itself or poetic bystanders of the Servant's success, his exaltation is certain, vindicating his sacrificial death. His comprehensive mediation is underscored by interceding on behalf of those whose sin he bore.

Isaiah 53 brings Levitical sacrifice to bear on the Servant's suffering. Sprinkling points toward two offerings. First, ordination of Aaron and his sons to the priesthood involved sprinkling blood (Lev 8), connected to the peace offering. Exodus 19:5–6 and 24:6–8 apply this sprinkling

---

17. Suggesting that this vision stretches the boundaries of Old Testament language and leaves initial audiences puzzled is Abernethy, *Discovering Isaiah*, 129–30.

18. The expectation of 53:11–12 that someone will bear others' guilt is unprecedented but is coherent with Isaiah's hope for extraordinary purification of the people and creation; so J. Alan Groves, "Atonement in Isaiah 53: 'For He Bore the Sins of Many,'" in *The Glory of the Atonement: Biblical, Theological and Practical Perspectives*, ed. Charles E. Hill and Frank A. James III (Downers Grove, IL: InterVarsity Press, 2004), 61–89.

to Israel's vocation, becoming a kingdom of priests.[19] Second, sprinkling is prominent again in Leviticus 14 amid cleansing rituals, within which guilt offerings made reparation for desecration of sacred things. Israel's exile indicated that she broke the covenant, desecrated the promised land, and needed cleansing.[20] Isaiah's Servant makes the reparative guilt offering for this defilement. Now the people can become the *sancta* they were called to be.[21] A pyramid effect connects the people with the Servant: the people as God's servant are led by particular servants (near context: a prophet like Moses; broader context: the anointed Cyrus); they will be rescued by the ultimate Servant, who gives rise to a redeemed remnant.[22] Despite the absence of verbal links, Zechariah 12:10–13 and Daniel 10–12 are also relevant: amid YHWH's saving victory, Israel will mourn the equivalent of a firstborn son whom they have pierced, yet wise men like Daniel will lead many to righteousness.[23] Furthermore, if the reference to light is original in Isaiah 53:11, then it may evoke the promised child from Isaiah 9.[24] Whether or not the Suffering Servant and the Davidic king coalesce within Isaiah itself, Christians find these hopes to be fulfilled in Jesus Christ.[25]

The Servant's cleansing, reparative sacrifice stands behind Mark's presentation of Jesus's expressed purpose in 10:45.[26] To catalog the

---

19. On the connection with Exodus 24 maintaining (for Luke, in the first instance) the Hebrew text's interpretation of Isaiah 53 as a guilt offering, see Ulrike Mittmann, "Jes 53 LXX–ein umstrittener urchristlicher Referenztext. Zum traditions–und rezeptionsgeschichtlichen Hintergrund der Einsetzungsworte," in *Die Weisheit und der Gottessohn: Studien zur Hermeneutischen Grundlegung einer Theologie des Neuen Testaments*, WUNT (Tübingen: Mohr Siebeck, 2021), chap. 8.

20. Seeing Leviticus 5:14–19 behind the *'āšām* or guilt offering of Isaiah 53:10 is Knight, *Servant Theology*, 176–77. He contrasts the Mosaic substitutionary offering with the Servant offering himself, noting on p. 180 that carrying away iniquity (Isa 53:4, 12) evokes the scapegoat of Leviticus 16:22, while the Servant's intercession evokes Moses's ministry from Exodus 32.

21. This proposal especially depends on Averbeck, "Christian Interpretations of Isaiah 53," 51–59. Touch points with prior Scripture include divine punishment and priestly ritual—although the Servant's deformities complicate his status as the sacrificial lamb—according to Abernethy, *Discovering Isaiah*, 126–27.

22. On Franz Delitzsch's pyramid of one and many along with Cyrus's significance (yet his distinction from the Servant), see Averbeck, "Christian Interpretations of Isaiah 53," 37–39.

23. As highlighted by Goldingay and Payne, *Isaiah 40–55*, 284–85. At several points, though, they opt for a different understanding than is proposed here.

24. As noted, albeit seeing light as a later addition, in Goldingay and Payne, *Isaiah 40–55*, 324.

25. Keeping the Suffering Servant (prophetic and priestly) and Davidic king (royal, focused on societal justice) hopes distinct, while citing G. B. Caird's famous line about a composite job description that only one applicant (Christ) could fulfill, is Abernethy, *Discovering Isaiah*, 133–34. But if Isaiah 9 anticipates a divine and not just Davidic Messiah, perhaps Isaianic hopes do not remain as distinct.

26. "Even critics recognize that it is difficult to deny some parallelism with Isa. 53:12," as noted by Rikk E. Watts, "Mark," in *CNTOT*, 203.

connections, from back to front: (1) Mark's last word, *pollōn* ("many"), repeatedly designates beneficiaries in Isaiah 53. (2) Mark's *anti* ("for") fits Isaiah 53 since that is the only Old Testament passage that anticipates someone bearing others' punishment. (3) Mark's reference to Jesus's "life" uses a word (*psychē*) that appears three times in the LXX of Isaiah 53:11–12 (with a synonym in 53:8). (4) Mark's servant vocabulary evokes the protagonist of Isaiah 53. (5) *Lutron* ("ransom") indirectly connects with Isaiah's Servant bearing sins and being an *'āšām* ("guilt offering").[27] Contextually, the prediction in Mark 10:33–34 evokes Isaiah 50:6 regarding mockery and scourging, while the condemnation to death may evoke Isaiah 53:8–9, 12.[28]

Of course, the ensuing question concerns how directly and fully to move from apparent Markan LXX connections to Jesus's self-understanding, and correspondingly from the *lutron* to the *'āšām*. In Isaiah, the Servant cannot simply bear preexilic sins for which Israel has already borne discipline (Isa 40:2) but addresses a fundamental breach in covenant faithfulness. The *'āšām* could enact ritual purification of lepers exiled from the community, or it could redress desecration of *sancta* when accompanied by appropriate remorse. The Servant having become the offering, all that remained for Israelites to join the many redeemed offspring was repentance, as expressed in Isaiah 53:4–6.[29] Mark's *lutron* appears only here (along with the Matthean parallel and the related phrase in 1 Tim 2:6) in the New Testament, while the LXX uses more general language for giving an offering. Although *lutron* focuses upon the result of release from slavery, not the mechanism of pardon from guilt, "the essential meaning is deliverance by the payment of an 'equivalent.'"[30] Along biblical-historical lines, then, we cannot know how specifically *'āšām* shaped Jesus's human self-understanding of how he would accomplish the *lutron*. Yet in either the Greek or Hebrew text, substitutionary death is integral to Isaiah 53, so "it is as if Jesus said, 'The Son of Man came to fulfil the task of the *'ebed Yahweh*.'"[31]

---

27. Some see Isaiah 43:3–4 in the background due to *ransom* language; so, e.g., Andrew T. LePeau, *Mark through Old Testament Eyes* (Grand Rapids: Kregel, 2017), 192. However, the focus on exchanging the nations for the unfaithful servant makes it doubtful that Mark's Jesus alludes to this text. Still, ransom language is common in Isaiah's broader context (35:9; 41:14; 43:1, 14; 44:22–24; 51:11; 52:3; 62:12; 63:9); so Peter G. Bolt, *The Cross from a Distance: Atonement in Mark's Gospel*, NSBT (Downers Grove, IL: IVP Academic, 2004), 72–73.

28. Watts, "Mark," 201.

29. As summarized in Watts, "Mark," 204–5.

30. France, *Mark*, 420.

31. Cullmann, *Christology of the NT*, 65.

II. ATONEMENT

Jesus's passive obedience involved heroic suffering "for us and for our salvation," ending in death by crucifixion. He lovingly chose to suffer (to be a "patient," to feel "passion") at human hands (John 10:18). Despite a natural aversion to death, he drank the cup that God the Father gave him (Matt. 26:39). Reticence is appropriate regarding the horrors of crucifixion, on which the Gospels do not linger.[32] Yet the evangelists could presuppose familiarity with crucifixion, whereas later generations fall into sentimental, symbolic appeals to the cross. In fact, Jesus's death began with scourging that already weakened him to the point of collapse, as reflected in struggling to carry the crossbar. Then his wrists were nailed to the cross to support his body weight. Eventually death stemmed from asphyxiation, after each breath required the agony of lifting himself. Other agonies included "bodily functions uncontrolled, insects feasting on wounds and orifices, unspeakable thirst, muscle cramps, bolts of pain from the severed median nerves in the wrists, scourged back scraping against the wooden *stipes*"—amid the degradations of nakedness, mockery, and imperial injustice.[33]

Dogmatic reflection on Christ's work has broader and narrower foci—both broader reconciliation, initiated by the incarnation, and narrower atonement (*at-one-ment*, as coined by William Tyndale) for sin, accomplished through the Mediator's passion.[34] Hebrews 2:14–18 corroborates the testimony of Philippians 2:5–11: incarnate solidarity with humanity was vital to the efficacy of Jesus's saving death. The ecumenical creeds tell the story of Christ's suffering, death, and burial for our sake, but they do not specify a *theory*—a large-scale explanatory vision—of what this passion accomplished.[35] No theory

---

32. These reflections rely on Fleming Rutledge, *The Crucifixion: Understanding the Death of Jesus Christ* (Grand Rapids: Eerdmans, 2015), 92–96. On p. 603 she notes that crucifixion "was especially designed to erase the memory of its victims as though they had never existed."

33. Despite its problematically passibilist and social Trinitarian account, there is an insightful connection between the historical and eschatological trials of Jesus in Jürgen Moltmann, *The Crucified God: The Cross of Christ as the Foundation and Criticism of Christian Theology*, trans. R. A. Wilson and John Bowden (New York: Harper & Row, 1974).

34. Thus, on the threefold office as an atonement framework, see Michael S. Horton, *Lord and Servant: A Covenant Christology* (Louisville: Westminster John Knox, 2005).

35. On the historical emergence of atonement theories from modern German Protestant theology rooted in Schleiermacher and F. C. Baur (1792–1860), see Adam J. Johnson, "Theories and *Theoria* of the Atonement: A Proposal," *IJST* 25, no. 1 (January 2021): 92–108. Johnson rightly commends recovering classic *theoria* as contemplation of multiple aspects of Christ's work, although that may not be inconsistent with the *particular* way of emphasizing penal substitution that is commended here.

could encompass the kaleidoscope of biblical images for atonement or the surplus of love that God poured out.[36] Gratefully marveling that "for us and for our salvation he came down from heaven" is the beginning of atonement theology.[37] Nevertheless, *atonement* became a rough equivalent for the Hebrew *kpr* group, which deals with sacrifices removing sin.[38] Therefore, moving beyond the ecumenical creeds to evangelical confessions and Protestant traditions, dogmatic theology ponders whether the Bible highlights certain *concepts*—thus supporting particular *models* of atonement or even specifying *means* by which Jesus accomplished it.[39] Such claims would not attain the orthodoxy-defining status of the ecumenical creeds. Biblical variety authorizes contextual prudence in gospel proclamation, as Luke-Acts illustrates. At minimum, however, Scripture establishes some kind of necessity for the cross (e.g., Acts 2:23).

Most evangelicals have emphasized sacrifice as the heart of Jesus's saving work.[40] Alongside the cleansing suggested by *kpr*, prominent metaphors include redemption (buying us back) and ransom (freeing us from captivity to Satan, sin, and death). The apparent paradox is that God both delivered fallen human beings over to these powers and

36. For a useful but excessive apocalyptic caution against economic logic constraining Christology to match soteriological need, see Walter Lowe, "Christ and Salvation," in *The Cambridge Companion to Postmodern Theology*, ed. Kevin J. Vanhoozer (Cambridge: Cambridge University Press, 2003), 235–51. The reason to avoid problem-exclusive soteriology is to honor dogmatically the first commandment—moving backward and forward from Christ's passion to expound the perfection of the triune God; so Webster, "'It Was the Will,'" in *God without Measure*, 1:143–45.

37. Highlighting narrative contexts of Christ's atoning work, while critiquing popular concepts of a works contract, is N. T. Wright, *The Day the Revolution Began: Reconsidering the Meaning of Jesus's Crucifixion* (New York: HarperOne, 2016). He acknowledges penal substitution, but elsewhere (e.g., p. 415) he rhetorically rejects any systematic theory in favor of a story, a meal, and loving service. Unfortunately, he adds confusion with the atoning function of his "covenant of vocation" and a penal judgment on "sin itself" (p. 287).

38. The piel *kipper* is most relevant. The less likely meaning "cover over" derives from an Arabic cognate. Passages like Leviticus 17:11 may involve a "ransom," but the commonest sense of "wiping clean" (with an Akkadian cognate) appears frequently in passages about cleansing rituals. So Christopher J. H. Wright, "Atonement in the Old Testament," in *The Atonement Debate: Papers from the London Symposium on the Theology of Atonement*, ed. Derek Tidball, David Hilborn, and Justin Thacker (Grand Rapids: Zondervan, 2008), 75–76.

39. These distinctions are similar to Joshua M. McNall, *The Mosaic of Atonement: An Integrated Approach to Christ's Work* (Grand Rapids: Zondervan Academic, 2019), 14n2. Mechanisms are distinct from models, since a multimechanism approach could constitute a model; so Crisp, *Word Enfleshed*, 121.

40. To illustrate that crucicentrism—without "anaemic squeamishness"—has made a watershed distinction between evangelical and liberal theologies, see Timothy Larsen, "Congregationalists and Crucicentrism," in *Evangelicalism and Dissent in Modern England and Wales*, ed. David Bebbington and David Ceri Jones (London: Routledge, 2021), 111–38.

mercifully delivers us from them while we are still rebellious. Many evangelicals understand this deliverance as incorporating penal substitution, that is, Jesus undergoing our penalty—propitiating God's wrath or at least expiating our sin. The ensuing account embraces that concept, albeit emphasizing its analogical nature: even while speaking within the framework of certain (1) biblical concepts, we must remain aware of (2) historical contexts and (3) ethical concerns that affect how (4) the theological core of atonement applies to the triune God.

A. Biblical Concepts

Notwithstanding the multitude of relevant metaphors, penal substitution encapsulates Scripture's central teaching about *how* Christ's death enacts the reconciliation that the incarnation initiated.[41] Some metaphors appear so often that they become concepts—habits for thinking and speaking: "The plurality of biblical imagery does not seem to be intended purely or even primarily as a selection box from which we may draw what we will according to our needs and the pre-understanding of our community."[42] Among the Bible's primary motifs, including penal execution, ransom, victory, and Passover, sacrifice is especially prominent.[43] Despite their complexity, some sacrifices prepared for Isaiah 53 to anticipate the Servant's death as substitutionary. Similarly, Hebrews epitomizes New Testament appeals to Old Testament sacrifices as foreshadowing Jesus's self-offering to cleanse our consciences. Beyond sacrifice per se, numerous passages contain "for us" language addressing sin and punishment. The Bible characterizes God as both being righteous and lovingly justifying sinners apart from works, treating union with Christ's sacrificial death as crucial for such forgiveness (e.g., Rom

---

41. The unity and authority of Scripture affect atonement theology. Challenges to penal substitution sometimes prioritize the Gospels' Jesus as a canon within the canon, critique verbal plenary inspiration, champion hermeneutics of suspicion, and/or strain credulity with exegetical explanations that deny divine judgment. Unfortunately, spatial limitations preclude detailed examples, but all of the above are variously on display in Brad Jersak and Michael Hardin, eds., *Stricken by God? Nonviolent Identification and the Victory of Christ* (Grand Rapids: Eerdmans, 2007).
42. Trevor Hart, *In Him Was Life: The Person and Work of Christ* (Waco, TX: Baylor University Press, 2019), 2. On atonement metaphors see Colin E. Gunton, *The Actuality of Atonement: A Study of Metaphor, Rationality and the Christian Tradition* (London: T&T Clark, 1988). Gunton treats three clusters as biblically primary—victory, justice, and sacrifice—concluding that both substitution and representation, objective and subjective elements, are involved.
43. On these metaphors (among other aspects of this section), see Henri A. G. Blocher, "Atonement," in *DTIB*, 72–76.

3:21–26).[44] Second Corinthians 5:14–21 suggests a "wonderful exchange" of sin and righteousness between us and Christ.[45]

Attempts to avoid the biblical prominence of penal substitution are unconvincing.[46] An apocalyptic critique sees penal substitution as a "contractual" emphasis that is inconsistent with the radical inbreaking of God's love in Christ. However, despite recovering Pauline insights that expose popular misunderstandings, this critique struggles with texts like Romans 3.[47] A missiological critique sees penal substitution as biblically secondary at most, laden with Western assumptions. However, despite recognizing Scripture's variety, this critique scarcely discusses texts like Romans 3 and functionally dismisses penal substitution rather than situating it.[48] An antiviolence critique sees retributive justice as inconsistent with Jesus's cross, laden with outdated appeals to sacrifice.[49] However, despite raising questions that expand our horizons and entail certain nuances, this critique strains credulity when denying that divine judgment occasions at least some sacrifice and "for us" texts.[50] When Isaiah 53 influences the paradigmatic gospel summary in 1 Corinthians 15:3,[51] integrating the Gospels' Jesus with Paul's Christ, it insists that he died "for our sins according to the Scriptures." Thus, substitution is not so much an image as the instrumental reality behind biblical motifs—

44. On Romans 3 see D. A. Carson, "Atonement in Romans 3:21–26," in *The Glory of the Atonement*, 119–39. On its connection with Exodus 34:6–7, see Jeremy J. Wynne, *Wrath Among the Perfections of God's Life*, SST (London: T&T Clark, 2010), 174–83. On Romans 5:6–8 vis-à-vis Graeco-Roman doom-averting deaths, see Simon J. Gathercole, *Defending Substitution: An Essay on Atonement in Paul*, ASBT (Grand Rapids: Baker Academic, 2015), 85–107.

45. Contra nonpenal, narrative Christus victor accounts that reflect the apocalyptic Pauline trend (plus René Girard's scapegoat theory via Raymund Schwager), like J. Denny Weaver, *The Nonviolent Atonement* (Grand Rapids: Eerdmans, 2001), 49–58. See pp. 133–34 in Carson's chapter, and Richard Gaffin, "Atonement in the Pauline Corpus: 'The Scandal of the Cross,'" in *The Glory of the Atonement*, 159. Both highlight parallels between 2 Corinthians 5 and Romans concerning divine righteousness.

46. See Gathercole, *Defending Substitution*, 29–46.

47. E.g., Douglas A. Campbell, *The Deliverance of God: An Apocalyptic Rereading of Justification in Paul* (Grand Rapids: Eerdmans, 2009). Campbell reads Romans 1–4 as largely reflecting views from Paul's opponents.

48. E.g., at least in extensive discussions since initial publication, Joel B. Green and Mark D. Baker, *Recovering the Scandal of the Cross: Atonement in New Testament and Contemporary Contexts* (Downers Grove, IL: InterVarsity Press, 2000).

49. Nonpenal understandings see sacrifice as only reflecting various gift-giving, ritual, and communal practices; see, e.g., chap. 3 of David A. Brondos, *Background*, vol. 1 of *Jesus' Death in New Testament Thought* (Mexico City: Comunidad Teológica de Mexico, 2018).

50. E.g., arguing against retributive justice (even regarding Romans 3) by purporting the Pauline prominence of *Sin* over *sins* is Stephen H. Travis, "Christ as Bearer of Divine Judgment in Paul's Thought about the Atonement," in *Jesus of Nazareth: Lord and Christ*, 332–45. But Paul's distribution of *Sin* and *sins* is relatively equal, while *sins* appears in pre-Pauline gospel formulae; see Gathercole, *Defending Substitution*, 47–53.

51. See Gathercole, *Defending Substitution*, 55–79.

effecting triumph, epitomizing divine love and eliciting human love, expiating sin from sacred space, and so forth. God satisfies justice by substituting personally for us.[52]

B. Historical Contexts

Given biblical concepts, the historical development of atonement doctrine should nuance, not displace, penal substitution. As typified by Gustaf Aulén (1879–1977), history suggests that penal substitution emerged gradually as a formal theory.[53] Aulén narrated a classical patristic emphasis upon victory: Christ liberating us by paying a ransom or tricking the devil or otherwise defeating sin and death. Objective satisfaction emerged when the medieval St. Anselm of Canterbury (1033–1109) compared God to a feudal lord whose honor human beings shamed. Protestant penal substitution models paralleled Anselm's focus on offenses against God. Subjective influence upon humanity—overwhelming us with God's love, encouraging us to imitate Christ—was initially championed by Peter Abelard (1079–1142), but largely awaited the Reformation-era Socinians, precursors of modern theological liberalism.

Although critiqued at points, Aulén's narrative plausibly captures basic emphases from various eras, yet the moral of his story is more debatable. Church fathers emphasized the incarnate Christ conquering death on humanity's behalf.[54] This emphasis upon victory resonates with non-Western contexts and recovers a biblical theme that some Protestants neglect. However, the fathers frequently cited Isaiah 53, relating Jesus's sacrifice to punishment.[55] And since Christ's victory was objective, Aulén's labels could turn a historical shift into a false dichotomy.[56] The

---

52. For a classic statement, see chap. 6 of John R. W. Stott, *The Cross of Christ* (Downers Grove, IL: InterVarsity Press, 1986). See also J. I. Packer, "What Did the Cross Achieve? The Logic of Penal Substitution," *TynBul* 25 (1974): 3–45. For caution regarding Stott's implication of strife between divine attributes, see Adonis Vidu, *Atonement, Law, and Justice: The Cross in Historical and Cultural Contexts* (Grand Rapids: Baker Academic, 2014), 257.

53. Gustaf Aulén, *Christus Victor: An Historical Study of the Three Main Types of the Idea of Atonement*, trans. A. G. Hebert (New York: Macmillan, 1969).

54. Conceding that sacrificial themes are present while contending that the fathers offer no theoretical mechanism (except the effect of releasing human nature from death) is Benjamin Myers, "The Patristic Atonement Model," in *Locating Atonement: Explorations in Constructive Dogmatics*, ed. Oliver D. Crisp and Fred Sanders (Grand Rapids: Zondervan, 2015), 71–88.

55. E.g., "He shared with us our punishment, but not our sin. Death is the punishment of sin. The Lord Jesus Christ came to die; he did not come to sin. By sharing with us the penalty without the sin, he canceled both the penalty and the sin." So Augustine, *Sermons on the Liturgical Seasons, For the Easter Season, Sermon 231.2*, in Oden and Hall, eds., *Mark*, 2:151–52.

56. See chaps. 6–7 in William Lane Craig, *Atonement and the Death of Christ: An Exegetical, Historical, and Philosophical Exploration* (Waco, TX: Baylor University Press, 2020).

medieval era did not contain two warring (Anselmian and Abelardian) theories; its treatments of sacrifice and satisfaction assumed an element of substitution as "metonymic representation" that somehow invites participation.[57] Pre-Reformation history should chasten myopically Pauline Protestant soteriology, enriching biblical holism. But Protestants also needed to recover Pauline soteriology for the church.

C. Ethical Concerns

Atonement theology must further address important ethical concerns, but these arise from misconstruing penal substitution rather than affirming the biblical doctrine. Versions that imply divine child abuse are heretically non-Trinitarian, fracturing the essential unity of the Father and the Son while neglecting Christ's voluntary heroism. Versions that lionize violence or passive victimization are likewise unbiblical.[58] A prominent biblical type must be carefully appropriated: God did not require that Abraham *actually* sacrifice Isaac (Genesis 22), nor did the Father ultimately *sacrifice* the Son, who in his divine nature as such could not die—being unable therein to undergo separation of body and soul. Of course, Christ's human death highlights the mystery of evil: willed in one way by the triune God, but willfully enacted by human leaders and crowds. It was heroically willed by Jesus since there was no other way to fulfill his loving mission.

Given its uniqueness, Christ's martyrdom should not promote victimization. When the New Testament appeals to Jesus's incredible sacrifice (1 Pet 1:18–19) to evoke grateful obedience (1 Cor 6:19–20), the call is limited to suffering for good rather than evil, responding nonviolently, and entrusting ourselves to God (1 Pet 2:20–23). By *his* wounds we have been healed (1 Pet 2:24). Christ's example should not entrench slaves, women, and other marginalized groups under oppression (1 Cor 7:21–24). Although 1 Peter 1 did not call for immediate (and inevitably unsuccessful) revolution against slavery, its careful encouragement of submission identified God as the true Master (1 Pet 2:18–19). Following Jesus's nonviolent example until the eschaton promises eventual justice

---

57. Caroline Walker Bynum, "The Power in the Blood: Sacrifice, Satisfaction, and Substitution in Late Medieval Soteriology," in *The Redemption: An Interdisciplinary Symposium on Christ the Redeemer*, ed. Stephen T. Davis, Daniel Kendall, SJ, and Gerald O'Collins, SJ (Oxford: Oxford University Press, 2004), 177–204.

58. Such concerns may also pertain to other models besides penal substitution, as noted by Garry Williams, "Penal Substitution: A Response to Recent Criticisms," in *The Atonement Debate*, 185.

and eternal reward because of his ultimate victory. Admittedly, penal substitution faces a shift of cultural plausibility, a moral burden of proof.[59] Some eyes see no sense in which Jesus's death could have fulfilled God's will.[60] What is at stake in these ethical concerns, though, is a theological question: whether justice is solely restorative or incorporates a properly retributive element that honors victims and God.[61]

D. A Theological Core

Thus succeeding paragraphs expound penal substitution, *formally defined*: Jesus propitiated divine wrath by undergoing the death penalty and thereby obtaining pardons for sinners who are united with him by faith. By contrast, contemporary accounts often retrieve select patristic elements while rejecting the traditional Protestant emphasis that people without Christ are not just wounded but dead in their sins (Eph 2:1–10). Complexities of nature and grace, ecumenical engagement, liberationist concerns, latent universalism, and perhaps lingering effects of Christendom foster accounts that emphasize humanity's continually graced nature and the incarnation as the primary mechanism of atonement, with the cross involving no sacrifice except from God to us.[62] For such nonretributive accounts, sin's wound is not fatal but hinders humanity's experience of divine presence; the incarnation, the cross, and the Holy Spirit gradually heal this wound, eliciting transformative openness to God.[63] Although their approaches to sin vary, such purely

---

59. On postmodern shifts, see Kevin J. Vanhoozer, "The Atonement in Postmodernity: Guilt, Goats and Gifts," in *The Glory of the Atonement*, 367–404. On a Foucauldian shift "in criminal justice from public ritual violence to private psychological violence," see Stephen R. Holmes, "Ransomed, Healed, Restored, Forgiven: Evangelical Accounts of the Atonement," in *The Atonement Debate*, 284.

60. E.g., there is internal tension within the volume, but rejecting any dimension involving God's will is J. Denny Weaver, "The Nonviolent Atonement: Human Violence, Discipleship and God," in *Stricken by God? Nonviolent Identification and the Victory of Christ*, ed. Brad Jersak and Michael Hardin (Grand Rapids: Eerdmans, 2007), 316–55.

61. Highlighting this issue is chap. 6, "Kathryn Tanner (1954–) on Incarnation as Atonement," in Oliver D. Crisp, *Revisioning Christology: Theology in the Reformed Tradition* (Burlington, VT: Ashgate, 2011), 111–31.

62. Models of atonement theology suffer from (1) notorious diversity; (2) their unappealing God; (3) outdated mechanisms; and (4) neglected aspects of the gospel story, according to Tanner, *Christ the Key*, 247–50. The quotation is from p. 252, and see further pp. 260–72. For another account that avoids speaking of Christ's "work" as "substitutionary" but focuses on the Mediator bringing the "end of sacrifice" (both Jewish and Roman), see Ingolf U. Dalferth, *Crucified and Resurrected: Restructuring the Grammar of Christology*, trans. Jo Bennett (Grand Rapids: Baker Academic, 2015), 304–13.

63. For another nonretributive account, which puts a second-person focus on mutual indwelling, taking Christ's cry of dereliction to unite all human psyches with his—healing them by eliciting free surrender to God—see Eleonore Stump, *Atonement*, OSAT (Oxford: Oxford

restorative accounts dismiss retributive aspects of biblical material on sin, sacrifice, and salvation.[64]

Hence penal substitution involved *undergoing the death penalty* deserved by sinners. Three core elements of "mere penal substitution" are substitution, penalty, and divine sanction.[65] Isaiah 53 has been a linchpin of biblical evidence for (1) substitution. Considering (2) the penalty raises the question of why those who are united with Christ still undergo physical death. In response, biblical euphemisms (such as sleep) diminish death's force, and metaphors deploy it to emphasize new life in Christ. By contrast, these euphemisms do not apply to Jesus's death, whereas language like *perishing* only applies to other human beings. Therefore, Jesus's death saves believers out of spiritual death in alienation from God—perishing—but physical death remains a temporal consequence of the fall and the curse. Christ underwent death with an experience like perishing so that we might avoid it.[66] Then (3) divine sanction goes beyond expiation to reach at least the threshold of propitiation. God goes beyond impersonally leaving sinners to the natural consequences of their actions, willing their punishment if they remain apart from Christ. Beyond struggling to account for biblical propitiation (e.g., 1 John 2:2), nonretributive views risk making Jesus's death a purposeless injustice: at best exemplary in its love, but not necessarily effective.[67] In accomplishing propitiation, however, God actively shows mercy.

Having undergone our death penalty through human injustice, Jesus *propitiated divine wrath*, which is "the redemptive mode of God's righteousness."[68] Wrath is not an immanent divine perfection like power, wisdom, love, and holiness; wrath is the economic response of God's

University Press, 2018). Pages 23–27 summarize objections to Anselmian accounts. Stump's contrast with a Thomistic account is complicated to evaluate; interpretations abound regarding Thomas, whereas her alternative still appeals to a Thomistic account of divine love. Her Marian alternative periodically mentions biblical texts. But it caricatures penal substitution (e.g., p. 393: "the notion of sacrifice as a present given to an offended deity as reparation for sin so that that deity will pardon the sin . . .") and summarily covers Romans 3:21–26 by citing Thomas. Stump's assumptions about forgiveness vis-à-vis divine love are among multiple problems highlighted by Craig, *Atonement*.

64. Further addressing objections to retributive justice (such as Nicholas Wolterstorff's) is Matthew Levering, "Creation and Atonement," in *Locating Atonement: Explorations in Constructive Dogmatics*, 43–70. Levering suggests that God's maintenance of creation order via retributive justice calls us away from retribution in dealings with each other. Noting that neo-Socinians need retributive justice for their critique of penal substitution—namely, that God would be wrongly punishing the innocent—is Craig, *Atonement*, 269.

65. McNall, *Mosaic of Atonement*, 101–7.

66. See Gathercole, *Defending Substitution*, 80–83.

67. Roger Nicole, "Postscript on Penal Substitution," in *The Glory of the Atonement*, 447.

68. Wynne, *Wrath Among the Perfections*, 173.

holy love to sin.[69] Many criticisms of penal substitution construe wrath as unhinged or self-absorbed anger. Yet classic formulations already recognized that propitiation does not turn divine wrath into love but lovingly enacts righteousness.[70] Biblical propitiation must be Trinitarian. It is not that God the Father was implacably angry while gentle Jesus, meek and mild, advocated for sinners. The Father lovingly initiated, the Son enacted, and the Spirit perfected the one operation of penal substitution. Jesus Christ embraced this mission as both the faithful Israelite and the divine Son.[71] Ultimately, God the Father did not sacrifice the Son, who could not die in his deity. In his humanity he suffered the mystery of evil, as human leaders and crowds unjustly resisted divine love, but the triune God willed to overcome this resistance for good.

Such forgiving mercy took the form of *obtaining pardons*. Although God "remembers our sins no more" (Jer 31:34; Heb 8:12), their historical reality is still acknowledged. Pardon is not acquittal, so in a sense the operation is executive rather than judicial.[72] The popular explanation of justification making me "just as if I had never sinned" conveys the truth of guilt removed—as liability to punishment.[73] Yet there is no legal fiction: the sinner is forgiven, but the sin has been punished, so to speak.[74] God's executive authority also underscores that divine wrath is not personal pique. Sinners' offenses oppose the just King of the universe, whose grace in showing patience and mercy upholds the right order of shalom. In holy love God undergoes the punishment.[75] That is why the justification of the ungodly is religiously unique.[76]

---

69. Treier, *Introducing Evangelical Theology*, 109–10.

70. Making this very point is, e.g., John Murray, *Redemption Accomplished and Applied* (Grand Rapids: Eerdmans, 1955), 31.

71. See Thomas H. McCall, *Forsaken: The Trinity and the Cross, and Why It Matters* (Downers Grove, IL: IVP Academic, 2012). On p. 38 he notes Christ's promise of paradise to the nearby thief—suggesting that, however Psalm 22 relates to the experience of God-abandonment, Jesus did not utterly despair.

72. Craig, *Atonement*, 60n16.

73. Craig, *Atonement*, 232.

74. Craig, *Atonement*, 184.

75. Because Jesus did not sin, he could not simply provide a vicarious penitence, as noted by Nicole, "Postscript," 451. Distinguishing strong, intermediate, and weak penal substitution—according to whether Christ was actually, possibly, or not punished—is Daniel J. Hill and Joseph Jedwab, "Atonement and the Concept of Punishment," in *Locating Atonement: Explorations in Constructive Dogmatics*, 139–53. In p. 150n25, they reproduce a rhetorical question about whether evangelicals actually say that God punished Christ, from I. Howard Marshall, "The Theology of the Atonement," in *The Atonement Debate*, 63. When they counter Marshall with numerous examples, however, they arguably misread his quotation's context—which opposes views in which God punishes Christ externally, as a human being separate from God.

76. Rutledge, *Crucifixion*, 571.

Christ's pardon becomes effective *as sinners are united with him by faith*. Perennial debate over the extent of the atonement—for the elect only or all of humanity—may speculatively replace a biblical dialectic with a false dichotomy. Neither set of proof texts is wholly compelling. On one hand, the gospel contains a genuine, universal invitation: "Be reconciled to God—Jesus is your saving Lord!"[77] Jesus divinely shared God's moral will and humanly longed for Israel's salvation (e.g., Matt 23:37). Giving himself as a ransom bearing Israel's curse for the world's benefit, Jesus died on behalf of the collective "many," who are urged to repent. On the other hand, the incarnate Son went to the cross in Trinitarian unity with the Father's electing love and the Spirit's effectual calling, paying a ransom rather than merely obtaining potential pardons. As Israel's Suffering Servant, the crucified curse-bearer had multifaceted aims: both generally reconciling created humanity's covenant history and specifically redeeming a faithful remnant. So the God-man's death was both sufficient for grounding a gospel call to the "many" and effective for granting pardons to those whom the Spirit unites with Christ. The faith evoked by the gospel is not an alternative condition to works, but a receptive form of agency through which pardoned sinners entrust themselves to God's grace.

This formal account functions *analogically*, nuancing the nature and necessity of Christ's sacrifice. "God was reconciling the world to himself in Christ" (2 Cor 5:19): this gospel connects an eternal determination with a temporal history.[78] God had no obligation to redeem sinners; biblical statements about the cross's *necessity* are contingent upon that free, loving divine decision. The cross was the historical way of being merciful and just toward sinners (Rom 3:21–26); Scripture does not address hypothetical alternatives beyond that. The cross's *nature* as a sacrifice is both a truth-bearing biblical concept and an analogical constraint upon speculation. Human analogies for penal substitution are limited at best (Rom 5:6–8). Prepared by divine providence, sacrifices biblically celebrate the extent of God's mercy and call us to honor God with embodied lives that have been redeemed at great cost. The jewel of conciliar Christology shines brightly here: statements about sacrifice can be true of Christ by virtue of his human nature, applied via the *communicatio idiomatum*,

---

77. On this content of the gospel call, see Jonathan Hoglund, *Called by Triune Grace: Divine Rhetoric and the Effectual Call*, SCDS (Downers Grove, IL: IVP Academic, 2016).

78. So Colin E. Gunton, introduction to *The Theology of Reconciliation*, ed. Colin E. Gunton (London: T&T Clark, 2003), 1.

that would not be true of his divine nature per se. The effectiveness of Christ's sacrifice depends on the analogical dissimilarity: the cross did not cost God any beatitude as eternal Spirit, but by virtue of incarnational union with fallen humanity, the Son could give his life as a ransom. God could do what no human sacrifice could; *sacrifice* therefore conveys God's incredible love in redeeming us and celebrates Jesus's heroic martyrdom. From a creaturely perspective, "greater love has no one than this: to lay down one's life for one's friends" (John 15:13), and the Son's assumption of a human nature facilitated the divine display of such love. Both opponents and proponents can fall into necessitarian, univocal reasoning when they grapple with logical puzzles about penal substitution—diminishing the proper appreciation: "And can it be . . . ?"

The theological core of *how* Christ enacted atonement should not marginalize other biblical aspects of his reconciling work. First, Jesus is our representative as well as our substitute: active obedience not only qualified him to bear our sins but also embodied righteousness that is imputed to those who are united with him. Second, focus should rest on reconciled relationships that judicial categories express: marriage is a noteworthy biblical analogy, in which a covenantal union is established that includes—yet transcends—a change in legal status. Third, these reconciled relationships are communal as well as personal: the cross and resurrection not only gain righteousness for forgiven sinners but also guarantee eventual justice and shalom. Thus, fourth, an array of metaphors can take proper contextual places in biblical proclamation: Christ's recapitulation of Adam's and Israel's stories is foundational; Christ's victory over hostile powers is climactic; and just as sanctification accompanies justification, so too does moral influence accompany penal substitution in the outworking of reconciliation with God— leading ultimately to the transforming glory of participation in divine fellowship.[79] The centrality of penal substitution consists in the *means* of enacting atonement, viewed specifically in terms of how Christ's passion ransomed us from sin and death. But this central aspect fits within a broader picture, in which the entire career of the incarnate Son and the manifold aspects of reconciliation should elicit our contemplative gaze.

---

79. The image of a mosaic—with recapitulation as the foundational feet, penal substitution as the beating heart, *Christus Victor* as the crowning head, and moral influence as the beckoning and restraining heart—comes from McNall, *Mosaic of Atonement*. On p. 310 he eschews both a defensive hierarchy of aspects (or, in Jeremy Treat's terms, "reductionism") and disconnected plurality (or "relativism").

III. DESCENT TO THE DEAD

Although often misunderstood or even denied by modern Protestants, Christ's "descent into hell" underscores the depth of God's reconciling love. Admittedly, there are exegetical complications in key biblical passages, including the referent of *hell*, which affects the identification of relevant texts. In fact, though, Christ's descent to *Sheol/Hades*, the realm of the dead, claims an early and widespread pedigree. Some have mistakenly isolated Rufinus (c. AD 390) as its only clear patristic affirmation.[80] However, its absence from some local creeds facilitated its function as a behind-the-scenes "password" that indicated genuine acquaintance with apostolic tradition. Other sources used the doctrine to counteract Apollinarianism by underscoring Jesus's full humanity.[81] Classic confessions of the descent included not only its eighth-century universal acceptance into the Apostles' Creed but also local predecessors and the fifth-century Athanasian Creed. Early confessors included Ignatius of Antioch, Polycarp, Justin Martyr, Hermas, Hippolytus, Irenaeus, Clement of Alexandria, Tertullian, Origen, Cyprian, Athanasius, Ambrose, Augustine, and Cyril of Alexandria.[82] Whatever the terminology and whomever the beneficiaries, its sphere was "Abraham's bosom," the realm of the righteous dead:[83]

> Christ, in remaining dead for three days, experienced death as all humans do: his body remained in the grave, and his soul remained in the place of the righteous dead. He did not suffer there, but, remaining the incarnate Son, proclaimed the victory procured by his penal substitutionary death to all those in the place of the dead— fallen angels, the unrighteous dead, and the OT saints.[84]

Therefore, Calvin significantly changed its locus when he had Jesus suffering the "hell" of divine wrath on the cross.[85]

---

80. Regarding errant reliance upon Philip Schaff here, see Matthew Y. Emerson, *"He Descended to the Dead": An Evangelical Theology of Holy Saturday* (Downers Grove, IL: IVP Academic, 2019), 68–69.

81. Emerson, *He Descended to the Dead*, 71.

82. Donald G. Bloesch, "Descent into Hell (Hades)," in *EDT*, 241–42.

83. Emerson, *He Descended to the Dead*, 81.

84. Emerson, *He Descended to the Dead*, 103.

85. Emerson, *He Descended to the Dead*, 92. For a table of historical views, see p. 98. On the tradition's common reference to Jesus breaking hell's power (at the initial stage of exaltation),

Beyond implicit biblical support from Christ's full humanity and genuine death, certain passages affirm not just his body's burial but also his soul's sojourn in Sheol. One crucial passage, 1 Peter 3:18–22, focuses on Christ's proclamation of victory over hostile spirits, not a gospel invitation to the unbelieving dead.[86] For another debated passage, Ephesians 4:9–10, although Jesus's descent "to the lower, earthly regions" has sometimes been related to incarnation on earth, the LXX supports a reference to the realm of the dead. Both LXX uses of the same phrase, Psalms 63:9 and 139:15, refer to the underworld.[87] Such texts fit the broader biblical arc, which traces a battle between YHWH and the serpent, involving their respective peoples and places.[88]

Therefore the descent was a complex hinge between humiliation and exaltation.[89] Traditionally, Reformed Christology has seen the descent as the nadir of humiliation, whereas others have focused on the beginning of exaltation.[90] In a sense, Christ's royal victory began at the cross, so arguments relating the descent to exaltation could actually move that focus earlier—per the dialectical aspect of the twofold state. Yet per its sequential aspect, the proclamation of 1 Peter 3:18–22 could favor a seamless exaltation that begins the defeat of hostile powers with Christ's triumph over the grave. Hence Ephesians 4:9–10 juxtaposes the descent with the subsequent ascent, parading the spoils of victory. The larger point is that Christ's death—with his body buried in the earth and his soul descended into Hades's Paradise—was the means of his victory, the necessary precursor of the resurrection that inaugurated the new creation. The descent to the dead continued the downward trajectory

---

see chaps. 2–4 of Alyssa Lyra Pitstick, *Light in the Darkness: Hans Urs von Balthasar and the Catholic Doctrine of Christ's Descent into Hell* (Grand Rapids: Eerdmans, 2007).

86. See William J. Dalton, *Christ's Proclamation to the Spirits: A Study of 1 Peter 3:18–4:6*, rev. ed., AnBib 23 (Roma: Editrice Pontifico Istituto Biblico, 1989).

87. Emerson, *He Descended to the Dead*, 40–41.

88. Emerson, *He Descended to the Dead*, 55.

89. Prioritizing exaltation while acknowledging the dénouement of humiliation is Emerson, *He Descended to the Dead*, 65. On pp. 167–68 he notes that few icons of the descent picture Jesus among the dead, having the exaltation's victory begin in the underworld after humiliation culminates at the cross (Phil 2:5–11). Page 207 offers a parallel between the cross on the sixth day, rest on the seventh day, and the resurrection as the eighth day of creation. Cautioning against relating the descent solely to victory is Alan E. Lewis, *Between Cross and Resurrection: A Theology of Holy Saturday* (Grand Rapids: Eerdmans, 2001), 40. His study helpfully contemplates the neglected Holy Saturday, but unfortunately it exaggerates death-of-God language.

90. Noting this contrast while focusing (as a Lutheran) on humiliation is McFarland, *Word Made Flesh*, 150–55. Cautiously proposing a universal first chance of hearing the gospel is Bloesch, "Descent into Hell," 242. Counteracting universal salvation in 1 Corinthians 15:24–28 is Emerson, *He Descended to the Dead*, 181. Focusing on exaltation does not entail either universal impetus, which must be evaluated otherwise.

of the passion even as it signaled the triumphant result. The descent completed what began with the manger, thus reassuring us that "neither death nor life, neither angels nor demons, neither the present nor the future, nor any powers, neither height nor depth, nor anything else in all creation, will be able to separate us from the love of God that is in Christ Jesus our Lord" (Rom 8:38–39).

IV. SON OF MAN

With Son of Man, Jesus's primary self-designation, the Gospels encapsulate the ministry of reconciliation upon which this chapter focuses. Granted, the name sometimes references exaltation: in Acts 7:56, Stephen saw "heaven open and the Son of Man standing at the right hand of God"; the quotation of Psalm 8:4–6 in Hebrews 2:6–9 and John's visions in Revelation (1:13; 14:14) also pertain to the ascended Christ. Otherwise the "title" comes from the earthly Jesus's lips whereas the early church did not use it.[91] Hence it is common to categorize Gospels sayings in relation to Jesus's present ministry, suffering, and future apocalypse.[92] Yet it is noteworthy that Mark's distribution focuses on suffering.[93]

Jesus's appropriation of Daniel 7:13–14 was apparently unprecedented.[94] There is good reason to affirm the Son of Man sayings' authenticity and at least occasional Danielic background. In addition

---

91. See, e.g., Richard N. Longenecker, *The Christology of Early Jewish Christianity* (Grand Rapids: Baker, 1970), 88–89. Quote marks around "title" defer to the possibility that Son of Man was only an indirect form of self-reference—a view that reportedly will receive a major defense from Richard Bauckham, who upholds the sayings' authenticity; see, currently, Bauckham, *Jesus*, 58. Doubtless "illegitimate totality transfer" should be avoided for all christological names; their backgrounds or collocated themes may not pertain in any given text. As for Son of Man, the key question is whether Daniel 7:13–14 is evoked at crucial moments like Mark 10:45.

92. With 17, 26, and 27 occurrences respectively, according to Darrell L. Bock and Benjamin I. Simpson, *Jesus the God-Man: The Unity and Diversity of the Gospel Portrayals* (Grand Rapids: Baker Academic, 2016), 82.

93. Chrys C. Caragounis, *The Son of Man: Vision and Interpretation*, WUNT (Tübingen: Mohr, 1986), 193.

94. For a representative denial that Jesus used the phrase as a title in fulfillment of Daniel 7, see Barnabas Lindars, SSF, *Jesus Son of Man: A Fresh Examination of the Son of Man Sayings in the Gospels in the Light of Recent Research* (Grand Rapids: Eerdmans, 1983), 170–89. Lindars highlights frequent settings of conflict with religious leaders. He also summarizes the influential work of Géza Vermes and Maurice Casey, who deny the Jewish existence of an apocalyptic title and relate the phrase to an Aramaic idiom. In that case, present- and passion-related sayings might be authentic but sayings about future messianic glory would not be. For a critique of such accounts, see Richard Bauckham, "The Son of Man: 'A Man in My Position' or 'Someone'?," *JSNT* 23 (1985): 23–33. For a collection of major texts, see Benjamin E. Reynolds, ed., *The Son of Man Problem: Critical Readings* (London: T&T Clark, 2018).

to Scripture's trustworthiness and multiple attestation, the sayings are likely authentic because later churchly invention would have offered no advantage for promoting Jewish messianism or motivation for believing the Easter message.[95] In the Daniel 7 background, then, are four beasts, with the final and most terrible one having ten horns that a little horn begins supplanting. The Ancient of Days takes his throne to enact judgment (7:9–10), and the beasts are slain (7:11–12). Daniel sees "one like a son of man coming with the clouds of heaven" and into God's presence (7:13), receiving universal and everlasting power and worship (7:14). The fulfillment of this Danielic vision surfaces in Jesus's words at his trial. Asked if he is "the Messiah, the Son of the Blessed One," Jesus replies, "I am," continuing, "And you will see the Son of Man sitting at the right hand of the Mighty One and coming on the clouds of heaven" (Mark 14:61–62). Stephen's postresurrection vision sees this exaltation coming to fruition. Jesus's prediction becomes the last straw, perceived as blasphemous, that elicits his crucifixion. Stephen's vision becomes the last straw, perceived as blasphemous, that elicits his stoning.

Hence *Son of Man* indicates a career of solidarity and suffering unto glory. Its Danielic ending of eschatological glory is unveiled among oppressive empires by a prophet suffering in exile. Likewise the Markan profile of Jesus's glory, as anticipated by his transfiguration and climactically announced before the high priest, challenges disciples not to shrink away from the cross, where he suffered with and for his people. As the Danielic Son of Man, though, Christ eschatologically represents God along with humanity.[96] Daniel 7 references God's chariot throne, elaborately described in Ezekiel, yet verse 9 mysteriously has multiple thrones being set in place (as does Ps 122:5). Scandalously, since even Moses could not see God's face and live (Exod 33:20), the Son of Man shares in the rule and worship proper to the Ancient of Days (Dan 7:14).[97] Whether the original context referred to a human or a heavenly being, Jesus's identification with the Son of Man "heightened the significance of the honorific language found in Psalms 2 and 110, whereby Israel's anointed king was thought of as God's son seated at God's right hand."[98] Indeed,

---

95. Craig A. Evans, "Jesus' Self-Designation 'The Son of Man' and the Recognition of His Divinity," in *The Trinity: An Interdisciplinary Symposium on the Trinity*, ed. Stephen Davis, Daniel Kendall, SJ, and Gerald O'Collins, SJ (Oxford: Oxford University Press, 1999), 46.

96. Walter Kasper, *Jesus the Christ*, trans. V. Green (repr., New York: Paulist, 1981), 108. See further III.II.1–3.

97. Evans, "Jesus' Self-Designation," 34–35.

98. Evans, "Jesus' Self-Designation," 31.

he saw himself as more than a popular messiah whose mission was to throw off the Roman yoke and restore the kingdom of Israel, as in the days of David and Solomon. The frequent appeal to the figure of Daniel 7 to define himself, his mission, his struggle, his death, and subsequent vindication strongly implies that Jesus understood himself in terms that transcend those of a mere mortal.[99]

In Mark 14, Jesus's response to Caiaphas was perceived as blasphemous for connecting Daniel 7:13 and Psalm 110:1, claiming that he would sit at God's right hand—sharing the divine throne and the prerogative of judgment.[100]

Along with divine sovereignty, this Son of Man enacts a priestly ministry. Since God's people are oppressed before reigning with the Most High (Dan 7:25–27), "the passage from Daniel is interpreted in light of the Suffering Servant of Isaiah 53 so that the Danielic Son of Man prophecy is being fulfilled in a 'hitherto unexpected manner.'"[101] As Isaiah's songs narrowed to one Suffering Servant, so the Son of Man narrowed to one who would be crucified before being exalted. In pre-Christian Judaism the phrase is anarthrous and general ("son of man") whereas in the Gospels it is articular and definite ("the" or "that" Son of Man).[102] Daniel 7 follows Daniel's rescue from the lions' den, which vindicates his faithfulness in prayer with a pagan decree favoring God's kingdom. Daniel 7 also parallels another vision in Daniel 2, after which a pagan image mimics the dimensions of Israel's temple(s).[103] Beyond prayer and the temple, additional priestly associations are possible, but in any case Daniel 7 goes beyond addressing the suffering of God's people to anticipate a holy sanctuary.[104] Passages like Mark 2:1–12 narrate the convergence of forgiveness and healing that is anticipated in texts like Psalm 103—outside the temple and eventually via Jesus's disciples.[105] The eschatological high priest inaugurates a royal priesthood.

99. Evans, "Jesus' Self-Designation," 40. To this evidence Evans adds Jesus's self-identification as God's wisdom, claims to more than honorific divine sonship, institution of Passover meals in his memory, and claim about sitting at God's right hand.
100. Evans, "Jesus' Self-Designation," 45.
101. David E. Garland, *A Theology of Mark's Gospel: Good News about Jesus the Messiah, the Son of God*, BTNT (Grand Rapids: Zondervan, 2015), 476.
102. Perrin, *Jesus the Priest*, 183.
103. Perrin, *Jesus the Priest*, 168–69.
104. Perrin, *Jesus the Priest*, 178–79.
105. Perrin, *Jesus the Priest*, 186–88.

Therefore, the Son of Man's triumph follows from his suffering as the Servant. His blood continues to be poured out *for* many at the Lord's Supper (Mark 14:24).[106] This celebration proclaims the Lord's death until he returns (1 Cor 11:26), giving the royal priesthood a prophetic ministry. Yet Son of Man texts not only articulate the threefold messianic office but also mysteriously anticipate eschatological divine sovereignty. Accordingly, despite not enshrining an atonement theory, conciliar Christology confesses an identity befitting the ultimate Son of Man's redemptive career. The Nicene Creed emphasizes that "for us and for our salvation" he became incarnate, and "for our sake" he was crucified, died, and was buried. A "wonderful exchange" incorporated both active obedience as humanity's righteous representative and passive obedience in dying as sinners' substitute. The Apostles' Creed identifies Christ fully with our plight when it affirms not only the burial of his body but also the descent of his soul to the dead. As the Son of Man, Jesus sinlessly identified with humanity's current condition and thereby fulfilled our triumphant destiny. For, in union with him and his suffering, we enjoy the glory God made for us to share as royal priests of creation.

---

106. On signaling a new Passover, see Brant Pitre, *Jesus and the Last Supper* (Grand Rapids: Eerdmans, 2015), 3. As pp. 514–16 argue, Jesus saw himself as the Danielic—apocalyptic and royal—Son of Man, yet without expecting the kingdom's fullness immediately, hence instituting the ritual meal for the interim. On eschatological tribulation as a two-stage event, with Jesus's death as a ransom returning Israel from exile, see Brant Pitre, *Jesus, the Tribulation, and the End of the Exile: Restoration Eschatology and the Origin of the Atonement* (Grand Rapids: Baker Academic, 2005). There Pitre argues on p. 40 that Jesus understood this return in traditional terms, rather than more metaphorically à la N. T. Wright.

CHAPTER 9

EXALTATION AS THE MEDIATOR

Hebrews 7:22–8:6

As epitomized in **Hebrews 7:22–8:6**, Jesus Christ is the theandric **Mediator** between God and humanity, whose bodily resurrection and ascension inaugurated his **exaltation**. *As his transfiguration anticipated, he now enjoys his heavenly session while shepherding his church on its earthly pilgrimage—incorporating participants in the new covenant through baptism, indwelling them by his Spirit, instructing them as their Lord, and interceding for them based on his completed work of atonement.*

The crucified Jesus is now the risen Lord and thereby the one redemptive Mediator between God and humanity. In a crucial text, Philippians 2:5–11, we primarily explored Christ's humiliation as he fulfilled the vocation of the Isaianic Servant of YHWH. But we also briefly encountered his exaltation. Exaltation was fitting because of his inclusion within the identity of YHWH—because the incarnate Son is eternally Lord. This exaltation also involved a new element, though: God gave a share in "the name that is above every name" to the theandric, once-dead-and-now-risen Messiah. Eschatological divine glory belongs to Jesus, in unexpected fulfillment of Old Testament hopes for God's human image bearers.

This exaltation is the subject of the present chapter. To begin with, our biblical study focuses on Hebrews's Christology, celebrating Jesus's exalted status as our everlasting priest. Then we explore a series of events that comprise the exaltation: its anticipation in the transfiguration, its inauguration in the resurrection, its apex in the ascension, and its continuation in the heavenly session. The chapter concludes by expounding the name Mediator, which encapsulates Christ's present lordship in the church as it draws the eternal Son's lordship over creation toward its ultimate form.

I. HEAVENLY PRIESTHOOD IN HEBREWS 7:22–8:6

Hebrews boasts a bevy of passages that name the person of Christ. Hebrews 1:1–4 immediately introduces God's Son as the revelatory protagonist; then 1:5–2:9 celebrates his superiority over angels (probably regarding the mediation of divine revelation); 2:10–18 insists on the necessity of his full humanity for our redemption; 3:1–6 celebrates his superiority over Moses as a covenant mediator; 4:14–16 introduces a lengthy treatment of the Son as high priest; 10:5–7 celebrates this priest's redemptive self-offering; 12:2 recapitulates the preceding emphases on Jesus's pioneering and perfecting of faith; 13:8 somehow indicates Christ's eternity; and 13:20 references the Lord Jesus's identity as the resurrected Messiah. To summarize, in Hebrews Jesus Christ is preeminently the Son of God and therefore superior to angels, Moses, or any other Old Testament figure. Along with being God's Son, he is also the high priest, requiring full identification with humanity. The superiority of his priesthood rests on its unique sacrifice, the faithful Son's once-for-all self-offering; its heavenly presentation and divine approval following the resurrection; and its everlasting implementation through the ascended pioneer's shepherding of his people.[1]

Manifesting the inextricable linkage between the person of Christ and his work, Hebrews also summarizes his benefits for us in numerous ways. Thanks to this Son and high priest, first of all we have salvation from sin—cleansing of the conscience, freedom from slavery, and forgiveness. Second, we are heirs of eternal rest, which is already anticipated in Christian worship despite not yet being realized in eschatological fullness. Third, salvation currently requires a pilgrimage,

---

1. Portions of this section are adapted from Daniel J. Treier, "'Mediator of a New Covenant': Atonement and Christology in Hebrews," in *So Great a Salvation: A Dialogue on the Atonement in Hebrews*, ed. Jon C. Laansma, George H. Guthrie, and Cynthia Long Westfall, LNTS (London: Bloomsbury T&T Clark, 2019), 105–19.

for which we have been set apart. Fourth, salvation includes ongoing divine aid for pilgrims. Fifth, a crucial vehicle of this aid is participation in Christ's approach to God. This pioneer provides more than just an extrinsic example; he is also the intrinsic perfecter of faith who accompanies pilgrims on the trail he has blazed. Sixth, the associated benefit is the perfection of our humanity, completing its process of maturation. Hence the benefits of Christ, the high priest who is Son, go beyond salvation from sin and arrive at eternal rest. Here and now Christ offers the redemptive help and hope that human beings need to reach their created end.

Correspondingly, the three essential elements of conciliar Christology—full deity, full humanity, and personal unity—are integral for Hebrews. The same holds true for Christ's threefold office: he is prophet, priest, and king in an integral fashion that is unprecedented. Each office presumes Jesus's humanity, in continuity with Israel's Scriptures, but they newly overlap in their ultimate fulfillment by Christ the divine Son. So initially the *munus triplex* correlates with Hebrews largely as expected: less emphasis on prophecy than the Gospels narrate in early encounters with Jesus, less emphasis on royalty than the Gospels present overall, and overwhelming emphasis on Christ's unique priesthood. That Hebrews integrates priesthood with the other two offices, however, hints at the Son's uniqueness as their unified bearer. In Hebrews's vision, Christ's priestly cleansing is integral to all the offices' fulfillment, thus reclaiming divine rule over the cosmos (so, e.g., Heb 1:3). As further exploration of his covenant mediation will establish, bringing such cleansing to bear on the conscience is now Jesus's prophetic focus.

While Son and high priest are Hebrews's two most prominent identifications of Christ, *Mediator* of the new covenant appears at crucial points and integrates their significance for his exaltation. This integration of Christ's person and work informs the present focus on Hebrews 7:22–8:6. Hebrews 1:1–4:13 clears comparative ground and builds a hortatory foundation, whereas 10:19–13:25 brings the main structure to its paraenetic apex. In between, 4:14–10:18 contains the central argument. After 4:14–5:10 introduces a forthcoming argument from Psalm 110 about Christ's Melchizedekian priesthood, 5:11–6:20 digresses with more exhortation (to remain stable in Christian hope and move past spiritual infancy). The central argument takes detailed shape beginning in 7:1, after *Mediator* language has appeared in 6:17 (and before that term celebrates the eschatological climax in 12:24). For present purposes, this name's crucial uses bookend our passage, appearing in 7:22 and 8:6 before coming to further fruition in 9:15.

In Hebrews 7:22 Jesus has become the guarantor (*enguos*) of a better covenant. While expounding Psalm 110:4 in relation to Melchizedek, Hebrews emphasizes covenantal change. The new covenant changes more than just the law in relation to priesthood (7:12). It grounds the ultimate priesthood in the power of an indestructible life (7:16), an appeal to a better hope (7:19), repetition now involving intercession rather than sacrifice (7:25), and the high priest's lack of need for his own sacrifice (7:26–28). These contrasts emerge from the psalm: an eternal oath regarding a priestly order. The phrase in 7:22 picks up the surrounding *better* language, integration of priesthood and law in terms of covenant, and the importance of the divine oath; in other words, it draws together the expository threads in anticipation of 8:1, which summarizes this main section's initial point. The *enguos* is not merely impersonal or passive: although the divine oath is the prior basis, Jesus's perfect sonship and ever-living intercession bring its fulfillment. Both God's appointment and the priest's actual ministry establish the guarantee. The audience has already been prepared for this guarantor by *mesiteuō* in 6:17, where God confirms the unchanging promise with an oath, the content of which unfolds in the ultimate priesthood of Hebrews 7.[2]

The first occurrence of "Mediator [*mesitēs*] of a (better) covenant" appears shortly after 7:22, in 8:6.[3] The central application of Psalm 110:4

---

2. The priesthood is inviolable, based on Psalm 110. But the Son's eternity precedes this appeal to Psalm 110:4, as Hebrews 1:1–14 already indicates: "The pastor clearly intends to affirm that both the quality and duration of his absolute priesthood are founded on the eternity of his person." See (with this quotation from p. 332) Gareth Lee Cockerill, *The Epistle to the Hebrews*, NICNT (Grand Rapids: Eerdmans, 2012), 330–34. It lies beyond our purview to wade into contemporary debate over when (according to Hebrews) Christ's priesthood—and, accordingly, Jesus's self-offering—begins. Today's welcome emphasis on Jesus's resurrection should not diminish the once-for-all significance of the cross. The profound linkage between the Son's eternity and his priesthood's inviolability suggests identifying him characteristically as a priest rather than restricting the epistle's priestly focus to particular (heavenly) ministrations. He is not an eternal priest because creation is not eternal. Yet, given the Son's eternal procession, it is fitting for his mission to be characterized by mediation.

3. To state the obvious: treating 7:22–8:6 as a unit reflects our theological purposes rather than a literary identification. For the latter, 8:1 would reflect a key transition that concludes what precedes and introduces what follows. The ensuing argument continues past 8:6, through the citation of Jeremiah's new covenant passage in 8:7–13 and into Hebrews 9. For theological purposes, though, 7:22–8:6 not only contains key instances of the Mediator title but also surrounds 8:1, and it stretches into the argument's preceding and succeeding sections. Notably, it raises

to the Son's priesthood having been established, the argument takes a new turn in Hebrews 8:1–10:18, focusing on the heavenly realm of the Son's ministry. Early in that context, 8:6 correlates his mediation with a superior ministry involving better promises. The rest of Hebrews 8 establishes another Old Testament basis for covenantal change by quoting Jeremiah 31. Hebrews 9:1–10 rehearses the symbolic function of the old covenant regulations, again highlighting the order's temporary character. When 9:11–14 resumes the broader argument, it emphasizes Christ's blood as that which purifies consciences through his heavenly self-presentation.

On that basis Mediator makes another appearance in 9:15, where Christ's new covenant enables the people to attain their promised inheritance. In 8:6 this key phrase arises in the context of Jesus's priesthood; in 9:15 the context is Christ's sacrifice. The former sets the stage for the detail of the latter. Of course, surrounding 9:15 wordplay treats *diathēkē* (covenant) as last will and testament, so that Christ's death and priestly presentation of his blood inaugurate a new situation, both purifying the heavenly sanctuary (the controlling thought down through 9:28) and perfecting human worshipers (10:1–10). At that point the argument's major moves have been made.

To move from establishing the importance of Mediator in Hebrews to addressing Christ's distinctive work turns us to *mesitēs* and Jeremiah 31:31–34. *Mesitēs* deals with what is in between multiple parties without precluding some identification with either or both. In Hebrews as in Galatians 3:19–20 and 1 Timothy 2:5, Jesus's humanity is the focus: he is superior to other agents of revelation and leaders of Israel. Amid many resonances between Hebrews and Jeremiah 31, the use of Jeremiah 31:31–34 in Hebrews 8:8–12 supports the former covenant's divinely planned obsolescence: it did not ensure that people would keep faith to reach the promised end. In the new covenant, God places the law inside the heart, evoking rather than enforcing obedience. External mediators like Moses give way since the new covenant internalizes knowledge of God. The passage's end adds another new aspect: God will be merciful, remembering sins no more. God promises this mercy personally, while according to Hebrews its means is Christ's mediation—priestly

---

the question of what gift(s) this high priest has to offer; the answer involves the next instance of Mediator in 9:15.

presentation of his self-sacrifice. This forgiveness is comprehensive, direct, and everlasting, in a way that the conscience can internalize. Such is the reassurance that people can truly know God, trusting the divine promise and obeying the divine instruction. Hebrews makes much of this argument in terms of priesthood and Jesus's humanity, but the broader concept of mediation ties that together with divine sonship: in Christ believers hear from God directly, hearing chiefly that they are forgiven.

Emphasis on the perfection of Jesus's humanity throughout the epistle prepares for the fourth Mediator text, Hebrews 12:24, where Christ's work is associated with "the sprinkled blood that speaks a better word than the blood of Abel." At multiple points between 7:22 and that climax, Hebrews emphasizes what Christ has to offer: he offered himself (7:27); he needed something to offer that would be fitting for the heavenly sanctuary and the new covenant's better promises (8:3–6); the high priest could only enter the inner sanctuary with an offering of blood (9:7), but a sacrifice that would truly cleanse the conscience must not be merely external and temporary (9:10); thus Christ offered his own blood (9:12) by the divine Spirit (9:14), effecting once-for-all heavenly purification. This contrast between animal blood and Christ's self-offering continues through 10:18 with the twofold appeal to Jeremiah 31:31–34 being reiterated in Hebrews 10:16–17.

Notwithstanding the emphasis on his perfect humanity, the priest's self-offering is accompanied by frequent references to eternity. The Creator's right hand (1:2–3), an indestructible life in contrast with earthly ancestry (7:16), Christ's first coming (9:11, 26; 10:5), his effects on Old Testament believers (11:26), and his perennial sameness (13:8) suggest inclusion in the identity of the eternal God rather than merely the inception of an enduring finitude. Troubled consciences can be confident that this self-offering is acceptable—they are really cleansed—because it is neither temporary nor merely external: the divine Son is the high priest. Not only has he purified sin and pioneered a path to follow; by the Holy Spirit he now presents perfect worship in the presence of God our Father. Eternal Son he always has been; royal priestly "son" he has become.[4]

---

4. Hence this treatment of Mediator coheres with the subsequent argument of Jamieson, *Paradox of Sonship*.

II. TRANSFIGURATION

The eventual exaltation of this Mediator was previewed in an earthly transfiguration before three of his disciples. The transfiguration garners little attention in modern systematic theologies, but the event instructively anticipates the risen Christ's ascension to heavenly glory on our behalf.[5] To be sure, his private manifestation upon a mountain was not a public act advancing salvation history. Still, the transfiguration is vital to Orthodox spirituality, valued in Catholic theology, and visible in historic liturgies.[6] Protestant emphasis on divine self-revelation should encourage more attention to this earthly anticipation of Christ's heavenly session and eschatological glory.

Fundamentally, the transfiguration reveals the glory of the God-man in his filial perfection. The event quickly follows Peter's recognition of Jesus as Messiah and Christ's prediction of his death (e.g., Matt 16:13–17:13). Not only did Jesus's face shine; his clothes became brilliantly white. The transfiguration reinforced the divine origin and reliability of the biblical message (2 Pet 1:12–21), the heart of which is Christ himself. As Moses and Elijah appeared to talk with Jesus, Peter proposed putting up three shelters to extend the dialogue. But the divine voice from the cloud responded by identifying Christ as the beloved Son who fulfills Psalm 2:7 to the uttermost. The disciples should listen uniquely to him; indeed, they would soon do so, because once they arose from prostrate terror, Moses and Elijah were gone. Nevertheless, this glorious revelation incorporated creaturely realities; both Scripture and creation mediate divine truth. In fact, Jesus's filial glory incorporated his humanity. Whereas he radiated inherent glory before the cloud's arrival, in contrast with Moses whose glory was derived (Exod 34:29–35), the transfiguration still involved a human face and creaturely garments. Likewise our glorification, via encounter

---

5. E.g., the following systematic theologies do not list the transfiguration in subject indexes and, at most, make passing biblical references: Berkhof; Bloesch; Erickson; Finger; Frame (whose volumes have no Christology as such); Gerrish; Grenz; Härle; Hinlicky; Hodge; Jenson; Mueller; Shedd; Spykman; Thiselton; Tillich; van Genderen and Velema; Weber.

6. On the significance for Eastern spirituality, see Andrew Louth, "From Doctrine of Christ to Icon of Christ: St. Maximus the Confessor on the Transfiguration of Christ," in *In the Shadow of the Incarnation: Essays on Jesus Christ in the Early Church in Honor of Brian E. Daley, S.J.*, ed. Peter W. Martens (Notre Dame: University of Notre Dame Press, 2008), 260–75. The transfiguration is one of the events in Christ's life that structures our participation in salvation, in, e.g., *Catechism of the Catholic Church*, 2nd ed. (Washington, DC: United States Catholic Conference, 1997), 142–43.

with Christ (2 Cor 3:7–4:6), incorporates rather than diminishes our humanity.[7]

Accordingly, the transfiguration offers a hermeneutical paradigm for christological fulfillment of the Old Testament.[8] The appearance of Moses and Elijah has manifold significance, but Moses may represent the Law and Elijah the Prophets: Moses had a founding ministry and Elijah a renewing ministry for God's people that Jesus now fulfills.[9] Both encountered God, albeit without direct sight, on mountains (in addition to Exodus 24 and 34, see 1 Kings 18–19); were forerunners of the Messiah (Deut 18:18; Mal 4:4–6); avoided normal human death (Deut 34:5–6; 2 Kgs 2:9–12); and suffered due to the resistance of God's people (e.g., Exod 32:19; Deut 32:5; 1 Kgs 19:1–10).[10] The implication is that Jesus fulfills their testimony and vocations so that now he has relocated Israel's sacred space. In and through him people encounter God—without an accompanying Aaron or Levitical priesthood. Elijah's restoring ministry has already come in John the Baptizer (Matt 17:9–13), but its purpose was not to renew the existing temple establishment, which opposed him too.

Consequently, the transfiguration's anticipation of Christ's exaltation cannot be separated from his looming humiliation on the cross. Even his disciples continued to misunderstand his messianic vocation. All three Gospel accounts contain the same sequence of Peter's confession, Jesus's passion prediction(s), and then the transfiguration. The anguished witticism that "Jesus came bringing the kingdom of God and ended up with the church" is not alien to the evangelists' narratives.[11] Matthew's transfiguration account is followed by the disciples' inability to heal a demon-possessed boy, so that an exasperated Jesus asks, "You unbelieving and perverse generation, how long shall I stay with you?"

---

7. These comments on the incorporation of Christ's humanity—discussing the Old Testament background and dogmatic implications—are informed by a future article from Michael Kibbe, "The (God-)Man on the Mountain: The Christology of the Transfiguration." On the contrast with Moses, see *Oration* 10 (especially p. 219) in John of Damascus, "Oration on the Transfiguration of Our Lord and Savior Jesus Christ," in *Light on the Mountain: Greek Patristic and Byzantine Homilies on the Transfiguration of the Lord*, ed. Brian E. Daley, SJ (New York: St. Vladimir's Seminary, 2013), 205–31.

8. Some of these reflections are shaped by Kevin J. Vanhoozer, "Ascending the Mountain, Singing the Rock: Biblical Interpretation Earthed, Typed, and Transfigured," *ModTheo* 28, no. 4 (October 2012): 794–97.

9. Michael S. Horton, *The Christian Faith: A Systematic Theology for Pilgrims on the Way* (Grand Rapids: Zondervan, 2011), 484.

10. LePeau, *Mark*, 157–63.

11. Attributed to Alfred Loisy by Benedict XVI, *Jesus: Baptism to Transfiguration*, 48.

(17:17). To the churchly foundation of Matthew 16 the exhortations of Matthew 18 add renovations of a ramshackle community: becoming like children, not causing others to stumble, imitating the Father's love for wayward sheep, enacting communal discipline, and continually forgiving as we have been forgiven. Similarly, Mark's transfiguration narrative (9:2–13) is sandwiched among three passion predictions and precedes the uncomprehending disciples' dispute about positions of honor. From the revelation of Christ's glory to Peter, James, and John, only self-aggrandizing aspirations emerged. Such is the extent of our resistance to a Messiah who must suffer first before glory follows. Whereas the disciples saw Jesus as a prophet, with Moses and Elijah as prototypes, the transfiguration was part of their preparation for his death and thereby his shift from preaching to being preached.[12] The transfiguration may also have provided vital confidence for Jesus from God as Father, given his impending doom.[13] Somewhat more publicly, likewise, the resurrection of Lazarus (John 11) foreshadowed eventual deliverance from the impending pathos.

Having highlighted connections to Christ's humanity, Old Testament precursors, and impending crucifixion, we return to contemplating divine glory. Of course, the cloud is associated with Yhwh's presence and activity. All three Gospel accounts speak of the cloud overshadowing them—with the same word being used for the Holy Spirit's ministry to Mary as the God-bearer (Luke 1:35).[14] Glory encompasses creaturely encounters with a summative divine perfection, "the cataphatic complement to the apophatic confession of God's invisibility":

In other words, it is because God is (cataphatically) revealed as the one who "dwells in unapproachable light" that God is (apophatically) confessed as the one "whom no one has ever seen or can see" (1 Tim. 6:16; cf. Isa. 6:1–5; Ezek. 1:26–28). So it is that on the Mount of Transfiguration, the revelation of the divine glory in Jesus takes the

---

12. Perhaps the systematic theology that most references the transfiguration—unsurprisingly, given his patristic focus—is Thomas C. Oden, *The Word of Life*, vol. 2 of *Systematic Theology* (Peabody, MA: Prince, 1998). On pp. 207, 288, he highlights this transition, while on pp. 263–68 he discusses the transfiguration more fully, noting that few Son of Man texts after the event reference Jesus's earthly ministry. On p. 281 he suggests that it was a key initial moment for recognition of Christ's mediatorial mission.

13. Adolf von Schlatter, *The History of the Christ: The Foundation for New Testament Theology*, trans. Andreas J. Köstenberger (Grand Rapids: Baker, 1997), 296–98.

14. J. Rodman Williams, *Renewal Theology: Systematic Theology from a Charismatic Perspective: Three Volumes in One* (Grand Rapids: Zondervan, 1996), 1:345.

form of an ineffable brightness on which the disciples cannot bear to look (see Matt. 17:2–5 and pars.; cf. Acts 7:55; Rev. 15:8; 21:23).[15]

The underlying metaphors of weight (Hebrew *kabod*) and brightness (Greek *doxa*) convey the twin aspects of divine glory: God's objective perfection, eliciting creatures' subjective perception.[16]

Thus, the transfiguration anticipated the resurrection and ascension as Jesus's completion and God's vindication of his earthly mission. Jesus's body was temporarily glorified,[17] affording "a clue to the nature of the resurrection": since "flesh and blood cannot inherit the kingdom of God" (1 Cor 15:50), yet the same body's appearance "changed," the eschatological kingdom must involve "the opening of a different realm with new conditions of life," and so "the resurrection entails a transformation of the present body that will fit it for a more glorious existence."[18] "This same" Jesus's ascension (Acts 1:11)—referenced as an *exodos*—was prefigured by and discussed with Moses and Elijah (Luke 9:31).[19] In the ensuing time we walk by faith rather than sight (2 Cor 5:7). The transfiguration obviously focuses on seeing, but that reality is temporal and transient, then oriented to words (e.g., Matt 17:3, 5, 7, 9). Nearly all subsequent disciples love Jesus without having physically seen him (1 Pet 1:8), relying on prophetic testimony from the initial eyewitnesses (2 Pet 1:12–21) and seeing with enlightened eyes of the heart (Eph 1:18).[20]

III. RESURRECTION

The resurrection is integral to the saving victory of Christ's passion. Between his death and resurrection, humiliation and exaltation were conjoined; the resurrection began his unmixed exaltation.[21] Jesus "was

---

15. McFarland, *Word Made Flesh*, 41.

16. Thus contra modern tendencies to reinterpret the event solely in terms of the disciples' (likely postresurrection) perception, as typified by John Macquarrie, *Jesus Christ in Modern Thought* (Philadelphia: Trinity Press International, 1990), 398–400.

17. Gordon R. Lewis and Bruce A. Demarest, *Our Primary Need: Christ's Atoning Provisions*, vol. 2 of *Integrative Theology* (Grand Rapids: Academie, 1990), 465.

18. Merrill C. Tenney, "The Historicity of the Resurrection," in *Jesus of Nazareth: Saviour and Lord*, ed. Carl F. H. Henry (Grand Rapids: Eerdmans, 1966), 143.

19. Oden, *Systematic Theology*, 2:504.

20. The quotation and surrounding reflections come from G. C. Berkouwer, *The Return of Christ*, ed. Marlin J. Van Elderen, trans. James Van Oosterom, Studies in Dogmatics (repr., Grand Rapids: Eerdmans, 1972), 366.

21. John Brown of Haddington, *Systematic Theology: A Compendious View of Natural and Revealed Religion* (repr., Grand Rapids: Reformation Heritage, 2015), 323–24.

delivered over to death for our sins and was raised to life for our justification" (Rom 4:25). The resurrection vindicated and applied his atoning work on the cross. The resurrection inaugurated the abundant life of a new humanity through the empowering presence of the same Holy Spirit who raised Jesus from the dead.[22] Shalom will only be complete once Christ's second coming ushers in eschatological consummation that includes the resurrection of our bodies; nevertheless, the inaugurated new creation already has cosmic, communal, and personal dimensions. Cosmically, in the resurrection God reaffirmed the good order of the material creation (Rom 8:18–25)—reinforcing the promise of a new heavens and earth where righteousness will be at home (2 Pet 3:13).[23] Communally, in the resurrection God initiated the fulfillment of Israel's promised restoration—regathering a covenantal remnant while including gentiles in the Spirit's outpouring (Acts 2:17–39). Personally, Jesus's resurrection comprised the first fruits of the new humanity—including a glorious restoration of physical life in which all members of Christ's body will participate (1 Cor 15:20–23) and a transformational realm of spiritual life into which union with him already incorporates us (Rom 6:1–14; Eph 1:15–2:10; 3:14–21).

In Jesus's context, resurrection did not simply mean "life after death" but dead people returning to new bodily life. The ancients were no more gullible than modern people regarding this strange notion.[24] Daniel 12 and possibly a few other Old Testament texts hinted at this hope. These hints were consistent with belief in YHWH as Creator and Judge of a cosmos that is essentially good. Resurrection became a disputed possibility: the Pharisees, consistent with more straightforward devotion to the Torah and expectation of judgment, embraced belief in resurrection whereas the Sadducees, consistent with aristocratic comfort, did not. Jesus's resurrection was the initial fulfillment of Israel's promised resurrection, as anticipated in Ezekiel 37's vision of the dry bones. Jesus's resurrection clarified that resurrection would be a personal and not just communal reality, while human immortality would not leave us

---

22. Portions of these sections on the resurrection and ascension are adapted from chap. 9 of Treier, *Introducing Evangelical Theology*.

23. The classic treatment of this reaffirmation remains O'Donovan, *Resurrection and Moral Order*.

24. For a reminder that the resurrection was baffling to early Christians themselves, see Rowan Williams, *Christ on Trial: How the Gospel Unsettles Our Judgement* (Grand Rapids: Eerdmans, 2000), 135–38.

disembodied.[25] Resurrection would involve a historical event, "bringing to birth God's future world in advance of its full appearing,"[26] signaling "the renewal and redemption of the entire cosmos (Rom. 8:18–25)." Accordingly, resurrection means "life after life after death," as we usually think of it, in which the present human body will be transformed into "a new type of physicality, incapable of corruption." Such is Paul's teaching in 1 Corinthians 15.

Confidence in Jesus's bodily resurrection rests on the Spirit's testimony in Scripture, but faith has good reasons for this understanding, especially the twofold attestation of an empty tomb and numerous appearances by the risen Christ. Of course, much modern theology reinterprets resurrection as merely a symbol of divine presence or empowerment. But these reinterpretations conflate Jesus's life with his original disciples' experience and substitute the disbelief of contemporary people for the latter.[27] Even some who apparently affirm the bodily resurrection suggest that it cannot be narrated in the same way as the events of Jesus's earthly ministry or that it was an eschatological event happening to the world rather than a miracle within history.[28] In return, some evangelicals overreact with rationalistic, undifferentiated affirmations of a historical resurrection. Both historicity and transcendence need to be clearly affirmed.[29] The Gospels would not identify Jesus as they do in relation to Israel's God if they did not culminate in narrating his bodily resurrection.[30] Resisting metaphorical reinterpretation of their historical claims is not the same as resting their truth on modern historical canons.

Exercising this theological freedom does not preclude historical investigation but respects its valuable, albeit limited, contribution.[31] In

---

25. See Robert H. Gundry, "The Essential Physicality of Jesus' Resurrection according to the New Testament," in *Jesus of Nazareth: Lord and Christ*, 204–19.

26. This paragraph largely summarizes a summary, from which the quotations are taken: N. T. Wright, "Resurrection of the Dead," in *DTIB*, 676–78. The article distills key aspects of N. T. Wright, *The Resurrection of the Son of God*, Christian Origins and the Question of God 3 (Minneapolis: Fortress, 2003).

27. See, e.g., this critique briefly made by Gerald O'Collins, SJ, "The Resurrection: The State of the Questions," in *The Resurrection: An Interdisciplinary Symposium on the Resurrection of Jesus*, ed. Stephen Davis, Daniel Kendall, SJ, and Gerald O'Collins, SJ (Oxford: Oxford University Press, 1997), 7–9.

28. For the former, see, e.g., McFarland, *Word Made Flesh*, 165–68. For the latter, see, e.g., Dalferth, *Crucified and Resurrected*, 79.

29. This is the upshot of the typology presented in George Hunsinger, "The Daybreak of the New Creation: Christ's Resurrection in Recent Theology," *SJT* 57, no. 2 (2004): 163–81.

30. So Frei, *Identity*.

31. Assessing Bultmann's indifference concerning how Easter faith arose in the disciples as "utterly amazing"—"It is not important to understand what happened in an event which has influenced the entire culture of the western world more than any other single event!"—Ladd

this regard, biblical scholarship is often out of step with classical histori-ography.[32] A miracle is "(1) an event which would never have occurred except for the action of a transcendent rational agent, (2) an event that has religious significance in the sense that it can reasonably be viewed as furthering God's purposes and (3) an event of such an extraordinary nature that it is either perceived as a directly supernatural interven-tion in the normal order of nature or immediately inferred as such."[33] Historical explanation cannot prove a miracle. Yet defenders of bodily resurrection can be too defensive about falling prey to "God of the gaps" reasoning; not all arguments about divine action as a probable cause put God into explanatory gaps that are vulnerable to being filled. Certain types of evidence in spiritually charged contexts suggest the propriety of supernatural causes.[34] In the present case, especially given the evidence concerning Jesus's life, philosophical argument can also support the propriety of a good God redeeming sinful, suffering human persons via incarnation and crowning that redemption with resurrection.[35] Like such philosophical arguments, spiritual experience—"You ask me how I know he lives: He lives within my heart"—can be profoundly true yet must not be allowed to rival Jesus's gracious self-testimony. Nevertheless, since his Spirit incorporates the church's proclamation in this testimony, historical reasoning is an appropriate aspect of faith.[36]

The nature of the resurrection body remains mysterious. The Gospels

---

follows Helmut Thielicke's suggestion that the necessity of historical research lies (at least) in anticriticism, indicating that there is no historical contradiction to Easter faith. See George Eldon Ladd, *I Believe in the Resurrection of Jesus* (Grand Rapids: Eerdmans, 1975), 137, 140–41.

32. Michael R. Licona, *The Resurrection of Jesus: A New Historiographical Approach* (Downers Grove, IL: IVP Academic, 2010). Licona evaluates six hypotheses (surveyed on pp. 21–22) vis-à-vis "bedrock" historical evidence and argues that bodily resurrection fares the best (even calling it "very certain" on p. 619). His case includes a defense of the historicity of Jesus's predictions and the relevance of Paul's conversion (summarized on pp. 617, 621) as well as the physicality of the body in 1 Corinthians 15 and the relevance of skeptical James's conversion (summarized on p. 618).

33. Robert A. Larmer, "The Meanings of Miracle," in *The Cambridge Companion to Miracles*, ed. Graham H. Twelftree (Cambridge: Cambridge University Press, 2011), 36. This definition avoids saying that miracles violate the laws of nature.

34. For a recent study that takes eyewitness experience seriously, see Craig S. Keener, *Miracles: The Credibility of the New Testament Accounts*, 2 vols. (Grand Rapids: Baker Academic, 2011).

35. See the summary (along with objections from chap. 11 to five "Rival Theories of What Happened" [pp. 174–86]) in Richard Swinburne, *The Resurrection of God Incarnate* (Oxford: Oxford University Press, 2003), 201–3.

36. Given the involvement of women as leading eyewitnesses, further reflection is needed on how to incorporate all dimensions of human knowing within the spiritual perception of the resurrection; so Sarah Coakley, "Response," in *The Resurrection: An Interdisciplinary Symposium on the Resurrection of Jesus*, ed. Stephen Davis, Daniel Kendall, SJ, and Gerald O'Collins, SJ (Oxford: Oxford University Press, 1997), 189–90.

underscore the body's physical reality by narrating Christ eating, showing his nail-scarred hands, and remaining located within time. Yet 1 Corinthians 15 calls the resurrected body "spiritual," contrasting it with "flesh and blood" that cannot inherit God's kingdom. Jesus went initially unrecognized in more than one case. He apparently passed through walls, suggesting new properties of location within space. If the transfiguration anticipated the resurrection, that would be consistent with Revelation's depictions, which contain both dazzling glory and physical forms. Although the Christian tradition has a mixed legacy concerning the body, its testimony about resurrection has consistently wrestled with the fascinating questions it raises.[37]

The resurrection is integral to knowing the triune God, as the Spirit of the risen Lord lives within and among us.[38] The resurrection links Jesus's person and work, vindicating the latter and revealing the former. Even so, Christ's renewed embodiment goes beyond demonstrating God's approval of his atoning work and the gospel's credibility to indicate the extension of earthly time and the permanence of the incarnation.[39] If Christ has not been raised as the first fruits of our resurrection, then Christian faith is futile and we remain in sin (1 Cor 15:17–20). But since Christ has been raised, God has given us victory in him and our labor is not in vain (1 Cor 15:54–58).

IV. ASCENSION AND HEAVENLY SESSION

The incarnation continues, as the risen Lord remains an embodied human being, now glorified at the right hand of God the Father. Resurrection initiated Jesus's triumphant, bodily ascent—and our ascent with him, giving us confidence for drawing near to God as Father, being empowered by his Spirit. The resurrection per se was an event; contemplating the ascension and the heavenly session explores

---

37. See Caroline Walker Bynum, *The Resurrection of the Body in Western Christianity, 200–1336* (New York: Columbia University Press, 1995). Augustine epitomizes the acknowledgment that we cannot really describe the heavenly body, yet he wrote "a good deal" on it anyway, as noted by Ola Sigurdson, *Heavenly Bodies: Incarnation, the Gaze, and Embodiment in Christian Theology*, trans. Carl Olsen (Grand Rapids: Eerdmans, 2016), 584–85.

38. Corinthian confusion about the resurrection coincided with ignorance of God (1 Cor 15:34)—as highlighted by my colleague Jon Laansma's inaugural lecture as the Gerald F. Hawthorne Professor of New Testament Greek and Exegesis, forthcoming in *JTI* as "'Some Have No Knowledge of God': The Resurrection and the Knowledge of God in 1 Corinthians."

39. See, contra Barth's view, Van Driel, *Incarnation Anyway*, 148, 161.

its implications by examining the risen Lord's present activity. New Testament salvation has three tenses: a past event, a present process, and a future destiny.[40] The ascension is the transitional point that moves from the past complex of events, the cross and resurrection, into the present process that unfolds during Christ's heavenly session.

The ascension visibly, even liturgically, marked the end of Jesus's earthly mission and announced his future return.[41] Despite Jesus's apparent departure, the disciples could be joyful because they knew they would not be abandoned.[42] His Spirit would be with them, and someday he would return. Since the ascension returned the Son to prior glory, the new element of exaltation involved his theandric identity as the God-man. Now, as Daniel 7 anticipated, the Son of Man has received royal-priestly authority at God the Father's right hand. For *Jesus* to share in the name above every name (Phil 2:9) exalted a human life to inaugurate our promised participation in God's reign. *Justification* terminology is used for Jesus's vindication by the Spirit (1 Tim 3:16); in the resurrection and ascension he attains divine approval that we come to share. The active obedience from which our justification follows is not merely a spartan compliance with divine commands but a heroic self-offering with which God is pleased.

In the heavenly session, Christ has begun to administer the new covenant, incorporating, indwelling, instructing, and interceding for his pilgrim people. He makes a heavenly presentation of his once-for-all sacrifice, and he becomes the life-giving head of a new social body, reconstituting a remnant of Israel and incorporating gentiles. Here dogmatic Christology should not annex territory that is properly the home of ecclesiology. Yet Jesus's work as the ascended shepherd of his church is integral to his identity as the risen Lord.

---

40. Anthony C. Thiselton, *Systematic Theology* (Grand Rapids: Eerdmans, 2015), 190.

41. Highlighting the ambiguity of when and where the ascension occurred—whether to identify it simply with Acts 1:1–11 or allow for other coming and going—is Gerrit Scott Dawson, *Jesus Ascended: The Meaning of Christ's Continuing Incarnation* (Phillipsburg, NJ: P&R, 2004), 36–37. Proposing two stages of exaltation and bodily transformation (the ascension ending Jesus's initial "flesh and blood" post-resurrection existence) is Millard J. Erickson, *The Word Became Flesh: A Contemporary Incarnational Christology* (Grand Rapids: Baker, 1991), 565–76. Much of the present account depends on Douglas Farrow, *Ascension and Ecclesia: On the Significance of the Doctrine of the Ascension for Ecclesiology and Christian Cosmology* (Grand Rapids: Eerdmans, 1999). See its discussion of story and metaphor in chap. 2.

42. Pope Benedict XVI, *Jesus of Nazareth: Holy Week; From the Entrance into Jerusalem to the Resurrection*, trans. Philip J. Whitmore (San Francisco: Ignatius, 2011), 281.

A. Incorporation

The heavenly session institutes a new form of God's presence with the covenant people,[43] having baptism as its initial sign and seal: Jesus pours out his Spirit on all flesh. Baptism with the Holy Spirit initiated a series of groups into the new covenant (1 Cor 12:13): the Jewish diaspora (Acts 2), Samaritans (Acts 8), gentiles (Acts 10), and followers of John the Baptizer (Acts 19).[44] Personal participation in this baptism follows. When members of these groups are united with Christ, his redeeming work claims them as his own (1 Cor 6:20), and his Spirit indwells them (Rom 8:9). Such incorporation makes us God's children by adoption, members of a royal-priestly family. Baptism in water makes this covenantal initiation public, uniting us not only with Christ the head (Rom 6:1–5) but also with others in the social body (Eph 2:11–22). The baptismal formula in Matthew 28:18–20 speaks of the triune God, naming the ultimate agent of Christian initiation. Texts like 1 Corinthians 12:13 speak of baptism in the Spirit, naming the instrumental agent within the Trinitarian economy. Other texts like Acts 2:38 speak of water baptism in Jesus's name because this Son—who claims all authority in heaven and earth, promising to be with his people till the end (Matt 28:18–20)—accomplished the redemptive work to which the ritual symbolism points.

As the earthly, ecclesial capstone of Easter, Pentecost's outpouring of Jesus's Spirit extended the reach of his reconciling grace in two ways.[45] First, Pentecost extended the reach of inclusion within this social body. Beyond including new people groups and languages, the Spirit's outpouring transcended prior boundaries like age, education, gender, marital status, and wealth (e.g., Acts 2:16–21, 42–47; 4:13; 1 Cor 9:5). Then, since the apostolic community was not obeying Jesus's command to go into all nations, persecution extended the church's witness to the ends of the earth (Acts 1:8; 8:1). Second, Pentecost also began extending the reach of empowerment within this social body. Beyond initially

---

43. Underscoring the complexity—and relative dogmatic neglect—of accounting for Christian experience of Jesus's presence is Markus Bockmuehl, "The Gospels on the Presence of Jesus," in *The Oxford Handbook of Christology*, ed. Francesca Aran Murphy (Oxford: Oxford University Press, 2015), 87–89. See also the biblical-theological treatment in Peter C. Orr, *Exalted Above the Heavens: The Risen and Ascended Christ*, NSBT (Downers Grove, IL: IVP Academic, 2018).

44. The classic treatment of this salvation-historical dimension is James D. G. Dunn, *Baptism in the Holy Spirit; A Re-Examination of the New Testament Teaching on the Gift of the Spirit in Relation to Pentecostalism Today* (Naperville, IL: Allenson, 1970).

45. "Capstone of Easter" comes from Carter, *Race: A Theological Account*, 315.

incorporating unschooled fishermen as leading spokesmen and women as key witnesses, the Spirit's outpouring of gifts soon valued unseen forms of service alongside visible *charismata* (e.g., 1 Cor 12:12–31). To every member, no matter how apparently able, Christ the head has apportioned some spiritual gift(s) with which to strengthen his body (Eph 4:7–16).

B. Indwelling

Via this Pentecostal outpouring, Jesus's Spirit indwells the church as his body in the world, which raises the question of the *totus Christus*. In John's Gospel (14:12) Jesus anticipates believers accomplishing even greater works than he did while physically on earth. Acts (1:1) speaks of what the earthly Jesus began to do and teach, implying that its apostolic narrative extends that ministry. Paul speaks of the church as the "body of Christ" (e.g., 1 Cor 12:27). How reality-depicting is that metaphor? Augustine's language of the "whole Christ" (*totus Christus*) presses that question. This new postresurrection entity is spiritual and metaphysical, yet not hypostatic.[46] Pockets of Reformed caution about the language stem from several possible objections: implying problematic ontological union(s); eclipsing the church's fallibility; extending medieval Catholicism's ecclesiastical inflation; ignoring the ascension; and, most seriously, eliding the Creator-creature distinction—diminishing Christ's divine perfection. In favor of the *totus Christus*, however, are not only "body of Christ" passages but also Jesus's praying of the Psalms and identification with his people's suffering (e.g., Acts 9:4; Col 1:24). Furthermore, there is an established Reformed tradition regarding Christ's "mystical body" in which our union with him, although soteriologically focused, transcends a strictly covenantal relationship. Marital imagery preserves a distinction between two subjects; however, becoming "one flesh" starts to suggest a mysterious new entity that is somewhat parallel to head and body. Defenders of the *totus* may have shown that the possible objections are not necessary or inevitable problems, rightly pressing critics to account for traditions of the mystical body and marital union. Indeed, associating churchly imperfections with Christ is all too biblically familiar (e.g., Rom 2:24). However, the nature of the ontological claim at stake—a

---

46. The rest of this paragraph largely summarizes and responds to J. David Moser, "*Totus Christus*: A Proposal for Protestant Christology and Ecclesiology," *ProEccl* 29, no. 1 (2020): 3–30. Moser's article and his rejoinder to interlocutors Michael Allen, Michael Horton, and Kevin Vanhoozer canvas other relevant literature; see further Webster, "Perfection and Participation."

united person with two distinct subjects—is awkwardly close to, yet worryingly different from, Chalcedon's hypostatic union. Therefore, it seems as if the conclusion of the matter must be prudential: in principle speaking of the *totus Christus* is permissible, and somehow acknowledging the basic concept is vital, but in practice remaining vigilant about the one Mediator's distinct personhood is also necessary. A complicated conceptual history permits but does not require the *totus* language when referring to Christ's mystical body.

Relatedly, there is good reason for exercising caution about *incarnational* language for the church, emphasizing mutual indwelling instead. Given the call in Philippians 2:5 for imitating Christ's self-giving humility, it has become relatively common for Catholics to speak of a "continuing incarnation" and for evangelicals to champion "incarnational ministry." However, rather than serving as a model for ministry, the incarnation points to the "more biblically faithful and theologically dynamic language of ministry as participation in Christ."[47] Contextualization is inevitable and appropriate, but the incarnation is not a general way to authorize the embodiment of our own culturally formed approaches. Too directly associating Christian ministry with the incarnation encourages either condescending "Messiah complexes" or cautious cultural avoidance mechanisms.[48] Speaking of "incarnational ministry" may overemphasize the church's sending relative to gathering, neglecting the living Christ's activity in drawing people to faith.[49] "Participation" communicates one side of the new relational reality: our realm of existence "in" Christ. The other side of this reality is Christ "in" us (Col 1:27) through his indwelling Spirit (Rom 8:10–11). The Pauline and Johannine language is too rich to systematize completely, but the indwelling—however asymmetrical—is mutual.

---

47. J. Todd Billings, *Union with Christ: Reframing Theology and Ministry for the Church* (Grand Rapids: Brazos, 2011), 124.

48. See Billings, *Union with Christ*, 131–35. Since (quoting R. S. Sugirtharajah's statement in "Complacencies and Cul-de-sacs," p. 22) "what is striking about systematic theology is the reluctance of its practitioners to address the relation between European colonialism and the field," it is appropriate to focus more on how "to critically unpack hidden power structures"; so Veli-Matti Kärkkäinen, *Christ and Reconciliation*, vol. 1 of *A Constructive Christian Theology for the Pluralistic World* (Grand Rapids: Eerdmans, 2013), 93.

49. Billings, *Union with Christ*, 156, 158. The incarnation offers an intriguing paradigm for the history of Christian mission, contemplating its distinctive tendencies concerning contextualization; so, e.g., chap. 2 in Andrew F. Walls, *The Cross-Cultural Process in Christian History: Studies in the Transmission and Appropriation of Faith* (Maryknoll, NY: Orbis, 2002). Considerable caution about this incarnational paradigm is necessary, however, given the pitfalls of indirect biblical support, grand historical narratives, and dubious future predictability.

C. Instruction

The Gospels and the epistles frame the risen Christ's instruction of his people in different yet complementary ways. In the Gospels, discipleship is rather literally a way of life. The twelve apostles and others followed Jesus as an itinerant rabbi and prophet. They walked with him on a pilgrimage that culminated in Jerusalem. They left their "nets" and families for this journey. They listened to him in public and private. They received instruction about prayer, but they also saw his practice and received correction when their persistence was inadequate. The privilege of physically following Jesus gave them insight as eyewitnesses, through which God has given us a distinctive framework for discipleship.

Whereas the Gospels narrate Jesus's instruction before the resurrection, in the epistles we continue to "learn Christ" despite his physical absence (Eph 4:20–21). Without literally following him around, we walk with him because he is present via the indwelling of his Holy Spirit, with whom we are to "keep in step" (Gal 5:16, 18, 25). As the Spirit implants the divine Word within us, our lives bear the fruit of Christlike love (John 15:1–17; Gal 5:22–23). As the good news about Christ dwells in us richly (Col 3:16), our speech edifies others (Eph 4:11–16). Of course, we may encounter divine speech as an external Word that corrects us (2 Tim 3:14–17; Heb 4:12–13); we are, after all, wandering sheep.[50] Yet this Word is never merely external to the church, for the Spirit of Jesus plants within us growing knowledge of God and incorporates us within the risen Lord's presentation to the world.

D. Intercession

As a royal priesthood the church experiences Christ's presence and absence dialectically. On one hand, because the Son remains incarnate, he is physically absent from earth; when the church fails to acknowledge this absence adequately, she becomes unduly triumphant about her earthly mediation of Christ's presence. Indeed, we do not currently know where heaven is. On the other hand, the church enjoys a new form of divine presence through the Holy Spirit. This new form is less tangible but more universally immediate and intimate. The Spirit can

---

50. On Scripture's relation to the resurrected Lord, see Webster, "Resurrection and Scripture," in *Domain of the Word*, chap. 2; Webster, "Prolegomena to Christology: Four Theses," in *Confessing God*, chap. 6; Webster, *Holy Scripture: A Dogmatic Sketch*, CIT (Cambridge: Cambridge University Press, 2003), 58–66, 108–9, 128.

make the risen Christ present to anyone, whereas if the Son remained on earth, that form of presence would be locally limited.[51]

Now God's people draw near to the heavenly throne in Jesus's name. He prays and advocates for us. When the church fails to focus on Jesus's human presence with God the Father, she fears the Son as if he were too divine to be of earthly, saving good. Then she threatens to displace the one Mediator between God and humanity with additional intermediaries: Mary, saints, and the like.[52] Given Christ's constant presentation of faithful covenant partnership in God's presence, though, Christians can pray boldly (Heb 4:14–16), participating in the theandric Son's heavenly fellowship and anticipating the fullness of future glory. This Mediator's ongoing intercession is not desperate pleading with an unrelenting Father. Instead, the Son intercedes as a constant reminder of earthly pilgrims' ongoing participation in a once-for-all self-offering with which God is delighted: "Unlike other priests, Christ does not *witness* to the work of God's salvation and mediation between Godself and creation but *is in His person* the work of God's salvation and mediation."[53] There is continuity between the Son's ongoing intercession in his heavenly session and his once-for-all intercession on the cross.[54]

V. MEDIATOR

This chapter's opening treatment of Hebrews's Christology highlighted the name Mediator to integrate Jesus's divine sonship and high priesthood. These emphases encapsulate the redemptive significance of his exaltation and his ultimate fulfillment of the *munus triplex*.[55] The unity of this threefold office integrates creation and redemption, and it nuances the nature of Christ's mediation—a priestly reign characterized by peace, exercised by personal speech, and rooted in reassurance of divine mercy. Whatever the exact occasion, Hebrews makes a theological virtue out of pastoral necessity: the singularity of Christ's self-offering proclaims

---

51. Confronting overemphasis on Jesus's earthly presence with the original disciples, highlighting his ongoing presence as the ascended Lord by the Spirit, are chaps. 8, 10 of Dietrich Bonhoeffer, *Discipleship*, ed. Martin Kuske and Ilse Todt, trans. Barbara Green and Reinhard Krauss, DBWE 4 (Minneapolis: Fortress, 2001).

52. For this argument and insight on the surrounding themes, see Farrow, *Ascension and Ecclesia.*

53. Italics original in Tom Greggs, *The Priestly Catholicity of the Church*, vol. 1 of *Dogmatic Ecclesiology* (Grand Rapids: Baker Academic, 2019), 69.

54. Greggs, *Dogmatic Ecclesiology*, 1:73.

55. Again, part of what follows is adapted from Treier, "Mediator."

God's reassuring invitation to draw near once believers realize that the high priest is both the sacrifice and the divine Son himself. Believers approach God boldly with nonatoning forms of bodily sacrifice—praise and good works (Heb 13:15)—for which the Old Testament called. In this Mediator there is no gap between human beings and God. The same Word promises in person that God will remember our sins no more.

Mediator adds a priestly dimension to a broadly Athanasian conviction about the immediacy of God's salvation in Christ, prompting Protestants to connect the earthly sacrifice and the heavenly session. Protestant accounts of atonement can myopically focus on the propitiatory death of a sinless human being. Such myopic accounts stammer regarding why Christ must be fully divine: the exaltation signals God's approval of the sacrifice, but the incarnation largely ensures that the sinless sacrifice makes it to the altar. At most, Christ's deity explains why one can substitute for many. Retrieving the Athanasian pattern reminds us that atonement involves not just a sacrifice but ultimately a high priest who is God's Son, in whom God redeems us personally. In return, a healthy Protestant focus provides a more holistically biblical perspective. Hebrews works out priesthood and sacrifice in ways that not only require but even emphasize Jesus's full humanity more clearly than patristic tradition did. Moreover, Christ's perfecting work follows from his pioneering path of perfect faith.

In Job 9:33–35, the protagonist laments, "If only there were someone to mediate between us, someone to bring us together, someone to remove God's rod from me, so that his terror would frighten me no more. Then I would speak up without fear of him, but as it now stands with me, I cannot." These words, speaking beyond what Job knew and using *mesitēs* ("Mediator") language in the LXX, find fulfillment in the Christ of Hebrews. Job needed an encounter with God, which first silenced and then reassured him, even establishing him as a kind of priest. The New Testament reserves *mesitēs* for Moses and Christ. Moses bears the title provisionally, whereas Christ "does not stand between the two parties: he is those two parties in his own person."[56] That is the intersection of Christ's person and work: as Mediator of the new covenant, Jesus is the fully divine Son, teaching fellow human beings to know God while reassuring them of forgiveness. Philip Melanchthon's famous axiom, "To know Christ is to know his benefits," is not fully

---

56. Bavinck, *Reformed Dogmatics*, 3:363.

reversible: we could not know the benefits in some transactional sense apart from knowing the living God, who says, "I will remember your sins no more."

The Son's identity as redemptive Mediator sheds light on the expectation of 1 Corinthians 15:24–28 concerning his submission upon handing over the kingdom to God the Father. To be sure, Paul does not speak with the precision of later dogma. But neither does Paul retract his identification of Christ as YHWH incarnate, and partitive exegesis is fitting for such passages.[57] In 1 Corinthians 15, as earlier in 1 Corinthians 8:6 and 12:3, Christ is *Kyrios* ("LORD," 15:57–58). Given his inclusion in YHWH's identity, Christ is worthy of worship as God's Son; given his incarnate identification with humanity, he is noteworthy for perfect obedience to God as Father. Acknowledging an appropriate Trinitarian order (*taxis*) and the incarnate Son's corresponding obedience does not require speaking of "eternal functional subordination" or projecting obedience into the Godhead as a divine attribute. Johannine language of mission and dogmatic language of reduplication provide the necessary concepts for both biblical aspects of Christ's kingship. As the eternal Son he shares God's sovereignty, which is comprehensive in principle; as Israel's Messiah he overcomes creaturely rebellion and reconciles all things, which establishes God's reign fully in practice. Thus, as theandric Mediator, he can appropriately be "made subject to him who put everything under him" (15:28). Calvin's view that this passage requires an eschatological conclusion of Christ's role as Mediator is unnecessary because, as we saw in chapter 2, the eternal Son mediates creational union and not just redemptive reconciliation.[58] Fulfillment of God's ultimate purposes through eschatological consummation in Christ (Eph 1:10) will be the focus of our final chapter.

Thus *Mediator* encompasses the fullness of Christ's exaltation. The glory anticipated in the transfiguration awaited the messianic Servant who suffered. The resurrection brought the earthly vindication of Jesus's ministry of reconciliation and inaugurated the new creation. The ascension dramatized the transition to a new phase of ministry, Christ's

---

57. See the helpful treatment of 1 Corinthians 15:24–28 vis-à-vis John 14:28 and other passages about Jesus "becoming" Lord and Son from Jamieson and Wittman, *Biblical Reasoning*, 167–76.

58. So Herman Bavinck, *Holy Spirit, Church, and New Creation*, ed. John Bolt, trans. John Vriend, vol. 4 of *Reformed Dogmatics* (Grand Rapids: Baker Academic, 2008), 685. See the extended discussion in chap. 14 of Berkouwer, *Return of Christ*.

heavenly session at God's right hand. As his Spirit empowers our mission to bear witness among all nations, the risen Lord incorporates, indwells, instructs, and intercedes for his people. Consequently, with Christ's authorization, disciples pray in his name, baptize new members into his body, and teach each other to follow him. The church's healthy life and fruitful activity flow from being united with her head. Hebrews ends by referring to the resurrection of "our Lord Jesus, that great Shepherd of the sheep" (13:20), praying that God would equip and effect "pleasing" sacrifices in the church "through Jesus Christ, to whom be glory for ever and ever" (13:21). Amen.

CHAPTER 10

CONSUMMATION AS THE BRIDEGROOM

Revelation 21:1–22:5

As epitomized in **Revelation 21:1–22:5**, Jesus Christ is the **Bridegroom**, whose return will bring the **consummation** of creation and redemption, glorifying the covenant people to be fully at home with God. *After the final judgment, only righteousness will fill the new cosmos; with history's struggles ended and tragedies redeemed, we will enjoy intimate communion with God and each other in Christ. Until then, the Lord's Supper nourishes faith with a foretaste of such communion.*

The subject of this book's final chapter is redemptive history's final chapter: the relation of Jesus Christ to the "last" things. Our first section expounds the christological implications of the eschatological holy city envisioned in Revelation 21:1–22:5. Each human being encounters only one last thing, either God's blessed presence or punishment. Thus, the second section explores eternal communion with God in Christ. More broadly, we already live in the last days (e.g., 1 Cor 10:11; 1 Pet 1:20; 1 John 2:18; Jude 18), which were inaugurated by Christ's incarnation, death, and resurrection. Therefore, because communion with God has multiple phases, this second section returns to the heavenly session, addressing Christ's presence in the Eucharist and the church's ministry of reconciliation prior to his return and the fullness of his blessed presence. Then the third section examines Christ's work of final judgment, whereby believers are rewarded and unbelievers are punished. The fourth section follows the examination of judgment by contemplating the nature of Christ's eternal communion with his glorified people, who will enjoy the beatific vision as participants in a new creation. Fifth and finally, Christ's identity as the Bridegroom recapitulates this chapter and the book as a whole.

I. THE HOLY CITY IN REVELATION 21:1–22:5

The final segment of John's Apocalypse depicts Christ's future work in "making everything new" (21:5). Although beginning in 21:9, the vision is introduced in 21:1–8, as John sees "a new heaven and a new earth" (21:1). Much of the ensuing material focuses on "the Holy City, Jerusalem, coming down out of heaven from God" (21:10): an initial view (21:9–14), its measurements (21:15–17), its material (21:18–21), its internal features (21:22–27), and its symbols pointing to God's presence (22:1–5).[1] This depiction of the city contains numerous details, evoking Old Testament texts like Ezekiel 40–48. Yet the focus here rests upon features that communicate the Christology of Revelation.

First, *Jesus's resurrection* bears on what a "new heaven and a new earth" means, the sense in which "the first earth had passed away" (Rev 21:1)—whether via renovation or annihilation and re-creation. Semantic and historical arguments are inconclusive. The newness (*kainos*) is more qualitative than temporal, but the contrast with the first (*protos*) obviously has temporal implications. Both annihilation and renovation eschatologies circulated in Second Temple Judaism. The language of passing away (*apēlthan*) might favor annihilation, but then the mention of the sea's removal could seem gratuitous. This removal is not literal, given the sea's varied significance throughout John's Apocalypse and a river's presence in Revelation 22. The sea's absence, though, highlights God's victory over the cosmic chaos with which the Old Testament associates it. Mentioning the removal seems unnecessary if annihilation and re-creation were in view.[2] Theologically, resurrection favors

---

1. G. K. Beale, *The Book of Revelation: A Commentary on the Greek Text*, NIGTC (Grand Rapids: Eerdmans, 1999), 1039, 1061.

2. For a discussion leaning closer to annihilation, see Grant R. Osborne, *Revelation*, BECNT (Grand Rapids: Baker Academic, 2002), 729–30. Leaning toward renovation is Beale, *Revelation*, 1040–43. Appealing to the sea's removal in favor of renovation is Bruce Riley Ashford and Craig G. Bartholomew, *The Doctrine of Creation: A Constructive Kuyperian Approach* (Downers Grove, IL: IVP Academic, 2020), 311.

renovation, maintaining continuity for Jesus's body and ours, however "spiritual" (1 Cor 15:42–44) their glorified form may be. Resurrection is not immediately explicit in Revelation 21:1, but in the near context the sea gives up her dead (20:13), Christ's bride is clothed (21:2), and metaphors invoke material activities (21:24–27) in a city. Metaphors like healing do not convey literal realities since there is no longer any curse (22:1–5), but there may be significance in their continuity with the present cosmos. It seems more likely that the risen Christ will dramatically reform current matter than simply annihilate and replace it. Nevertheless, it may be tempting for comfortable modern exegetes to emphasize material continuity and understate qualitative renovation.[3] When 21:4 reiterates that the "old order of things has passed away," as God wipes every tear from our eyes, it signals a definite end of cosmic history as we know it.

Second, *covenantal communion with Christ* is the core emphasis of the mixed metaphors introduced in Revelation 21:2. In the ensuing vision John sees a place, "the Holy City, the new Jerusalem, coming down out of heaven from God." Yet this New Jerusalem is "prepared as a bride beautifully dressed for her husband." It is possible to emphasize the symbolic character of the vision enough to find a people here while excluding a place.[4] It is also possible to insist on a place, emphasizing the direct object in 21:2 while noticing the simile ("prepared as") involving the bride: "Babylon was both a people and a place, and [given the contrast in play] that is the better answer here."[5] If the renovated cosmos contains embodied people who interact, then some kind of visible, material realm seems likely. God's dwelling with God's people is the master theme, fulfilling a host of Old Testament promises regarding a new covenant.[6] Correspondingly, there is overlap between God as the place's renovator and Christ as the people's Bridegroom. God is the agent of the dwelling (21:3), the redemptive comfort (21:4), and presumably the

---

3. See reflections on how Galatians and Hebrews construe "the New Testament grand narrative" as a "journey through history to the fulfillment of a promise that transcends history," contra immanentist modern tendencies, in (quoting p. 389) David Lyle Jeffrey, "(Pre) Figuration: Masterplot and Meaning in Biblical History," in *"Behind" the Text: History and Biblical Interpretation*, ed. Craig Bartholomew et al., SHS 4 (Grand Rapids: Zondervan, 2003), 363–93.

4. E.g., Beale, *Revelation*, 1045.

5. So Osborne, *Revelation*, 733. Topological theory, to which Geoffrey Fulkerson has introduced me, recognizes that *place* involves a relationally constituted world and is more than just meaningful *space*—suggesting that there would be a union of people and place here even if no material cosmos were in view. Nevertheless, the simile does not completely identify the city with the saints (see also Osborne, 747).

6. See further Osborne, *Revelation*, 734–35.

newness (21:5a).[7] Yet the biblical Christ is associated with emphatically declaring true words (21:5b), accomplishing redemption (21:6a), and giving living water (21:6b). The covenantal communion at the heart of this new creation depends upon the church's marriage to Christ as her Passover Lamb.

Third, ultimate enjoyment of *God's immediate, glorious presence in Christ* is celebrated by splendid, temple-related imagery. The *Shekinah* dwelling language of Revelation 21:3 introduces this theme. The brilliant jewels of the twelve foundation stones (21:18–21) further the theme, since most of them appear in the priestly ephod (Exod 28:17–20; 39:8–14).[8] Then Revelation 21:22 underscores the point: "I did not see a temple in the city, because the Lord God Almighty and the Lamb are its temple," fulfilling John 2:19–22. Indeed, God's glory illuminates the entire city, whereas a temple would distinguish sacred from "secular" space in a way that is no longer fitting. John envisions not the end of the church but the end of religion.[9] The church comes to enjoy her true end, being at home with God. The angel that has been a harbinger of judgment now renders "a more pleasing and natural form of service: leading the seer on a tour of the heavenly city."[10] The tour celebrates the brilliance of God's glory and the splendor of God's gracious presence, especially if the city is constructed of gold—not just overlaid with it.[11] The tour also celebrates the order and blessed safety of dwelling with God. The city is a cube of extraordinary size.[12] By comparison its wall is laughably small. Ultimately the one wall celebrates unity, and it is not defensive (by the end of Revelation 20 enemies have been vanquished) but decorative (providing demarcation that the ancients valued).[13]

Fourth, this celestial vision reinforces *the divine identity of Jesus Christ.* As the Lamb of God, he is the husband of the churchly bride in Revelation 21:2—with God's renovation of the cosmos as a divine dwelling place immediately following (21:3). To be at home in God's

7. The "Behold!" of 21:3 calls attention to an apocalyptic divine act, according to Joseph L. Mangina, *Revelation*, BTCB (Grand Rapids: Brazos, 2010), 238.
8. Beale, *Revelation*, 1080–82.
9. Mangina, *Revelation*, 242.
10. Mangina, *Revelation*, 240.
11. So Osborne, *Revelation*, 755.
12. Something like the distance from Toronto to Miami, according to Amos Yong, *Revelation*, Belief (Louisville: Westminster John Knox, 2021), 251n2. The size may correspond to the limits of the known Hellenistic world, thus incorporating the nations rather than corresponding to Ezekiel's temple vision; so Beale, *Revelation*, 1074.
13. On unity see Beale, *Revelation*, 1078. The measurements are symbolic, frequently multiples of twelve.

household is to be united with Christ. We have already noted that true words, completed redemption, and living water indicate the Lamb's shared agency in God's renewing work. To these indications we can add, "I am the Alpha and the Omega, the Beginning and the End" (21:6). Said simply of Israel's God, to the exclusion of the Lamb, these words would be tautologous. "I will be their God" (21:7) surely includes God in the speaking. But how could John see this One "seated on the throne" (21:5) if not for the Lamb? The Lamb too is the Alpha and Omega, whose twelve apostles mark the city's boundaries (21:14), who comprises the city's temple along with the Lord God Almighty (21:22), who illuminates the city with the effulgence of divine glory (21:23–25), and whose book of life is the basis for judgment (21:27).[14] In that context the shared "throne of God and of the Lamb" (22:1, 3; see also 3:21) is no surprise.[15] The Lamb's servants will see his face and bear his name (22:4), even as they are illuminated by the Lord God (22:5).

Fifth, *traces of Trinitarian theology elsewhere in Revelation* corroborate the Lamb's divine identity. Revelation 1:1–8 indicates a Trinitarian source for this revelation, perhaps especially in the greeting of 1:4–5 from "him who is, and who was, and who is to come, and from the seven spirits before his throne, and from Jesus Christ." The "someone like a son of man" in 1:9–20 elicits worship that angels refuse, and this One is "the First and the Last." This Son of God is the eschatological judge (2:18) who dispenses God's Spirit (3:1–5) and holds the key of David (3:7). He is "the Amen, the faithful and true witness, the ruler of God's creation" (3:14). Only this Lamb on the heavenly throne is worthy to break the seals of history's scroll, whereupon he receives worship (5:1–14). His wrath enacts divine judgment (6:15–17), as does the rider on the white horse (19:11–16), who is named "Faithful and True" as the Word of God. Both the Lamb's name and his Father's name are written on the foreheads of the 144,000 redeemed people, whom they receive together as first fruits (Rev 14:1–5). The Lamb is "Lord of lords and King of kings" (17:14); the former may indicate his deity and the latter his humanity.[16] Christ receives priestly activity and rules with God (20:6). Climactically,

---

14. The "book of life" may involve an epexegetical genitive, "the book that is life," evoking a roll of the city's citizens; so Osborne, *Revelation*, 766.

15. See Beale, *Revelation*, 1113.

16. For the evidence in this paragraph, see Smith, *Trinity in Revelation*. Smith interacts carefully with alternative readings that deny the Lamb's divine identity and interpret *spirit* language in terms of angels. Regarding 17:14, Smith appeals to Peter J. Leithart, *Revelation 12–22*, ITC (London: T&T Clark, 2018), 199. See also essays on the worship of Jesus and the role of the

this One who is "coming soon" to judge names himself ("I am") "the Alpha and the Omega, the First and the Last, the Beginning and the End" (22:12–13). Much of this litany focuses on Christ's divine identity, but the sevenfold Spirit's accompanying activity in revelation (notably in Revelation 1–3, e.g., in 1:4–5) and lack of participation in rendering worship like angels (Rev 4–5) suggests a proto-Trinitarian theology of the Holy Spirit. Intriguingly, John's visionary procession "in the Spirit" to a mountain view of the holy city (21:10) uses the same terminology as later creeds used for the procession of the Spirit.[17]

Sixth, given his identification yet distinction vis-à-vis God (the Father), the Lamb is *the crucial agent of divine revelation and the fulfillment of Israel's redemptive history.* Among Old Testament allusions besides Ezekiel 40–48 and the temple, Isaiah 52 and 61–62 (if not all of 56–66) are prominent, evoking a new creation and new exodus in which the Lamb recapitulates foundational events of Israel's covenant history. Furthermore, the Lamb's twelve apostles, named on the foundation stones (21:14), are integrated with Israel's twelve tribes, named on the city gates (21:12). The city's universal reach, signaled even by the unusually plural *peoples* (*laoi* in 21:3), fulfills rather than supplants Israel's expectations regarding the nations' pilgrimage to Jerusalem (21:24–27).[18] Indeed, twelve crops of fruit provide healing to the nations (22:2), as the tree of life epitomizes the escalation of Edenic delight via Ezekiel's eschatological fulfillment.[19] Thanks to the Lamb, Israel fulfills her destiny as a vehicle of universal blessing. However ambiguous the extent of ongoing cultural activity may be, Babylon is not simply thrown into the lake of fire but gives way to the New Jerusalem: "John thereby sees a new grand-central station, so to speak."[20]

Seventh, Revelation lauds *the identity of the messianic, victorious Lion of Judah with the slain Passover Lamb* (5:5–6). The powerful Lion of Judah (Gen 49:9) grows up from the fledgling Root of Jesse (Isa 11:1, 10) to

Spirit in Richard Bauckham, *The Climax of Prophecy: Studies on the Book of Revelation* (Edinburgh: T&T Clark, 1993).

17. Mangina, *Revelation*, 246.

18. With the entire city being God's temple, spatial restrictions upon gentiles and nonpriests no longer apply, as noted by Beale, *Revelation*, 1047. The fullness of consummation is underscored by the addition of *all* to intertexts from Isaiah 43:19, 65:17, and 66:22 (p. 1052).

19. Beale, *Revelation*, 1103.

20. Yong, *Revelation*, 257. On Babylon not being thrown into the lake of fire, see Mangina, *Revelation*, 239, 242–43. Yong and Mangina may be unduly inclined to see ongoing cultural exchange with others outside the city, whereas John more modestly celebrates the new cosmos within the Old Testament's earthly framework.

defeat the dragon of Revelation 12 *by* becoming the sacrificial Lamb of God who takes away the world's sin (John 1:29).[21] The Lamb still bears the marks of his counterintuitive means of victory. Judgment there will be, but in the first instance it warns potential cowards among God's people to endure the world's opposition faithfully.[22] Revelation proclaims redemption, seeking transformation rather than terror: those who overcome will enjoy the light of God's countenance as participants in the Lion's reign.[23] The Lamb both shares the divine throne and gives us a share in God's reign by giving it a creaturely face (Rev 22:3–5). He is both Lord of all "lords" and king of all earthly kings.

II. COMMUNION

The fundamental theme of Revelation 21–22 is communion with God as God's people, the restoration and perfection of what Adam and Eve lost. In the person of the Suffering Servant and slain Lamb, YHWH has inaugurated this restoration, but Christ's return has an unexpected two-stage character: until his second coming, he nourishes his people in the Eucharist and thus nurtures their participation in his ministry of reconciliation.

A. Eucharist

In the sacrament of the Lord's Supper, Christ nourishes his pilgrim people with signs and seals of his covenant promises. When the Heidelberg Catechism begins by asking, "What is your only comfort in life and in death?" it famously answers, "That I am not my own, but belong—body and soul, in life and in death—to my faithful Savior, Jesus Christ." The Catechism unfolds this Savior's faithfulness in three ways: (1) fully paying for all our sins and freeing us from the devil's power; (2) preserving us providentially so that all things work together for our salvation; and (3) assuring us of eternal life and making us ready to live for God. By proclaiming his redemptive work (the Savior's first activity), the sacrament contributes to preservation and assurance (his second and

---

21. See chap. 6 of Bauckham, *Climax of Prophecy.*
22. Beale, *Revelation*, 1059–60.
23. Thus fulfilling texts like Numbers 6:25 and Daniel 7:18, 27; see Osborne, *Revelation*, 774–76. With the Lamb's name on their foreheads, saints become priests; whether or not they participate in the Lamb's act of judgment or have animals to rule over, at least they share his reign with respect to angels (1 Cor 6:3). See Beale, *Revelation*, 1115–17.

third activities). In eating the Supper, we celebrate our participation in the Savior's victory over death.[24]

The Eucharist—which means thanksgiving—reorients our pilgrimage in time through remembrance, communion, and hope: "Specifically, through the Supper, the Father's adopted children delight in a foretaste of heavenly fellowship with Christ, their spouse."[25] Encountering God's promise through covenantal signs and seals rekindles faith. Thanksgiving is transformative because ingratitude lay at the heart of human rebellion.[26] God's promised gift is Jesus Christ himself, who fosters our *hope* of eternal communion. The Supper anticipates the celestial banquet, at which—together with all of God's people, rich and poor, from every tribe and tongue (e.g., Isa 25:6)—we will feast with the slain Lamb. This hope is rooted in *remembrance*: we "proclaim the Lord's death until he comes" (1 Cor 11:26). Both sacraments—baptism and the Lord's Supper—tangibly signify Christ's death and resurrection. Our participation is a grateful response to Christ's once-for-all self-offering. Thus, earthly *communion* is situated by remembrance and hope. As we remember Christ's sacrifice, we weep and rejoice; as we remember his promises, we delight in a secure faith and lament in hope for what we do not yet see.[27] We not only commune with Christ but also seek and celebrate unity with the rest of his churchly body.

Christ is really, spiritually present at the meal. *Really*: "This is my body, which is for you." "This cup is the new covenant in my blood." The Supper is a "participation in" his body and blood (1 Cor 10:16; 11:24–25). "Whoever eats my flesh and drinks my blood remains in me, and I in them" (John 6:56). This special form of Christ's presence—action at a distance to give himself in relational nearness for fellowship ("participation") with his people—depends upon a divinely promised, genuine bond ("is") between the physical signs and the realities they represent. Jesus's Last Supper ritually evoked the Passover to establish new covenantal communion. "This is my body" is a promise that only a

---

24. Highlighting this theme from neglected places—Isaiah 25, "with its vision of a future banquet where God will swallow death forever," and Purim, "with its celebration of the overthrow of death among diasporic Jews"—is Andrew T. Abernethy, "Canonical Imagination, COVID-19, and the Communion: Illumination from Isaiah's Banquet and Purim in Esther," *JTI*, forthcoming.

25. Billings, *Remembrance, Communion, and Hope*, 57. Subsequent sentences draw from summary theses that begin on p. 68.

26. As noted with reference to Romans 1:18–22 (amid a larger emphasis on an eschatological "thanksgiving parade") in Michael S. Horton, *People and Place: A Covenant Ecclesiology* (Louisville: Westminster John Knox, 2008), 291.

27. See Billings, *Remembrance, Communion, and Hope*, 111, 132, 170.

human being "can offer and . . . only a divine agent can keep."[28] Given the divine agency, the promise is kept *spiritually*: in contrast with the epiclesis in much modern liturgy, "Christ is not brought down from heaven so much as we are raised up to heaven to feed upon him there."[29] This upward spiritual movement underscores that we do not yet enjoy the full immediacy of Christ's presence. Corollary to our experience of this reality via faith rather than sight, gospel words remain "central to Protestantism," yet the Lord's Table communicates the Word in a way that dramatically incorporates sensory participation.[30] Beyond merely remembering, we eat and drink so that we may commune with Christ and each other in a distinctive way. The upward spiritual movement of this communion is Trinitarian—being taken up by the Spirit through faith to be nourished afresh in our union with the Son, thus drawing near to God as Father.

Accordingly, at the Supper we both "feed on Christ in our hearts by faith" and fellowship with him as our future Bridegroom. If "this is my body" precludes mere memorialism, neither does it necessitate transubstantiation or impanation. Admittedly, such direct identification of the bread with Christ's body can take various forms, while seeming ecumenically advantageous. However, Eucharistic realism took a long and winding historical road; impanation hardly qualifies for a Vincentian canon of what has been believed by everyone, everywhere. Meanwhile, impanation metaphorically clashes with Jesus's desire to be the host at the table, feasting with his disciples (Matt 26:29). His real presence at the Supper is spiritual and multifaceted—as host and bread of life—rather than primarily located in the physical elements. However directly or indirectly John 6 speaks of the Eucharist, its theology of abiding (which anticipates John 15:1–17) simultaneously underscores the reality-depicting importance and the nonliteral character of the feeding metaphor: its focus is upon nourishing union with Christ. The "Reformed" view of real yet spiritual presence incorporates the Holy Spirit's ministry more focally than impanation. Of course, this view further appeals to the ascension, with Jesus's resurrected body remaining located in whatever

---

28. Hinlicky, *Beloved Community*, 518.

29. Carl Trueman, "The Incarnation and the Lord's Supper," in *The Word Became Flesh: Evangelicals and the Incarnation*, ed. David Peterson (Carlisle, Cumbria, UK: Paternoster, 2003), 196–97. Given this formulation, Trueman's later hesitation about spiritual eating seems overwrought.

30. Trueman, "Incarnation and the Lord's Supper," 203–5.

"place" comprises the heavenly sanctuary. By contrast, impanation so focuses Christ's presence and the Spirit's power upon the earthly elements that personal communion and inaugurated eschatology are displaced by overrealized literalism.[31] Even sacramental impanation that allows for both descent and ascent motifs may still struggle to celebrate Jesus as the table's host.[32] Both participation (1 Cor 10:16) and remembrance (1 Cor 11:24–25) focus spiritual attention on together encountering the living Christ, not eating consecrated elements as such.

Although the language appears early and often in church history, the Eucharist only involves a sacrifice in a carefully qualified sense.[33] Technical explanations were lacking prior to transubstantiation, which activated Protestant allergies: whether its sacrifice is unbloody or not, the Mass's propitiatory repetition obscures the cross's singular accomplishment. For these allergies the proper prescription is to refine the Reformed emphasis upon Christ's heavenly session. Sacrificial animals were not killed on the altar; instead, their blood and perhaps body parts were subsequently presented there. Similarly, Jesus's death occurred "outside the camp" (Heb 13:13) prior to the heavenly presentation that completed his sacrifice. Jesus's ongoing intercession temporally extends this heavenly self-offering until the eschaton; hence communicants can participate in his sacrifice, perhaps even in its aftermath of priestly eating, despite its singular and otherwise-finished character. This account of eating and sacrifice construes the Eucharist's place in accord with our initial account of its time: if remembrance, communion, and hope relate our pilgrimage to the past, present, and future, then the Supper's spiritual movement is upward and forward, proleptically enjoying communion with Christ as the Spirit enables us to participate in the heavenly presentation of his unique sacrifice.

---

31. As in, e.g., Marilyn McCord Adams, *Christ and Horrors: The Coherence of Christology*, CIT (Cambridge: Cambridge University Press, 2006), 296–309.

32. See the sophisticated "sacramental impanation" view of Arcadi, *An Incarnational Model of the Eucharist*, 253. (See also the "transelementation" view with which Arcadi triangulates, from George Hunsinger, *The Eucharist and Ecumenism: Let Us Keep the Feast*, CIT [Cambridge: Cambridge University Press, 2008].) Arcadi believes that Calvinists could apply their pneumatology to embrace his model, with both ascent and descent motifs (p. 253) and the Spirit bridging the "spatial gap between the elements and the human body in Christ" (pp. 273–74). Yet it is unclear how the causal power would remain that of Christ's human body, with the Spirit "only providing the requisite connection" between it and the elements. And the question remains whether extension via part-whole synecdoche rightly construes the biblical relation between *this* and *the body of Christ* (so p. 264)—or is overly literal.

33. This paragraph summarizes the proposal of Stephen R. Holmes, "A Reformed Account of Eucharistic Sacrifice," *IJST* 24, no. 2 (April 2022): 191–211.

B. Reconciliation

Until his return, Jesus Christ not only nourishes his people in the Eucharist but also nurtures their participation in his ministry of reconciliation. As we have seen throughout, the gift of reconciliation is personal, communal, and cosmic in scope. *Personal*: The new creation has come (2 Cor 5:17) once sinners are reconciled to God through Christ (2 Cor 5:18). *Communal*: Beyond "not counting people's sins against them," this reconciling God teaches those who are "in Christ" to stop regarding others "from a worldly point of view" (2 Cor 5:16, 19). *Cosmic*: Passages like Ephesians 1 and Colossians 1 celebrate "all things" as the object of reconciliation. In between individual sinners and all things Christ has placed the church as the new form of a reconciled and reconciling humanity.[34]

The church participates in Jesus's ministry of reconciliation by evangelizing, embodying the forgiveness it proclaims (thus "discerning the body," 1 Cor 11:29), and enduring necessary hardship. *Evangelism*: The connection between the Eucharist and gospel proclamation is not accidental (e.g., Luke 24:13–35, 45–49; Acts 2:41–47; 1 Cor 11:26). The Lord's Supper not only proclaims the gospel to the gathered community with visible words but also strengthens and sends Christ's body to bear witness.[35] *Forgiveness*: The church must embody what it proclaims, going beyond verbal formulas or inner feelings to the merciful pursuit of restored fellowship.[36] Forgiveness must often be granted without reconciliation being certain or even achievable because offenders may resist repentance or temporal obstacles may persist.[37] Even so, practices of forgiveness join verbal proclamation to bear a more compelling witness regarding God's mercy. *Endurance*: The need to practice forgiveness— both internally and externally—signals that like her Lord the church will encounter hardship, often at others' hands. Some of this hardship may involve direct persecution for the gospel's sake, but there will also be indirect demands of temporal ascesis and communal solidarity with

34. For the church as a "mediocosm" between the individual and the universe, see (without embracing its universalistic trappings) Adams, *Christ and Horrors*, 200–204.

35. See chapter 7 regarding the insights of missional theology and integral mission, but for perceptive concerns here see Michael Niebauer, *Virtuous Persuasion: A Theology of Christian Mission*, Studies in Historical and Systematic Theology (Bellingham, WA: Lexham, 2022).

36. See L. Gregory Jones, *Embodying Forgiveness: A Theological Analysis* (Grand Rapids: Eerdmans, 1995); Miroslav Volf, *Exclusion and Embrace: A Theological Exploration of Identity, Otherness, and Reconciliation*, rev. ed. (Nashville: Abingdon, 2019).

37. Unexpectedly, perhaps, the parable of the prodigal son does not end in complete reconciliation, as noted by Green, *All Things Beautiful*, 108.

suffering people. Jesus died as a singular martyr, but for the gospel's sake he also paradigmatically knew homelessness and scorn.[38]

This ministry of reconciliation orients Christian life eschatologically, around participation in Christ. The church's moral economy is summarized in Colossians 1:28: "He is the one we proclaim, admonishing and teaching everyone with all wisdom, so that we may present everyone fully mature in Christ." Since "the mystery that has been kept hidden for ages and generations . . . is now disclosed" (Col 1:26), "set your hearts on things above, where Christ is, seated at the right hand of God . . . not on earthly things" (Col 3:1–2). Already "you died, and your life is now hidden with Christ in God" so that "when Christ, who is your life, appears, then you also will appear with him in glory" (Col 3:3–4). Yet

> to seek these realities is not to escape from creaturely relations. "Above" and "below" are not equivalent to "transcendent" and "temporal"—indeed, whatever else may be said of the so-called Colossian heresy, it appears to have fallen into precisely this all-too-worldly notion of the "above," which *inflamed* fascination with the flesh rather than checking it (2:23). To seek what is above, therefore, is to be directed in one's moral history by the reality which grounds that history and toward which that history moves, namely "Christ is." This seeking is not apart from the mundane realities of holy action—dealing with desire, governing speech, forbearing others, handling church, domestic, and economic relations. . . . Truly to seek what is above is not to flee embodied social existence but to see it as caught up in the entire reorientation of created life in the kingdom of Christ.[39]

This reorientation means traveling at "the speed the love of God walks," lovingly attending to others like Jesus would rather than depending on

---

38. Protestant tradition has often proclaimed a Jesus who suffers *for* but not *with* us, so it must listen carefully to liberationist critiques; see Mouw and Sweeney, *Suffering and Victorious*, 95. Yet we all have an idolatrous tendency to identify Jesus primarily with our own suffering, so "liberation" cannot simply displace biblical teaching as Christology's fundamental criterion. Here I am also influenced by conversations with Joel Miles.

39. This paragraph's discussion of Colossians (quoting p. 23) depends on "'Where Christ Is,'" in Webster, *God without Measure*, vol. 2. See also the call for an ecclesial ethics to be "genuinely eschatological," lest we otherwise embrace "a fundamentally non-dramatic Christology," in Webster, "Christ, Church and Reconciliation," in *Word and Church*, 229. For an exposition of this new realm as Paul's master theme, see Douglas J. Moo, *A Theology of Paul and His Letters: The Gift of the New Realm in Christ*, BTNT (Grand Rapids: Zondervan, 2021).

our own "resourcefulness" in "carrying" God to them.[40] Hope means that our labor is not in vain, insofar as it participates in Christ's ministry of reconciliation—bearing witness to redemption already accomplished and being applied.[41]

C. Return

The fullness of our communion with Christ awaits his return to earth, about which Jesus spoke both directly and indirectly (e.g., in the Olivet Discourse of Matthew 24–25). He promised to prepare a place for followers and to return for them (John 14:3). The angels at his ascension reiterated that he would return (Acts 1:11), and this promise became part of the kerygma (Acts 3:21). New Testament epistles anticipate Jesus's return frequently (e.g., the Thessalonian letters; 1 Cor 15:23; Phil 3:20; Col 3:4; 2 Tim 4:8; Titus 2:13; Heb 9:28). "Maranatha" ("O Lord, come!") appears in very early Christian material (e.g., 1 Cor 16:22).[42]

Christ's return will be personal, bodily, and visible. New Testament terminology encapsulates these aspects: *parousia* conveys presence, coming, or arrival, while *apocalypse* means revelation, and *epiphany* manifestation. With variations on *erchomai*, Jesus is referenced as "the coming one" (Heb 10:37, evoking Isa 26:20–21; Hab 2:3) and associated with the Lord God as "him who is, and who was, and who is to come" (Rev 1:4, 8).[43] Whatever the complexities of the Olivet Discourse, Jesus's coming may not be reduced to a secret or inner presence (Matt 24:26–27). The same Lord who ascended will return in the same manner (Acts 1:11). Like the transfiguration, the ascension may not have been universally visible, but texts like Matthew 24:30 suggest that Christ's return will be: unbelieving people "will mourn when they see the Son of Man coming on the clouds of heaven, with power and great glory."

To be precise, rather than a repetitive second coming, we await the climactic return of earth's rightful King.[44] Jesus's self-reference as Son

---

40. Kosuke Koyama, *Three Mile an Hour God: Biblical Reflections* (Maryknoll, NY: Orbis, 1979), 7, 35, 52.

41. For an effective use of *participation* in this vein, see Jules A. Martinez-Olivieri, *A Visible Witness: Christology, Liberation, and Participation*, ES (Minneapolis: Fortress, 2016).

42. David Wenham, *Jesus in Context: Making Sense of the Historical Figure* (Cambridge: Cambridge University Press, 2021), 235. The rest of this paragraph and parts of the next two summarize an excellent summary: Millard J. Erickson, "Second Coming of Christ," in *EDT*, 793–95.

43. Bavinck, *Reformed Dogmatics*, 4:686.

44. Thomas C. Oden, *Life in the Spirit*, vol. 3 of *Systematic Theology* (Peabody, MA: Prince, 1998), 410.

of Man persists throughout the Olivet Discourse until Matthew 25:34, when he takes his throne to participate in divine judgment. From then on, he refers to himself as "the King." His arrival completes Yhwh's multistage return in the person of the Davidic Messiah. It is as if the church is an embassy representing another realm, bearing witness—in presence, word, and deed—to the coming return of the King against whom earth-dwellers rebelled.[45] With the babe in Mary's womb, the incarnation began in apparent humiliation; Christ's return will manifest his exaltation and the range of human responses to him. Lament is an appropriate corollary of inaugurated eschatology, of living "between the times" until we enjoy our King's everlasting, immediate presence.[46] In anticipation of that blessed day of the Lord, Jesus exhorts people to watch (Matt 24:36–51), to prepare to wait (Matt 25:1–13), and to work faithfully (Matt 25:14–30).

III. JUDGMENT

At the final judgment, Christ will make public the moral truth, and make right the moral course, of earthly history. Judgment is the act of distinguishing between good and evil now that fallen creatures have sought such knowledge independently. Before Christ's first advent, the old covenant prepared for judgment pedagogically by giving the law and demonstrating the failure of even redeemed people to keep it adequately. After the penultimate judgments of exile, Jesus's first advent proclaimed the looming arrival of eschatological judgment. His death and resurrection inaugurated a new covenant that pronounced a favorable verdict on humanity in him, while signaling an end to God's patience with creaturely rebellion (e.g., Acts 17:30–31).[47] At the final judgment, God will make public the destinies of persons and nations that have been determined privately upon their deaths. God will also make right injustices suffered during postlapsarian providence. Whereas God's patience may permit evil to seem unpunished,

45. See Jonathan Leeman, *Political Church: The Local Assembly as Embassy of Christ's Rule*, SCDS (Downers Grove, IL: IVP Academic, 2016).

46. Thanks to Grant Flynn for highlighting this point from Rebekah Eklund, *Jesus Wept: The Significance of Jesus' Laments in the New Testament*, LNTS (London: T&T Clark, 2016), 2.

47. Judgment often becomes associated primarily with punishment. See, e.g., lack of a specific definition along with certain collocations (such as "condemning justice") in James M. Hamilton Jr., *God's Glory in Salvation through Judgment: A Biblical Theology* (Wheaton, IL: Crossway, 2010), 56–59, 377–78.

judgment eventually executes what is right; to vindicate the good, the gap between rendering a verdict and rectifying a situation must be closed.[48] In judgment, God acts personally: it is true that "you reap what you sow," but nature does not simply take its course, because the honor of God's name is at stake.[49] God undertakes judgment in Christ, the theandric Mediator, the "Son of Man" to whom the Father "has entrusted all judgment" (John 5:22, 27).

Because the final judgment will occur in Christ, its criteria reflect the unity of law and gospel, calling for faith in God's gracious Mediator rather than meritorious works. Faith is not a humanly creative actualization of salvation as a divinely offered possibility, but the divinely enabled reception of Christ himself as offered in the gospel.[50] Jesus's discussion of "the sheep and the goats" (Matt 25:31–46) is much debated, but both the widest and narrowest readings seem unlikely.[51] Wide readings promote humanitarianism or inclusion as salvation's basis, tending toward optimism about ethical or religious people who lack explicit faith in Christ. But such readings create tension with Matthean realism about human sinfulness and public religiosity (e.g., Matt 5:3–12; 6:1–8; 7:21–23), not to mention the cross itself. Narrow readings restrict Jesus's comments to promoting care for his disciples, thus denying salvific import for good works and tending toward soteriological pessimism. But such readings create tension with the functional focus of Matthean righteousness (e.g., 5:17–20). Although the scope of family language in Matthew ("the least of these brothers or sisters of mine," 25:40 NET) narrows to Jesus's followers, judgment encompasses not only whose names are written in the Lamb's book of life but also what people have done. God graciously enables those who are in Christ to do good works, forgives their imperfections, and then rewards them; God punishes those who reject grace in Christ with respect to their deeds.[52] Addressing a conflicted context in which

---

48. On judgment as the activity of executing right, see O'Donovan, *Desire of the Nations*. For debate about some nuances, see essays (especially by R. W. L. Moberly, Andrew Lincoln, Jonathan Chaplin, and James Skillen, with O'Donovan's responses) in Craig G. Bartholomew et al., eds., *A Royal Priesthood? The Use of the Bible Ethically and Politically*, SHS 3 (Grand Rapids: Zondervan, 2002).

49. Bavinck, *Reformed Dogmatics*, 4:699.

50. On the unity of law and gospel, see Bavinck, *Reformed Dogmatics*, 4:700. On faith as foremost, see the discussion beginning on p. 408 in Berkouwer, *Return of Christ*.

51. For a good exegetical summary, see Turner, *Matthew*, 603–11.

52. See, e.g., 1 Cor 3:10–15; 2 Cor 5:9–10; and Eph 2:10, as treated in Calvin, *Institutes*, 1:788–833 (III.15–18).

Jesus's followers were a reassembled form of broader Israel, Matthew 25 does not answer every intervening question about those who have not heard the gospel. Addressing those who (think they) know the Lord's name, it underscores potential surprise regarding who is saved. Whereas Matthew 7:21–23 and 25:41–46a warn about eschatological disappointment for those who perform religious deeds without love, 25:34–40 offers eschatological hope for those who are humbly righteous unawares. This hope offers no clear basis for "inclusivist" soteriology or "anonymous Christians" based on implicit faith, focusing instead on the surprise of encountering Jesus in serving others. But the passage should unsettle the certainties of current human judgments, underscoring a divine and not just human perspective. Whereas we are inclined to analyze ourselves and others according to criteria inferred from 25:35–46, the King's discourse begins with electing grace: "Come, you who are blessed by my Father; take your inheritance, the kingdom prepared for you since the creation of the world" (25:34). This invitation hearkens back to the gracious emphasis of 11:25–30: all who are weary and burdened receive the invitation to come to Christ; those who do so are the childlike beneficiaries of divine revelation.

Christ judges the idolatry and injustice of communities and nations, not just the eternal destiny of individual persons. In Matthew 11:20–24, Jesus contrasts the response—and, correspondingly, the punishment—of towns like Chorazin and Bethsaida with Tyre and Sidon. In the background lie passages like Isaiah 13–23, with oracles of judgment addressing various nations.[53] Since this social dimension accounts for both complicity and victimization, Christology offers "a type of critical theory" for addressing idolatry and injustice.[54] As the God-man, Jesus will exercise representative authority, speaking for the dead who have been wronged.[55] The Judge will make the world right so that relationships will bring only joy; neither interpersonal nor systemic evil will last forever. Such joy will make it possible to forget harm we have endured; any lingering marks will identify healing rather than evoke traumatic memories.[56]

---

53. Thanks to Andrew Abernethy for this reminder.
54. Martinez-Olivieri, *A Visible Witness*, 207.
55. Brent Waters, "The Incarnation and the Christian Moral Life," in *Christology and Ethics*, ed. F. LeRon Shults and Brent Waters (Grand Rapids: Eerdmans, 2010), 30.
56. See Miroslav Volf, *The End of Memory: Remembering Rightly in a Violent World* (Grand Rapids: Eerdmans, 2006), 205–14. Memory and identity are complicated, garnering new attention in spheres like disability theology. Without making glib pronouncements on complex issues, we

Despite enduring tensions regarding eternal punishment, biblical warnings remain in force—not least from Jesus himself. Admittedly, the connection between resurrection and life generates apparent tension with the resurrection of human beings apart from Christ—unto punishment.[57] The persistence of hell generates apparent tension with the "all things" God reconciles in Christ.[58] Given divine simplicity, God's wrathful absence generates apparent tension with God's loving presence.[59] Yet modernity trumpets divine love in ways that may distort our perception of these tensions.[60] Luke's relatively humanitarian Jesus epitomizes a larger theme when he warns, "Unless you repent, you too will all perish" (Luke 13:5). Acknowledging Christ's work of final judgment, including its retributive element, requires loving zeal for the honor of his name and the harm borne by evil's victims. At the same time, Jesus's zealous followers themselves depend upon what the cross climactically demonstrates: God takes no delight in punishing the wicked (Ezek 18:23–32; Lam 3:33).

---

can agree with Volf that (1) if remembering evils is an obligation, then it becomes incumbent (yet almost impossibly burdensome) to remember them all (so that forgetting can be an eschatological gift); (2) forgiving is a moral aspiration whereas sometimes reconciliation is not (and may currently be impossible); (3) letting memories go may be appropriate, since forgetting does not lose one's identity automatically; (4) there is a distinction between the transition to the eternal state (where judgment still seems to involve remembering evils) and the ongoing eternal state; and (5) heavenly rejoicing is what enables nonremembering without inappropriate loss of identity.

57. For traditional biblical evidence (e.g., Dan 12:2; John 5:28–29) see Oden, *Systematic Theology*, 3:398. On early Christian tension in this regard, see Thomas D. McGlothlin, *Resurrection as Salvation: Development and Conflict in Pre-Nicene Paulinism* (Cambridge: Cambridge University Press, 2018). Resurrection is both a prerequisite for the judgment of all and an outworking of salvation (p. 265). Beyond the embodiment on which 1 Corinthians 15 focuses, passages like Romans 6, Romans 8, and Colossians 3 along with larger connections to Daniel 12, John 5, and Revelation 20 (p. 266), pose a theological challenge (p. 268): "How can Christians take seriously the claim that resurrection is Spirit-produced conformity to the resurrected Christ without getting rid of the resurrection of all to face judgment?"

58. Admittedly, this tension is spatially framed. Yet other topological tensions are similar, such as the Creator-creature distinction vis-à-vis divine infinity. For a stimulating shift to focusing on temporality, contrasting metronomic time (devastated by death as an artifact of the fall) with systolic time (tensed for life-giving action), see Paul J. Griffiths, *Decreation: The Last Things of All Creatures* (Waco, TX: Baylor University Press, 2014). Griffiths, however, argues for hell's annihilation and the possible salvation of its occupants, even Satan. Too much biblical evidence resists this possibility.

59. For problematic but thought-provoking reflection, see Donald G. Bloesch, *The Last Things: Resurrection, Judgment, Glory*, vol. 7 of *Christian Foundations* (Downers Grove, IL: IVP Academic, 2004), 216–28.

60. Earlier modern Christology associated God's kingdom with ethical values at the expense of apocalyptic emphasis; so McGrath, *Making of Modern German Christology*, 215. By contrast, postmodernity celebrated apocalyptic themes, but again at the expense of divine judgment. On the attendant new spirituality (especially parallels to paganism and Gnosticism, noted on p. 145)—a contextual Christology for "the West"—see David F. Wells, *Above All Earthly Pow'rs: Christ in a Postmodern World* (Grand Rapids: Eerdmans, 2005).

IV. GLORIFICATION

As Christ completes his work of judgment, he will glorify those who are united with God in him: beyond graciously rewarding their good deeds, he will grant them the beatific vision and unending life in the splendor of the new cosmos. The nature of heavenly beatitude has garnered newfound debate over how new creation and beatific vision relate. Emphasis on new creation prioritizes the earthiness of Old Testament hope, the embodied and social character of human existence, and Jesus's bodily resurrection. Its proponents understandably oppose gnostic tendencies in popular eschatology.[61] Emphasis on beatific vision prioritizes the God-centered and personal character of Christian hope, the symbolic ambiguities of biblical eschatology, and the spiritual nature of the resurrected body. Its proponents understandably oppose loose critiques of Platonism, loss of contact with Christian tradition, and a potentially idolatrous shift amid recent enthusiasm about new creation.[62] Both sides can agree that God in Christ should be the center, with creation and culture the circumference, of our blessed hope.[63] Again Christology comes to the fore: Jesus's resurrection suggests that God will renovate rather than annihilate the existing cosmos, maintaining physical continuity in redemption. Yet Jesus's resurrection also suggests that the beatific vision will be our ultimate joy, making our Savior's face the focus of our contemplative gaze upon God's glory.[64] When we enjoy the redemption of the cosmos, we will no longer be making history. In eternal rest (Heb 4:9–10), activity will no longer

---

61. E.g., J. Richard Middleton, *A New Heaven and a New Earth: Reclaiming Biblical Eschatology* (Grand Rapids: Baker Academic, 2014); N. T. Wright, *Surprised by Hope* (New York: HarperOne, 2008).

62. E.g., Michael Allen, *Grounded in Heaven: Recentering Christian Hope and Life on God* (Grand Rapids: Eerdmans, 2018); Hans Boersma, *Seeing God: The Beatific Vision in Christian Tradition* (Grand Rapids: Eerdmans, 2018); Matthew Levering, *Jesus and the Demise of Death: Resurrection, Afterlife, and the Fate of the Christian* (Waco, TX: Baylor University Press, 2012).

63. Michael E. Wittmer, "Conclusion," in *Four Views on Heaven*, ed. Michael E. Wittmer, Counterpoints (Grand Rapids: Zondervan Academic, 2022), 207. This volume surfaces partial correlations between, on one hand, emphasizing beatific vision and affirming purgatory (as in Peter Kreeft's position) and, on the other hand, emphasizing new creation and denying an intermediate state of the soul after death (as in Richard Middleton's position). These correlations highlight useful cautions for evangelical development of such views.

64. To engage recent theological literature on whether a resurrected body is essential to beatific vision and how the latter incorporates Christ's humanity vis-à-vis intellectual apprehension of the divine essence, see Marc Cortez, "The Body and the Beatific Vision," in *Being Saved: Explorations in Human Salvation*, ed. Marc Cortez, Joshua R. Farris, and S. Mark Hamilton (London: SCM, 2018), 326–43.

change us for relative better or worse but will deepen enjoyment of God and God's works.[65]

Glorification is biblically preferable terminology for the perfected participation in Christ that patristic and medieval theology often called "deification" or *theosis*. Glorification names the consummation of the Holy Spirit's glorious new covenant ministry, which removes the veil that obscures God's presence in the proclamation of revelation. As we contemplate God's glory in Christ with unveiled faces, we "are being transformed into his image with ever-increasing glory" (2 Cor 3:18). Someday glory "will be revealed in us." Creation itself will be "brought into the freedom and glory" of God's children. Glorification concludes the "golden chain" of salvation for those whom God "predestined to be conformed to the image of his Son" (Rom 8:18, 21, 29–30). First Corinthians 15 uses *splendor* and *glory* language to speak of our future immortal bodies, when we "bear the image of the heavenly man" (15:49). By contrast, the direct biblical support for *theosis* language comes primarily from 2 Peter 1:4, which anticipates that we will "participate in the divine nature, having escaped the corruption in the world caused by evil desires."[66] Something like that concept has been widespread among Christian traditions.[67] Salvation ultimately includes not only forgiveness of sin but also conformity to Christ's godly, loving character and even filial participation in the fellowship of the triune God. Yet fully bearing the divine image and escaping postlapsarian corruption are more frequently associated with glory in Scripture than the ontological vocabulary of deification.

Contra some associations of deification with purgatory, glorification's final transformation will be immediate—"in a flash, in the twinkling of an eye, at the last trumpet" (1 Cor 15:52). Purgatory does not reflect the importance of bodily, social, and temporal life for human sanctification, since it operates outside of those realms; instead, notwithstanding revisionist accounts, it connotes personal punishment that obscures Jesus's

---

65. On recognizing God's blessing upon the completion of human activity, see Oliver O'Donovan, *Entering into Rest*, vol. 3 of *Ethics as Theology* (Grand Rapids: Eerdmans, 2017). On Gregory of Nyssa's notion of *epektasis*, integrating movement within stasis through perpetual progress in God's love, see Euntaek D. Shin, "A Theology of Rest" (PhD diss., Wheaton, IL, Wheaton College Graduate School, 2022).

66. To be sure, there is a trend toward speaking of *theosis* in Pauline theology, championed via themes like "cruciformity" in Michael Gorman's work. But terminological association or similarity does not establish that deification is necessary vocabulary for Pauline teaching.

67. Carl Mosser, "Deification: A Truly Ecumenical Concept," *Perspectives*, August 2015, 8–14.

completed sin-bearing work. Saints' ultimate renewal in Christ is not ontological in terms of qualifying our being to see God in a quasi-metaphysical sense. Instead, Christ will make us new morally, spiritually, and relationally, "for we shall see him as he is" (1 John 3:2) when "we shall see face to face" and know him as we are known—in the fullness of love (1 Cor 13:12).

V. BRIDEGROOM

The name Bridegroom recapitulates Scripture's christological drama. In the garden of Eden, God created the covenantal union of marriage because "it is not good for the man to be alone" (Gen 2:18), and then, in some mysterious fashion, Adam and Eve walked and talked with God (Gen 3:8). After the fall, a series of covenants provided redemptive mediation to reestablish communion. In the centuries before Christ, these covenants reinforced the extent of human wickedness, as Israel typified our tendency to fall away from God's love into spiritual adultery. In the Gospels, as Jesus proclaimed a new covenant, he named himself the Bridegroom (Matt 9:15; cf. John 3:29) and used weddings parabolically to prepare for his return (Matt 22:1–14; 25:1–13). He instituted a ritual celebration of the new covenant (Matt 26:26–30) before experiencing the loss of communion with God to redeem his people (Matt 27:46). He prepared followers for his departure by suggesting that he would go to his Father's house and prepare a place for living with them (John 14:1–4). In metaphorical keeping with ancient customs, it is as if we are currently betrothed, legally committed, to Christ but not yet living as his bride in his Father's house.

This marital metaphor complements the filial metaphor of adoption for understanding union with Christ. Adoption underscores taking on the character appropriate to being in God's family, being called to live as apprentices of God our Father, experiencing by grace a filial relationship like Christ enjoys by nature as the divine Son, and thus relating to Jesus as a fellow human, our brother. Marriage underscores yearning to live in deeper intimacy with God, experiencing this intimacy through coming to know Christ who, as a slain Lamb, is the merciful embodiment of a loving God. Both adoption and marriage reflect the New Testament's inaugurated yet not fully realized eschatology. Adoption reminds us, through the Holy Spirit's guarantee, that we have not yet received our full inheritance. Marriage reminds us that our garments are not yet spotless with good deeds, and our body is not yet fully formed with all its members.

The unitive name Bridegroom relates Christ to nature, grace, and glory. The incarnation's unitive end and redemptive focus must be held together in a mysterious harmony: "Holy Scripture indicates that the Father appointed the Son as redeemer and head of the elect not merely out of his desire to redeem sinners but also ultimately out of his desire to manifest the glory of his beloved Son in and among his creatures" (Ps 2:7–8; Heb 1:2; Col 1:18; Eph 1:9–10).[68] Confessing this christological end does not speak of Christ apart from the divine decree but rather within it. Celebrating this end does not reduce creation and fall to mere means but rather highlights the Father's love for the Son in the Spirit.[69] The triune God is glorified by the beautiful work of creation and the gracious work of redemption, yet this glory is magnified by the communicative work of consummation: giving creatures an eternal share in divine beatitude manifests the glory of God's love most fully. The cause of Christ's work is love for the church; its course runs from saving self-sacrifice to sanctification through Word and sacrament; its end is nuptial (Eph 5:25–27, 32): "Knowing Christ the bridegroom is the final end of all his saving and sanctifying activities. . . . In the institution of marriage, God has written into the very fabric of creation a sign pointing to the ultimate end of the saving 'mystery' to which both Old and New Testaments attest."[70]

Dogmatic Christology discerns the ontological arc implicit in the biblical drama and confesses accordingly that Jesus Christ is our saving Lord. The work of creation and redemption reveals this Son to be the Mediator through whom the triune God communicates the divine goodness.[71] The consummation of our creaturely communion with God likewise reveals our theandric Mediator as the Bridegroom, the prince to whom we are betrothed in anticipation of a royal wedding feast. If Jesus were

---

68. Scott R. Swain, "Covenant of Redemption," in *Christian Dogmatics: Reformed Theology for the Church Catholic*, ed. Michael Allen and Scott R. Swain (Grand Rapids: Baker Academic, 2016), 123.

69. Swain, "Covenant of Redemption," 124.

70. Scott R. Swain, "The (Nuptial) End of Biblical Interpretation," *Reformed Blogmatics* (blog), February 16, 2022.

71. On the communicative or "self-diffusive" nature of the Good, see I.4–I.6 in St. Thomas Aquinas, *Summa Theologica*, vol. 1 (Allen, TX: Christian Classics, 1948).

not fully human, then the Bridegroom would present no face with which to commune; if he were not fully divine, then the Bridegroom would not unite us with God; if not for the personal unity of Jesus Christ as Lord, then our hope for a heavenly banquet on a renewed earth would be lost. Yet the Holy Spirit enables the church to confess, however imperfectly, the biblical truth "Jesus is Lord," to the glory of God the Father.

> O how my speech falls short, how faint it is
> For my conception! And for what I saw
> It is not enough to say that I say little.
>
> O eternal light, existing in yourself alone,
> Alone knowing yourself; and who, known to yourself
> And knowing, love and smile upon yourself!
>
> . . .
>
> Like a geometer who sets himself
> To square the circle, and is unable to think
> Of the formula he needs to solve the problem,
>
> So was I faced with this new vision:
> I wanted to see how the image could fit the circle
> And how it could be that that was where it was;
>
> But that was not a flight for my wings:
> Except that my mind was struck by a flash
> In which what it desired came to it.
>
> At this point high imagination failed;
> But already my desire and my will
> Were being turned like a wheel, all at one speed,
>
> By the love which moves the sun and the other stars.[72]

---

72. *Paradiso* XXXIII, lines 121–26, 133–45, in Dante, *The Divine Comedy*, trans. C. H. Sisson, OWC (Oxford: Oxford University Press, 2008), 499.

WORKS CITED

Abernethy, Andrew T. "Canonical Imagination, COVID-19, and the Communion: Illumination from Isaiah's Banquet and Purim in Esther." *JTI*, forthcoming.

———. *Discovering Isaiah: Content, Interpretation, Reception*. London: SPCK, 2021.

———. *The Book of Isaiah and God's Kingdom: A Thematic-Theological Approach*. NSBT. Downers Grove, IL: IVP Academic, 2016.

Abernethy, Andrew T., and Gregory Goswell. *God's Messiah in the Old Testament: Expectations of a Coming King*. Grand Rapids: Baker Academic, 2020.

Adams, Marilyn McCord. *Christ and Horrors: The Coherence of Christology*. CIT. Cambridge: Cambridge University Press, 2006.

Allen, Michael. "Christ." In *The T&T Clark Companion to the Doctrine of Sin*, edited by Keith Johnson and David Lauber, 451–66. Bloomsbury Companions. London: T&T Clark, 2018.

———. *The Christ's Faith: A Dogmatic Account*. SST. London: T&T Clark, 2011.

———. "Covenant in Recent Theology." In *Covenant Theology: Biblical, Theological, and Historical Perspectives*, edited by Guy Prentiss Waters, J. Nicholas Reid, and John R. Muether, 427–44. Wheaton, IL: Crossway, 2020.

———. *Grounded in Heaven: Recentering Christian Hope and Life on God*. Grand Rapids: Eerdmans, 2018.

Anatolios, Khaled. *Retrieving Nicaea: The Development and Meaning of Trinitarian Doctrine*. Grand Rapids: Baker Academic, 2011.

Anderson, Paul N. "On Guessing Points and Naming Stars: Epistemological Origins of John's Christological Tensions." In *The Gospel of John and Christian Theology*, edited by Richard Bauckham and Carl Mosser, 311–45. Grand Rapids: Eerdmans, 2008.

Anizor, Uche. *Kings and Priests: Scripture's Theological Account of Its Readers.* Eugene, OR: Pickwick, 2014.

Anizor, Uche, and Hank Voss. *Representing Christ: A Vision for the Priesthood of All Believers.* Downers Grove, IL: IVP Academic, 2016.

Aquinas, St. Thomas. *Summa Theologica.* Vol. 1. Allen, TX: Christian Classics, 1948.

Arcadi, James M. *An Incarnational Model of the Eucharist.* CIT. Cambridge: Cambridge University Press, 2018.

Ashford, Bruce Riley, and Craig G. Bartholomew. *The Doctrine of Creation: A Constructive Kuyperian Approach.* Downers Grove, IL: IVP Academic, 2020.

Athanasius, St. "Four Discourses Against the Arians." In *Athanasius: Select Works and Letters,* edited by Philip Schaff and Henry Wace. *NPNF2* 4. Reprint, Peabody, MA: Hendrickson, 2004.

———. *On the Incarnation.* Translated by John Behr. PP 44A. New York: St. Vladimir's Seminary, 2011.

Atkins, Christopher S. "Rethinking John 1:1: The Word Was Godward." *NovT* 63 (2021): 44–62.

Auden, W. H. *For the Time Being: A Christmas Oratorio.* Edited by Alan Jacobs. Princeton: Princeton University Press, 2013.

Augustine, St. *The Trinity.* Edited by John E. Rotelle, OSA. Translated by Edmund Hill, OP. Hyde Park, NY: New City, 1991.

Aulén, Gustaf. *Christus Victor: An Historical Study of the Three Main Types of the Idea of Atonement.* Translated by A. G. Hebert. New York: Macmillan, 1969.

Averbeck, Richard E. "Christian Interpretations of Isaiah 53." In *The Gospel according to Isaiah 53: Encountering the Suffering Servant in Jewish and Christian Theology,* edited by Darrell L. Bock and Mitch Glaser, 33–60. Grand Rapids: Kregel, 2012.

Ayres, Lewis. *Augustine and the Trinity.* Cambridge: Cambridge University Press, 2010.

———. *Nicaea and Its Legacy: An Approach to Fourth-Century Trinitarian Theology.* Oxford: Oxford University Press, 2004.

Bäck, Allan. *On Reduplication: Logical Theories of Qualification.* Leiden: Brill, 1996.

Baillie, D. M. *God Was in Christ: An Essay on Incarnation and Atonement.* New York: Scribner's, 1948.

Baker, David W. *Two Testaments, One Bible: A Study of the Theological*

Relationship between the Old and New Testaments. Rev. ed. Downers Grove, IL: InterVarsity Press, 1991.

Barclay, John M. G. "Kenosis and the Drama of Salvation in Philippians 2." In *Kenosis: The Self-Emptying of Christ in Scripture and Theology*, edited by Paul T. Nimmo and Keith L. Johnson, 7–23. Grand Rapids: Eerdmans, 2022.

———. *Paul and the Gift*. Grand Rapids: Eerdmans, 2015.

Barnes, Michel René. "On *The Unity of Christ* by Christopher A. Beeley." *Nova et Vetera* 14, no. 1 (2016): 331–41.

Barrett, Matthew. *Canon, Covenant and Christology: Rethinking Jesus and the Scriptures of Israel*. NSBT. Downers Grove, IL: IVP Academic, 2020.

Barth, Karl. "Epheser 1,1–14 (Safenwil, Sonntag, Den 4. Mai 1919)." In *Predigten 1919*, edited by Hermann Schmidt, 39:173–80. Karl Barth Gesamtausgabe. Zurich: Theologischer Verlag Zürich, 2003.

———. *The Doctrine of God*. Edited by G. W. Bromiley and T. F. Torrance. Vol. II/2 of *Church Dogmatics*. Edinburgh: T&T Clark, 1957.

———. *The Doctrine of Reconciliation*. Edited by G. W. Bromiley and T. F. Torrance. Vol. IV/1 of *Church Dogmatics*. Edinburgh: T&T Clark, 1956.

———. *The Epistle to the Ephesians*. Edited by R. David Nelson. Translated by Ross M. Wright. Grand Rapids: Baker Academic, 2017.

———. "The Preface to the Second Edition." In *The Epistle to the Romans*, translated by Edwyn C. Hoskyns, 2–15. Oxford: Oxford University Press, 1968.

Barth, Markus. *Ephesians 1–3: A New Translation with Introduction and Commentary*. AB. New York: Doubleday, 1974.

Bartholomew, Craig G., Jonathan Chaplin, Robert Song, and Al Wolters, eds. *A Royal Priesthood? The Use of the Bible Ethically and Politically*. SHS 3. Grand Rapids: Zondervan, 2002.

Bates, Matthew W. "A Christology of Incarnation and Enthronement: Romans 1:3–4 as Unified, Nonadoptionist, and Nonconciliatory." *CBQ* 77 (2015): 107–27.

———. *The Birth of the Trinity: Jesus, God, and Spirit in New Testament and Early Christian Interpretations of the Old Testament*. Oxford: Oxford University Press, 2015.

———. *The Hermeneutics of the Apostolic Proclamation: The Center of Paul's*

Method of Scriptural Interpretation. Waco, TX: Baylor University Press, 2012.

Bauckham, Richard J. "Christology." In *Dictionary of Jesus and the Gospels*, 2nd ed., edited by Joel B. Green et al., 125–34. Downers Grove, IL: IVP Academic, 2013.

———. "Is 'High Human Christology' Sufficient? A Critical Response to J. R. Daniel Kirk's *A Man Attested by God*." *BBR* 27, no. 4 (2017): 503–25.

———. *Jesus: A Very Short Introduction*. Oxford: Oxford University Press, 2011.

———. *Jesus and the Eyewitnesses: The Gospels as Eyewitness Testimony*. Grand Rapids: Eerdmans, 2006.

———. *Jesus and the God of Israel:* God Crucified *and Other Studies on the New Testament's Christology of Divine Identity*. Grand Rapids: Eerdmans, 2008.

———. "Monotheism and Christology in the Gospel of John." In *Contours of Christology in the New Testament*, edited by Richard N. Longenecker, 148–66. Grand Rapids: Eerdmans, 2005.

———. *The Climax of Prophecy: Studies on the Book of Revelation*. Edinburgh: T&T Clark, 1993.

———. "The Son of Man: 'A Man in My Position' or 'Someone'?" *JSNT* 23 (1985): 23–33.

Bavinck, Herman. *Reformed Dogmatics*. Edited by John Bolt. Translated by John Vriend. 4 vols. Grand Rapids: Baker Academic, 2003–08.

Beale, G. K. *The Book of Revelation: A Commentary on the Greek Text*. NIGTC. Grand Rapids: Eerdmans, 1999.

———. *The Temple and the Church's Mission: A Biblical Theology of the Dwelling Place of God*. NSBT. Downers Grove, IL: InterVarsity Press, 2004.

Beeley, Christopher A. *The Unity of Christ: Continuity and Conflict in Patristic Tradition*. New Haven, CT: Yale University Press, 2012.

Behr, John. *Formation of Christian Theology*. 2 vols. in 3 parts. Crestwood, NY: St. Vladimir's Seminary, 2001–04.

Benedict XVI, Pope. *Jesus of Nazareth: From the Baptism in the Jordan to the Transfiguration*. Translated by Adrian J. Walker. New York: Image, 2015.

———. *Jesus of Nazareth: Holy Week; From the Entrance into Jerusalem to the Resurrection*. Translated by Philip J. Whitmore. San Francisco: Ignatius, 2011.

———. *Jesus of Nazareth: The Infancy Narratives*. Translated by Philip J. Whitmore. New York: Image, 2012.

Berkouwer, G. C. *The Person of Christ*. Translated by John Vriend. Studies in Dogmatics. Grand Rapids: Eerdmans, 1954.

———. *The Return of Christ*. Edited by Marlin J. Van Elderen. Translated by James Van Oosterom. Studies in Dogmatics. Reprint, Grand Rapids: Eerdmans, 1972.

Billings, J. Todd. *Remembrance, Communion, and Hope: Rediscovering the Gospel at the Lord's Table*. Grand Rapids: Eerdmans, 2018.

———. *Union with Christ: Reframing Theology and Ministry for the Church*. Grand Rapids: Brazos, 2011.

Bird, Michael F. *Jesus Is the Christ: The Messianic Testimony of the Gospels*. Downers Grove, IL: IVP Academic, 2012.

———. *Jesus the Eternal Son: Answering Adoptionist Christology*. Grand Rapids: Eerdmans, 2017.

Blenkinsopp, Joseph. *Isaiah 1–39: A New Translation with Introduction and Commentary*. AB. New York: Doubleday, 2000.

Blocher, Henri A. G. "Atonement." In *Dictionary for Theological Interpretation of the Bible*, edited by Kevin J. Vanhoozer et al., 72–76. Grand Rapids: Baker Academic, 2005.

———. *Songs of the Servant: Isaiah's Good News*. Reprint, Vancouver: Regent College, 2005.

Bloesch, Donald G. "Descent into Hell (Hades)." In *Evangelical Dictionary of Theology*, 3rd ed., edited by Daniel J. Treier and Walter A. Elwell, 241–42. Grand Rapids: Baker Academic, 2017.

———. *The Last Things: Resurrection, Judgment, Glory*. Vol. 7 of *Christian Foundations*. Downers Grove, IL: IVP Academic, 2004.

Blomberg, Craig L. "'Your Faith Has Made You Whole': The Evangelical Liberation Theology of Jesus." In *Jesus of Nazareth: Lord and Christ: Essays on the Historical Jesus and New Testament Christology*, edited by Joel B. Green and Max Turner, 75–93. Grand Rapids: Eerdmans, 1994.

Bock, Darrell L. *Luke 1:1–9:50*. BECNT. Grand Rapids: Baker Academic, 1994.

Bock, Darrell L., and Benjamin I. Simpson. *Jesus the God-Man: The Unity and Diversity of the Gospel Portrayals.* Grand Rapids: Baker Academic, 2016.

Bock, Darrell L., and Robert L. Webb, eds. *Key Events in the Life of the Historical Jesus: A Collaborative Exploration of Context and Coherence.* Grand Rapids: Eerdmans, 2010.

Bockmuehl, Markus. "The Gospels on the Presence of Jesus." In *The Oxford Handbook of Christology*, edited by Francesca Aran Murphy, 87–102. Oxford: Oxford University Press, 2015.

———. *This Jesus: Martyr, Lord, Messiah.* Downers Grove, IL: InterVarsity Press, 1994.

Boersma, Hans. *Heavenly Participation: The Weaving of a Sacramental Tapestry.* Grand Rapids: Eerdmans, 2011.

———. *Seeing God: The Beatific Vision in Christian Tradition.* Grand Rapids: Eerdmans, 2018.

Boff, Leonardo. *Jesus Christ Liberator: A Critical Christology for Our Time.* Maryknoll, NY: Orbis, 1978.

Bolt, Peter G. *The Cross from a Distance: Atonement in Mark's Gospel.* NSBT. Downers Grove, IL: IVP Academic, 2004.

Bonhoeffer, Dietrich. *Discipleship.* Edited by Martin Kuske and Ilse Todt. Translated by Barbara Green and Reinhard Krauss. DBWE 4. Minneapolis: Fortress, 2001.

———. *Ethics.* Edited by Clifford J. Green. Translated by Reinhard Krauss, Douglas W. Stott, and Charles C. West. DBWE 6. Minneapolis: Fortress, 2005.

———. "Lectures on Christology (Student Notes)." In *Berlin: 1932–1933*, edited by Larry L. Rasmussen, translated by Isabel Best and David Higgins, 299–360. DBWE 12. Minneapolis: Fortress, 2009.

Brakel, Wilhelmus à. *The Christian's Reasonable Service.* 4 vols. Edited by Joel R. Beeke. Translated by Bartel Elshout. Grand Rapids: Reformation Heritage, 1992–2015.

Brondos, David A. *Background.* Vol. 1 of *Jesus' Death in New Testament Thought.* Mexico City: Comunidad Teológica de Mexico, 2018.

Brown, Jeannine K. "Jesus's Messiah as Isaiah's Servant of the Lord: New Testament Explorations." *JETS* 53, no. 1 (March 2020): 51–69.

Brown, John, of Haddington. *Systematic Theology: A Compendious View of Natural and Revealed Religion.* Reprint, Grand Rapids: Reformation Heritage, 2015.

Brown, Raymond E. *The Gospel according to John*. 2nd ed. AB. New Haven, CT: Yale University Press, 1986.

Bruce, Matthew J. Aragon. "Election." In *The Oxford Handbook of Karl Barth*, edited by Paul Dafydd Jones and Paul T. Nimmo, 309–24. Oxford: Oxford University Press, 2020.

Bruner, Frederick Dale. *The Christbook: Matthew 1–12*. Rev. ed. Vol. 1 of *Matthew: A Commentary*. Grand Rapids: Eerdmans, 2004.

Bultmann, Rudolf. *Jesus Christ and Mythology*. New York: Scribner's, 1958.

———. *The New Testament and Mythology and Other Basic Writings*. Edited by Schubert Ogden. Philadelphia: Fortress, 1984.

Burney, C. F. "Christ as the ΑΡΧΗ of Creation." *JTS* 27 (1925): 160–77.

Bynum, Caroline Walker. "The Power in the Blood: Sacrifice, Satisfaction, and Substitution in Late Medieval Soteriology." In *The Redemption: An Interdisciplinary Symposium on Christ the Redeemer*, edited by Stephen T. Davis, Daniel Kendall, SJ, and Gerald O'Collins, SJ, 177–204. Oxford: Oxford University Press, 2004.

———. *The Resurrection of the Body in Western Christianity, 200–1336*. New York: Columbia University Press, 1995.

Calvin, John. *Commentary on a Harmony of the Evangelists, Matthew, Mark, and Luke*. Vol. 3. Translated by William Pringle. Vol. 17 of *Calvin's Commentaries*. Reprint, Grand Rapids: Baker, 1993.

———. *Commentary on the Holy Gospel of Jesus Christ according to John*. Translated by William Pringle. Vol. 17 of *Calvin's Commentaries*. Reprint, Grand Rapids: Baker, 1993.

———. *Commentary on the Prophet Isaiah*. Vol. 1. Translated by William Pringle. Vol. 7 of *Calvin's Commentaries*. Reprint, Grand Rapids: Baker, 1993.

———. *Institutes of the Christian Religion*. Vol. 1. Edited by John T. McNeill. LCC 20. Philadelphia: Westminster, 1960.

Campbell, Constantine R. *Paul and Union with Christ: An Exegetical and Theological Study*. Grand Rapids: Zondervan, 2012.

Campbell, Douglas A. *The Deliverance of God: An Apocalyptic Rereading of Justification in Paul*. Grand Rapids: Eerdmans, 2009.

Canlis, Julie. "The Fatherhood of God and Union with Christ in Calvin." In *"In Christ" in Paul: Explorations in Paul's Theology of Union and Participation*, edited by Michael J. Thate, Kevin J. Vanhoozer, and

Constantine R. Campbell, 399–425. WUNT II. Tübingen: Mohr Siebeck, 2014.

Capes, David B. *The Divine Christ: Paul, the Lord Jesus, and the Scriptures of Israel*. Grand Rapids: Baker Academic, 2018.

Caragounis, Chrys C. *The Son of Man: Vision and Interpretation*. WUNT. Tübingen: Mohr, 1986.

Carnes, Natalie. *Image and Presence: A Christological Reflection on Iconoclasm and Iconophilia*. Encountering Traditions. Stanford, CA: Stanford University Press, 2018.

Carson, D. A. "Atonement in Romans 3:21–26." In *The Glory of the Atonement: Biblical, Theological and Practical Perspectives*, edited by Charles E. Hill and Frank A. James III, 119–39. Downers Grove, IL: InterVarsity Press, 2004.

———. *Jesus the Son of God: A Christological Title Often Overlooked, Sometimes Misunderstood, and Currently Disputed*. Wheaton, IL: Crossway, 2012.

———. "John 5:26: *Crux Interpretum* for Eternal Generation." In *Retrieving Eternal Generation*, edited by Fred Sanders and Scott R. Swain, 79–97. Grand Rapids: Zondervan, 2017.

Carter, Craig A. *Interpreting Scripture with the Great Tradition: Recovering the Genius of Premodern Exegesis*. Grand Rapids: Baker Academic, 2018.

Carter, J. Kameron. *Race: A Theological Account*. New York: Oxford University Press, 2008.

Catechism of the Catholic Church. 2nd ed. Washington, DC: United States Catholic Conference, 1997.

Chappell, Paul G. "Heal, Healing." In *Evangelical Dictionary of Theology*, 3rd ed., edited by Daniel J. Treier and Walter A. Elwell, 368–69. Grand Rapids: Baker Academic, 2017.

Childs, Brevard S. *Isaiah: A Commentary*. OTL. Louisville: Westminster John Knox, 2000.

Coakley, Sarah. *Christ without Absolutes: A Study of the Christology of Ernst Troeltsch*. Oxford: Clarendon, 1988.

———. "*Kenōsis* and Subversion: On the Repression of 'Vulnerability' in Christian Feminist Writing." In *Powers and Submissions: Spirituality, Philosophy and Gender*, 3–39. CCT. Oxford: Blackwell, 2002.

———. "Response." In *The Resurrection: An Interdisciplinary Symposium on the Resurrection of Jesus*, edited by Stephen Davis, Daniel Kendall,

SJ, and Gerald O'Collins, SJ, 184–90. Oxford: Oxford University Press, 1997.

———. "What Does Chalcedon Solve and What Does It Not? Some Reflections on the Meaning and Status of the Chalcedonian 'Definition.'" In *The Incarnation: An Interdisciplinary Symposium on the Incarnation of the Son of God*, edited by Stephen T. Davis, Daniel Kendall, SJ, and Gerald O'Collins, SJ, 143–63. Oxford: Oxford University Press, 2002.

Cockerill, Gareth Lee. *The Epistle to the Hebrews*. NICNT. Grand Rapids: Eerdmans, 2012.

Cole, Graham A. *The God Who Became Human: A Biblical Theology of Incarnation*. NSBT. Downers Grove, IL: IVP Academic, 2013.

Colón-Emeric, Edgardo. "Jesus Was Born in Guatemala: Toward a Latinx Wesleyan Christology." In *Methodist Christology: From the Wesleys to the Twenty-First Century*, edited by Jason E. Vickers and Jerome Van Kuiken, 143–60. Nashville: Wesley's Foundery, 2020.

Cone, James H. *The Cross and the Lynching Tree*. Maryknoll, NY: Orbis, 2011.

Coogan, Jeremiah. "Rethinking Adoptionism: An Argument for Dismantling a Dubious Category." *SJT*, forthcoming.

Cooper, John W. *Body, Soul, and Life Everlasting: Biblical Anthropology and the Monism-Dualism Debate*. Grand Rapids: Eerdmans, 2000.

Copeland, Rebecca L. *Created Being: Expanding Creedal Christology*. Waco, TX: Baylor University Press, 2020.

Cortez, Marc. "The Body and the Beatific Vision." In *Being Saved: Explorations in Human Salvation*, ed. Marc Cortez, Joshua R. Farris, and S. Mark Hamilton, 326–43. London: SCM, 2018.

Craig, William Lane. *Atonement and the Death of Christ: An Exegetical, Historical, and Philosophical Exploration*. Waco, TX: Baylor University Press, 2020.

Cranfield, C. E. B. "Some Reflections on the Subject of the Virgin Birth." *SJT* 41 (1988): 177–89.

Crisp, Oliver D. "Desiderata for Models of the Hypostatic Union." In *Christology, Ancient and Modern: Explorations in Constructive Dogmatics*, edited by Oliver D. Crisp and Fred Sanders, 19–41. Grand Rapids: Zondervan, 2013.

———. *Divinity and Humanity: The Incarnation Reconsidered*. CIT. Cambridge: Cambridge University Press, 2007.

————. *God Incarnate: Explorations in Christology.* New York: T&T Clark, 2009.

————. "Incarnation without the Fall." *JRT* 10 (2016): 215–33.

————. *Revisioning Christology: Theology in the Reformed Tradition.* Burlington, VT: Ashgate, 2011.

————. *The Word Enfleshed: Exploring the Person and Work of Christ.* Grand Rapids: Baker Academic, 2016.

Cross, Frank Moore. "Kinship and Covenant in Ancient Israel." In *From Epic to Canon: History and Literature in Ancient Israel*, 3–21. Baltimore: Johns Hopkins University Press, 1998.

Cullmann, Oscar. *Christ and Time: The Primitive Christian Conception of Time and History.* Translated by Floyd Filson. London: SCM, 1951.

————. *The Christology of the New Testament.* Translated by Shirley C. Guthrie and Charles A. M. Hall. Rev. ed. NTL. Philadelphia: Westminster, 1963.

Cunningham, Mary Kathleen. *What Is Theological Exegesis? Interpretation and Use of Scripture in Barth's Doctrine of Election.* Valley Forge, PA: Trinity Press International, 1995.

Cyril of Alexandria, St. *On the Unity of Christ.* Translated by John Anthony McGuckin. Crestwood, NY: St. Vladimir's Seminary, 2000.

Daley, Brian E., SJ. "Antioch and Alexandria: Christology as Reflection on God's Presence in History." In *The Oxford Handbook of Christology*, edited by Francesca Aran Murphy, 121–38. Oxford: Oxford University Press, 2015.

————. *God Visible: Patristic Christology Reconsidered.* Oxford: Oxford University Press, 2018.

Dalferth, Ingolf U. *Crucified and Resurrected: Restructuring the Grammar of Christology.* Translated by Jo Bennett. Grand Rapids: Baker Academic, 2015.

Dalton, William J. *Christ's Proclamation to the Spirits: A Study of 1 Peter 3:18–4:6.* Rev. ed. AnBib 23. Roma: Editrice Pontifico Istituto Biblico, 1989.

Dante. *The Divine Comedy.* Translated by C. H. Sisson. OWC. Oxford: Oxford University Press, 2008.

Davidson, Ivor J. "Christ." In *The Oxford Handbook of Reformed Theology*, edited by Michael Allen and Scott R. Swain, 446–72. Oxford: Oxford University Press, 2020.

Davidson, Richard M. *Typology in Scripture: A Study of Hermeneutical*

Τύπος *Structures*. Berrien Springs, MI: Andrews University Press, 1981.

Davies, Oliver. *A Theology of Compassion: Metaphysics of Difference and the Renewal of Tradition*. Grand Rapids: Eerdmans, 2003.

Dawson, Gerrit Scott. *Jesus Ascended: The Meaning of Christ's Continuing Incarnation*. Phillipsburg, NJ: P&R, 2004.

Dawson, John David. *Christian Figural Reading and the Fashioning of Identity*. Berkeley: University of California Press, 2002.

DeHart, Paul J. *Unspeakable Cults: An Essay in Christology*. Waco, TX: Baylor University Press, 2021.

Dempsey, Michael T., ed. *Trinity and Election in Contemporary Theology*. Grand Rapids: Eerdmans, 2011.

Dorner, I. A. "System of Christian Doctrine Part II: Special Doctrines: The Doctrine of Christ." In *God and Incarnation in Mid-Nineteenth Century Theology: Thomasius, Dorner, Biedermann*, edited by Claude Welch, 181–284. A Library of Protestant Thought. New York: Oxford University Press, 1965.

Duby, Steven. *God in Himself: Scripture, Metaphysics, and the Object of Christian Theology*. SCDS. Downers Grove, IL: IVP Academic, 2019.

———. *Jesus and the God of Classical Theism: Biblical Christology in Light of the Doctrine of God*. Grand Rapids: Baker Academic, 2022.

Duncan, Ligon. "Foreword." In *Covenant Theology: Biblical, Theological, and Historical Perspectives*, edited by Guy Prentiss Waters, J. Nicholas Reid, and John R. Muether, 23–30. Wheaton, IL: Crossway, 2020.

Dunn, James D. G. *Baptism in the Holy Spirit; A Re-Examination of the New Testament Teaching on the Gift of the Spirit in Relation to Pentecostalism Today*. Naperville, IL: Allenson, 1970.

———. "Christology as an Aspect of Theology." In *The Future of Christology: Essays in Honor of Leander E. Keck*, edited by Abraham J. Malherbe and Wayne A. Meeks, 202–12. Minneapolis: Fortress, 1993.

———. *Christology in the Making: A New Testament Inquiry into the Origins of the Doctrine of the Incarnation*. 2nd ed. Grand Rapids: Eerdmans, 1996.

———. "Review of Simon Gathercole, *The Pre-Existent Son: Recovering the Christologies of Matthew, Mark, and Luke* (Grand Rapids: Eerdmans, 2006)." *RBL*, April 2007.

———. *The Epistles to the Colossians and Philemon*. NIGTC. Grand Rapids: Eerdmans, 1996.

Eastman, Susan G. "Oneself in Another: Participation and the Spirit in Romans 8." In *"In Christ" in Paul: Explorations in Paul's Theology of Union and Participation*, edited by Michael J. Thate, Kevin J. Vanhoozer, and Constantine R. Campbell, 103–25. WUNT II. Tübingen: Mohr Siebeck, 2014.

Eklund, Rebekah. *Jesus Wept: The Significance of Jesus' Laments in the New Testament*. LNTS. London: T&T Clark, 2016.

Ellis, Brannon. *Calvin, Classical Trinitarianism, and the Aseity of the Son*. Oxford: Oxford University Press, 2012.

Elowsky, Joel C., ed. *John 1–10*. ACCSNT 4a. Downers Grove, IL: IVP Academic, 2006.

Emerson, Matthew Y. *"He Descended to the Dead": An Evangelical Theology of Holy Saturday*. Downers Grove, IL: IVP Academic, 2019.

Erickson, Millard J. "Second Coming of Christ." In *Evangelical Dictionary of Theology*, 3rd ed., edited by Daniel J. Treier and Walter A. Elwell, 793–95. Grand Rapids: Baker Academic, 2017.

———. *The Word Became Flesh: A Contemporary Incarnational Christology*. Grand Rapids: Baker, 1991.

Escobar, J. Samuel. *In Search of Christ in Latin America: From Colonial Image to Liberating Savior*. Downers Grove, IL: IVP Academic, 2019.

Evans, C. Stephen, ed. *Exploring Kenotic Christology: The Self-Emptying of God*. Oxford: Oxford University Press, 2006.

———. *The Historical Christ and the Jesus of Faith: The Incarnational Narrative as History*. Oxford: Clarendon, 1996.

Evans, Craig A. "Jesus' Self-Designation 'The Son of Man' and the Recognition of His Divinity." In *The Trinity: An Interdisciplinary Symposium on the Trinity*, edited by Stephen Davis, Daniel Kendall, SJ, and Gerald O'Collins, SJ, 29–47. Oxford: Oxford University Press, 1999.

Evans, Craig A., and Lidija Novakovic. "Typology." In *Dictionary of Jesus and the Gospels*, 2nd ed., edited by Joel B. Green et al., 986–90. Downers Grove, IL: IVP Academic, 2013.

Fairbairn, Donald. *Grace and Christology in the Early Church*. OECS. Oxford: Oxford University Press, 2003.

Fairbairn, Donald, and Ryan M. Reeves. *The Story of Creeds and Confessions: Tracing the Development of the Christian Faith*. Grand Rapids: Baker Academic, 2019.

Farmer, Craig S., ed. *John 1–12*. RCSNT 4. Downers Grove, IL: IVP Academic, 2014.

Farrow, Douglas. *Ascension and Ecclesia: On the Significance of the Doctrine of the Ascension for Ecclesiology and Christian Cosmology*. Grand Rapids: Eerdmans, 1999.

Fee, Gordon D. *God's Empowering Presence: The Holy Spirit in the Letters of Paul*. Peabody, MA: Hendrickson, 1994.

———. *Pauline Christology: An Exegetical-Theological Study*. Peabody, MA: Hendrickson, 2007.

———. *Paul's Letter to the Philippians*. NICNT. Grand Rapids: Eerdmans, 1995.

Finn, Daniel K. "What Is a Sinful Social Structure?" *TS* 77, no. 1 (2016): 136–64.

Fitzmyer, Joseph A. *The Gospel according to Luke I–IX: Introduction, Translation, and Notes*. AB. Garden City, NY: Doubleday, 1981.

Fletcher-Louis, Crispin. *Christological Origins: The Emerging Consensus and Beyond*. Vol. 1 of *Jesus Monotheism*. Eugene, OR: Cascade, 2015.

———. "'The Being That Is in a Manner Equal with God' (Phil. 2:6c): A Self-Transforming, Incarnational, Divine Ontology." *JTS* 71, no. 2 (2020): 581–627.

Fogelin, Robert J. *A Defense of Hume on Miracles*. Princeton: Princeton University Press, 2003.

France, R. T. *Jesus and the Old Testament*. London: Tyndale, 1971.

———. *The Gospel of Mark*. NIGTC. Grand Rapids: Eerdmans, 2002.

Frankfurt, Harry G. "Freedom of the Will and the Concept of a Person." *Journal of Philosophy* 68 (1971): 5–20.

Fredriksen, Paula. "How High Can Early High Christology Be?" In *Monotheism and Christology in Greco-Roman Antiquity*, edited by Matthew N. Novenson, 293–319. NovTSup. Leiden: Brill, 2020.

Frei, Hans W. *The Eclipse of Biblical Narrative: A Study in Eighteenth and Nineteenth Century Hermeneutics*. New Haven, CT: Yale University Press, 1974.

———. *The Identity of Jesus Christ: The Hermeneutical Bases of Dogmatic Theology*. Eugene, OR: Wipf & Stock, 1997.

Friedeman, Caleb. *The Revelation of the Messiah: The Christological Mystery of Luke 1–2 and Its Unveiling in Luke-Acts*. SNTSMS. Cambridge: Cambridge University Press, 2022.

Gaffin, Richard. "Atonement in the Pauline Corpus: 'The Scandal of the Cross.'" In *The Glory of the Atonement: Biblical, Theological and Practical Perspectives*, edited by Charles E. Hill and Frank A. James III, 140–62. Downers Grove, IL: InterVarsity Press, 2004.

Garland, David E. *A Theology of Mark's Gospel: Good News about Jesus the Messiah, the Son of God*. BTNT. Grand Rapids: Zondervan, 2015.

Gathercole, Simon J. *Defending Substitution: An Essay on Atonement in Paul*. ASBT. Grand Rapids: Baker Academic, 2015.

———. *The Preexistent Son: Recovering the Christologies of Matthew, Mark, and Luke*. Grand Rapids: Eerdmans, 2006.

Gavrilyuk, Paul L. *The Suffering of the Impassible God: The Dialectics of Patristic Thought*. OECS. Oxford: Oxford University Press, 2004.

Gibson, Scott M., and Matthew D. Kim, eds. *Homiletics and Hermeneutics: Four Views on Preaching Today*. Grand Rapids: Baker Academic, 2018.

Gioia, Luigi, OSB. *The Theological Epistemology of Augustine's* De Trinitate. OTM. Oxford: Oxford University Press, 2008.

Goldingay, John, and David Payne. *Isaiah 40–55*. ICC. London: T&T Clark, 2006.

González, Antonio. *The Gospel of Faith and Justice*. Translated by Joseph Owens. Maryknoll, NY: Orbis, 2005.

González, Justo L. *From the Beginnings to the Council of Chalcedon*. Vol. 1 of *A History of Christian Thought*. Nashville: Abingdon, 1987.

———. *Luke*. Belief. Louisville: Westminster John Knox, 2010.

———. *The Early Church to the Dawn of the Reformation*. Vol. 1 of *The Story of Christianity*. New York: Harper One, 2010.

Goppelt, Leonhard. *Typos: The Typological Interpretation of the Old Testament in the New*. Grand Rapids: Eerdmans, 1982.

Gordon, James R. "Dialectic." In *Evangelical Dictionary of Theology*, 3rd ed., edited by Daniel J. Treier and Walter A. Elwell, 244–45. Grand Rapids: Baker Academic, 2017.

———. *The Holy One in Our Midst: An Essay on the Flesh of Christ*. ES. Minneapolis: Fortress, 2016.

Gorman, Michael J. *Inhabiting the Cruciform God: Kenosis, Justification, and Theosis in Paul's Narrative Soteriology*. Grand Rapids: Eerdmans, 2009.

———. *The Death of the Messiah and the Birth of the New Covenant: A (Not So) New Model of the Atonement*. Eugene, OR: Cascade, 2014.

Green, Chris E. W. *All Things Beautiful: An Aesthetic Christology*. Waco, TX: Baylor University Press, 2021.

Green, Gene L., Stephen T. Pardue, and K. K. Yeo, eds. *Jesus without Borders: Christology in the Majority World.* MWT. Grand Rapids: Eerdmans, 2014.

Green, Joel B. "Good News to Whom? Jesus and the 'Poor' in the Gospel of Luke." In *Jesus of Nazareth: Lord and Christ: Essays on the Historical Jesus and New Testament Christology,* edited by Joel B. Green and Max Turner, 59–74. Grand Rapids: Eerdmans, 1994.

———. *The Gospel of Luke.* NICNT. Grand Rapids: Eerdmans, 1997.

Green, Joel B., and Mark D. Baker. *Recovering the Scandal of the Cross: Atonement in New Testament and Contemporary Contexts.* Downers Grove, IL: InterVarsity Press, 2000.

Greene, Colin J. D. *Christology in Cultural Perspective: Marking Out the Horizons.* Grand Rapids: Eerdmans, 2004.

Greggs, Tom. *The Priestly Catholicity of the Church.* Vol. 1 of *Dogmatic Ecclesiology.* Grand Rapids: Baker Academic, 2019.

Greidanus, Sidney. *Preaching Christ from the Old Testament: A Contemporary Hermeneutical Method.* Grand Rapids: Eerdmans, 1999.

Grenholm, Cristina. "Mary Among Stereotypes and Dogmas: A Feminist Critique and Reinterpretation of the Patriarchal Cornerstone of Motherhood." *Journal of the European Society of Women in Theological Research* 15 (2007): 15–35.

Griffiths, Paul J. *Decreation: The Last Things of All Creatures.* Waco, TX: Baylor University Press, 2014.

Grillmeier, Aloys, SJ. *From the Apostolic Age to Chalcedon (451).* Translated by John Bowden. Vol. 1 of *Christ in Christian Tradition.* Atlanta: John Knox, 1975.

Grindheim, Sigurd. *God's Equal: What Can We Know about Jesus' Self-Understanding in the Synoptic Gospels?* LNTS. London: T&T Clark, 2011.

Groenhout, Ruth. "Kenosis and Feminist Theory." In *Exploring Kenotic Christology: The Self-Emptying of God,* edited by C. Stephen Evans, 291–312. Oxford: Oxford University Press, 2006.

Groves, J. Alan. "Atonement in Isaiah 53: 'For He Bore the Sins of Many.'" In *The Glory of the Atonement: Biblical, Theological and Practical Perspectives,* edited by Charles E. Hill and Frank A. James III, 61–89. Downers Grove, IL: InterVarsity Press, 2004.

Guite, Malcolm. *Sounding the Seasons: Seventy Sonnets for the Christian Year.* London: Canterbury, 2012.

Gundry, Robert H. *Jesus the Word according to John the Sectarian: A Paleofundamentalist Manifesto for Contemporary Evangelicalism, Especially Its Elites, in North America.* Grand Rapids: Eerdmans, 2002.

———. *Mark: A Commentary on His Apology for the Cross.* Grand Rapids: Eerdmans, 1993.

———. "The Essential Physicality of Jesus' Resurrection according to the New Testament." In *Jesus of Nazareth: Lord and Christ: Essays on the Historical Jesus and New Testament Christology,* edited by Joel B. Green and Max Turner, 204–19. Grand Rapids: Eerdmans, 1994.

Gunton, Colin E. "And in One Lord, Jesus Christ . . . Begotten, Not Made." In *Nicene Christianity: A Future for a New Ecumenism,* edited by Christopher R. Seitz, 35–48. Grand Rapids: Brazos, 2001.

———. *Christ and Creation: The Didsbury Lectures.* Grand Rapids: Eerdmans, 1993.

———. "Introduction." In *The Theology of Reconciliation,* edited by Colin E. Gunton, 1–11. London: T&T Clark, 2003.

———. *The Actuality of Atonement: A Study of Metaphor, Rationality and the Christian Tradition.* London: T&T Clark, 1988.

———. *The Christian Faith: An Introduction to Christian Doctrine.* Oxford: Blackwell, 2002.

———. *The Triune Creator: A Historical and Systematic Study.* Edinburgh Studies in Constructive Theology. Grand Rapids: Eerdmans, 1998.

———. *Yesterday and Today: A Study of Continuities in Christology.* Grand Rapids: Eerdmans, 1983.

Habets, Myk. "Spirit Christology: The Future of Christology?" In *Third Article Theology: A Pneumatological Dogmatics,* edited by Myk Habets, 207–32. Minneapolis: Fortress, 2016.

Haight, Roger, SJ. "The Case for Spirit Christology." *JTS* 53 (1992): 257–87.

Hamilton, James M., Jr. *God's Glory in Salvation through Judgment: A Biblical Theology.* Wheaton, IL: Crossway, 2010.

Hanson, R. P. C. *The Search for the Christian Doctrine of God: The Arian Controversy, 318–381.* Edinburgh: T&T Clark, 1988.

Harris, Murray J. *Colossians and Philemon.* EGNT. Grand Rapids: Eerdmans, 1991.

———. *Jesus as God: The New Testament Use of Theos in Reference to Jesus.* Grand Rapids: Baker, 1992.

Hart, Trevor. *In Him Was Life: The Person and Work of Christ*. Waco, TX: Baylor University Press, 2019.

Harvey, Van Austin. *The Historian and the Believer: The Morality of Historical Knowledge and Christian Belief*. New York: Macmillan, 1966.

Hawthorne, Gerald F. *The Presence and the Power: The Significance of the Holy Spirit in the Life and Ministry of Jesus*. Dallas: Word, 1991.

Hays, Christopher M., and Milton Acosta. "Jesus as Missional Migrant: Latin American Christologies, the New Testament Witness, and Twenty-First Century Migration." In *Who Do You Say I Am? On the Humanity of Jesus*, edited by George Kalantzis, David B. Capes, and Ty Kieser, 158–77. Eugene, OR: Cascade, 2020.

Hays, Richard B. *Echoes of Scripture in the Gospels*. Waco, TX: Baylor University Press, 2016.

Healy, Nicholas M. "Karl Barth, German-Language Theology, and the Catholic Tradition." In *Trinity and Election in Contemporary Theology*, edited by Michael T. Dempsey, 229–43. Grand Rapids: Eerdmans, 2011.

Hector, Kevin W. "God's Triunity and Self-Determination: A Conversation with Karl Barth, Bruce McCormack, and Paul Molnar." In *Trinity and Election in Contemporary Theology*, edited by Michael T. Dempsey, 29–46. Grand Rapids: Eerdmans, 2011.

Hellerman, Joseph H. *Philippians*. EGGNT. Nashville: B&H Academic, 2015.

Hengel, Martin. "The Prologue of the Gospel of John as the Gateway to Christological Truth." In *The Gospel of John and Christian Theology*, edited by Richard Bauckham and Carl Mosser, 265–94. Grand Rapids: Eerdmans, 2008.

Heppe, Heinrich. *Reformed Dogmatics*. Edited by Ernst Bizer. Translated by G. T. Thomson. Reprint, Eugene, OR: Wipf & Stock, 2007.

Hesslein, Kayko Driedger. *Dual Citizenship: Two-Natures Christologies and the Jewish Jesus*. London: Bloomsbury, 2015.

Hick, John, ed. *The Myth of God Incarnate*. Philadelphia: Westminster, 1977.

Hill, Daniel J., and Joseph Jedwab. "Atonement and the Concept of Punishment." In *Locating Atonement: Explorations in Constructive Dogmatics*, edited by Oliver D. Crisp and Fred Sanders, 139–53. Grand Rapids: Zondervan, 2015.

Hill, Daniel Lee, and Ty Kieser. "Social Sin and the Sinless Savior: Delineating Supra-Personal Sin in Continuity with Conciliar Christology." *ModTheo* 38, no. 3 (July 2022): 568–91.

Hill, Wesley. *Paul and the Trinity: Persons, Relations, and the Pauline Letters.* Grand Rapids: Eerdmans, 2015.

Hinlicky, Paul R. *Beloved Community: Critical Dogmatics after Christendom.* Grand Rapids: Eerdmans, 2015.

Hoang, Bethany Hanke, and Kristen Deede Johnson. *The Justice Calling: Where Passion Meets Perseverance.* Grand Rapids: Brazos, 2016.

Hoch, Carl B., Jr. *All Things New: The Significance of Newness for Biblical Theology.* Grand Rapids: Baker, 1995.

Hoehner, Harold W. *Ephesians: An Exegetical Commentary.* Grand Rapids: Baker Academic, 2002.

Hoglund, Jonathan. *Called by Triune Grace: Divine Rhetoric and the Effectual Call.* SCDS. Downers Grove, IL: IVP Academic, 2016.

Holmes, Stephen R. "A Reformed Account of Eucharistic Sacrifice." *IJST* 24, no. 2 (April 2022): 191–211.

———. "Ransomed, Healed, Restored, Forgiven: Evangelical Accounts of the Atonement." In *The Atonement Debate: Papers from the London Symposium on the Theology of Atonement,* edited by Derek Tidball, David Hilborn, and Justin Thacker, 267–92. Grand Rapids: Zondervan, 2008.

———. "Reformed Varieties of the *Communicatio Idiomatum.*" In *The Person of Christ,* edited by Stephen R. Holmes and Murray A. Rae, 70–86. London: T&T Clark, 2005.

Holwerda, David E. *Jesus and Israel: One Covenant or Two?* Grand Rapids: Eerdmans, 1995.

Horton, Michael S. *Justification.* Vol. 2. NSD. Grand Rapids: Zondervan, 2018.

———. *Lord and Servant: A Covenant Christology.* Louisville: Westminster John Knox, 2005.

———. *People and Place: A Covenant Ecclesiology.* Louisville: Westminster John Knox, 2008.

———. *The Christian Faith: A Systematic Theology for Pilgrims on the Way.* Grand Rapids: Zondervan, 2011.

Hoskins, Paul M. *Jesus as the Fulfillment of the Temple in the Gospel of John.* Paternoster Biblical Monographs. Waynesboro, GA: Paternoster, 2006.

House, Paul. *Isaiah*. Vol. 1, *Chapters 1–27*. A Mentor Commentary. Ross-shire, UK: Christian Focus, 2018.

Hughes, Kyle R. *The Trinitarian Testimony of the Spirit: Prosopological Exegesis and the Development of Pre-Nicene Pneumatology*. Leiden: Brill, 2018.

Hunsinger, George. "Karl Barth's Christology: Its Basic Chalcedonian Character." In *Disruptive Grace: Studies in the Theology of Karl Barth*, 131–47. Grand Rapids: Eerdmans, 2000.

———. *Reading Barth with Charity: A Hermeneutical Proposal*. Grand Rapids: Baker Academic, 2015.

———. "The Daybreak of the New Creation: Christ's Resurrection in Recent Theology." *SJT* 57, no. 2 (2004): 163–81.

———. *The Eucharist and Ecumenism: Let Us Keep the Feast*. CIT. Cambridge: Cambridge University Press, 2008.

Hurtado, Larry W. *Lord Jesus Christ: Devotion to Jesus in Earliest Christianity*. Grand Rapids: Eerdmans, 2003.

———. "Monotheism." In *Dictionary for Theological Interpretation of the Bible*, edited by Kevin J. Vanhoozer et al., 519–21. Grand Rapids: Baker Academic, 2005.

Inbody, Tyron. *The Many Faces of Christology*. Nashville: Abingdon, 2002.

Irons, Charles Lee. "A Lexical Defense of the Johannine 'Only Begotten.'" In *Retrieving Eternal Generation*, edited by Fred Sanders and Scott R. Swain, 98–116. Grand Rapids: Zondervan, 2017.

Jamieson, R. B. *The Paradox of Sonship: Christology in the Epistle to the Hebrews*. SCDS. Downers Grove, IL: IVP Academic, 2021.

Jamieson, R. B., and Tyler R. Wittman. *Biblical Reasoning: Christological and Trinitarian Rules for Exegesis*. Grand Rapids: Baker Academic, 2022.

Jeffrey, David Lyle. *Luke*. BTCB. Grand Rapids: Brazos, 2012.

———. "(Pre) Figuration: Masterplot and Meaning in Biblical History." In *"Behind" the Text: History and Biblical Interpretation*, edited by Craig Bartholomew, C. Stephen Evans, Mary Healy, and Murray Rae, 363–93. SHS 4. Grand Rapids: Zondervan, 2003.

Jennings, Willie James. *The Christian Imagination: Theology and the Origins of Race*. New Haven, CT: Yale University Press, 2011.

Jenson, Robert W. "Christ in the Trinity: *Communicatio Idiomatum*." In *The Person of Christ*, edited by Stephen R. Holmes and Murray A. Rae, 61–69. London: T&T Clark, 2005.

———. "Identity, Jesus, and Exegesis." In *Seeking the Identity of Jesus: A Pilgrimage*, edited by Beverly Roberts Gaventa and Richard B. Hays, 43–59. Grand Rapids: Eerdmans, 2008.

Jersak, Brad, and Michael Hardin, eds. *Stricken by God? Nonviolent Identification and the Victory of Christ*. Grand Rapids: Eerdmans, 2007.

Jipp, Joshua W. "Ancient, Modern, and Future Interpretations of Romans 1:3–4: Reception History and Biblical Interpretation." *JTI* 3, no. 2 (2009): 241–59.

———. *Christ Is King: Paul's Royal Ideology*. Minneapolis: Fortress, 2015.

———. *The Messianic Theology of the New Testament*. Grand Rapids: Eerdmans, 2020.

John of Damascus. "Exposition of the Orthodox Faith." In *Hilary of Poitiers, John of Damascus*. Edited by Philip Schaff and Henry Wace. NPNF2 9. Reprint, Peabody, MA: Hendrickson, 2004.

———. "Oration on the Transfiguration of Our Lord and Savior Jesus Christ." In *Light on the Mountain: Greek Patristic and Byzantine Homilies on the Transfiguration of the Lord*, edited by Brian E. Daley, SJ, 205–31. New York: St. Vladimir's Seminary, 2013.

Johnson, Adam J. "Theories and *Theoria* of the Atonement: A Proposal." *IJST* 25, no. 1 (January 2021): 92–108.

Jones, L. Gregory. *Embodying Forgiveness: A Theological Analysis*. Grand Rapids: Eerdmans, 1995.

Josephson-Storm, Jason Ä. *The Myth of Disenchantment: Magic, Modernity, and the Birth of the Human Sciences*. Chicago: University of Chicago Press, 2017.

Jowers, Dennis W. "The Meaning of μορφῇ in Philippians 2:6–7." *JETS* 49, no. 4 (December 2006): 739–66.

Juel, Donald. *Messianic Exegesis: Christological Interpretation of the Old Testament in Early Christianity*. Philadelphia: Fortress, 1988.

Just, Arthur A., Jr., ed. *Luke*. ACCSNT 3. Downers Grove, IL: InterVarsity Press, 2003.

Kaiser, Walter C., Jr. "The Identity and Mission of the 'Servant of the Lord.'" In *The Gospel according to Isaiah 53: Encountering the Suffering Servant in Jewish and Christian Theology*, edited by Darrell L. Bock and Mitch Glaser, 87–107. Grand Rapids: Kregel, 2012.

Kapic, Kelly. "The Son's Assumption of a Human Nature: A Call for Clarity." *IJST* 3 (2001): 154–66.

Kärkkäinen, Veli-Matti. *Christ and Reconciliation*. Vol. 1 of *A Constructive*

Christian Theology for the Pluralistic World. Grand Rapids: Eerdmans, 2013.

———. *Christology: A Global Introduction*. Grand Rapids: Baker Academic, 2003.

Kasper, Walter. *Jesus the Christ*. Translated by V. Green. Reprint, New York: Paulist, 1981.

Katz, Steven T. "The Language and Logic of 'Mystery' in Christology." In *Christ, Faith and History: Cambridge Studies in Christology*, edited by S. W. Sykes and J. P. Clayton, 239–61. Cambridge: Cambridge University Press, 1972.

Keener, Craig S. *Christobiography: Memory, History, and the Reliability of the Gospels*. Grand Rapids: Eerdmans, 2019.

———. *Miracles: The Credibility of the New Testament Accounts*. 2 vols. Grand Rapids: Baker Academic, 2011.

Khalaf, Ghassan. "Jesus and Judaism: His Identity and Relationship to Judaism." In *Arabic Christian Theology: A Contemporary Global Evangelical Perspective*, edited by Andrea Zaki Stephanous, 89–210. Grand Rapids: Zondervan, 2019.

Kieser, Ty. "Theandric and Triune: John Owen and a Case for Classically Reformed Christological Agency." PhD diss., Wheaton College Graduate School, 2020.

Kilner, John F. *Dignity and Destiny: Humanity in the Image of God*. Grand Rapids: Eerdmans, 2015.

Kinzig, Wolfram, and Markus Vinzent, "Recent Research on the Origin of the Creed," *JTS* 50, no. 2 (October 1999): 535–59.

Kirk, J. R. Daniel. *A Man Attested by God: The Human Jesus of the Synoptic Gospels*. Grand Rapids: Eerdmans, 2016.

Kirkpatrick, David C. *A Gospel for the Poor: Global Social Christianity and the Latin American Left*. Philadelphia: University of Pennsylvania Press, 2019.

Knight, George A. F. *Servant Theology: A Commentary on the Book of Isaiah 40–55*. ITC. Edinburgh: Handsel, 1984.

Kooi, Cornelis van der, and Gijsbert van den Brink. *Christian Dogmatics: An Introduction*. Translated by Reinder Bruinsma and James D. Bratt. Grand Rapids: Eerdmans, 2017.

Köstenberger, Andreas J. "The Deity of Christ in John's Gospel." In *The Deity of Christ*, edited by Christopher W. Morgan and Robert A. Peterson, 91–114. TC. Wheaton, IL: Crossway, 2011.

Köstenberger, Andreas J., and Scott R. Swain. *Father, Son and Spirit: The Trinity and John's Gospel*. NSBT. Downers Grove, IL: IVP Academic, 2008.

Koyama, Kosuke. *Three Mile an Hour God: Biblical Reflections*. Maryknoll, NY: Orbis, 1979.

Kreitzer, Beth, ed. *Luke*. RCSNT 3. Downers Grove, IL: IVP Academic, 2015.

Kugler, Chris. "New Testament Christology: A Critique of Hurtado's Influence." *BBR* 30, no. 3 (2020): 367–78.

Küster, Volker. *The Many Faces of Jesus Christ: Intercultural Christology*. Translated by John Bowden. Maryknoll, NY: Orbis, 2001.

Laansma, Jon C. "'Some Have No Knowledge of God': The Resurrection and the Knowledge of God in 1 Corinthians." *JTI* (forthcoming).

Ladd, George Eldon. *I Believe in the Resurrection of Jesus*. Grand Rapids: Eerdmans, 1975.

Lane, William L. *The Gospel of Mark*. NICNT. Grand Rapids: Eerdmans, 1974.

Larmer, Robert A. "The Meanings of Miracle." In *The Cambridge Companion to Miracles*, edited by Graham H. Twelftree, 36–54. Cambridge: Cambridge University Press, 2011.

Larsen, Timothy. "Congregationalists and Crucicentrism." In *Evangelicalism and Dissent in Modern England and Wales*, edited by David Bebbington and David Ceri Jones, 111–38. London: Routledge, 2021.

———, ed. *The Oxford Handbook of Christmas*. Oxford: Oxford University Press, 2020.

Leeman, Jonathan. *Political Church: The Local Assembly as Embassy of Christ's Rule*. SCDS. Downers Grove, IL: IVP Academic, 2016.

Legge, Dominic, OP. *The Trinitarian Christology of St Thomas Aquinas*. Oxford: Oxford University Press, 2017.

Leithart, Peter J. *Revelation 12–22*. ITC. London: T&T Clark, 2018.

LePeau, Andrew T. *Mark through Old Testament Eyes*. Grand Rapids: Kregel, 2017.

Letham, Robert. *The Message of the Person of Christ*. BST. Downers Grove, IL: InterVarsity Press, 2013.

Levering, Matthew. "Creation and Atonement." In *Locating Atonement: Explorations in Constructive Dogmatics*, edited by Oliver D. Crisp and Fred Sanders, 43–70. Grand Rapids: Zondervan, 2015.

———. *Jesus and the Demise of Death: Resurrection, Afterlife, and the Fate of the Christian*. Waco, TX: Baylor University Press, 2012.

Levine, Amy-Jill, and Marc Zvi Brettler. *The Bible with and without Jesus: How Jews and Christians Read the Same Stories Differently*. New York: HarperOne, 2020.

Levison, Jack. *A Boundless God: The Spirit according to the Old Testament*. Grand Rapids: Baker Academic, 2020.

Lewis, Alan E. *Between Cross and Resurrection: A Theology of Holy Saturday*. Grand Rapids: Eerdmans, 2001.

Lewis, Gordon R., and Bruce A. Demarest. *Our Primary Need: Christ's Atoning Provisions*. Vol. 2 of *Integrative Theology*. Grand Rapids: Academie, 1990.

Licona, Michael R. *The Resurrection of Jesus: A New Historiographical Approach*. Downers Grove, IL: IVP Academic, 2010.

Lightfoot, J. B. *St. Paul's Epistles to the Colossians and Philemon*. Reprint, Peabody, MA: Hendrickson, 1993.

Lincoln, Andrew T. *Born of a Virgin? Reconceiving Jesus in the Bible, Tradition, and Theology*. Grand Rapids: Eerdmans, 2013.

Lindars, Barnabas, SSF. *Jesus Son of Man: A Fresh Examination of the Son of Man Sayings in the Gospels in the Light of Recent Research*. Grand Rapids: Eerdmans, 1983.

Lindbeck, George A. "Postcritical Canonical Interpretation: Three Modes of Retrieval." In *Theological Exegesis: Essays in Honor of Brevard S. Childs*, edited by Christopher Seitz and Kathryn Greene-McCreight, 26–51. Grand Rapids: Eerdmans, 1999.

Loades, Ann. "On Mary: Constructive Ambivalence?" *The Way* 34, no. 2 (April 1994): 138–46.

Loke, Andrew Ter Ern. *A Kryptic Model of the Incarnation*. London: Routledge, 2014.

Lonergan, Bernard. *The Way to Nicea: The Dialectical Development of Trinitarian Theology*. Translated by Conn O'Donovan. Philadelphia: Westminster, 1976.

Longenecker, Richard N. *The Christology of Early Jewish Christianity*. Grand Rapids: Baker, 1970.

Louth, Andrew. "From Doctrine of Christ to Icon of Christ: St. Maximus the Confessor on the Transfiguration of Christ." In *In the Shadow of the Incarnation: Essays on Jesus Christ in the Early Church in Honor of Brian E. Daley, S.J.*, edited by Peter W. Martens, 260–75. Notre Dame: University of Notre Dame Press, 2008.

Lowe, Walter. "Christ and Salvation." In *Christian Theology: An Introduction to Its Traditions and Tasks*, edited by Peter C. Hodgson and Robert H. King, 222–48. Minneapolis: Fortress, 1994.

———. "Christ and Salvation." In *The Cambridge Companion to Postmodern Theology*, edited by Kevin J. Vanhoozer, 235–51. Cambridge: Cambridge University Press, 2003.

Luy, David J. "Chalcedonian Christology and the Partitive Impulse." Online. *The Henry Center, Trinity Evangelical Divinity School*, October 30, 2020. https://henrycenter.tiu.edu/2020/10/perceiving-the-word-made-flesh.

———. *Dominus Mortus: Martin Luther on the Incorruptibility of God in Christ*. Minneapolis: Fortress, 2014.

Macaskill, Grant. "Christian Scriptures and the Formation of Intellectual Humility." *Journal of Psychology and Theology* 46, no. 4 (2018): 243–52.

———. "Christology, Divine Aseity, and the I Am Sayings in the Fourth Gospel." *JTI* 12, no. 2 (2018): 217–41.

———. "Incarnational Ontology and the Theology of Participation in Paul." In *"In Christ" in Paul: Explorations in Paul's Theology of Union and Participation*, edited by Michael J. Thate, Kevin J. Vanhoozer, and Constantine R. Campbell, 87–101. WUNT II. Tübingen: Mohr Siebeck, 2014.

Macchia, Frank D. *Jesus the Spirit Baptizer: Christology in Light of Pentecost*. Grand Rapids: Eerdmans, 2018.

MacDonald, Nathan. *Deuteronomy and the Meaning of "Monotheism."* 2nd ed. FZAW, II. Tübingen: Mohr Siebeck, 2012.

Macleod, Donald. *The Person of Christ*. Contours of Christian Theology. Downers Grove, IL: InterVarsity Press, 1998.

Macquarrie, John. *Jesus Christ in Modern Thought*. Philadelphia: Trinity Press International, 1990.

Malbon, Elizabeth Struthers. "The Christology of Mark's Gospel: Narrative Christology and the Markan Jesus." In *Who Do You Say That I Am? Essays on Christology*, edited by Mark Allan Powell and David R. Bauer, 33–48. Louisville: Westminster John Knox, 1999.

Mangina, Joseph L. *Revelation*. BTCB. Grand Rapids: Brazos, 2010.

Marion, Jean-Luc. "They Recognized Him; And He Became Invisible to Them." *ModTheo* 18, no. 2 (April 2002): 145–52.

Marshall, I. Howard. *The Gospel of Luke: A Commentary on the Greek Text*. NIGTC. Grand Rapids: Eerdmans, 1995.

———. "The Theology of the Atonement." In *The Atonement Debate: Papers from the London Symposium on the Theology of Atonement*, edited by Derek Tidball, David Hilborn, and Justin Thacker, 49–68. Grand Rapids: Zondervan, 2008.

Martin, Ralph P., and Brian J. Dodd, eds. *Where Christology Began: Essays on Philippians 2*. Louisville: Westminster John Knox, 1998.

Martinez-Olivieri, Jules A. *A Visible Witness: Christology, Liberation, and Participation*. ES. Minneapolis: Fortress, 2016.

McCall, Thomas H. *Analytic Christology and the Theological Interpretation of the New Testament*. OSAT. Oxford: Oxford University Press, 2021.

———. *Forsaken: The Trinity and the Cross, and Why It Matters*. Downers Grove, IL: IVP Academic, 2012.

McCaulley, Esau. "Toward a Black Anthropology and Social Ethic: Why the Humanity and Jewishness of Jesus Matters." In *Who Do You Say I Am? On the Humanity of Jesus*, edited by George Kalantzis, David B. Capes, and Ty Kieser, 143–57. Eugene, OR: Cascade, 2020.

McClymond, Michael J. *Familiar Stranger: An Introduction to Jesus of Nazareth*. Grand Rapids: Eerdmans, 2004.

McCormack, Bruce L. "Grace and Being: The Role of God's Gracious Election in Karl Barth's Theological Ontology." In *The Cambridge Companion to Karl Barth*, edited by John Webster, 92–110. Cambridge: Cambridge University Press, 2000.

———. *The Humility of the Eternal Son: Reformed Kenoticism and the Repair of Chalcedon*. CIT. Cambridge: Cambridge University Press, 2021.

———. *Karl Barth's Critically Realistic Dialectical Theology: Its Genesis and Development 1909–1936*. Oxford: Clarendon, 1995.

———. *Orthodox and Modern: Studies in the Theology of Karl Barth*. Grand Rapids: Baker Academic, 2008.

———. "The Person of Christ." In *Mapping Modern Theology: A Thematic and Historical Introduction*, edited by Kelly M. Kapic and Bruce L. McCormack, 149–73. Grand Rapids: Baker Academic, 2012.

McCready, Douglas. *He Came Down from Heaven: The Preexistence of Christ and the Christian Faith*. Downers Grove, IL: InterVarsity Press, 2005.

McDonough, Sean M. *Christ as Creator: Origins of a New Testament Doctrine*. Oxford: Oxford University Press, 2010.

McDowell, Catherine. "'In the Image of God He Created Them': How Genesis 1:26–27 Defines the Divine–Human Relationship and Why It Matters." In *The Image of God in an Image Driven Age: Explorations in Theological Anthropology*, edited by Beth Felker Jones and Jeffrey W. Barbeau, 29–46. Downers Grove, IL: IVP Academic, 2016.

McFarland, Ian A. "Perceiving the Word Made Flesh." Online. *The Henry Center, Trinity Evangelical Divinity School*, October 30, 2020. https://henrycenter.tiu.edu/2020/10/perceiving-the-word-made-flesh.

———. "Perceiving the Word Made Flesh: A Rejoinder." Online. *The Henry Center, Trinity Evangelical Divinity School*, October 30, 2020. https://henrycenter.tiu.edu/2020/10/perceiving-the-word-made-flesh.

———. *The Divine Image: Envisioning the Invisible God*. Minneapolis: Fortress, 2005.

———. *The Word Made Flesh: A Theology of the Incarnation*. Louisville: Westminster John Knox, 2019.

McGlothlin, Thomas D. *Resurrection as Salvation: Development and Conflict in Pre-Nicene Paulinism*. Cambridge: Cambridge University Press, 2018.

McGrath, Alister E. *The Making of Modern German Christology: From the Enlightenment to Pannenberg*. Oxford: Blackwell, 1986.

McGrew, Timothy. "Review of Fogelin." *Mind* 114, no. 453 (January 2005): 145–49.

McGuckin, John A. *Saint Cyril of Alexandria and the Christological Controversy: Its History, Theology, and Texts*. Crestwood, NY: St. Vladimir's Seminary, 2004.

McIntyre, John. *The Shape of Christology: Studies in the Doctrine of the Person of Christ*. 2nd ed. Edinburgh: T&T Clark, 1998.

McKinion, Steven A. *Isaiah 1–39*. ACCSOT 10. Downers Grove, IL: InterVarsity Press, 2004.

McKnight, Scot. *The Letter to the Colossians*. NICNT. Grand Rapids: Eerdmans, 2018.

McNall, Joshua M. *The Mosaic of Atonement: An Integrated Approach to Christ's Work*. Grand Rapids: Zondervan Academic, 2019.

Michaels, J. Ramsey. *The Gospel of John*. NICNT. Grand Rapids: Eerdmans, 2010.

Michelson, Jared. "Covenantal History and Participatory Metaphysics:

Formulating a Reformed Response to the Charge of Legal Fiction." *SJT* 71, no. 4 (2018): 391–410.

Middleton, J. Richard. *A New Heaven and a New Earth: Reclaiming Biblical Eschatology.* Grand Rapids: Baker Academic, 2014.

Milbank, Alison. "Seeing Double: The Crucified Christ in Western Mediaeval Art." In *The Oxford Handbook of Christology,* edited by Francesca Aran Murphy, 215–32. Oxford: Oxford University Press, 2015.

Miller, Ike. *Seeing by the Light: Illumination in Augustine's and Barth's Readings of John.* SCDS. Downers Grove, IL: IVP Academic, 2020.

Mittmann, Ulrike. *Die Weisheit und der Gottessohn: Studien zur Hermeneutischen Grundlegung einer Theologie des Neuen Testaments.* WUNT. Tübingen: Mohr Siebeck, 2021.

Moberly, R. W. L. "Isaiah and Jesus: How Might the Old Testament Inform Contemporary Christology." In *Seeking the Identity of Jesus: A Pilgrimage,* edited by Beverly Roberts Gaventa and Richard B. Hays, 232–48. Grand Rapids: Eerdmans, 2008.

———. *The Bible, Theology, and Faith: A Study of Abraham and Jesus.* CSCD. Cambridge: Cambridge University Press, 2000.

Moltmann, Jürgen. *The Crucified God: The Cross of Christ as the Foundation and Criticism of Christian Theology.* Translated by R. A. Wilson and John Bowden. New York: Harper & Row, 1974.

———. *The Way of Jesus Christ: Christology in Messianic Dimensions.* Translated by Margaret Kohl. Minneapolis: Fortress, 1993.

Moo, Douglas J. *A Theology of Paul and His Letters: The Gift of the New Realm in Christ.* BTNT. Grand Rapids: Zondervan, 2021.

Morris, Leon. *The Gospel according to John.* NICNT. Grand Rapids: Eerdmans, 1989.

Morris, Thomas V. *The Logic of God Incarnate.* Ithaca, NY: Cornell University Press, 1986.

Moser, J. David. "Tools for Interpreting Christ's Saving Mysteries in Scripture: Aquinas on Reduplicative Propositions in Christology." *SJT* 73, no. 4 (November 2020): 285–94.

———. "*Totus Christus*: A Proposal for Protestant Christology and Ecclesiology." *ProEccl* 29, no. 1 (2020): 3–30.

Mosser, Carl. "Deification: A Truly Ecumenical Concept." *Perspectives* (August 2015): 8–14.

Motyer, J. Alec. *The Prophecy of Isaiah: An Introduction and Commentary.* Downers Grove, IL: InterVarsity Press, 1993.

Moule, C. F. D. *The Origin of Christology.* Cambridge: Cambridge University Press, 1977.

Mouw, Richard J., and Douglas A. Sweeney. *The Suffering and Victorious Christ: Toward a More Compassionate Christology.* Grand Rapids: Baker Academic, 2013.

Muller, Richard A. *Post-Reformation Reformed Dogmatics.* 2nd ed. 4 vols. Grand Rapids: Baker Academic, 2003.

Murphy, Francesca Aran. "Afterword: The Breadth of Christology: The Beautiful Work of Christ." In *The Oxford Handbook of Christology*, edited by Francesca Aran Murphy, 628–48. Oxford: Oxford University Press, 2015.

Murray, John. *Redemption Accomplished and Applied.* Reprint, Grand Rapids: Eerdmans, 1968.

Myers, Benjamin. "The Patristic Atonement Model." In *Locating Atonement: Explorations in Constructive Dogmatics*, edited by Oliver D. Crisp and Fred Sanders, 71–88. Grand Rapids: Zondervan, 2015.

Myers, Stephen G. *God to Us: Covenant Theology in Scripture.* Grand Rapids: Reformation Heritage, 2021.

Newman, Carey C., ed. *Jesus and the Restoration of Israel: A Critical Assessment of N. T. Wright's* Jesus and the Victory of God. Downers Grove, IL: InterVarsity Press, 1999.

———. *Paul's Glory-Christology: Tradition and Rhetoric.* NovTSup. Leiden: Brill, 1992.

Nichols, Aidan, OP. "Image Christology in the Age of the Second Council of Nicaea." In *The Oxford Handbook of Christology*, edited by Francesca Aran Murphy, 169–82. Oxford: Oxford University Press, 2015.

Nichols, Stephen J. "The Deity of Christ Today." In *The Deity of Christ*, edited by Christopher W. Morgan and Robert A. Peterson, 25–38. TC. Wheaton, IL: Crossway, 2011.

Nicole, Roger. "Postscript on Penal Substitution." In *The Glory of the Atonement: Biblical, Theological and Practical Perspectives*, edited by Charles E. Hill and Frank A. James III, 445–52. Downers Grove, IL: InterVarsity Press, 2004.

Niebauer, Michael. *Virtuous Persuasion: A Theology of Christian Mission.*

Studies in Historical and Systematic Theology. Bellingham, WA: Lexham, 2022.

Niebuhr, H. Richard. *The Kingdom of God in America*. New York: Harper & Row, 1937.

Nimmo, Paul T. "Ethics." In *A Companion to the Theology of John Webster*, edited by Michael Allen and R. David Nelson, 280–96. Grand Rapids: Eerdmans, 2021.

Novakovic, Lidija. *Philippians: A Handbook on the Greek Text*. Waco, TX: Baylor University Press, 2020.

Novenson, Matthew N. "Introduction." In *Monotheism and Christology in Greco-Roman Antiquity*, edited by Matthew N. Novenson, 180:1–8. NovTSup. Leiden: Brill, 2020.

———, ed. *Monotheism and Christology in Greco-Roman Antiquity*. NovTSup. Leiden: Brill, 2020.

Oakes, Edward T., SJ. *Infinity Dwindled to Infancy: A Catholic and Evangelical Christology*. Grand Rapids: Eerdmans, 2011.

O'Collins, Gerald, SJ. "The Resurrection: The State of the Questions." In *The Resurrection: An Interdisciplinary Symposium on the Resurrection of Jesus*, edited by Stephen Davis, Daniel Kendall, SJ, and Gerald O'Collins, SJ, 5–28. Oxford: Oxford University Press, 1997.

Oden, Thomas C. *Systematic Theology*. 3 vols. Peabody, MA: Prince, 1998.

Oden, Thomas C., and Christopher A. Hall, eds. *Mark*. ACCSNT 2. Downers Grove, IL: InterVarsity Press, 1998.

O'Donovan, Oliver. *Entering into Rest*. Vol. 3 of *Ethics as Theology*. Grand Rapids: Eerdmans, 2017.

———. *Resurrection and Moral Order: An Outline for Evangelical Ethics*. 2nd ed. Grand Rapids: Eerdmans, 1994.

———. *The Desire of the Nations: Rediscovering the Roots of Political Theology*. Cambridge: Cambridge University Press, 1996.

Orr, Peter C. *Exalted Above the Heavens: The Risen and Ascended Christ*. NSBT. Downers Grove, IL: IVP Academic, 2018.

Ortlund, Dane. *Gentle and Lowly: The Heart of Christ for Sinners and Sufferers*. Wheaton, IL: Crossway, 2020.

Ortlund, Raymond C., Jr. "The Deity of Christ and the Old Testament." In *The Deity of Christ*, edited by Christopher W. Morgan and Robert A. Peterson, 39–59. TC. Wheaton, IL: Crossway, 2011.

Osborne, Grant R. *Revelation*. BECNT. Grand Rapids: Baker Academic, 2002.

Oswalt, John N. *The Book of Isaiah, Chapters 1–39*. NICOT. Grand Rapids: Eerdmans, 1986.

Owen, John. "Christologia: Or, a Declaration of the Glorious Mystery of the Person of Christ." In *The Works of John Owen*, vol. 1, edited by William H. Goold, 1–272. Reprint, London: Banner of Truth Trust, 1965.

Packer, J. I. *Knowing God*. Reprint, Downers Grove, IL: InterVarsity Press, 2018.

———. "What Did the Cross Achieve? The Logic of Penal Substitution." *TynBul* 25 (1974): 3–45.

Paddison, Angus. "Christology and Jewish-Christian Understanding: Reading the Fourth Gospel as Scripture." In *Christology and Scripture: Interdisciplinary Perspectives*, edited by Andrew T. Lincoln and Angus Paddison, 41–57. New York: T&T Clark, 2008.

Padilla, C. René. "Toward a Contextual Christology from Latin America." In *Conflict and Context: Hermeneutics in the Americas*, edited by Mark Lau Branson and C. René Padilla, 81–91. Grand Rapids: Eerdmans, 1986.

Pannenberg, Wolfhart. *Jesus—God and Man*. Translated by Lewis L. Wilkins and Duane A. Priebe. 2nd ed. Philadelphia: Westminster, 1977.

Pao, David W., and Eckhard J. Schnabel. "Luke." In *Commentary on the New Testament Use of the Old Testament*, edited by G. K. Beale and D. A. Carson, 251–414. Grand Rapids: Baker Academic, 2007.

Pardue, Stephen T. *The Mind of Christ: Humility and the Intellect in Early Christian Theology*. SST. London: T&T Clark, 2013.

Parvis, Sara. "Christology in the Early Arian Controversy: The Exegetical War." In *Christology and Scripture: Interdisciplinary Perspectives*, edited by Andrew T. Lincoln and Angus Paddison, 120–37. New York: T&T Clark, 2008.

Pawl, Timothy. *In Defense of Conciliar Christology: A Philosophical Essay*. OSAT. Oxford: Oxford University Press, 2016.

Peeler, Amy. "Protestants Need to Talk More About Mary." *Didaktikos: Journal of Theological Education* 3, no. 3 (November 2019): 12–13.

———. *Women and the Gender of God*. Grand Rapids: Eerdmans, 2022.

Perkins, Pheme. "The Gospel of Mark." In *New Interpreter's Bible*, 8:509–733. Nashville: Abingdon, 1995.

Perkins, William. *A Warning Against Idolatry of the Last Times (1601)*. Edited by Shawn D. Wright. The Works of William Perkins 7. Grand Rapids: Reformation Heritage, 2018.

Perrin, Nicholas. *Jesus the Priest*. Grand Rapids: Baker Academic, 2018.

———. *Jesus the Temple*. Grand Rapids: Baker Academic, 2010.

Perrin, Nicholas, and Richard B. Hays, eds. *Jesus, Paul and the People of God: A Theological Dialogue with N. T. Wright*. Downers Grove, IL: IVP Academic, 2011.

Pierce, Madison N. *Divine Discourse in the Epistle to the Hebrews: The Recontextualization of Spoken Quotations of Scripture*. SNTSMS. Cambridge: Cambridge University Press, 2020.

———. "Hebrews 1 and the Son Begotten 'Today.'" In *Retrieving Eternal Generation*, edited by Fred Sanders and Scott R. Swain, 117–31. Grand Rapids: Zondervan, 2017.

Piotrowski, Nicholas G. "Nazarene." In *Dictionary of Jesus and the Gospels*, 2nd ed., edited by Joel B. Green et al., 624–25. Downers Grove, IL: IVP Academic, 2013.

Pitre, Brant. *Jesus and the Last Supper*. Grand Rapids: Eerdmans, 2015.

———. *Jesus, the Tribulation, and the End of the Exile: Restoration Eschatology and the Origin of the Atonement*. Grand Rapids: Baker Academic, 2005.

Pitstick, Alyssa Lyra. *Light in the Darkness: Hans Urs von Balthasar and the Catholic Doctrine of Christ's Descent into Hell*. Grand Rapids: Eerdmans, 2007.

Placher, William C. *Jesus the Savior: The Meaning of Jesus Christ for Christian Faith*. Louisville: Westminster John Knox, 2001.

———. *Mark*. Belief. Louisville: Westminster John Knox, 2010.

Poobalan, Ivor. "Christology in Asia: Rooted and Responsive." In *Asian Christian Theology: Evangelical Perspectives*, edited by Timoteo D. Gener and Stephen T. Pardue, 83–100. Carlisle, Cumbria, UK: Langham Global Library, 2019.

Price, Robert B. "Barth on the Incarnation." In *The Wiley Blackwell Companion to Karl Barth: Barth and Dogmatics*, edited by George Hunsinger and Keith L. Johnson, 137–45. London: Wiley-Blackwell, 2020.

Provan, Iain W. "The Messiah in the Books of Kings." In *The Lord's*

Anointed: Interpretation of Old Testament Messianic Texts, edited by Philip E. Satterthwaite, Richard S. Hess, and Gordon J. Wenham, 67–85. Grand Rapids: Baker, 1995.

———. *The Reformation and the Right Reading of Scripture*. Waco, TX: Baylor University Press, 2017.

Reynolds, Benjamin E., ed. *The Son of Man Problem: Critical Readings*. London: T&T Clark, 2018.

Richard, Guy M. "The Covenant of Redemption." In *Covenant Theology: Biblical, Theological, and Historical Perspectives*, edited by Guy Prentiss Waters, J. Nicholas Reid, and John R. Muether, 43–62. Wheaton, IL: Crossway, 2020.

Riches, Aaron. *Ecce Homo: On the Divine Unity of Christ*. Interventions. Grand Rapids: Eerdmans, 2016.

Riesner, Rainer. "Archeology and Geography." In *Dictionary of Jesus and the Gospels*, 2nd ed., edited by Joel B. Green et al., 44–59. Downers Grove, IL: IVP Academic, 2013.

Roberts, Kyle. *A Complicated Pregnancy: Whether Mary Was a Virgin and Why It Matters*. Theology for the People. Minneapolis: Fortress, 2017.

Robertson, Jon M. *Christ as Mediator: A Study of the Theologies of Eusebius of Caesarea, Marcellus of Ancyra, and Athanasius of Alexandria*. OTM. Oxford: Oxford University Press, 2007.

Rowe, C. Kavin. "Biblical Pressure and Trinitarian Hermeneutics." *ProEccl* 11, no. 3 (2002): 295–312.

———. *Early Narrative Christology: The Lord in the Gospel of Luke*. Grand Rapids: Baker Academic, 2009.

———. *World Upside Down: Reading Acts in the Graeco-Roman Age*. New York: Oxford University Press, 2009.

Runia, Klaas. *The Present-Day Christological Debate*. Downers Grove, IL: InterVarsity Press, 1984.

Rutledge, Fleming. *The Crucifixion: Understanding the Death of Jesus Christ*. Grand Rapids: Eerdmans, 2015.

Ryan, Jordan. *The Role of the Synagogue in the Aims of Jesus*. Minneapolis: Fortress, 2017.

Samuel, Vinay, and Chris Sugden, eds. *Sharing Jesus in the Two Thirds World: Evangelical Christologies from the Contexts of Poverty, Powerlessness and Religious Pluralism*. Bangalore: Partnership in Mission–Asia, 1983.

Sánchez M., Leopoldo A. *Receiver, Bearer, and Giver of God's Spirit: Jesus'*

Life in the Spirit as a Lens for Theology and Life. Eugene, OR: Pickwick, 2015.

Sanders, Fred. "Eternal Generation and Soteriology." In *Retrieving Eternal Generation*, edited by Fred Sanders and Scott R. Swain, 260–70. Grand Rapids: Zondervan, 2017.

———. "Introduction to Christology: Chalcedonian Categories for the Gospel Narrative." In *Jesus in Trinitarian Perspective: An Intermediate Christology*, edited by Fred Sanders and Klaus Issler, 1–41. Nashville: B&H Academic, 2007.

———. *The Triune God.* NSD. Grand Rapids: Zondervan, 2016.

Sanders, Kirsten. "The Logic of Chalcedon and the Burning Bush." Online. *The Henry Center, Trinity Evangelical Divinity School*, October 30, 2020. https://henrycenter.tiu.edu/2020/10/perceiving-the-word-made-flesh.

Sarisky, Darren. "Augustine and Participation: Some Reflections on His Exegesis of Romans." In *"In Christ" in Paul: Explorations in Paul's Theology of Union and Participation*, edited by Michael J. Thate, Kevin J. Vanhoozer, and Constantine R. Campbell, 357–74. WUNT II. Tübingen: Mohr Siebeck, 2014.

———. "Judgments in Scripture and the Creed: Reflections on Identity and Difference." *ModTheo* 37, no. 3 (July 2021): 703–20.

Satterthwaite, Philip E., Richard S. Hess, and Gordon J. Wenham, eds. *The Lord's Anointed: Interpretation of Old Testament Messianic Texts.* Grand Rapids: Baker, 1995.

Schibler, Daniel. "Messianism and Messianic Prophecy in Isaiah 1–12 and 28–33." In *The Lord's Anointed: Interpretation of Old Testament Messianic Texts*, edited by Philip E. Satterthwaite, Richard S. Hess, and Gordon J. Wenham, 87–104. Grand Rapids: Baker, 1995.

Schipper, Jeremy. *Disability and Isaiah's Suffering Servant.* Biblical Refigurations. Oxford: Oxford University Press, 2011.

Schlatter, Adolf von. *The History of the Christ: The Foundation for New Testament Theology.* Translated by Andreas J. Köstenberger. Grand Rapids: Baker, 1997.

Schleiermacher, Friedrich. *Christian Faith: A New Translation and Critical Edition.* Translated by Terrence N. Tice, Catherine L. Kelsey, and Edwina Lawler. 2 vols. Louisville: Westminster John Knox, 2016.

Schröter, Jens. "Präexistenter Sohn und Messias Israels. Zu einer Christologischen Denkstruktur bei Paulus." In *Perspektiven zur*

Präexistenz im Frühjudentum und Frühen Christentum, edited by Jörg Frey, Friederike Kunath, and Jens Schröter, 107–28. WUNT. Tübingen: Mohr Siebeck, 2021.

Schultz, Richard. "The King in the Book of Isaiah." In *The Lord's Anointed: Interpretation of Old Testament Messianic Texts*, edited by Philip E. Satterthwaite, Richard S. Hess, and Gordon J. Wenham, 141–65. Grand Rapids: Baker, 1995.

Schwarz, Hans. *Christology*. Grand Rapids: Eerdmans, 1998.

Schwöbel, Christoph. "Christ For Us—Yesterday and Today: A Response to 'The Person of Christ.'" In *The Person of Christ*, edited by Stephen R. Holmes and Murray A. Rae, 182–201. London: T&T Clark, 2005.

Scobie, Charles H. H. *The Ways of Our God: An Approach to Biblical Theology*. Grand Rapids: Eerdmans, 2003.

Scott, James M., ed. *Exile: A Conversation with N. T. Wright*. Downers Grove, IL: IVP Academic, 2017.

Seitz, Christopher R. *Colossians*. BTCB. Grand Rapids: Brazos, 2014.

———. *Isaiah 1–39*. Int. Louisville: Westminster John Knox, 1993.

Shannon, Nathan D. *Absolute Person and Moral Experience: A Study in Neo-Calvinism*. T&T Clark Enquiries in Theological Ethics. London: T&T Clark, 2022.

Shin, Euntaek D. "A Theology of Rest." PhD diss., Wheaton College Graduate School, 2022.

Sigurdson, Ola. *Heavenly Bodies: Incarnation, the Gaze, and Embodiment in Christian Theology*. Translated by Carl Olsen. Grand Rapids: Eerdmans, 2016.

Silva, Moisés. "Galatians." In *CNTOT*, edited by G. K. Beale and D. A. Carson, 785–812. Grand Rapids: Baker Academic, 2007.

Smith, Brandon D. *The Trinity in the Book of Revelation: Seeing Father, Son, and Holy Spirit in John's Apocalypse*. SCDS. Downers Grove, IL: IVP Academic, 2022.

Smith, D. Blair. "Perceiving Christ in Faith." Online. *The Henry Center, Trinity Evangelical Divinity School*, October 30, 2020. https://henry-center.tiu.edu/2020/10/perceiving-the-word-made-flesh.

Smith, Gary V. *Isaiah 1–39*. NAC 15A. Nashville: B&H, 2007.

Sokolowski, Robert. *The God of Faith and Reason: Foundations of Christian Theology*. Washington, DC: Catholic University of America Press, 1995.

Sonderegger, Katherine. "Christ as Infinite and Finite: Rowan Williams' *Christ the Heart of Creation*." *ProEccl* 30, no. 1 (February 2021): 98–113.

———. "Jesus Christ." In *A Companion to the Theology of John Webster*, edited by Michael Allen and R. David Nelson, 208–22. Grand Rapids: Eerdmans, 2021.

———. "Jesus Christ and the Incarnation." In *The Oxford Handbook of Christmas*, edited by Timothy Larsen, 90–101. Oxford: Oxford University Press, 2020.

———. "The Humility of the Son of God." In *Christology, Ancient and Modern: Explorations in Constructive Dogmatics*, edited by Oliver D. Crisp and Fred Sanders, 60–73. Grand Rapids: Zondervan, 2013.

———. "The Sinlessness of Christ." In *Theological Theology: Essays in Honour of John Webster*, edited by R. David Nelson, Darren Sarisky, and Justin Stratis, 267–75. London: Bloomsbury T&T Clark, 2015.

Sosa Siliezar, Carlos Raúl. *Savior of the World: A Theology of the Universal Gospel*. Waco, TX: Baylor University Press, 2019.

Soulen, R. Kendall. "*Generatio, Processio Verbi, Donum Nominis*: Mapping the Vocabulary of Eternal Generation." In *Retrieving Eternal Generation*, edited by Fred Sanders and Scott R. Swain, 132–46. Grand Rapids: Zondervan, 2017.

———. *The God of Israel and Christian Theology*. Minneapolis: Augsburg Fortress, 1996.

Spencer, Aída Besançon. "From Artemis to Mary: Misplaced Veneration versus True Worship of Jesus in the Latino/a Context." In *Jesus without Borders: Christology in the Majority World*, edited by Gene L. Green, Stephen T. Pardue, and K. K. Yeo, 123–40. MWT. Grand Rapids: Eerdmans, 2014.

Stackhouse, John G., Jr. "Jesus Christ." In *The Oxford Handbook of Evangelical Theology*, edited by Gerald R. McDermott, 146–58. New York: Oxford University Press, 2010.

Stamps, R. Lucas. "Perception, Incarnation, and the Flesh of Christ." Online. *The Henry Center, Trinity Evangelical Divinity School*, October 30, 2020. https://henrycenter.tiu.edu/2020/10/perceiving-the-word-made-flesh.

Steinmetz, David C. "Uncovering a Second Narrative: Detective Fiction and the Construction of Historical Method." In *The Art of Reading Scripture*, edited by Ellen F. Davis and Richard B. Hays, 54–65. Grand Rapids: Eerdmans, 2003.

Stewart, Bryan A., and Michael A. Thomas, eds. *John: Interpreted by Early Christian and Medieval Commentators.* CB. Grand Rapids: Eerdmans, 2018.

Stinton, Diane B. *Jesus of Africa: Voices of Contemporary African Christology.* Maryknoll, NY: Orbis, 2004.

Stiver, Dan R. *Life Together in the Way of Jesus Christ: An Introduction to Christian Theology.* Waco, TX: Baylor University Press, 2009.

Stott, John R. W. *The Cross of Christ.* Downers Grove, IL: InterVarsity Press, 1986.

Strauss, Mark L. "Jesus and the Spirit in Biblical and Theological Perspective: Messianic Empowering, Saving Wisdom, and the Limits of Biblical Theology." In *The Spirit and Christ in the New Testament and Christian Theology: Essays in Honor of Max Turner*, edited by I. Howard Marshall, Volker Rabens, and Cornelis Bennema, 266–84. Grand Rapids: Eerdmans, 2012.

Stump, Eleonore. *Atonement.* OSAT. Oxford: Oxford University Press, 2018.

Sugirtharajah, R. S., ed. *Asian Faces of Jesus.* Faith and Cultures. Maryknoll, NY: Orbis, 1993.

Swain, Scott R. "Covenant of Redemption." In *Christian Dogmatics: Reformed Theology for the Church Catholic*, edited by Michael Allen and Scott R. Swain, 107–25. Grand Rapids: Baker Academic, 2016.

———. "New Covenant Theologies." In *Covenant Theology: Biblical, Theological, and Historical Perspectives*, edited by Guy Prentiss Waters, J. Nicholas Reid, and John R. Muether, 551–69. Wheaton, IL: Crossway, 2020.

———. "The (Nuptial) End of Biblical Interpretation." *Reformed Blogmatics* (blog), February 16, 2022.

———. "The Radiance of the Father's Glory: Eternal Generation, the Divine Names, and Biblical Interpretation." In *Retrieving Eternal Generation*, edited by Fred Sanders and Scott R. Swain, 29–43. Grand Rapids: Zondervan, 2017.

———. *The Trinity: An Introduction.* Short Studies in Systematic Theology. Wheaton, IL: Crossway, 2020.

———. *The Trinity and the Bible: On Theological Interpretation.* Bellingham, WA: Lexham, 2021.

Swain, Scott R., and Michael Allen. "The Obedience of the Eternal Son:

Catholic Trinitarianism and Reformed Christology." In *Christology, Ancient and Modern: Explorations in Constructive Dogmatics*, edited by Oliver D. Crisp and Fred Sanders, 74–95. Grand Rapids: Zondervan, 2013.

Swinburne, Richard. *The Resurrection of God Incarnate*. Oxford: Oxford University Press, 2003.

———. *Was Jesus God?* Oxford: Oxford University Press, 2008.

Sykes, S. W. "The Theology of the Humanity of Christ." In *Christ, Faith and History: Cambridge Studies in Christology*, edited by S. W. Sykes and J. P. Clayton, 53–72. Cambridge: Cambridge University Press, 1972.

Tanner, Kathryn. *Christ the Key*. CIT. Cambridge: Cambridge University Press, 2010.

———. *God and Creation in Christian Theology: Tyranny or Empowerment?* Minneapolis: Fortress, 1988.

———. "Jesus Christ." In *The Cambridge Companion to Christian Doctrine*, edited by Colin E. Gunton, 245–72. Cambridge: Cambridge University Press, 1997.

Tanner, Norman P., SJ, ed. *Nicaea I to Lateran V.* Vol. 1 of *Decrees of the Ecumenical Councils*. London: Sheed & Ward, 1990.

Tennent, Timothy C. *Theology in the Context of World Christianity: How the Global Church Is Influencing the Way We Think about and Discuss Theology*. Grand Rapids: Zondervan, 2007.

Tenney, Merrill C. "The Historicity of the Resurrection." In *Jesus of Nazareth: Saviour and Lord*, edited by Carl F. H. Henry, 133–44. Grand Rapids: Eerdmans, 1966.

Thate, Michael J. "Paul and the Anxieties of (Imperial?) Succession: Galatians and the Politics of Neglect." In *"In Christ" in Paul: Explorations in Paul's Theology of Union and Participation*, edited by Michael J. Thate, Kevin J. Vanhoozer, and Constantine R. Campbell, 209–50. WUNT II. Tübingen: Mohr Siebeck, 2014.

Thielman, Frank. *Ephesians*. BECNT. Grand Rapids: Baker Academic, 2010.

Thiessen, Matthew. *Jesus and the Forces of Death: The Gospels' Portrayal of Ritual Impurity within First-Century Judaism*. Grand Rapids: Baker Academic, 2020.

Thiselton, Anthony C. *Hermeneutics: An Introduction*. Grand Rapids: Eerdmans, 2009.

———. *Systematic Theology*. Grand Rapids: Eerdmans, 2015.

Thompson, Marianne Meye. *Colossians and Philemon*. THNTC. Grand Rapids: Eerdmans, 2005.

———. *The God of the Gospel of John*. Grand Rapids: Eerdmans, 2001.

———. *The Promise of the Father: Jesus and God in the New Testament*. Louisville: Westminster John Knox, 2000.

Thompson, William M. *The Struggle for Theology's Soul: Contesting Scripture in Christology*. New York: Crossroad, 1996.

Thornton, L. S. *Revelation and the Modern World*. Vol. 1 of *The Form of a Servant*. London: Dacre, 1950.

Thurman, Howard. *Jesus and the Disinherited*. Boston: Beacon, 1976.

Tillich, Paul. *Systematic Theology*. 3 vols. Chicago: University of Chicago Press, 1951–63.

Tilling, Chris. *Paul's Divine Christology*. WUNT II. Tübingen: Mohr Siebeck, 2012.

Torrance, Alan. "Being of One Substance with the Father." In *Nicene Christianity: A Future for a New Ecumenism*, edited by Christopher R. Seitz, 49–61. Grand Rapids: Brazos, 2001.

Torrance, Iain R. *Christology After Chalcedon: Severus of Antioch and Sergius the Monophysite*. Reprint, Eugene, OR: Wipf & Stock, 1998.

Torrance, T. F. *The Christian Doctrine of God: One Being, Three Persons*. Edinburgh: T&T Clark, 1996.

———. *The Mediation of Christ*. Grand Rapids: Eerdmans, 1984.

———. *The Trinitarian Faith*. Reprint, Edinburgh: T&T Clark, 1995.

Travis, Stephen H. "Christ as Bearer of Divine Judgment in Paul's Thought about the Atonement." In *Jesus of Nazareth: Lord and Christ: Essays on the Historical Jesus and New Testament Christology*, edited by Joel B. Green and Max Turner, 332–45. Grand Rapids: Eerdmans, 1994.

Treat, Jeremy R. *The Crucified King: Atonement and Kingdom in Biblical and Systematic Theology*. Grand Rapids: Zondervan, 2014.

Treier, Daniel J. "'Christian Platonism' and Christological Interpretation: A Response to Craig A. Carter, *Interpreting Scripture with the Great Tradition*." *Journal of Reformed Faith and Practice* 5, no. 3 (December 2020): 40–54.

———. "Christology and Commentaries: Examining and Enhancing Theological Exegesis." In *On the Writing of New Testament Commentaries: Festschrift for Grant R. Osborne on the Occasion of His*

Seventieth Birthday, edited by Stanley E. Porter and Eckhard J. Schnabel, 299–316. Leiden: Brill, 2012.

———. "*Heavenly Participation: The Weaving of a Sacramental Tapestry*—A Review Essay." *CSR* 41, no. 1 (Fall 2011): 67–71.

———. "Incarnation." In *Christian Dogmatics: Reformed Theology for the Church Catholic*, edited by Michael Allen and Scott R. Swain, 216–42. Grand Rapids: Baker Academic, 2016.

———. *Introducing Evangelical Theology*. Grand Rapids: Baker Academic, 2019.

———. *Introducing Theological Interpretation of Scripture: Recovering a Christian Practice*. Grand Rapids: Baker Academic, 2008.

———. "Jesus Christ, Doctrine of." In *Dictionary for Theological Interpretation of the Bible*, edited by Kevin J. Vanhoozer et al., 363–71. Grand Rapids: Baker Academic, 2005.

———. "'Mediator of a New Covenant': Atonement and Christology in Hebrews." In *So Great a Salvation: A Dialogue on the Atonement in Hebrews*, edited by Jon C. Laansma, George H. Guthrie, and Cynthia Long Westfall, 105–19. LNTS. London: Bloomsbury T&T Clark, 2019.

———. *Proverbs and Ecclesiastes*. BTCB. Grand Rapids: Brazos, 2011.

———. "Systematic Theology." In *Evangelical Dictionary of Theology*, 3rd ed., edited by Daniel J. Treier and Walter A. Elwell, 853–55. Grand Rapids: Baker Academic, 2017.

———. "Typology." In *Dictionary for Theological Interpretation of the Bible*, edited by Kevin J. Vanhoozer et al., 823–27. Grand Rapids: Baker Academic, 2005.

———. "Virgin Territory?" *ProEccl* 23, no. 4 (Fall 2014): 373–79.

Trueman, Carl. "The Incarnation and the Lord's Supper." In *The Word Became Flesh: Evangelicals and the Incarnation*, edited by David Peterson, 185–208. Carlisle, Cumbria, UK: Paternoster, 2003.

Turner, David L. *Matthew*. BECNT. Grand Rapids: Baker Academic, 2008.

Turretin, Francis. *Institutes of Elenctic Theology*. 3 vols. Edited by James T. Dennison Jr. Translated by George Musgrave Giger. Phillipsburg, NJ: P&R, 1992–97.

Valiente, O. Ernesto. *Liberation through Reconciliation: Jon Sobrino's Christological Spirituality*. New York: Fordham University Press, 2016.

Van Driel, Edwin Chr. *Incarnation Anyway: Arguments for Supralapsarian Christology.* AARAS. Oxford: Oxford University Press, 2008.

————. *Rethinking Paul: Protestant Theology and Pauline Exegesis.* CIT. Cambridge: Cambridge University Press, 2021.

Van Kuiken, E. Jerome. *Christ's Humanity in Current and Ancient Controversy: Fallen or Not?* London: T&T Clark, 2017.

Van Mastricht, Petrus. *Theoretical-Practical Theology.* 3 vols. Edited by Joel R. Beeke. Translated by Todd M. Rester. Grand Rapids: Reformation Heritage, 2018–21.

VanDrunen, David. "Iconoclasm, Incarnation and Eschatology: Toward a Catholic Understanding of the Reformed Doctrine of the 'Second' Commandment." *IJST* 6, no. 2 (2004): 130–47.

Vanhoozer, Kevin J. "Ascending the Mountain, Singing the Rock: Biblical Interpretation Earthed, Typed, and Transfigured." *ModTheo* 28, no. 4 (October 2012): 781–803.

————. "Christology in the West: Conversations in Europe and North America." In *Jesus without Borders: Christology in the Majority World*, edited by Gene L. Green, Stephen T. Pardue, and K. K. Yeo, 11–36. MWT. Grand Rapids: Eerdmans, 2014.

————. "From 'Blessed in Christ' to 'Being in Christ': The State of Union and the Place of Participation in Paul's Discourse, New Testament Exegesis, and Systematic Theology Today." In *"In Christ" in Paul: Explorations in Paul's Theology of Union and Participation*, edited by Michael J. Thate, Kevin J. Vanhoozer, and Constantine R. Campbell, 3–33. WUNT II. Tübingen: Mohr Siebeck, 2014.

————. "The Atonement in Postmodernity: Guilt, Goats and Gifts." In *The Glory of the Atonement: Biblical, Theological and Practical Perspectives*, edited by Charles E. Hill and Frank A. James III, 367–404. Downers Grove, IL: InterVarsity Press, 2004.

————. "The Origin of Paul's Soteriology: Election, Incarnation, and Union with Christ in Ephesians 1:4 (with Special Reference to Evangelical Calvinism)." In *Reconsidering the Relationship between Biblical and Systematic Theology in the New Testament: Essays by Theologians and New Testament Scholars*, edited by Benjamin E. Reynolds, Brian Lugioyo, and Kevin J. Vanhoozer, 177–211. WUNT II. Tübingen: Mohr Siebeck, 2014.

————. "Wrighting the Wrongs of the Reformation? The State of the Union with Christ in St. Paul and Protestant Soteriology." In *Jesus,*

Paul and the People of God: A Theological Dialogue with N. T. Wright, edited by Nicholas Perrin and Richard B. Hays, 235–59. Downers Grove, IL: IVP Academic, 2011.

Vanhoozer, Kevin J., and Daniel J. Treier. *Theology and the Mirror of Scripture: A Mere Evangelical Account*. SCDS. Downers Grove, IL: IVP Academic, 2015.

Velde, Dolf te, ed. *Disputations 1–23*. Translated by Riemer A. Faber. Vol. 1 of *Synopsis Purioris Theologiae: Synopsis of a Purer Theology: Latin Text and English Translation*. Leiden: Brill, 2014.

Vidu, Adonis. *Atonement, Law, and Justice: The Cross in Historical and Cultural Contexts*. Grand Rapids: Baker Academic, 2014.

———. *The Same God Who Works All Things: Inseparable Operations in Trinitarian Theology*. Grand Rapids: Eerdmans, 2021.

Volf, Miroslav. *Exclusion and Embrace: A Theological Exploration of Identity, Otherness, and Reconciliation*. Rev. ed. Nashville: Abingdon, 2019.

———. *The End of Memory: Remembering Rightly in a Violent World*. Grand Rapids: Eerdmans, 2006.

Wainwright, Geoffrey. *Doxology: The Praise of God in Worship, Doctrine, and Life: A Systematic Theology*. New York: Oxford University Press, 1980.

———. *For Our Salvation: Two Approaches to the Work of Christ*. Grand Rapids: Eerdmans, 1997.

Wallace, Daniel B. *Greek Grammar Beyond the Basics: An Exegetical Syntax of the New Testament*. Grand Rapids: Zondervan, 1996.

Walls, Andrew F. *The Cross-Cultural Process in Christian History: Studies in the Transmission and Appropriation of Faith*. Maryknoll, NY: Orbis, 2002.

Walsh, Brian J., and Sylvia C. Keesmaat. *Colossians Remixed: Subverting the Empire*. Downers Grove, IL: InterVarsity Press, 2004.

Warfield, Benjamin Breckinridge. *The Person and Work of Christ*. Edited by Samuel G. Craig. Philadelphia: Presbyterian and Reformed, 1950.

Waters, Brent. "The Incarnation and the Christian Moral Life." In *Christology and Ethics*, edited by F. LeRon Shults and Brent Waters, 5–31. Grand Rapids: Eerdmans, 2010.

Watts, Rikk E. "Mark." In *Commentary on the New Testament Use of the Old Testament*, edited by G. K. Beale and D. A. Carson, 111–249. Grand Rapids: Baker Academic, 2007.

Weaver, J. Denny. *The Nonviolent Atonement*. Grand Rapids: Eerdmans, 2001.

————. "The Nonviolent Atonement: Human Violence, Discipleship and God." In *Stricken by God? Nonviolent Identification and the Victory of Christ*, edited by Brad Jersak and Michael Hardin, 316–55. Grand Rapids: Eerdmans, 2007.

Webb, Robert L. "The Historical Enterprise and Historical Jesus Research." In *Key Events in the Life of the Historical Jesus: A Collaborative Exploration of Context and Coherence*, edited by Darrell L. Bock and Robert L. Webb, 9–93. Grand Rapids: Eerdmans, 2009.

Webster, Douglas D. *A Passion for Christ: An Evangelical Christology*. Grand Rapids: Zondervan, 1987.

Webster, John. *Confessing God: Essays in Christian Dogmatics II*. London: T&T Clark, 2005.

————. *The Culture of Theology*. Edited by Ivor J. Davidson and Alden C. McCray. Grand Rapids: Baker Academic, 2019.

————. *The Domain of the Word: Scripture and Theological Reason*. London: T&T Clark, 2012.

————. *God without Measure: Working Papers in Christian Theology*. Vol. 1, *God and the Works of God*. London: Bloomsbury T&T Clark, 2016.

————. *God without Measure: Working Papers in Christian Theology*. Vol. 2, *Virtue and Intellect*. London: Bloomsbury T&T Clark, 2016.

————. *Holy Scripture: A Dogmatic Sketch*. CIT. Cambridge: Cambridge University Press, 2003.

————. "Jesus Christ." In *The Cambridge Companion to Evangelical Theology*, edited by Timothy Larsen and Daniel J. Treier, 51–63. Cambridge: Cambridge University Press, 2007.

————. "Kenotische Christologie." In *Die Religion in Geschichte und Gegenwart: Handworterbuch für Theologie und Religionswissenschaft*, edited by Hans Dieter Betz et al., 4:929–31. Tübingen: Mohr Siebeck, 2006.

————. "Perfection and Participation." In *The Analogy of Being: Invention of the Antichrist or the Wisdom of God?*, edited by Thomas Joseph White, OP, 379–94. Grand Rapids: Eerdmans, 2011.

————. *Word and Church: Essays in Christian Dogmatics*. New York: T&T Clark, 2001.

Weinandy, Thomas G., OFM, Cap. *In the Likeness of Sinful Flesh: An Essay on the Humanity of Christ*. Edinburgh: T&T Clark, 1993.

————. *Jesus: Essays in Christology*. Ave Maria, FL: Sapientia, 2014.

Welch, Claude, ed. *God and Incarnation in Mid-Nineteenth Century German*

Theology: Thomasius, Dorner, Biedermann. Translated by Claude Welch. A Library of Protestant Thought. New York: Oxford University Press, 1965.

Wells, David F. *Above All Earthly Pow'rs: Christ in a Postmodern World.* Grand Rapids: Eerdmans, 2005.

Wellum, Stephen J. *God the Son Incarnate: The Doctrine of Christ.* FET. Wheaton, IL: Crossway, 2016.

Wenham, David. *Jesus in Context: Making Sense of the Historical Figure.* Cambridge: Cambridge University Press, 2021.

White, Thomas Joseph, OP. *The Incarnate Lord: A Thomistic Study in Christology.* Washington, DC: Catholic University of America Press, 2015.

White, Vernon. *Identity.* London: SCM, 2002.

Wilcoxen, Matthew A. *Divine Humility: God's Morally Perfect Being.* Waco, TX: Baylor University Press, 2019.

Wiles, Maurice. *Archetypal Heresy: Arianism through the Centuries.* Oxford: Clarendon, 1996.

Wiley, H. Orton. *Christian Theology.* Vol. 2. Kansas City: Beacon Hill, 1952.

Wilken, Robert Louis, ed. *Isaiah: Interpreted by Early Christian and Medieval Commentators.* With Angela Russell Christman and Michael J. Hollerich. CB. Grand Rapids: Eerdmans, 2007.

Williams, Garry. "Penal Substitution: A Response to Recent Criticisms." In *The Atonement Debate: Papers from the London Symposium on the Theology of Atonement*, edited by Derek Tidball, David Hilborn, and Justin Thacker, 172–91. Grand Rapids: Zondervan, 2008.

Williams, J. Rodman. *Renewal Theology: Systematic Theology from a Charismatic Perspective: Three Volumes in One.* Grand Rapids: Zondervan, 1996.

Williams, Rowan. *Arius: Heresy and Tradition.* Rev. ed. Grand Rapids: Eerdmans, 2002.

———. *Christ on Trial: How the Gospel Unsettles Our Judgement.* Grand Rapids: Eerdmans, 2000.

———. *Christ the Heart of Creation.* London: Bloomsbury Continuum, 2018.

———. "Christology." In *The Vocation of Anglican Theology*, edited by Ralph McMichael, 77–110. London: SCM, 2014.

———. "A History of Faith in Jesus." In *The Cambridge Companion to*

Jesus, edited by Markus Bockmuehl, 220–36. Cambridge: Cambridge University Press, 2001.

Willis, E. David. *Calvin's Catholic Christology: The Function of the So-Called Extra Calvinisticum in Calvin's Theology*. Leiden: Brill, 1966.

Willis, John T. "The Meaning of Isaiah 7:14 and Its Application in Matthew 1:23." *Restoration Quarterly* 21 (1978): 1–18.

Wilson, Brittany E. *The Embodied God: Seeing the Divine in Luke-Acts and the Early Church*. Oxford: Oxford University Press, 2021.

Wilson, Jonathan R. *God So Loved the World: A Christology for Disciples*. Grand Rapids: Baker Academic, 2001.

Witherington, Ben, III. *Isaiah Old and New: Exegesis, Intertextuality, and Hermeneutics*. Minneapolis: Fortress, 2017.

Wittmer, Michael E. "Conclusion." In *Four Views on Heaven*, edited by Michael E. Wittmer, 205–8. Counterpoints. Grand Rapids: Zondervan Academic, 2022.

———, ed. *Four Views on Heaven*. Counterpoints. Grand Rapids: Zondervan, 2022.

Wolters, Albert M. *Creation Regained: Biblical Basics for a Reformational Worldview*. Grand Rapids: Eerdmans, 1985.

Work, Telford C. *Jesus—the End and the Beginning: Tracing the Christ-Shaped Nature of Everything*. Grand Rapids: Baker Academic, 2019.

———. "Jesus' New Relationship with the Holy Spirit, and Ours: How Biblical Spirit–Christology Helps Resolve a Chalcedonian Dilemma." In *Christology, Ancient and Modern: Explorations in Constructive Dogmatics*, edited by Oliver D. Crisp and Fred Sanders, 171–83. Grand Rapids: Zondervan, 2013.

Wright, Christopher J. H. "Atonement in the Old Testament." In *The Atonement Debate: Papers from the London Symposium on the Theology of Atonement*, edited by Derek Tidball, David Hilborn, and Justin Thacker, 69–82. Grand Rapids: Zondervan, 2008.

Wright, N. T. "The Biblical Formation of a Doctrine of Christ." In *Who Do You Say That I Am? Christology and the Church*, edited by Donald Armstrong, 47–68. Grand Rapids: Eerdmans, 1999.

———. *The Climax of the Covenant: Christ and the Law in Pauline Theology*. Minneapolis: Fortress, 1992.

———. *The Day the Revolution Began: Reconsidering the Meaning of Jesus's Crucifixion*. New York: HarperOne, 2016.

—————. *How God Became King: The Forgotten Story of the Gospels*. New York: HarperOne, 2012.

—————. *Jesus and the Victory of God*. Christian Origins and the Question of God 2. Minneapolis: Fortress, 1996.

—————. "Resurrection of the Dead." In *Dictionary for Theological Interpretation of the Bible*, edited by Kevin J. Vanhoozer et al., 676–78. Grand Rapids: Baker Academic, 2005.

—————. *The Resurrection of the Son of God*. Christian Origins and the Question of God 3. Minneapolis: Fortress, 2003.

—————. *Surprised by Hope*. New York: HarperOne, 2008.

Wynne, Jeremy J. *Wrath Among the Perfections of God's Life*. SST. London: T&T Clark, 2010.

Wyschogrod, Michael. "A Jewish Perspective on Incarnation." *ModTheo* 12, no. 2 (April 1996): 195–209.

Yancy, George, ed. *Christology and Whiteness: What Would Jesus Do?* New York: Routledge, 2012.

Yeago, David S. "The New Testament and the Nicene Dogma: A Contribution to the Recovery of Theological Exegesis." *ProEccl* 3 (1994): 152–64.

Yoder, John Howard. *The Politics of Jesus: Vicit Agnus Noster*. 2nd ed. Grand Rapids: Eerdmans, 1994.

Yong, Amos. *Revelation*. Belief. Louisville: Westminster John Knox, 2021.

Young, Frances M. *Biblical Exegesis and the Formation of Christian Culture*. Cambridge: Cambridge University Press, 1997.

—————. *From Nicaea to Chalcedon: A Guide to the Literature and Its Background*. Philadelphia: Fortress, 1983.

Zachhuber, Johannes. *Luther's Christological Legacy: Christocentrism and the Chalcedonian Tradition*. Milwaukee: Marquette University Press, 2017.

Zehnder, Markus. "The Question of the 'Divine Status' of the Davidic Messiah." *BBR* 30, no. 4 (2020): 485–514.

SUBJECT INDEX

SCRIPTURE INDEX

2 Corinthians

Galatians

Ephesians

PROPER NAME INDEX